THE ANIMAL/HUMAN BOUNDARY

STUDIES IN COMPARATIVE HISTORY

ESSAYS FROM THE

SHELBY CULLOM DAVIS CENTER

FOR HISTORICAL STUDIES

Animals in Human Histories: The Mirror of Nature and Culture
Edited by Mary J. Henninger-Voss

The Animal/Human Boundary: Historical Perspectives
Edited by Angela N. H. Creager and William Chester Jordan

A Publication of the
Shelby Cullom Davis Center for Historical Studies
Princeton University

THE ANIMAL/HUMAN BOUNDARY:

Historical Perspectives

EDITED BY

ANGELA N. H. CREAGER

AND

WILLIAM CHESTER JORDAN

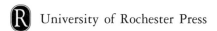 University of Rochester Press

University of Rochester Press
668 Mt. Hope Avenue
Rochester, New York, 14620, USA
Boydell & Brewer, Ltd.
P.O. Box 9, Woodbridge, Suffolk 11P12 3DF, UK
www.urpress.com
ISSN 1539-4905

Library of Congress Cataloging-in-Publication Data

The animal-human boundary : historical perspectives / edited by Angela N. H. Creager and William Chester Jordan ; contributors, Piers Beirne . . . [et al.].
p. cm. — (Studies in comparative history, ISSN 1539-4905 ; 2)
Includes bibliographical references and index.
ISBN 1-58046-120-4 (pbk. : alk. paper)
1. Animals and civilization.   2. Animals—Symbolic aspects.   3. Bestiality.   I. Creager, Angela N. H.   II. Jordan, William C., 1948-   III. Series.

QL85.A5143 2002
306—dc21
2002072458

British Library Cataloguing-in-Publication Data

A catalogue record for this book is available from the British Library

This publication is printed on acid-free paper
Printed in the United States of America
Designed and typeset by Straight Creek Bookmakers

CONTENTS

ACKNOWLEDGMENTS

We have relied on the help of many generous friends and colleagues in publishing this volume. The scholars who participated in the Shelby Cullom Davis Center's seminars on "Animals and Human Society" stimulated our thinking about the themes raised here. We especially thank the center's fellows in 1997–98: Mary Fissell, Maryanne Kowaleski, Susan Lederer, Rob Meens, Gregg Mitman, François Pouillon, and James Serpell, for their lively contributions. (Some also contributed essays to this collection.) Anthony Grafton, current director of the Davis Center, supported this volume during its preparation. Suzanne Marchand, Elizabeth Lunbeck, Karen Merrill, and Jeremy Adelman, editors of previous Davis Center volumes, imparted valuable guidance. Kari Hoover took care of many administrative and bureaucratic matters, and Eric Ash provided inestimable assistance in preparing the manuscript. Finally, Gavin Lewis did a masterful job editing the entire volume. We thank them all.

We also acknowledge other publishers for allowing us to include material that previously appeared elsewhere. Chapter 3 was originally published by Ruth Mazo Karras in *Conflicted Identities and Multiple Masculinities: Men in the Medieval West,* ed. Jacqueline Murray (New York: Garland Publishing, 1999). An earlier version of chapter 4 was published by Mary Fissell in *History Workshop Journal* 47 (1999): 1–29, and an earlier version of chapter 5 appeared in *Pennsylvania History* 65 (1998): special issue, *Explorations in Early American Culture,* pp. 8–43. Chapter 7 is a revised and expanded version of Piers Beirne's essay "Rethinking Bestiality," which appeared in *Theoretical Criminology* 1, no. 3 (1997): 317–40, a shorter version of which was reprinted in *Companion Animals and Us,* ed. Anthony Podberscek, Elizabeth Paul, and James A. Serpell (Cambridge: Cambridge University Press, 2000), pp. 313–31. All are reprinted here by permission.

INTRODUCTION

ANGELA N. H. CREAGER AND WILLIAM CHESTER JORDAN

If we choose to let conjecture run wild, then animals, our fellow brethren in pain, diseases, death,
suffering, and famine—our slaves in the most laborious works, our companions in our amusements—they
may partake {of} our origins in one common ancestor—we may be all netted together.
—*Charles Darwin*

So Darwin wrote in his secret notebook in 1837,[1] as he began to sketch out
the ideas culminating in his theory of evolution by natural selection. Darwin's conjecture that humans and animals are part of a unified family tree
transformed scientific and social thought about the natural world, but his
preoccupation with the permeability of the boundary between humans and
animals has deep historical antecedents. The human-animal boundary is the
connecting theme that runs through this volume of essays, one of two
volumes culled from a year's worth of seminars at Princeton University's
Shelby Cullom Davis Center for Historical Studies.[2]

The way in which humans articulate identities, social hierarchies, and
their inversions through relations with animals has been a very fruitful
topic in anthropological and historical investigations of the last several
decades. One need think only of Clifford Geertz's "Balinese Cockfight" and
Robert Darnton's "The Great Cat Massacre."[3] The contributors to this volume similarly call attention to the symbolic meanings of animals, from the
casting of first-year students as goats in medieval universities to the representation of vermin as greedy thieves in early modern England. But the
essays in this volume are also concerned with the more material and bodily
aspects of human-animal relations, like bestiality, eating regulations, xenotransplantation, and aggression. Our contributors draw attention to the
shifting grounds for distinguishing humans from animals, and the diverse
historical and cultural motivations for regulating this divide.

Modern biologists have increasingly problematized the animal-human
boundary. Since Descartes's differentiation of the body (as automaton) from
the soul as the seat of consciousness and the defining essence of "man,"

ix

physiological and psychological studies of mind have consistently detached from the soul attributes once assigned to it. Researchers have also challenged the supposedly unique ability of humans to use language. Chimpanzees and gorillas, it has been argued, have learned to communicate using American Sign Language. In addition, some scientists regard the sophistication of modes of communication in species like dolphins and songbirds as undermining the view of humans as uniquely capable of complex expressions. And, now, studies of nonhuman primates threaten to compromise the long-held assumption that only humans possess self-awareness. In the 1960s, an entire generation of Americans, through National Geographic's popular television specials, witnessed the behavior of Koko, the "signing" gorilla, behavior which certain researchers concluded was evidence of her self-consciousness and moral sensibility.[4] If they are correct and if tool use and the cultural transmission of knowledge, once considered benchmarks of humanity, are also not confined to *Homo sapiens,* the question becomes: How can one firmly differentiate human beings from other animals?[5]

Yet, despite scientific misgivings, the sense of the "otherness" of animals remains generally intact in contemporary, secular society. As Thomas Nagel argued in his classic essay, "What Is It Like to Be a Bat?" we can scarcely imagine the experiences of other animals, even as we recognize that they do have experiences, some of which (hunger, thirst, fatigue, sexual desire) are similar to our own.[6] In Nagel's view, this predicament, and the limited understanding of consciousness available to us, render the entire mind-body problem intractable.[7] For our purposes, however, the refractoriness of our similarity to animals to scientific study serves as counterpoint to a rich history of imagined connections and distinctions between humans and other creatures. Both the diverse cultural contexts and material circumstances of men and women have shaped their understanding of and interactions with animals.

The first three essays in this volume examine the ways in which medieval Europeans conceptualized and invoked the boundary between themselves and animals. One of the most intimate aspects of humans' relations with animals, for example, is our consumption of them. Because eating is a behavior we share with animals, it also reminds us of our closeness to other creatures. Rob Meens looks to the issue of food prohibitions as a window on the human/animal boundary in medieval European society. He focuses on the proscription against eating horsemeat in medieval Ireland, which carried a heavier penance than either bestiality or murder to revenge close kin. Meens argues that this abhorrence of horsemeat was not principally related to struggles against paganism, as other historians have suggested, but rather reflected the intimate association of humans with horses—the close contact of humans with horses through riding gave these creatures an ambiguous or anomalous standing, perhaps even a status as residually human. Other animals viewed as unfit for consumption (although not necessarily forbidden) included dogs, cats, and mice, which also lived in intimate relations with humans, whether as companions or pests. Considered impure, they could contaminate acceptable food (or, in the case of mice, the Eucharist itself). Abstaining from impure foods, which reflected cultural anxiety to maintain a clear boundary between humans and animals, could also serve as a marker of social identity. Pariahs—thieves and outlaws—might eat horsemeat, but aristocrats and clergy would not so defile themselves.

Paul Freedman explores the ways in which elites represented peasants as beasts and, to some extent, treated them that way, drawing on texts and other sources from many regions over the course of the Middle Ages in order to demonstrate the pervasiveness of the effort at dehumanization. Many of these representations occur in humorous and ribald literature (as in the *fabliaux*); yet, they reinforced a deeply serious cultural evaluation of peasants as suited by their very nature to their lot of hard work and servitude. To be sure, not all images of the medieval peasant were contemptuous. Peasants also represented exemplary Christians, an implicit denunciation of their treatment as mere brutes.

The images of the peasant were not static during the Middle Ages. The peasants' revolts beginning in the fourteenth century polarized the cultural uses of such representations. Peasants tended to be viewed either as savage beasts or as exploited humans, and in the latter case the comparison with animals served as a political argument for treatment with more dignity or equality. Freedman's essay not only expands our historical understanding of the complex animal images of peasants, but also challenges (as he himself points out) a simplistic or homogeneous view of the "other" in medieval European society. While representations of peasants as bestial overlapped with images marginalizing other groups, such as Jews, Muslims, and lepers, the peasants were part of the Christian order and in most regions of Europe were more familiar figures than Jews or Muslims. In this sense the imagery used to represent peasants, like that used to depict women, expresses the intense ambivalence about these intimate subordinates, whose similarities to those in higher stations remained a constant and troubling reminder of the earthly inequalities experienced in a Christian society.

The persistent references to peasants and rustics as animal-like also contributed a stock of images used in the ritual identification of liminal statuses, like that of new university students, as Ruth Mazo Karras demonstrates in her essay, "Separating the Men from the Goats." If the initiation rituals of twentieth-century university social groups, such as fraternities, can be said to represent a repudiation of the feminine, then initiation rites for the *beani* (first-year students) in medieval universities focused symbolically on exorcising the bestial and uncivilized. A *beanus* could expect to suffer harassment from his peers (such as having urine or feces thrown at him) or might be required to put on a grand feast for other students. The focus on the animal nature of initiates, with hazing rites involving food, excrement, and sex, is graphically illustrated in a particular initiation rite, described in the *Manuale Scholarium,* in which the *beanus* is dressed like a goat and harassed, his horns and "teeth" removed in a process of humanization. The symbolic shedding of one's animality was clearly gendered, reinforcing particular masculine ideals of university life. Students may have feasted, gotten drunk, and had consorts, but these habits were to be urbane, not bestial. Above all, university rituals of identification and hazing symbolically differentiated students from peasants and rustics.

By the early modern period, a growing print culture allowed for a wider dissemination of Latin and vernacular writings, which often represented animals in text and illustrations. The three essays addressing this era point to the diversity of opinions between, among others, Protestants and Catholics, and Europeans and colonial Americans, on the proper relationship of humans to animals living in their close proximity, like vermin, farm beasts, and companions.

Vermin in the early modern period were perceived not principally as pests but as thieves—poachers of human food. They were frequently represented in cheap print, from vermin-killing manuals to cookbooks to jokebooks, and Mary Fissell draws on these sources to explore the production of meanings about vermin in late seventeenth- and eighteenth-century England. Three principal characteristics defined vermin in this context: their dependence on human food, their wiliness, and their greed, especially as seen in their lack of manners in eating. The various depictions of vermin thus offered, through a negative portrait, an implicit picture of the civilizing process that differentiated humans from brutes. However, complicating the stark contrast between humans and vermin as beasts was a suspicion that vermin could communicate using signs and language, showing a disturbing similarity to the humans they stole from. Perhaps for this reason, humans almost never consumed animals classified as vermin (the exception being waterbirds).

As for farm animals, John Murrin offers the most comprehensive portrait to date of bestiality as it was prosecuted in colonial America. Colonial Christians tended to view both sodomy and bestiality as "unnatural" sexual acts, equally violating God's design and law. Yet, there was wide variation, within the colonies, as within Europe, concerning the specific sexual acts and suspects that were prosecuted. During the decades in colonial America when women were the chief suspects for witchcraft, they were rarely accused of unnatural sexual acts, whereas those accused of bestiality and sodomy were almost always men. Particularly in New England, "bestiality discredited men in the way that witchcraft discredited women."[8] Both witchcraft and perverse sexual acts were viewed in theological terms, yet bestiality came under additional censure due to the common belief that sexual unions between animals and humans could produce monstrous progeny. Bestiality depraved men, reducing them to brutes; it also left a human residue in animals, justifying their punishment (by execution) along with the punishment of the human perpetrators.

The frequency with which magistrates prosecuted men suspected of bestiality did not correlate positively with the ratio of men to women in a particular colony. Nearly all trials for sodomy and bestiality took place in New England, a region that had been settled by families, rather than in the southern colonies, where male laborers vastly outnumbered women. It is hard, too, to evaluate the importance of religious factors in dealing with these crimes. Religious leaders strongly condemned both sodomy and bestiality. Yet even among Protestants the punishment for sodomy might be mitigated. Men convicted of bestiality were almost always hanged.

Based on the vigor with which magistrates prosecuted accusations of bestiality in New England, some historians have argued that bestiality was relatively common there. The numbers simply do not support this interpretation, in Murrin's view; he argues that even if one extrapolates from all recorded instances of bestiality and sodomy to the general population, these were still relatively rare events. Murrin finds more creditable the notion that the Puritan roots of New England led to a stronger abhorrence and prosecution of bestiality than in the other colonies. Even this intensity was specific to a particular period. In New England in the 1640s there was a striking increase in the number of men (mostly young men) convicted and executed for bestiality. Murrin refers to this flurry of prosecutions in New England as the "bestiality panic," and argues that only the outbreak of decades-long fighting in 1675 against Indians and, later, New France curtailed the steady stream of accusations and trials concerning bestiality. Whereas most of those prosecuted during the 1640s were young male servants, as men from more respectable households began to be accused, the passion for executing those convicted (perhaps predictably) waned. Ultimately, even the punishments for bestiality became, like those for sodomy, less stringent in the northern colonies.

Witchcraft and bestiality were not only symmetrically linked in the way they were gendered (women being accused of witchcraft and men of bestiality), but both involved intimate associations of humans with animals, whether real or imagined. James Serpell explores the peculiar role of animal-like familiars in witchcraft, a distinctively English preoccupation for which various historical explanations have been offered. Building on Keith Thomas's interpretation, Serpell has previously argued that the persecution of women's animal companions as demonic familiars was an extension of viewing pet-keeping generally as heretical. Whereas bestiality was abhorred for turning humans into beasts, "pet-keeping turned beasts into humans."[9] Giving pets human names, talking to them as if they could understand human language, and having them occupy the home disturbed cultural assumptions about the essential divide between humans and animals. Here, Serpell offers a more comprehensive, quantitative study of witches' familiars. His analysis points to a conflation of factors in the conception of the familiar, pet-keeping being only one.

The frequent inclusion of both toads and vermin (such as mice and rats) among familiars suggests the desire to impute supernatural powers to animals. Popular and learned culture already associated toads with witchcraft, perhaps based on the (pharmacological) properties of their skin secretions. As Mary Fissell shows, people believed that vermin were able to communicate using language. To account for the English peculiarity of associating animal familiars with witchcraft, Serpell draws on the work of Norman Cohn and Richard Kieckhefer. He points out that witchcraft in England was more closely associated with popular belief systems than on the Continent, where learned officials of the Inquisition strongly shaped both the perception and persecution of witchcraft. Serpell also finds some compelling similarities between the role of animals in early modern English magic and more contemporary shamanistic practices in non-Western cultures.

The final group of essays brings modern philosophical and scientific perspectives to bear on the question of the human/animal divide. Piers Beirne seeks to reevaluate the immorality of bestiality in terms of the harm inflicted upon animals as sentient beings rather than as a violation of traditional Judeo-Christian proscriptions. The new sociological understanding he puts forward relies on a transformed sense of our relation to other creatures. While traditional censure of bestiality has fixed on upholding the essential divide between humans and animals—and so seeks to protect against the degeneration of humans into bestial behavior—Beirne argues for a notion of animal abuse that minimizes the ethical and legal distance between humans and animals (or at least mammals). Bestiality, he argues, should be considered a form of sexual assault, like rape or pederasty.

Beirne's argument for a new definition of bestiality draws some inspiration from a larger social movement since the 1970s to grant animals basic rights. Since the first publication of Peter Singer's *Animal Liberation* in 1975, citizens and scholars have challenged the traditional acceptance of human dominance over animals. The Great Ape Project, which aims to have legislation passed granting great apes some basic rights (such as would protect them from being subjected to biomedical experimentation), provides perhaps the most vivid and interesting current example of how a reconsideration of the human/animal boundary may transform law. In one respect, such a development would seem to be the culmination of a strain of liberalism, in which traditional religious beliefs have been supplanted by a new secular (humanist) ethic. However, as Beirne points out, the decreasing legitimacy of religious norms as the basis for laws has led to a greater acceptance and decriminalization of bestiality, in the name of relaxing sexual proscriptions. Thus, ironically, arguments against bestiality have not received the attention they might have from political liberals or animal rights activists.

H. Peter Steeves uses the examples of liminal persons—from feral children to less well-documented creatures such as Bigfoot—to offer a philosophical analysis of how poorly defined is the category "human." Physical characteristics that have been posited by anthropologists as unique to "man" evince, upon closer inspection, an ethnocentric bias. Nonphysical markers of human identity have not proved any more resilient. Notions of "culture" and language use have been gradually extended to other primates, and reliance on technology has significantly displaced our everyday "tool-making" activities. Despite the deeply emotional connotations of the term "human," Steeves argues, a firm, scientific, objective definition proves elusive. Increasingly, we now appeal to genetics, not so much for a definition as for a concrete source of measurable differences between our species and others. But what sort of ethics will this understanding of the "human" produce? For his part, Steeves argues for a phenomenological view, that some categorizations, specifically those that do not rely on a sharp animal/human demarcation, are more useful ethically than traditional schemes of difference. Indeed, the narratives that humans construct about our world, which seems such a distinctive property of our species, often point to the interconnectedness of animal and human life. The alterity of animals is, in his view, "a construct without clear criteria."

The biological similarities between humans and animals have prompted many twentieth-century scientists to argue that even social aspects of humans, such as behavior, can be better understood through studying animals. Richard Burkhardt's essay examines the role of such research in offering "biological insights into the human condition." Analogies drawn from animal studies to humans have been most controversial when addressing aggression and sexuality. The emergence in the 1930s of the discipline of ethology, based on field observations of animal behavior, provided a strong scientific platform for such theorizing, but the early spokesmen for this field were also deeply affected by the social and geographical dislocations of World War II and its aftermath. Both of ethology's founding fathers, Niko Tinbergen and Konrad Lorenz, spent years imprisoned during the war (Tinbergen in a concentration camp in his native Holland, the Austrian Lorenz as a war prisoner of the Russians). Both studied animal aggression at a time when awareness of human brutality was overwhelming. Yet the effects of this context on ethological knowledge were complex. Lorenz tended to view humans as degenerate animals, having suffered from the absence of natural selection in weeding out maladaptive traits and other weaknesses. Human aggression, he argued, was instinctive, building up spontaneously as a biological drive until its release in aggressive action was inevitable. During the Cold War years, when Lorenz was the most publicly visible representative of ethology, his theories on aggression indicated how poorly biologically prepared humans were to handle the consequences of our rapid cultural evolution. With the threat of imminent nuclear war and the lack of an innate instinct in the human species against killing its kind, Lorenz seemed to offer support for the view that humanity was a doomed species.

At another level, Lorenz remained strangely unreflective about the relationship between his theorizing and the political ideologies and circumstances of his time, even though his sympathetic association with National Socialism during the Third Reich damaged his career prospects in the postwar period and received press attention when he was awarded the Nobel Prize in 1973. Lorenz continued to advance his early theory of autonomous instincts, but other ethologists in the postwar period, including his friend Tinbergen, sought more complex (and politically palatable) explanations for aggression. If the human internal drive to fight could not be eliminated, then, Tinbergen suggested, it might be sublimated or controlled through science. For the next generation of ethologists, the problem of altruism took center stage from the biology of aggression, but the fundamental similarities between animals and humans as social creatures remained axiomatic. The ascendance of sociobiology has continued to provide the public with stories about our evolutionary scripted behaviors and to provoke controversy about whether differences between other animals and ourselves can be ignored.[10]

Susan Lederer's historical study of "heterotransplantation" explores the medical implications of our differences from animals. "Heterotransplantation" or "heterografting," the transfer of tissues or organs from one species onto another (now commonly referred to as "xenotransplantation"), arose in the early twentieth century as a surgical strategy of last resort to treat severe burn and industrial accident victims. It began to get public attention in the 1910s, as newspapers reported on experimental grafting surgeries. Whereas accounts of transplantation surgeries involving human donors had used the imagery of sacrifice and nobility, stories of animals as donors of tissues and organs unsettled traditional assumptions about the differences between humans and animals. However, American patients did not for this reason reject the prospect of transplants (often skin grafts) from animals. Rather, contemporary reports suggest that patients found the prospect of incorporating frog or pig skin interesting and novel, even though the transplants frequently failed. And in the case of "rejuvenation" procedures, very popular in the early 1920s, men seeking enhanced virility sought to have chimpanzee, baboon, or even goat testicular tissue grafted into their own glands. The main moral reservations that were raised against heterotransplantation came from antivivisectionists, who particularly objected to a case in which a dog was used as a source of bone for an injured boy, in a procedure that required the animal and human to be surgically conjoined for nearly a fortnight. Yet, there was surprisingly little comment in the U.S., except some Catholic objections, on the unnaturalness of human-animal unions in heterotransplantation, particularly when compared to sustained objections against smallpox vaccination on these grounds. And one cannot predict whether current medical hopes for xenotransplantation, based on genetic techniques intended to overcome the immunological differences between humans and animals, will give rise to strong negative reactions.[11] In a word, the story this book tells is a still unfolding one.

NOTES

1. Paul H. Barrett, Peter J. Gautrey, Sandra Herbert, David Kohn, and Sydney Smith, eds., *Charles Darwin's Notebooks, 1836–1844: Geology, Transmutation of Species, Metaphysical Enquiries* (Ithaca, N.Y.: Cornell University Press, 1987), p. B232. The punctuation has been regularized.

2. The companion to this book is a group of essays on cultural representations of animals edited by Mary J. Henninger-Voss, *Animals in Human Histories: The Mirror of Nature and Culture* (Rochester, N.Y.: University of Rochester Press, 2002).

3. Clifford Geertz, "Deep Play: Notes on the Balinese Cockfight," in *The Interpretation of Cultures: Selected Essays* (New York: Basic Books, 1973),

pp. 412–53; Robert Darnton, "Workers Revolt: The Great Cat Massacre of the Rue Saint-Séverin," *The Great Cat Massacre and Other Episodes in French Cultural History* (1984; reprint, New York: Vintage Books, 1985), pp. 75–104.

4. Donna Haraway, *Primate Visions: Gender, Race, and Nature in the World of Modern Science* (New York: Routledge, 1989), chap. 7.

5. See, e.g., *Chimpanzee Cultures,* ed. Richard W. Wrangham (Cambridge, Mass.: Harvard University Press in cooperation with the Chicago Academy of Sciences, 1994).

6. Thomas Nagel, "What Is It Like to Be a Bat?" *Philosophical Review* 83 (1974): 435–50.

7. Despite the philosophical problems with understanding animal experience, the past quarter-century has seen a blossoming of studies of animal cognition and affect. See Donald R. Griffin, *The Question of Animal Awareness: Evolutionary Continuity of Mental Experience* (New York: Rockefeller University Press, 1976), and, more recently, Marc D. Hauser, *Wild Minds: What Animals Really Think* (New York: Henry Holt, 2000). A useful summary of Hauser's work is offered by Jennifer Schuessler, "Monkeys Who Think and the Neuroscientist Who Loves Them," *Linguafranca* 10 (April 2000): 56–64.

8. See below, p. 140.

9. James Serpell, *In the Company of Animals: A Study of Human-Animal Relations* (Oxford: Blackwell, 1986), p. 158.

10. On the sociobiology debate, see Ullica Segerstråle, *Defenders of the Truth: The Battle for Science in the Sociobiology Debate and Beyond* (Oxford: Oxford University Press, 2000).

11. In the United States, biotechnology companies Novartis and Nextran are competing to be the first to provide transplantable hearts, kidneys, and livers from genetically altered pigs. Tinker Ready, "Pork Futures: The Promise—and Peril—of Xenotransplantation," *Utne Reader Online,* Body, Jan./Feb, 2000 [http://www.utne.com/bBody.tmpl?command=search&db=dArticle. db&eqheadlinedata=Pork%20Futures]

PART ONE

PURITY AND CIVILIZATION: REPUDIATION OF THE BESTIAL IN MEDIEVAL EUROPEAN SOCIETY

I

EATING ANIMALS IN THE EARLY MIDDLE AGES
CLASSIFYING THE ANIMAL WORLD AND BUILDING GROUP IDENTITIES

ROB MEENS

And it must be said that the system—at least, the system as Noah understood it—made very little sense. What was so special about cloven-footed ruminants, one asked oneself? Why should the camel and the rabbit be given second-class status? Why should a division be introduced between fish that had scales and fish that did not? The swan, the pelican, the heron, the hoopoe: are these not some of the finest species? yet they were not awarded the badge of cleanliness. Why round on the mouse and the lizard—which had enough problems already, you might think—and undermine their self-confidence further? If only we could see a glimpse of logic behind it all; if only Noah had explained it better.
—*Julian Barnes,* A History of the World in 10½ Chapters *(1989)*

When the Irish saint Moling was seeking refuge in the little village of Tnuthel, he found no welcome there, except in a certain house on the edge of town. The woman of the house bade him and his companion welcome and offered them cow's milk for refreshment. When the man of the house returned home, the couple wanted to invite their guests to dinner, but they only had some horse-steak on offer. As they put this in the cauldron, the saint, who knew they were preparing horsemeat, blessed the house and the cauldron, whereby he changed the steak into a wonderful quarter of mutton.

This anecdote from a saint's life shows that in Ireland in the eleventh or twelfth century, when this text was written, it was not done to eat horsemeat.[1] This paper will start with investigating the problem of eating horse in the early medieval period and then will turn to a discussion of other animals that were held unsuitable to be served at the table. In conclusion the discussion will turn to the reasons for and functions of these taboos in early medieval society.

3

HORSES AS FOOD

That there was a taboo on the consumption of horses in medieval Ireland is corroborated by evidence from the important canon law collection, dating from somewhere around the year 700, known as the *Collectio Hibernensis.* This collection contains a section titled "On the Prohibition of Eating Horses," the first decree of which stipulates: "The Law forbids, and Jerome even says in his controversy with Arnubius: 'The horse and the dog are always unclean animals.'" It further cites a canon from the seventh-century penitential of Archbishop Theodore of Canterbury stressing that it is not customary to eat horse, and a canon attributed to a council of Carthage stipulating that although the Church does not forbid eating horse, it is, however, not to be allowed.[2] From this miscellaneous group of texts, which is quite typical for this collection, it seems clear that consuming horsemeat constituted a problem in the Irish Church around the year 700 and that the compilers of this collection were convinced that eating such meat was not to be allowed. The "Law" (*lex*) cited in the first decree of the *Collectio* has never been identified. A prohibition on eating horsemeat is, however, not to be found in the Old Testament, which is usually referred to by the word *lex.* Maybe the *Collectio* here refers to an older Irish text, the *Canones Hibernenses,* a small miscellaneous collection of legislative material dating from the seventh century, which prescribes a penance of four years of fasting for eating horseflesh. If the *Canones* are not the *lex* referred to in the *Collectio,* they do confirm that there existed a taboo on eating horsemeat in Ireland prior to the *Collectio Hibernensis.* That such a taboo persisted in later times is shown by the *Old Irish Penitential,* probably compiled somewhere in the eighth century, which imposes a penance of three and a half years for such an offense.[3]

The penances imposed in these texts are unusually high. The Old Irish Penitential, for example, imposes only a two years' penance for engaging in bestiality, and a four years' penance for killing someone in revenge for close kin.[4] The severe penances for eating horse suggest that this was regarded as more serious than just an ordinary transgression of a dietary law. The Old Irish Penitential only imposes penances ranging from one to forty days for other transgressions of dietary prescriptions.[5] The *Canones Hibernenses* impose a penance of seven and a half years for drinking blood or urine, but for other violations of dietary rules penances range from five days to one year.[6] The severe penances assigned by these Irish texts in this particular case, therefore, hint at the existence of some ritual abhorred by the ecclesiastical lawgivers in which consumption of a horse played an important role. As we will see, there exists a description of such a ritual that would explain the repugnance of our ecclesiastical authors. But let us first see whether this taboo on eating horsemeat was only an Irish affair.

Secret penance (a term that is to be preferred to the usual expression "private penance")[7] originated in Ireland and the Celtic fringes of the British Isles. From there it spread to Anglo-Saxon England and to the Continent. As a consequence of this development Irish penitentials, in particular those written by Columbanus and Cummean, had a formative influence on Anglo-Saxon and Continental texts of this kind.[8] Nevertheless in continental works there is no mention of a rule prohibiting eating horsemeat. Irish texts, however, have come down to us mainly in Continental manuscripts. So it is with the *Canones Hibernenses,* but this text is only known from a single manuscript written in the beginning of the tenth century in Brittany by a scribe called Arbecoc.[9] Its Continental dissemination will therefore have remained limited. This is different with the *Collectio Hibernensis,* which is known from a great many continental manuscripts.[10] It remains unsure, however, how the section on eating horsemeat was read, especially since it included Archbishop Theodore's rule which did not actually forbid the consumption of horsemeat. It is also uncertain how influential this section has been.[11]

The fact that Theodore's penitential addressed the question of eating horsemeat suggests that there was some discussion of the matter in Anglo-Saxon England.[12] The archbishop did not forbid the consumption of horse, nor did he prescribe a penance for people doing such thing. He merely stated that it was not forbidden to eat horsemeat, but that it was not customary to do so. Which customs precisely he is referring to here is not clear, but it seems likely that he alluded to Roman or Greek customs, rather than to Anglo-Saxon ones, for Theodore was constantly referring to the customs of the Romans or the Greeks when dealing with delicate Anglo-Saxon problems.[13] Since Theodore's penitential was widely known on the Continent, where five versions of it circulated, his view was much more influential than the Irish ones.[14] Theodore's canon was also widely adopted in later penitentials.[15] The discussion to which Theodore's canon alludes may well have been sparked off by Irish penitential texts circulating in England at that time, or by Irish missionaries working there.

The question of eating horsemeat also worried another Anglo-Saxon church leader, Boniface, in the course of his mission to Germany in the eighth century. The anxious missionary, in a letter that has not survived, requested advice from the pope how to deal with people eating questionable sorts of food. Apparently, he made a distinction between eating wild horses (*agrestem caballum*) and tame ones (*domesticum*). The former were only eaten by a few (*aliquanti*), the latter, however, by many (*pleri*). The pope responded that

Boniface should stop this practice for it was something unclean and horrible, and that he should impose a proper penance on people doing such things.[16] That Anglo-Saxons themselves, in this respect also, did not always live up to the ideal that Boniface held up to the Germanic peoples he was trying to Christianize, is apparent from a canon of the legatine council held in the year 786. The Roman legates Georgius and Theophactylus there scorned the English for still clinging to their custom of eating horsemeat, "a thing no Christian from the East (*nullus christianorum in orientalibus*) does."[17]

The formulation chosen by the papal legates confirms Theodore of Canterbury's suggestion that it was not customary (in Rome or in Greece) to eat horsemeat. The same is implied by Pope Gregory's reply to Boniface. While in Rome this seems to have been evident, so that there was no need to legislate on it (as Theodore already noted), the position was different in newly converted lands such as Ireland, Anglo-Saxon England, and the German territories, where there seem to have existed traditions of consuming horses. Archaeological findings from Gaul, England, and Denmark do indeed suggest that in the northern areas of Europe horsemeat was used for consumption.[18] It should be borne in mind, however, that archaeologically it is difficult to establish such a consumption. Horse bones containing marks of butchery might as well be evidence of the feeding of horses to dogs.[19] In Gaul in the first century B.C. horses make up between 1 and 10 percent of the animal remains that can be linked to human consumption.[20] Percentages of numbers of animals, however, are no reflection of the relative importance of different types of food in terms of meat weight, which would be greater in the case of the horse because of its size. In the southern French village of Lunel Viel (Hérault) the horse accounted for 5.2 percent of the meat diet in the third century, rising to 12.3 percent in the fourth century and to 23.7 percent in the years 450–600. In the tenth and eleventh centuries, the next period for which there is archaeological evidence, the proportion had dropped to 10 percent. Interestingly enough, there seems to have been a "negative correlation" of the consumption of horsemeat and beef.[21] In Iron Age Britain, horseflesh apparently also formed an important part of people's diet. In West Stow horses were the "second most important meat source" after cattle.[22] Though the proportion of horseflesh in the diet declined in the Romano-British and Anglo-Saxon periods, apparently horsemeat did not become obsolete until the later Middle Ages, when horses were mainly used as riding and draft animals.[23] In Carolingian Saxony the animal bones found by archaeologists, however, do not indicate human consumption of the horse.[24] The princely grave of Valsgärde VII dating from around the year 675 contained horse bones with indications of human consumption.[25]

When the Icelanders converted to Christianity around the year 1000, so Ari Thorgilsson tells us in his *Íslendingabók,* they did so under the condition that they be allowed to continue the practice of eating horses and exposing their unwanted children.[26] Eating horsemeat and infanticide were, therefore, seen—at least by the historian Ari when he wrote this work probably between 1122 and 1132—as two native traditions that were incompatible with Christianity. The emphasis on eating horseflesh in this account seems rather surprising. It might result from Irish missionary practices, for in Ireland, as we have seen, this practice was heavily condemned. Irish *peregrini* are known to have visited Iceland, even before its inhabitants decided collectively to convert to Christianity, but the impact of Christian women and slaves from Ireland and the British Isles was also an important factor in the Christianization of the Viking island.[27] Some authors have explained these exemptions mainly as ecologically necessary measures. Horsemeat, in this view, was such an integral part of the staple diet of many Icelanders that it would have been considered too drastic to forbid it instantly.[28] According to the *Íslendingabók,* however, the Icelanders gave up both "un-Christian" practices in just a few years. If horsemeat was such an important part of the diet in Iceland, this was an extremely swift change of consumption patterns, and one might consider the possibility whether Ari's narrative was not in fact covering up the influence of the Norwegian king in the process of Christianization. For Norwegian law forbade the consumption of horseflesh on pain of a fine of three marks to be paid to the bishop.[29] Possibly, however, Ari was criticizing contemporary practices by idealizing the first generation of Icelandic Christians.

That horses were not to be used for human consumption by Christians is also implied in a moving story related by Folcuin of Lobbes (ca. 935–990) in his description of the death of his namesake and relative, Folcuin bishop of Thérouanne (816–55). When the bishop died his horse would not tolerate any other rider, for after having carried the limbs of such a great bishop, it would not bear to serve the passions (*voluptatibus*) of any other man. When the horse died not long after his master and was fed to the dogs, these did not even touch the corpse. The dogs were unable to devour the carcass of an animal on which hymns in praise of Christ had so often been sung. When the people (*cives*) saw this, they decided to give the animal, which wild beasts and birds also did not dare to touch, a human burial (*humano more sepelierunt*).[30] Folcuin seems somehow to distrust this story, for twice he declares that he relates this from hearsay (*fertur, ferunt*). In this passage, however, the historiographer reveals in passing what might happen to a dead horse: it was fed to the dogs.

Pierre Bonnassie, surveying the evidence from early medieval annals, has shown how people in times of famine resorted to eating all kinds of food, including meat from impure animals.[31] The annals speak of unclean things (*immundicias*), meat from impure animals and reptiles (*immundorum animalium et reptilium carnes*), or of unclean animals in general (*immunda animalia*), but only once mention a specific kind of animal: the dog (*canum carnes*).[32] Italian chronicles of a later period mention also cats and mice.[33] The first continuator of the *Gesta Treverorum,* writing around 1132, however, informs us about the poor of Trier devouring the horses of Archbishop Poppo (1016–1047) and some of his followers. It was in a time of severe famine that the archbishop, riding a noble horse (*equus nobilis*) and dressed in his paschal tunic, went to one of the churches in the town to celebrate Mass. A great crowd of paupers came to meet him and asked for anything to sustain their lives (*aliquid vitae subsidium*). When the bishop "in his usual manner," gave his treasurer the order to distribute money to the poor, they cried in one voice "that coins were no use to them" (*nummos sibi opus non esse*). Money couldn't buy them any food, they objected. When the bishop replied that he didn't have anything else with which to help them, they said: "if this is so, then give us the fat of your horse, so that our hunger will at least be tempered by eating some flesh." And the bishop, though unwilling, said: "He who asks for things beloved, shall give something beloved" a saying which, according to the continuator of the *Gesta,* was later turned into a proverb in the vernacular.[34] He gave his horse to the poor people and persuaded some of his followers to do the same. And the horses were devoured and swallowed on the spot before their very eyes.[35] Archbishop Poppo's deed of actually providing horsemeat in time of necessity is in line with the provision of Theodore of Canterbury regarding the consumption of horsemeat and the one permitting the consumption of food that is considered to be unclean in cases of necessity. The monks of Corbie, where Theodore's penitential was surely known, did not exclude horsemeat from the food they supplied to the poor in the ninth century, though they expressed some kind of reservation in this particular case.[36] The animal bones found in the dependent villages of the royal monastery of St. Denis indicate that the peasants there also ate horsemeat, although the monks, of course, refrained from doing so.[37] A thirteenth-century penitential handbook attributed to Robert Grosseteste declared that it is no serious offense when a poor man out of necessity eats the meat of a donkey or a horse.[38]

The vehemence with which a native tradition of eating horse was opposed in Ireland, however, suggests that this practice meant something different in Ireland from what it did in England or the German lands. Whereas in the latter it was discouraged, mainly by referring to Theodore's decree, in Ireland it seems to have instilled such horror that extremely heavy penances were prescribed for offenses of this kind.[39] Yet, the *Life of*

Moling does not condemn the fact that the couple who welcomed the saint, apparently living some sort of marginal life on the edge of town, kept horsemeat in their house. As we have seen, Theodore of Canterbury had permitted the use of unclean food in cases of necessity.[40] From the evidence provided by the *Collectio Hibernensis* it is clear that Theodore's penitential was known in Ireland at an early date and was also regarded as an authoritative text. The passage giving permission to use unclean food in times of necessity was also included in the *Old Irish Penitential*.[41] This Theodorian influence would explain the use of horsemeat by Moling's hosts. On the other hand, the Irish saint Columba could rebuke a man by uttering the apparently ominous words: "The time will come when in a wood, with thieves, you will chew the flesh of a stolen mare."[42] From this passage it seems that eating horse functioned as some sort of social stigma. Some people (thieves, outlaws?), apparently, were not fully human and could therefore eat horsemeat, whereas this was forbidden to normal members of society. Probably the *Canones Adomnani* also referred to outlaws when they permitted "bestial men" (*bestiales homines*) to eat from animals that had been fed upon by other animals. "For it seems to him [Adomnan] fitting that human beasts [*humanae bestiae*] should eat the flesh that has been served to beasts."[43]

That eating horsemeat was taboo is also suggested by that intriguing king-making rite described by Gerald of Wales in his *Topography of Ireland*. This *rite de passage* is characterized by a number of transgressions of society's fundamental rules. Gerald describes it as follows:

> There is in the northern and farther part of Ulster, namely in Kenell-cunill, a certain people which is accustomed to appoint its king with a rite altogether outlandish and abominable. When the whole people of that land has been gathered together in one place, a white mare is brought forward into the middle of the assembly. He who is to be inaugurated, not as a chief, but as a beast, not as a king but as an outlaw, has bestial intercourse with her before all, professing himself to be a beast also. The mare is then killed immediately, cut up in pieces, and boiled in water. He sits in the bath surrounded by all his people, and all, he and they, eat of the meat of the mare which is brought to them. He quaffs and drinks of the broth in which he is bathed, not in any cup, or using his hand, but just dipping his mouth into it around him. When this unrighteous rite has been carried out, his kingship and dominion have been conferred.[44]

Gerald's account of this rite has raised some serious doubts among historians regarding its authenticity. His description of the Irish in this work, did, indeed, serve as a rationale for English colonization.[45] Yet all the elements mentioned in Gerald's narrative are also found in penitential texts from Ireland as being in some way or another impure. This holds true, for example, for men sexually abusing animals, for consuming something that came into contact with a dead animal or with the extremities of one's body, and also, as we have seen, eating horsemeat. This suggests that Gerald was not letting his imagination run wild, but was, with all his biases, in fact describing some sort of Irish king-making ritual.[46] Rituals such as this could also explain the vehemence with which eating meat from horses was combated by Irish churchmen.

Historians have often regarded dietary taboos as an aspect of the struggle against paganism.[47] One wonders whether this is true. Some canons do indeed specify that people have to do penance after having eaten food sacrificed to the pagan gods. But even here it was not always out of religious motives, so it seems, that people took part in such rituals. Obviously, people confessing their sins and willing to do penance for them are to be considered as Christians. Nevertheless, they seem to have taken part in rituals that were held to be pagan by the authors of penitential texts. Columbanus distinguished between different motives for partaking in pagan rituals. It could be done out of ignorance, out of real reverence for the pagan deities (*pro cultu daemonum aut honore simulacrorum*), or people might take part just for the food and drink (*gulae tantum vitio*).[48] The pagan cult centered around a huge cask of beer that Columbanus encountered near Bregenz gives us some clue why this last motive mattered.[49]

Sometimes people expected magical effects from eating unclean food, but this is not necessarily to be regarded as a symptom of paganism. On the contrary, people might be seduced into doing something that was forbidden by Christianity, just for magical reasons. In the tripartite St. Gall penitential, rules regarding the consumption of blood and of unclean meat that has been gnawed upon by a wolf are found under the rubric of "magical deeds" (*de maleficis*).[50] In the eleventh century Paris penitential, we also find dietary rules among those that deal with magical acts.[51] This indicates that people did eat forbidden foods for magical purposes, but rather than this being the cause of the taboo on these kinds of food, to judge by the date of these texts this must be seen rather as a later development. There is a striking parallel with forbidden sexual activities on a Sunday that were also grouped under the rubric of "magic." The typically Christian rule concerning sexual abstinence on a holy day is here appropriated and given a peculiar twist.[52] There is, therefore, no conclusive evidence that links dietary prescriptions with food used in pagan sacrifices. An exception might be the cases of the horse and the dog. The king-making ritual among the Kenellcunill might have had a religious content, but this is not obvious from Gerald's description. It could also have functioned as some sort of "civic" ritual, with no necessary religious connotations, as Robert Markus has argued for late antique rituals of the fourth century.[53] On the Continent the practice of burying horses and dogs might point to a religious custom of sacrificing these animals.[54] The archaeological context, however, seems to favor an interpretation of these archaeological finds as burial gifts instead of as sacrifices. In that case the link between pagan rituals and food taboos disappears altogether.[55]

IMPURE ANIMALS PAR EXCELLENCE: DOGS, CATS, AND MICE

The life of the Irish saint Declan, written some time after the life of Moling, recounts that when Declan was entertained by a certain Dercanus, this *vir gentilis* tried to pull a trick on the saint. He asked his servants to kill a dog, to hide its head and legs by burying them, and to prepare its meat for the saint and his disciples. They should take care to choose a fat dog, so that the meat would resemble mutton. Declan, however, being a saint, suspected that he was served unlawful (*illicitum*) food, and discovered in the food offered to them a dog's claw, which Dercanus's servants had overlooked when slaughtering the animal.[56] Just like horses, dogs, so we may conclude from this story, were not regarded as proper food in Ireland in the twelfth century either. Unlike in the case of the horse, however, no ecclesiastical or secular ruling forbade the consumption of dog meat. From this we must conclude that, while there was some discussion about the permissibility of horsemeat, such a discussion was unthinkable in the case of dogs. Only in times of famine did people apparently resort to canine meat.[57]

The fact that dogs are found in the same archaeological context as horses strengthens the view that dietary rules were not primarily aiming to obliterate pagan sacrifices. If the practice of burying horses reflected pagan rituals in which horses were ritually consumed, we would also expect such rituals in the case of dogs, which are found in similar archaeological circumstances. Yet, there was no early medieval rule forbidding the consumption of dog meat. Apparently people in this period did not need to be warned against eating dogs.[58] Archaeological evidence suggests that while in ancient Gaul dogs were used as food, they were no longer regarded as such in early medieval times. In the absence of any regulation forbidding the consumption of dogs such a shift seems more the result of a Romanizing process than of an influence of Christian norms.[59] The first reference to eating dog meat comes from the beginning of the thirteenth century, when Robert Grosseteste imposed a three days' penance on a poor man who ate a dog in time of need.[60] This contrast between eating horse or canine meat is already clear in the stories of Moling and Declan. While the couple offering Moling food in fact had horsemeat in the house for consumption, the *vir gentilis* Dercanus was clearly trying to test the holy man.

The dog was not only unthinkable as food, it was also held to be impure.[61] This, at least in part, seems an explanation for the ignominious character of the ritual of reconciliation that involved carrying a dog.[62] Food touched by dogs was held to be unclean. The *Paenitentiale Bigotianum* imposes a one-year penance for drinking something "contaminated" by a dog (*quod intinxit canis*).[63] A similar canon is implied by Theodore of Canterbury when he says that it doesn't matter if a dog, a mouse or an(other?) unclean animal that eats blood, touches food.[64] Cummean imposed a penance of three special fasts (*superpositiones*) for someone who ate or drank something that was contaminated by "a household animal that is a mouse-catcher" (*familiaris bestia quae est muriceps*).[65] A similar provision is to be found in the *Canones Hibernenses*.[66] These passages have been translated as rules concerning contamination of food by cats, but they surely apply to dogs as well, as shown by the gloss added to this sentence in the *P. Ps.-Theodori* and the *P. Ps.-Egberti*.[67] The canon from the *Old Irish Penitential*, translated by Binchy as "Anyone who drinks the leaving of a cat does five days' penance," should possibly also be interpreted as regarding something polluted by a dog.[68] For information on what sorts of food people might have eschewed, it is also useful to look at works in which foreign peoples and their habits are described. In one of these, the *Cosmographia* of Aethicus Ister—an enigmatic text that might or might not have been composed by the Irishman Virgil of Salzburg, but was surely composed in the eighth century and was also well known in southern Germany by that time—the "Turchi" are said to feed on several abominable things, one of which is meat from dogs.[69] This does not tell us much about the Turks (whatever people the author may have had in mind when using that term, possibly the Avars), but quite a lot about the prevalent conceptions of proper food in the time and region in which the author was writing.

That the dog was not held in high esteem might partly be the result of Proverbs 26:11, which speaks about the sinner returning to his former sins just as the dog returns to his vomit, a text well known to authors of penitentials.[70] All sorts of food that had become impure, and therefore unsuitable for human consumption, was to be given to the dogs. As we have seen, dogs were fed not only meat from dead horses but also the remains of animals that had been gnawed upon by wild beasts or animals that had had to be killed because they had been polluted by sexual contact with humans.[71] Especially the holy had to be safeguarded against the impure; thus, vomiting the Eucharist could be regarded as an act requiring reparation by a forty days' penance. Even in case of sickness, a penance was required, though only one of seven days. The penance for this act was, however, increased to a hundred days if dogs licked up the vomit containing the Holy Eucharist.[72] Anxieties about the possible contamination of the Holy Eucharist inspired a whole group of *sententiae* concerning the Host, which proved to be highly influential.[73]

One of the concerns expressed in these canons is that the Eucharist, if it is not well guarded, will be nibbled on by a mouse.[74] This brings us to another category of animals held to be impure: mice. We already have seen that mouse-catching was seen as a characteristic of impure animals like the cat and the dog. Mice were also held to be able to contaminate food. If a mouse or a chicken or something else falls into wine or water, nobody should drink from it.[75] Such rules have been read as hygienic rules, meant to educate the barbarian pagans.[76] They should, however, rather be read as careful demarcations of the pure and the impure. Another text, for example, makes a distinction between a clean bird (*avis munda*) on the one hand, and an unclean bird or a mouse (*immunda avis aut sorix*) on the other, when dealing with wine, oil, or honey polluted by such animals falling into them. In the first case a ritual cleansing will make the food acceptable again, while in the second case the food cannot be used, and whoever sells this polluted substance to someone else should do penance for a year.[77] The equation between the mouse and an unclean bird suggests that the mouse is also seen as an unclean animal. In some instances the mouse is associated with the weasel, which, therefore, might also be reckoned among unclean animals. We might indeed have to interpret terms like *mus* and *sorex* as denoting several kinds of small rodents.[78] In fact Theodore grouped the dog, the cat, and the mouse together when he decided that it does no harm to eat food touched by these animals or by an(other) animal that feeds on blood.[79] Here, therefore, the dogs, cats and mice seem to be grouped together as the "impure animals" par excellence, leaving room, however, for other unclean animals feeding on blood.

UNCLEAN BIRDS AND THE IMPORTANCE
OF FEEDING

The *Hubertense* penitential makes a clear distinction between pure and impure animals, though it remains hard to find out which animals were regarded as such. It also speaks of pure and impure birds, but again doesn't specify which birds belong to which group.[80] Species of birds are mentioned in Irish texts only. They name the eagle, the hawk, the crow, the scaldcrow, the daw, the magpie, the cock, and the hen, as birds that are able to contaminate food by touching it.[81] The *Collectio Hibernensis* attributes the following remark to Jerome: "The meat of birds is permitted to clerics; it does not so much satisfy, but rather incites pain, and yet the law teaches that almost all birds are denied."[82] The *Cosmographia* of Aethicus Ister, when describing the abominable habits of the "Turks," also names several birds: the vulture, the kite, and the eagle owl.[83]

The birds mentioned in the *Cosmographia,* though not identical with those mentioned by Irish texts, clearly belong to a similar group: that of carrion-eating birds. The fact that chickens and hens are also mentioned here may at first seem surprising, because they clearly served as food in these times. They should, however, be compared to pigs, animals wandering around the house and from time to time overstepping the boundary that separated man from the animals. Since it was probably the things they fed upon that made birds impure, the same could apply to chickens, hens, and pigs. These animals were not impure by nature, but one should always keep in mind what they had fed upon. For "if pigs by chance eat meat from carcasses or [drink] human blood, we do not believe that they should be rejected, nor chickens; so pigs that have tasted human blood can be consumed. But if they have eaten from the bodies of the dead, their meat should not be eaten until they have grown thin again and after a year," so Theodore of Canterbury decided.[84] His decision shows something of the anxieties people were living with. One gets the impression that Theodore, with the kindness of a stranger—since he had been born in the Greek-speaking town of Tarsus and had spent quite some time in Rome before coming to Canterbury—tried to soften a rigid system of food taboos by declaring some of these void and others invalid in time of necessity. In Irish texts like the *Canones Adomnani* or the *Canones Hibernenses,* however, one still can feel something of the harshness of such a rigid set of taboos.

MOTIVATIONS

It is hard to identify the motives on account of which certain animals were regarded as unclean. It has been argued that certain animals were eschewed because they played a significant role in pagan rituals. We have seen that there is no compelling reason to suppose this. Another reason advanced is that these dietary rules were inspired by ideas of hygiene. This would, however, suppose some kind of knowledge about bacteria and infections. Mary Douglas has argued persuasively that, though there may be a "marvelous correspondence" between medically based avoidance and ritual avoidance, the latter should be regarded on its own terms, that is as a kind of ritual expression.[85] Yet another reason advanced for these dietary rules is that they were a means whereby the Church was trying to civilize the barbaric peoples of the North.[86] There might, indeed, be some kind of Romanizing, rather than civilizing, aspect to the rules. The proportion of horsemeat in the diet in West Stow seems to have declined from Romano-British times onwards. Apart from this, biblical precedents probably also played a role, though they surely did not dictate the whole program, as is shown by the acceptance of pork and the taboo on horsemeat. In our material several allusions to the biblical *lex* can be found, mostly to the Old Testament, but also to Acts (15:28–29), where the consumption of blood and strangled animals is prohibited.[87]

Animals' feeding patterns were also of importance, as is, for example, suggested by the *Canones Adomnani,* discussing food contaminated by cows and pigs. In the first case the food can be consumed with a good conscience, for "cows feed only on grass and the leaves of trees." In the case of swine, however, the food should be cooked and could only be distributed to "unclean men" (*inmundis hominibus*), for "swine eat things clean and unclean."[88] Animals that fed on carrion, blood, and human corpses apparently could not be consumed by humans with a clear conscience. The polluting power of these three substances seems to have been so great that it could reach human beings through the food they took in, and for this reason carnivores were not regarded as proper human food.[89]

That improper behavior on the part of animals made them impure is suggested by another canon from the *Canones Adomnani,* referring to Old Testament legislation on the bull "that pushes with the horn" (Ex. 21:29–36), a biblical text that was also included in the *Collectio Hibernensis.*[90] The canon reads: "Swine that taste the flesh or blood of men are always forbidden. For in the Law an animal that pushes with the horn, if it kills a man, is forbidden; how much more those that eat a man."[91] This suggests that animals somehow transgressing the conceived natural order between man and beast are regarded as impure, for the proper order is that men kill cattle and eat them, not the other way around. Such animals were also regarded as somehow dangerous, as is shown by Theodore of Canterbury's rule that bees that had killed a human being were to be put to death swiftly.[92] There were some doubts as to whether one still could use the honey produced by such homicidal bees. Theodore admitted its use, while other texts prohibited it; the question whether the honey had come into physical contact with the bees, and hence had in a way become contaminated by them, played a prominent part in this discussion.[93]

Some of these dietary rules presumably aimed at distinguishing humans from animals. This seems to be the motive behind rules forbidding the consumption of animals that have been sexually abused by humans, and of food that has been gnawed upon by animals.[94] Such a reason can hardly, however, be applied to the taboo on certain specific animals like the horse. In this case the place of the animal in question in the early medieval worldview must be of importance. Early medieval dietary prescriptions seem in a way to reflect the concept of pollution as depicted by Mary Douglas.[95] Could it be that those animals that were to be avoided were in a sense anomalous or ambiguous creatures? Such an interpretation is suggested by the impurity attached to animals like the dog, cat, and mouse, which lived around human dwellings, in the marginal area between house and forest, culture and nature.

If animals became impure by eating certain types of food and by occupying an anomalous position between human society and wild nature, this still does not explain why people also had to abstain from horsemeat. Though horses were in those days much smaller than they are now, they were much bigger than dogs and cats.[96] Horses would in an agricultural context be more on a par with cattle. In the case of the horse, however, a social distinction seems to be in order. Apparently for poor people it was not a real problem to eat horses. For clerics and nobles, however, it was. Could it not be that this distinction, somehow, reflected different attitudes toward (different types of) horses? Early medieval law codes differentiate between several kinds of horses. Farmers only possessed horses as working animals, designated in our sources as *vilior equus, miserabilis caballus,* or *deterior equus.*[97] Aristocrats, secular and ecclesiastical, used a different kind of horse for a different purpose, namely riding. Archbishop Poppo of Trier rode a "noble horse" (*equus nobilis*). Corbinian rode an "Iberus," a Spanish horse, to save someone who had been sentenced to death. The count of Trient stole such an "Iberus" to breed with his own mares. Charlemagne send Harun el Rashid Spanish horses and mules as a gift.[98] This difference in the use of horses might also explain the different attitudes toward the animal's meat. Riding a horse brings someone into more intimate contact with the animal than using it as a working animal does. The personal bond that tied rider to horse, exemplified in the story about Abbot Folcuin and his horse—but which might also be read in the archaeological records of burying horses in clearly aristocratic graves— might explain why these animals were regarded as somehow more "human" than cattle or pigs, and were thus also in a way anomalous. The noble human emotions attributed to Abbot Folcuin's horse may be seen as an example of the anthropomorphizing tendency toward horses.

CONCLUSION

Explaining the impurity attached to early medieval animals remains a hazardous exercise, if only because we have no complete catalogue of such animals, but only a few scattered references that are mainly to be found in penitential handbooks for confessors. Even if we had such a complete catalogue, it would still remain difficult to explain the motives on account of which animals were held to be impure, because we know so little about early medieval views of the animal world and its classification. There are of course the encyclopedic works of Isidore of Seville and Hrabanus Maurus, building on the foundations laid by Pliny, which classify the animal world, but these theoretical works do not necessarily reflect the classifications ordinary people lived by. The evidence seems, however, to imply that feeding habits and inappropriate behavior contributed to the impurity of some species, while others were set apart from animals that could serve as food on grounds of closeness to humans.

Our sources also seem to indicate that there was no uniform classification of the pure and the impure with regard to animals. Medieval society was much more open to outside influences than early Jewish society was. Therefore, history and geography seem of more importance in the medieval case. In Ireland an exceptionally rigid set of dietary rules seems to have been in use, which accords with the strict rules regarding marriage and sexuality that we find in Irish penitentials. It is unclear, however, to whom these rules applied. Possibly Irish penitentials were only applied to the dependents of monasteries, the *manaig,* which could explain their concern for purity.[99] Monks had to avoid all meat and some decrees even forbade them to eat food touched by impure people.[100] This suggests a concentric world view with the most pure, i.e. the monks, in the center, the less pure, the *manaig,* in a second orbit, and in an outer circle the not fully human, the *homines bestiales.*[101] Theodore's penitential was clearly meant to be used at all levels of society. The dietary prescriptions found in his work were intended to moderate some of the Irish rules, and might reflect a less "monastic" view of the world, with less strict boundaries (less "grid and group," to use the terminology of Mary Douglas). The fact that Theodore came from a different culture from that of the Irish might also have contributed to the fact that he seems to act much more independently when discussing the distinctions between food pure and impure. The Theodorian view was clearly the one that appealed to Continental compilers of penitential books, for they adopted most of his dietary canons, while the stricter Irish rules are only to be found in a handful of continental manuscripts.

Apart from geographical diversity, social distinctions seem to have been important. The horse appears to have been used as food by the poor without great difficulty, while it was taboo for the secular and ecclesiastical aristocracy. This will reflect different views of the horse, but it probably also served as a powerful symbol of social differences. Eating horsemeat showed that you were poor and did not belong to the aristocracy. Using and abstaining from certain types of food, therefore, could function as strong markers of identity. Definitions of the "other" in terms of what they eat seem very powerful indeed. In the process, the other becomes less human, as exemplified by the *homines bestiales,* who ate bestial food. For Gerald of Wales the different food patterns of the Irish were one element in his depiction of them as less civilized than Anglo-Normans and therefore as proper subjects of conquest and domination.[102]

Food taboos may be said to function as rituals of exclusion. The power of such rituals becomes clearer when we consider the social bonds forged by eating and drinking together.[103] People, on the other hand, who refused to eat the same food, or did not admit others to their table, made strong social statements. When the Irish bishop Dagan refused to share a meal with his Roman colleagues Laurentius, Mellitus, and Justus who were working among the Anglo-Saxons, and would not even enter the house in which they were dining, the three bishops were so indignant that they concluded that the Irish were as bad as the Britons.[104] When the priest Ingo, working among the Karantanians in the eighth century, served Christian servants in his house with golden cups, he fed their pagan masters "like dogs" outside, serving them with filthy jugs (*fusca vasa*) and providing these "dogs" with bread and meat.[105] What kind of meat Ingo served them is not revealed, but bearing in mind the expression coined by Ludwig Feuerbach, "Der Mensch ist was er ißt,"[106] it is not implausible that in those unclean vessels Ingo served them food impure for Christians. Accidentally, he thereby may have mirrored the story about Declan being served a dog by the pagan Dercanus. This episode may serve as a reminder how food can be used as a powerful language that seems particularly apt to constitute groups and to define outsiders—literally, in Ingo's case!

NOTES

1. W. Stokes, "The Birth and Life of St. Moling," *Revue Celtique* 27 (1906): 292–93. According to J. F. Kenney, *The Sources for the Early History of Ireland: An Introduction and Guide,* vol. 1: *Ecclesiastical* (1929; reprint ed., Blackrock: Four Courts Press, 1993), p. 462, the text "has much importance for the light it throws on social and moral conditions in the eleventh and twelfth centuries."

2. *Collectio Hibernensis* LIV.13, ed. H. Wasserschleben, in *Die irische Kanonensammlung,* 2d ed. (Leipzig: Bernhard Tauchnitz, 1885), p. 218; except for the canon from Theodore's penitential, the citations are not identified. For a recent discussion of our state of knowledge of the *Collectio Hibernensis,* see L. Mair Davies, "Isidorian Texts and the *Hibernensis,*" *Peritia* 11 (1997): 207–49, esp. pp. 209–18; see also R. Meens, "The Oldest Manuscript Witness of the *Collectio canonum Hibernensis,*" *Peritia* 14 (2000) 1–19.

3. *Canones Hibernenses* I.13, ed. L. Bieler, in *The Irish Penitentials, with an appendix by D. A. Binchy,* Scriptores Latini Hiberniae, vol. 5 (Dublin: Dublin Institute for Advanced Studies, 1963), p. 160; *Old Irish Penitential* (hereafter *OIP*) I.2, in Bieler, *The Irish Penitentials,* p. 259.

4. *OIP* II.24 and V.3, pp. 264 and 271.

5. Ibid. II.3–4, p. 260.

6. *Canones Hibernenses* I.12–21, ed. Bieler, in *The Irish Penitentiaries,* pp. 160–62.

7. See M. de Jong, "What Was Public about Public Penance? *Paenitentia publica* and Justice in the Carolingian World," in *La giustizia nell'alto medioevo,* vol. 2: *Secoli IX–XI,* Settimane di Studio, vol. 44 (Spoleto: Centro Italiano di Studi sull'Alto Medioevo, 1997), pp. 863–904; and R. Meens, "The Frequency and Nature of Early Medieval Penance," in *Handling Sin: Confession in the Middle Ages,* ed. P. Biller and A. J. Minnis, York Studies in Medieval Theology, vol. 2 (York: York Medieval Press, 1998), pp. 47–52.

8. See R. Kottje, "Überlieferung und Rezeption der irischen Bussbücher auf dem Kontinent," in *Die Iren und Europa im früheren Mittelalter,* ed. H. Löwe, 2 vols. (Stuttgart: Klett-Cotta, 1982) 1:511–24; T. Charles-Edwards, "The Penitential of Theodore and the *Iudicia Theodori,*" in *Archbishop Theodore: Commemorative Studies on His Life and Influence,* ed. M. Lapidge, Cambridge Studies in Anglo-Saxon England, vol. 11 (Cambridge: Cambridge University Press, 1995), pp. 141–74, for the influence of the penitential of Theodore of Canterbury; and R. Meens, *Het tripartite boeteboek: Overlevering en betekenis van vroegmiddeleeuwse biechtvoorschriften (met editie en vertaling van vier tripartita)* (Hilversum: Verloren, 1994) for the influence on continental penitentials.

9. Bieler, *The Irish Penitentials,* pp. 14, 26.

10. P. Fournier, "De l'influence de la collection irlandaise sur la formation des collections canoniques," *Nouvelle revue historique de droit français et étranger* 23 (1899): 27–78; H. Mordek, *Kirchenrecht und Reform im Frankenreich: Die Collectio Vetus Gallica, die älteste systematische Kanonessammlung des fränkischen Gallien: Studien und Edition,* Beiträge zur Geschichte und Quellenkunde des Mittelalters, vol. 1 (Berlin: Walter de Gruyter, 1975), pp. 255–59; R. Reynolds, "Unity and Diversity in Carolingian Canon Law Collections:

The Case of the *Collectio Hibernensis* and Its Derivatives," in *Carolingian Essays,* ed. U.-R. Blumenthal, Andrew W. Mellon Lectures in Early Christian Studies (Washington, D.C.: Catholic University of America Press, 1983), pp. 99–135.

11. As far as I know it was not adopted from the *Hibernensis* into other collections of canon law.

12. *P. Theodori U* II.11.4, ed. P. W. Finsterwalder, in *Die Canones Theodori Cantuariensis und ihre Überlieferungsformen* (Weimar: Böhlaus Hof-Buchdruckerei, 1929), p. 299; cf. *P. Theodori G* 144, D 22, and Co 121, pp. 267, 241, 279; *Canones Basilienses* 24c, ed. F. B. Asbach, in *Das Poenitentiale Remense und der sogen. Excarpsus Cummeani: Überlieferung, Quellen und Entwicklung zweier kontinentaler Bußbücher aus der 1. Hälfte des 8. Jahrhunderts* (Regensburg, 1975), appendix, p. 82.

13. Cf. J. E. Salisbury, *The Beast Within: Animals in the Middle Ages* (New York: Routledge, 1994), p. 56, and A. Meaney, "Anglo-Saxon Idolaters and Ecclesiasts from Theodore to Alcuin: A Source Study," *Anglo-Saxon Studies in Archaeology and History* 5 (1992): 105, both suggesting that Theodore referred to Anglo-Saxon customs here. For Theodore's references in cases of doubt to Roman and Greek customs, see S. Hollis, *Anglo-Saxon Women and the Church: Sharing a Common Fate* (Woodbridge: The Boydell Press, 1992), pp. 60–61. Theodore's thorough knowledge of the Greek and Roman world is brought out by his biblical commentaries, see Lapidge, *Archbishop Theodore: Commemorative Studies,* and especially B. Bischoff and, M. Lapidge, eds., *Biblical Commentaries from the Canterbury School of Theodore and Hadrian* (Cambridge: Cambridge University Press, 1994).

14. On the manuscript tradition of Theodore's penitential, see R. Kottje, "Paenitentiale Theodori," in *Handwörterbuch zur deutschen Rechtsgeschichte,* vol. 3 (Berlin: Schmidt, 1984), cols. 1413–16. Two other manuscripts were identified by M. M. Woesthuis, "A Note on Two Manuscripts of the 'Penitentiale Theodori' from the Library of De Thou," *Sacris Erudiri* 34 (1994): 175–84; see also Meens, *Het tripartite boeteboek,* pp. 30–36.

15. For example, in the *Excarpsus Cummeani* I.23, the *P. Remense* III.30, the *P. Vindobonense* B, II.10, the *P. Capitula Iudiciorum XXIII,* 1i, and the *P. Parisiense compositum* 84. Meens, *Het tripartite boeteboek,* pp. 527, 534.

16. Boniface, letter 28, ed. R. Rau, in *Briefe des Bonifatius: Willibalds Leben des Bonifatius, Nebst einigen zeitgenössischen Dokumenten,* Ausgewählte Quellen zur deutschen Geschichte des Mittelalters: Freiherr vom Stein-Gedächtnisausgabe, vol. 4b (Darmstadt: Wissenschaftliche Buchgesellschaft, 1968), p. 100.

17. Ed. E. Dümmler, in *MGH: Epistolae Karol. Aevi,* vol. 4 (Berlin, 1895), p. 27. For Alcuin's influence on the formulation of these canons, see C.

Cubitt, *Anglo-Saxon Church Councils c. 650–c. 850* (London: Leicester University Press, 1995), pp. 153–90. A connection between the canons propounded by the papal legates and the legislative activity of Offa of Mercia has been suggested by P. Wormald, "In Search of King Offa's 'Law-Code,'" in *People and Places in Northern Europe 500–1600: Essays in Honour of Peter Hayes Sawyer,* ed. I. Wood and N. Lund (Woodbridge, 1991), pp. 24–45, who also suggests that some rules might be a reaction to Pictish customs (p. 33).

18. For the archaeological evidence on consumption of horsemeat, see the index constructed by F. Audoin-Rouzeau, *Hommes et animaux en Europe: Corpus de données archéozoologiques et historiques* (Paris: CNRS, 1993), under "consommation de Equus caballus."

19. J. Coy, "The Animal Bones," in J. Haslam, "A Middle Saxon Iron Smelting Site at Ramsbury, Wiltshire," *Medieval Archaeology* 24 (1980): 41–51: "Such butchery might only mean that horses were fed to dogs as they are today but the presence of these fragments alongside food remains with not necessarily more evidence of chewing makes it likely that they were eaten by people."

20. P. Méniel, *Les sacrifices d'animaux chez les Gaulois* (Paris: Editions Errance, 1992), pp. 136, 138

21. C. Raynaud et al., *Le village Gallo-Romain et médiéval de Lunel Viel (Hérault): La fouille du quartier ouest (1981–1983)* (Paris: Les Belles Lettres, 1990), p. 304, and tables on pp. 308–9.

22. P. Crabtree, "Zooarchaeology at Early Anglo-Saxon West Stow," in *Medieval Archaeology: Papers of the Seventeenth Annual Conference of the Center for Medieval and Early Renaissance Studies,* ed. C. Redman, Medieval & Renaissance Texts & Studies, vol. 60 (Binghamton, N.Y.: Center for Medieval and Renaissance Studies, 1989), p. 206.

23. Ibid.; A. Grant, "Medieval Animal Husbandry: The Archaeozoological Evidence," in *Animals and Archaeology,* vol. 4: *Husbandry in Europe,* ed. C. Grigson and J. Clutton-Brock, BAR International Series 227 (Oxford, 1984), pp. 181–82; despite its title this paper deals only with evidence from Britain.

24. Monika Doll, "'Im Essen jedoch konnte er nicht so enthaltsam sein . . .': Fleischverzehr in der Karolingerzeit," in *799: Kunst und Kultur der Karolingerzeit: Karl der Große und Papst Leo III in Paderborn: Beiträge zum Katalog der Ausstellung Paderborn 1999,* ed. C. Stiegemann and M. Wemhoff (Mainz: Philip von Zabern, 1999), pp. 445–49, based on evidence from the royal palace in Paderborn and the nearby villages of Soest and Höxter.

25. W. Janssen, "Das Tier im Spiegel der archäologischen Zeugnisse," in *L'uomo di fronte al mondo animale nell'alto medioevo,* Settimane di Studio, vol.

31 (Spoleto: Centro Italiano di Studi sull' Alto Medioevo, 1985), p. 1247. According to Janssen the interpretation of the bones as pointing to the consumption of horsemeat was not completely convincing at the time he was writing his contribution.

26. A. Thorgillson, *The Book of Icelanders (Íslendingabók)*, ed. and trans. Halldór Hermannsson, Islandica, vol. 20 (Ithaca, N.Y.: Cornell University Library, 1930), chap. 7, pp. 64–67. On the conversion of Iceland, see now J. Jochens, "Late and Peaceful: Iceland's Conversion through Arbitration in 1000," *Speculum* 74 (1999): 621–55.

27. S. Rafnsson, "The Penitential of St. Thorlakur in Its Icelandic Context," *Bulletin of Medieval Canon Law* 15 (1985): 19–30; for the relation between infanticide and eating horsemeat, see J. Jochens, *Women in Old Norse Society* (Ithaca, N.Y.: Cornell University Press, 1995), pp. 87–88; for the evidence for Irish *peregrini* in Iceland, see D. Strömbäck, *The Conversion of Iceland* (London: University College London, 1975), pp. 62–63; the influence of women and slaves is stressed in R. Fletcher, *The Conversion of Europe: From Paganism to Christianity* (London: Fontana Press, 1997), pp. 397–400, and Jochens, "Late and Peaceful," pp. 633–40.

28. See S. Nordal, *Icelandic Culture* (Ithaca, N.Y.: Cornell University Press, 1990), p. 178; M. Magnusson, *Icelandic Saga* (London: Bodley Head, 1987), p. 141; the latter also provides as a reason for the emphasis on eating horse, though without any underpinning from sources, that this was associated with pagan cults, especially that of Freyr.

29. *Gulathing Law* 20, trans. L. M. Larson, in *The Earliest Norwegian Laws Being the Gulathing Law and the Frostathing Law* (New York: Columbia University Press, 1935), p. 48.

30. Folcuin of Lobbes, *Gesta abbatum S. Bertini Sithiensium,* c. 62, *MGH SS* 13, p. 619.

31. P. Bonnassie, "Consommation d'aliments immondes et cannibalisme de survie dans l'occident du Haut Moyen Age," *Annales ESC* 44 (1989): 1035–56.

32. Ibid., p. 1046.

33. G. Ortalli, "Gli animali nella vita quotidiana dell'alto medioevo: Termini di un rapporto," in *L'uomo di fronte al mondo animale,* pp. 1389–1443.

34. "Carum quisque dabit, qui cara recipere quaerit." Cf. H. Walther, *Proverbia sententiaeque latinitatis medii aevi: Lateinische Sprichwörter und Sentenzen des Mittelalters in alphabetischer Anordnung,* 9 vols. (Göttingen: Vandenhoeck, 1963–86), no. 17,083: "Nolens cara dare, non cara memeris habere."

35. *Gesta Treverorum: Additamentum et continuatio prima,* c. 6, ed. G. Pertz, MGH SS 8, p. 180.

36. *Statuta Adalhardi*, ed. J. Semmler, in *Corpus Consuetudinum Monasticarum*, vol. 1, ed. K. Hallinger (Siegburg: F. Schmitt, 1963), p. 374: "similiter omnem quintum decimae de pecudis, id est in uitulis, in berbicibus uel omnibus quae dantur de gregibus portario, etiam in caballis." Ms. Berlin, Staatsbibliothek Preußischer Kulturbesitz, Hamilton 132 (H), containing the U version of Theodore's penitential, was written in Corbie in the beginning of the ninth century; see R. Kottje, "Bußpraxis und Bußritus," in *Segni e riti nella chiesa altomedievale occidentale*, Settimane di studio, vol. 33 (Spoleto: Centro Italiano di Studi sull' Alto Medioevo, 1987), p. 374 n. 24.

37. J.-H. Yvinec, "L'élevage et la chasse," in *Un village au temps de Charlemagne: Moines et paysans de l'abbaye de Saint-Denis du VIIe siècle à l'An Mil*, ed. J. Cuisenier and R. Guadagnin (Paris: Editions de la Réunion des musées nationaux, 1988), pp. 229–31.

38. *De Confessione* 50, ed. J. Goering and F. A. C. Mantello, in "The Early Penitental Writings of Robert Grosseteste," *Recherches de théologie ancienne et médiévale* 54 (1987): 102.

39. This geographical distinction was not observed by Bonnassie, "Consommation d'aliments immondes," p. 1037.

40. *P. Theodori U* I.7.6–7, p. 299.

41. *OIP* I.4: "Theodore says that although food be touched by the hand of one polluted or by a dog, cat, mouse, or unclean animal that drinks blood, this does the food no harm" (p. 260).

42. *Vita Columbae* I.21, ed. A. O. and M. A. Anderson, in *Adomnan's Life of Columba* (Oxford: Clarendon Press, 1991), p. 48; a similar rebuke is made by Enda of Aran, see C. Plummer, ed., *Vitae Sanctorum Hiberniae*, vol. 2 (Oxford: Clarendon Press, 1968), p. 73.

43. *Canones Adomnani* 4 and 18, ed. Bieler, in *The Irish Penitentials*, pp. 176 and 180.

44. Gerald of Wales, *Topographia Hiberniae* III.102, ed. J. O'Meara, "Giraldus Cambrensis, *Topographia Hibernie*: Text of the First Recension," *Proceedings of the Royal Irish Academy* 52C (1948–50): 168; John J. O'Meara, trans., *Gerald of Wales, The History and Topography of Ireland* (Harmondsworth: Penguin Books, 1982), p. 110.

45. R. Bartlett, *Gerald of Wales 1146–1223* (Oxford: Clarendon Press, 1982), pp. 38–45, and 170–71.

46. R. Meens, "Van koningen en paarden: Gerald van Wales en het inauguratieritueel van de koningen van Kenellcunill," *Millennium* 9 (1995): 14–26.

47. M. Muzzarelli, "Norme di comportamento alimentare nei libri penitenziali," *Quaderni Medievali* 13 (1982): 45–80; Bonnassie, "Consommation

d'aliments immondes"; A. Gurjewitsch, *Mittelalterliche Volkskultur* (Munich: Beck, 1986), p. 147.

48. *Paenitentiale Columbani* B 24, ed. Bieler, in *The Irish Penitentials,* p. 104.

49. *Vita Columbani* I.27, in *Quellen zur Geschichte des 7. und 8. Jahrhunderts,* H. Wolfram, in Ausgewählte Quellen zur deutschen Geschichte des Mittelalters: Freiherr vom Stein-Gedächtnisausgabe (AQ), vol. 4a (Darmstadt: Wissenschaftliche Buchgesellschaft, 1982), pp. 482–84; for a similar pagan ritual involving beer, see Jonas's *Vita Vedasti,* c. 7, ed. B. Krusch, in *MGH SS Rer. Mer.* 3 (Hanover, 1896), pp. 410–11.

50. *P. Sangallense tripartitum* II.36–37, ed. Meens, in *Het tripartite boeteboek,* p. 342.

51. *P. Parisiense compositum,* 18–19, ed. Meens, in *Het tripartite boeteboek,* p. 488.

52. See R. Meens, "Magic and the Early Medieval World View," in *The Community, the Family, and the Saint: Patterns of Power in Early Medieval Europe,* ed. J. Hill and M. Swan (Turnhout: Brepols, 1998), pp. 285–95.

53. R. A. Markus, *The End of Ancient Christianity* (Cambridge: Cambridge University Press, 1990).

54. M. Müller-Wille, "Pferdegrab und Pferdeopfer im frühen Mittelalter," *Berichten van de Rijksdienst voor het Oudheidkundig Bodemonderzoek* 20–21 (1970–71): 119–248.

55. J. Oexle, "Merowingerzeitliche Pferdebestattungen—Opfer oder Beigaben?" *Frühmittelalterliche Studien* 18 (1984): 122–72. Cf. B. Young, "Paganisme, christianisation et rites funéraires mérovingiens," *Archéologie Médiévale* 7 (1977): 58–59; A. Dierkens, "Cimetières mérovingiens et histoire du Haut Moyen Age: Chronologie—société—religion," *Acta Historica Bruxellensia,* vol. 4: *Histoire et Méthode* (Brussels: Université de Bruxelles, 1981), pp. 43–44.

56. *Vita Declani,* c. 25, ed. Plummer, in *Vitae Sanctorum Hiberniae,* 2:50. This life was possibly written in the years 1171–1210; see R. Sharpe, *Medieval Irish Saints' Lives: An Introduction to "Vitae Sanctorum Hiberniae"* (Oxford: Clarendon Press, 1991), pp. 31–32. The story is also included in the Irish version of this life; see P. Power, ed., *Life of St. Declan of Ardmore and Life of St. Mochuda of Lismore, with Introduction, Translation and Notes* (London: Irish Texts Society, 1914), pp. 48–51.

57. See above, pp. 8.

58. W. Janssen, "Das Tier im Spiegel der archäologischen Zeugnisse," pp. 1251–53, interpreted the Merovingian remains of cats and dogs found at Brébières (near Arras) as food remains, which seems not very probable.

59. For the practice of eating dogs in Gaul, see P. Méniel, "Les animaux dans l'alimentation des Gaulois," in *L'animal dans l'alimentation humaine: Les critères de choix. Actes du colloque international de Liège, 26–29 novembre 1986, Anthropozoologica,* special issue 2, ed. L. Bodson (1988): 118, 120; for its abolishment in early medieval times, see J.-H. Yvinec, "Alimentation carnée au début du Moyen Age," ibid., pp. 123–26.

60. *De Confessione,* 50, ed. J. Goering and F. A. C. Mantello, in "The Early Penitential Writings of Robert Grosseteste," p. 102.

61. For a succinct cross-cultural overview of the ambivalent relationship between man and dog, see J. Serpell, "From Paragon to Pariah: Some Reflections on Human Attitudes to Dogs," in *The Domestic Dog: Its Evolution, Behaviour and Interactions with People,* ed. J. Serpell (Cambridge: Cambridge University Press, 1995), pp. 245–56.

62. For the ritual see B. Schwenk, "Das Hundentragen: Ein Rechtsbrauch im Mittelalter," *Historisches Jahrbuch* 110 (1990). 289–308; Schwenk, however, regards the dog in too positive a light; cf. M. Hageman, "De gebeten hond? Het gebruik van honden in rituelen van vernedering," *Madoc* 12 (1998): 265–70.

63. *P. Bigotianum* I.5.5, ed. Bieler, in *The Irish Penitentials,* p. 216.

64. *P. Theodori U* I.7.7, ed. Finsterwalder, in *Die Canones Theodori,* p. 299.

65. *P. Cummeani* (XI).18, ed. Bieler, in *The Irish Penitentials,* p. 130.

66. *Canones Hibernenses* I.18, ed. Bieler, in *The Irish Penitentials,* p. 162.

67. *P. Ps.-Theodori* XVI.22, ed. Wasserschleben, *in Die irische Kirchensammlung,* p. 603: "Familiari bestia, id est, cane et catto"; *P. Ps.-Egberti* XIII.4, ibid., p. 244: "a familiari bestia, id est cane vel catto"; see also the *P. mixtum Bedae-Egberti,* XXII.2, ed. as "Liber de remediis peccatorum," ibid., p. 270. On the penitentials attributed to Bede and Egbert, see R. Haggenmüller, *Die Überlieferung der Beda und Egbert zugeschriebenen Bußbücher* (Frankfurt a. M.: Peter Lang, 1991).

68. As suggested to me by Bart Jaski.

69. O. Prinz, ed., *Die Kosmographie des Aethicus, MGH Quellen zur Geistesgeschichte des Mittelalters* 14, p. 120. This negative view of "Turkish" food patterns seems incompatible with the editor's idea that the author of this text might have belonged to a "Turkish" group, like the Avars (p. 18).

70. Already cited in Vinnian's penitential, 21, ed. Bieler, in *The Irish Penitentials,* p. 80.

71. *P. Theodori U,* II.11.1 and 9, ed. Finsterwalder, in *Die Canones Theodori,* pp. 325–26. These canons were included in many later penitentials.

72. *P. Cummeani* I.8–10 and (XI).7–9, ed. Bieler, in *The Irish Penitentials,* pp. 112, 130.

73. Such canons, originally from the *P. Ambrosianum,* influenced later texts mainly through *P. Cummeani* (XI): "De questionibus sacrificii," ed. Bieler, in *The Irish Penitentials,* pp. 130–32, see also (IX).1, ibid., p. 124. On the influence of these canons, see Meens, *Het tripartite boeteboek,* pp. 286–87, and H. Lutterbach, "The Mass and Holy Communion in the Medieval Penitentials (600–1200): Liturgical and Religio-Historical Perspectives," in *Bread of Heaven: Customs and Practices Surrounding Holy Communion: Essays in the History of Liturgy and Culture,* ed. C. Caspers, G. Lukken, and G. Rouwhorst (Kampen: Kok Pharos, 1995), pp. 61–82.

74. *P. Cummeani* (XI).1, ed. Bieler, in *The Irish Penitentials,* p. 130.

75. *P. Oxoniense,* in *Paenitentalia Minora Franciae et Italiae saeculi VIII–IX,* ed. R. Kottje, Corpus Christianorum Series Latina 156 (Turnhout: Brepols, 1994), II.54, p. 200.

76. C. Vogel, *Les "Libri Paenitentiales,"* Typologie des sources du moyen âge occidental, vol. 27 (Turnhout: Brepols, 1978), pp. 110–11, and Gurjewitsch, *Mittelalterliche Volkskultur,* p. 147.

77. *P. Hubertense,* 61, ed. Kottje, in *Paenitentialia Minora,* p. 115; cf. *P. Merseburgense* b, 16, ibid., p. 174.

78. As suggested by J. McNeill and H. Gamer, *Medieval Handbooks of Penance,* 2d ed. (New York: Columbia University Press, 1990), p. 191 n. 76.

79. Though Bieler (*The Irish Penitentials,* p. 217) translates *pilax* as "watchdog," the translation "cat" as proposed by McNeill and Gamer, *Medieval Handbooks of Penance,* p. 191, seems to be preferable; cf. R. Spindler, *Das altenglische Bußbuch (sog. Confessionale Pseudo-Egberti)* (Leipzig: Bernhard Tauchnitz, 1934), J. F. Niermeyer, *Mediae Latinitatis lexicon minus* (Leiden: Brill, 1993), p. 797, and R. Latham, *Revised Medieval Latin Word-List from British and Irish Sources* (London: British Academy, 1965), p. 351.

80. *P. Hubertense,* 34, 58, 61, ed. Kottje, in *Paenitentialia minora,* pp. 111, 114–15; cf. *P. Merseburgense* B, 14 and 16, ibid., p. 174.

81. *Canones Hibernenses* I.17; *Canones Adomnani* 12 and 13; *P. Bigotianum* I.V.6; *OIP* I.3, pp. 162, 178, 216, 260.

82. *Collectio Hibernensis* LIV.9, ed. Wasserschleben, in *Die irische Kanonensammlung,* p. 217: "De esu avium licito. Hieronimus: Caro avium clericis licita est; non tam enim pascit, quam incitat dolorem, sed et paene totas aves inlicitas lex docet."

83. Aethicus Ister, ed. Prinz, *Die Kosmographie des Aethicus,* p. 120.

84. *P. Theodori* U, II.11.7–8, ed. Finsterwalder, in *Die Canones Theodori,* p. 326.

85. M. Douglas, *Purity and Danger: An Analysis of the Concepts of Pollution and Taboo* (1966; reprint ed., London: Routledge, 1980), pp. 29–32.

86. A. Gurjewitsch, *Mittelalterliche Volkskultur,* pp. 147–48.

87. S. Boulc'h, "Le statut de l'animal et la notion de pureté dans les prescriptions alimentaires chrétiennes du haut Moyen Age occidental," in *Le statut éthique de l'animal: Conceptions anciennes et nouvelles. Journée d'étude Université de Liège, 18 mars 1995,* ed. L. Bodson (Liège: Université de Liège, Institut de Zoologie, 1996), p. 50; H. Lutterbach, "Die Speisegesetzgebung in den frühmittelalterlichen Bußbüchern (600–1200): Religionsgeschicht-liche Perspektive," *Archiv für Kulturgeschichte* 80 (1998): 28–36. It does not seem very fruitful to regard early medieval dietary rules as a "Rearchäisierung des Denk- und Verstehenshorizontes" (p. 37) of an originally ethical Christian interpretation of the Old Testament prescriptions, as Lutterbach does.

88. *Canones Adomnani* 10–11, ed. Bieler, in *The Irish Penitentials,* p. 178.

89. Boulc'h, "Le statut de l'animal," pp. 48–52.

90. *Collectio Hibernensis* LIII.3, ed. Wasserschleben, in *Die irische Kirchen-sammlung,* pp. 213–14.

91. *Canones Adomnani* 7, ed. Bieler, in *The Irish Penitentials,* p. 176.

92. *P. Theodori* U II.11.6, ed. Finsterwalder, in *Die Canones Theodori,* p. 325.

93. *Confessionale Ps.-Egberti,* 34e, ed. R. Spindler, in *Das altenglische Bußbuch,* p. 193 (the *Scriftboc,* as Allen Frantzen calls it in *The Literature of Penance in Anglo-Saxon England* [New Brunswick, N.J.: Rutgers University Press, 1983], pp. 133–34) and *P. Martenianum* LV.14, ed. W. von Hörmann, in "Bußbücherstudien IV," *Zeitschrift der Savigny-Stiftung für Rechtsgeschichte Kan. Abt.* 4 (1914): 412.

94. Bonnassie, "Consommation d'aliments immondes," p. 1040.

95. R. Meens, "Pollution in the Early Middle Ages: The Case of the Food Regulations in Penitentials," *Early Medieval Europe* 4 (1995): 3–19; Douglas, *Purity and Danger.*

96. On the size of horses, see Salisbury, *The Beast Within,* p. 29.

97. W. Schneider, "Animal laborans: Das Arbeitstier und sein Einsatz in Transport und Verkehr der Spätantike und des frühen Mittelalters," in *L'uomo di fronte al mondo animale nell'alto medioevo,* pp. 522–23.

98. Ibid., p. 524.

99. On the semimonastic status of the *manaig,* see L. Bitel, *Isle of the Saints: Monastic Settlement and Christian Community in Early Ireland* (Ithaca, N.Y.: Cornell University Press, 1990), pp. 124–28.

100. *Canones Hibernenses* I.22–24, ed. Bieler, in *The Irish Penitentials,* p. 162; *P. Bigotianum* I.6–7, ibid., pp. 216–18; *OIP* I.3, ibid., p. 260; cf. Bitel, *Isle of the Saints,* p. 210: "The refusal to eat certain foods, at certain times, with certain people brought spiritual purity to fleshbound holy men and women."

101. See P. Brown, *The Rise of Western Christendom: Triumph and Diversity AD 200–1000* (Oxford: Blackwell, 1996), p. 313; cf. Bitel, *Isle of the Saints,* and K. McCone, *Pagan Past and Christian Present in Early Irish Literature* (Maynooth: An Sagart, 1990), pp. 203–32.

102. Bartlett, *Gerald of Wales,* pp. 161–62, 176–77.

103. See especially the work of G. Althoff, *Verwandte, Freunde und Getreue: Zum politischen Stellenwert der Gruppenbindungen in früheren Mittelalter* (Darmstadt: Wissenschaftliche Buchgesellschaft, 1990), pp. 202–12; Althoff, "Der frieden-, bündnis- und gemeinschaftstiftende Charakter des Mahles im früheren Mittelalter," in *Essen und Trinken im Mittelalter und Neuzeit,* ed. I. Bitsch et al. (Sigmaringen: Thorbecke, 1987), pp. 13–25; D. Bullough, *Friends, Neighbours and Fellow-Drinkers: Aspects of Community and Conflict in the Early Medieval West,* H. M. Chadwick Memorial Lectures, vol. 1 (Cambridge: Department of Anglo-Saxon, Norse and Celtic, 1991); and R. Meens, "Dronkenschap in de vroege middeleeuwen," *Tijdschrift voor Geschiedenis* 109 (1996): 424–42.

104. Bede, *Historia Ecclesiastica gentis Anglorum* II.4; in *Bede's Ecclesiastical History of the English People,* ed. B. Colgrave and R. A. B. Mynors, 2d ed. (Oxford: Clarendon Press, 1992), p. 146.

105. *Conversio Bagoariorum et Carantanorum,* c.7, ed. F. Lošek, in *Die "Conversio Bagoariorum et Carantanorum" und der Brief des Erzbischofs Theotmar von Salzburg,* Schriften der MGH, Studien und Texte 15 (Hanover: Hahnsche Buchhandlung, 1997), pp. 112–14. Cf. H. Wolfram, *Conversio Bagoariorum et Carantanorum: Das Weißbuch der Salzburger Kirche über die erfolgreiche Mission in Karantanien und Pannonien* (Vienna: Böhlau Verlag, 1979); and W. Pohl, "'Das sanfte Joch Christi': Zum Christentum als gestaltende Kraft im Mitteleuropa des frühen Mittelalters," in *Karantanien und der Alpen-Adria-Raum im Frühmittelalter: 2. St. Veiter Historikergespräche,* ed. G. Hödl and J. Grabmayer (Vienna: Böhlau Verlag, 1993), pp. 259–89.

106. For Feuerbach's expression, see H.-J. Teuteberg, "Homo edens: Reflexionen zu einer neuen Kulturgeschichte des Essens," *Historische Zeitschrift* 265 (1997): 1–4.

2

THE REPRESENTATION OF MEDIEVAL PEASANTS AS BESTIAL AND AS HUMAN

PAUL H. FREEDMAN

The privileged orders of Europe have at times regarded rural life with a certain admiration for its productivity, or a degree of sentimental praise for its pastoral simplicity.[1] At the same time the countryside was frequently considered alien, populated with beings of a lower order resembling more the beasts they tended than humanity. This attitude survives in the work of well-known scholars who have sought to overturn an excessively sentimental view of rural life in times past. Eugen Weber's *Peasants into Frenchmen*, for example, devotes considerable attention to the degraded condition of peasants before the late nineteenth century, especially in a first chapter entitled "A Country of Savages," in which peasant life is depicted as bestial by eighteenth- and early-nineteenth century observers, a view accepted by the author as well.[2]

One of the best-known evocations of the unfortunate degradation of the peasant comes in a passage of La Bruyère's. He describes a landscape whose denizens seem at first glance to be ferocious animals, dark, burned by the sun, attached to the soil that they work with stubborn persistence. Yet these creatures can speak. When they lift themselves upright from their bent-over positions of toil they display a human countenance, indeed they are human.[3]

The same oscillation between animal and human is more poignantly evoked in Carlo Levi's twentieth-century memoir of exile in Lucania. Here the peasants lament: "We're not Christians. . . . Christ stopped short of here, at Eboli." Levi goes on to explain: "'Christian,' in their way of speaking means 'human being,' and this almost proverbial phrase that I have heard so often may be no more than the expression of a hopeless feeling of inferiority. 'We're not Christians, we're not human beings; we're not thought of as men but simply as beasts, beasts of burden, or even less than beasts, mere creatures of the wild.'"[4]

29

La Bruyère and Levi present an ambivalent and enduring image of the peasant that shifts back and forth between animal and human. There is, however, a significant difference between La Bruyère's distant, uneasy pity for the condition of rustics and the sharper contrast drawn by Levi between their humanity and the treatment meted out to them. The despairing, ironic lament of the Lucanian peasants is, after all, a reproach that those who are in fact Christians should be treated in a way that denies their fundamental equality with the powerful, their common humanity. To be Christian meant to be fully human according to prevailing ideas shared by peasants and their masters during the Middle Ages. As I hope to show, this amounted to something more than a rhetorical flourish; it was a truism that could even be used to justify rebellion.

Nevertheless, the most common purpose served by associating peasants with animals during the Middle Ages was to convey an amused contempt. A medieval German rhyme observed that the peasant resembles the ox except that he lacks horns: "Der Bauer ist an Ochsen statt, nur daß er keine Hôrner hat."[5] A Catalan saying, not quite extinct even now, defines the peasant as "the animal who most closely resembles man."[6]

A second function of such imagery was to denounce ill-treatment. That peasants were treated like animals was not because of their intrinsic nature but by reason of a terrible injustice. Peasants were fully human, and not merely under some conveniently vague rubric that might grudgingly encompass even the most outcast peoples, because peasants were not outcasts. They might indeed commonly be likened to animals or contemned as filthy, lazy, larcenous, and stupid, but they were not marginal to Christian Europe in the sense that Jews, Saracens, lepers, or the imagined "monstrous races" of the East were. They constituted a majority of the population, they were necessary for the survival of society, and they were members, perhaps even exemplars, of the Christian community.[7]

There are, therefore, two sorts of animal images, one expressing contempt, the other an assertion of humanity implying what it is not completely anachronistic to call human rights or liberties.

DERISION AND DANGER

Animal metaphors form part of an immense vocabulary of disdain for peasants. Entire medieval literary genres such as the German *Schwankliteratur* or the French *fabliaux* were partly or wholly devoted to peasants as comical figures: their stupidity, their foolish violence, their association with excrement. Bestial imagery was often blended with these other topoi of ridicule, for example in mock taxonomies or "grammars" of rusticity. A French text of the late thirteenth century divides *vilains* into twenty-three categories. Some resemble pigs, dogs, or asses (*vilains porcins, vilains chenins, vilains asnins*), while others are merely ferocious, deformed, or dirty.[8] A fifteenth-century Latin "Peasant Catechism" from Germany begins with the statement that the word *rusticus* is of Hebrew derivation because a peasant is as inept and wicked as a Jew. It is a noun of the third declension for "before the cock had crowed twice, the rustic shat three times." Almost as an afterthought, rustics are said to belong to the "asinine race."[9]

Within the large realm of unfavorable depiction of peasants there are a number of subdivisions. Peasants might be represented as filthy in one work and dishonest in another, but more often what is presented is a lexicon of negative imagery organized thematically but also according to several usually pejorative axes: the peasant as object of ridicule versus the peasant as dangerous; the peasant as lowly but useful as opposed to completely base and evil; the peasant as human exemplar versus his grotesque or bestial nature. Behind these oppositions lies a fundamental distinction between what might be regarded as "social" descriptions (denunciations of the avarice of peasants, for example) and fanciful, usually ludicrous, hyperbole (peasants as animals). Thus a condemnation of rustics by Bernard of Cluny for evading tithes differs in its straightforward serious tone from comical Italian accusations that peasants crucified Christ or that they resemble asses, wolves, and dogs.[10]

The physical appearance of the rustic was the most common way of conveying a strange and subhuman nature—an emblem at once of otherness and of useful, exploited labor. Bestial attributes shade into disquisitions on color or deformity. In his chronicle, Froissart describes the French peasant rebels of the Jacquerie as small, dark, and ill-armed.[11] During a legal dispute concerning servile condition that took place at Mantua in about 1200, a witness testified that the father of the man in question had been well-formed, nearly white, and tall. Another witness stated he had been small and fat, but agreed he had been white and reasonably good-looking. Here color and stature were considerations in evaluating servile status.[12]

Peasants were frequently presented in literary works as misshapen—unnaturally large, or dwarfish, or simply hideously ugly; their deviance from a normal appearance was emphasized by exaggerated animal metaphors. The two guards of the chamber of Laris in the *Romance of Claris and Laris,* are rustics (*vilains*) fifteen feet tall, of an ugliness "never before seen." They are covered with black hair, their nails are as long as snakes, and their eyes are fiery. Their teeth resemble those of a wild boar, their noses are like those of cats, while their snouts are those of wolves.[13] In the *Yvain* of Chrétien de Troyes, the knight Calogrenant, lost in the forest, encounters a herdsmen. This rustic not only "resembles a Moor" but is likened to no less than six animals. In response to Calogrenant's jocular but uneasy question "come, tell me if you are a good or evil thing," the herdsman says that he is a man. Calogrenant then inquires "what sort of man are you," to which the herdsman replies with simple dignity, "just as you see me and no different."[14] Not only does he prove to be human after all, but he helps the knight find his way.

Such shifts from bestial to human were a commonplace image of the forest and its solitary rustic denizens.[15] In historical chronicles Count Geoffrey of Anjou and the young Philip Augustus become lost while hunting and meet hideous, deformed, or blackened rustics who are nevertheless harmless and well-meaning.[16] In the former instance the count recognizes his interlocutor as a fellow victim of the sentence against Adam by which all are forced to suffer in this world, this common ancestry being an already venerable theme of human equality.

Another knight lost in the forest is the protagonist in a dialogue between a noble and a rustic written in 1443 by Felix Hemmerli, a canon of Zurich and a ferocious hater of peasants. The rustic is black, hirsute, bestial. His head is overlarge, his face twisted, his expression "asinine." A little surprisingly, under the circumstances, he speaks correct and florid Latin.[17] Like Calogrenant, but with more hostility, the noble asks if he is a devil or a man, and the rustic responds that he is a man, the same as the noble only better. Even here, where the debate is carried by the knight, the rustic is reasonably adept in disputation and eventually shows the way out of the forest, parting as the knight's friend.

None of the rustics in these stories and putative histories is the equal of the aristocracy, but they lose their original beastly semblance to come into focus as human, an alternation characteristic of medieval consideration of strange peoples, a nagging but inconsistent concentration on separation between cultivated and barbaric accompanied by a refrain of similarity.

More definitively savage are rebellious peasants whose insurrections are likened to uncontrolled wildness. Peasants were not threatening as individuals, however large and frighteningly bestial their appearance, but as a mass they were dangerous. Froissart, as earlier noted, mocks the ill-equipped Jacquerie; but once they have formed in sufficient numbers to capture nobles, their frenzy knows no limits according to the same chronicler's descriptions of peasant atrocities. Now the peasants are mad dogs.[18] Pope Gregory IX, in a Crusade letter of 1233 directed against the Stedinger rebels in northern Germany, likened them to beasts, "only even crueler."[19]

The abbot of Vale Royal, in a dispute with the men of the villages of Darnall and Over in 1326, described the peasants who had attacked his entourage as "bestial men of Rutland."[20] The Swiss, archetypes of peasant rebels, were called "mountain beasts" by their Austrian adversaries.[21]

In the most sustained, hysterical depiction of a peasant revolt, John Gower's lurid dream vision at the opening of his *Vox clamantis,* the English peasants of 1381 are likened first to domestic beasts that have escaped their bonds, and then to wild, verminous creatures such as foxes, flies, and frogs.[22] With the suppression of the revolt, the peasants become draught animals, oxen returned to the yoke after a terrifying interlude during which they left the fields, forgot their nature (normally docile), and turned into panthers, lions, bears.

Here with Gower is encapsulated a contrast between two images of peasants as animals: the wild peasant (whether comically savage or frighteningly dangerous) versus the domesticated peasant whose animal characteristics reinforce and symbolize his aptness for tedious but necessary toil. In one case the peasant is remote, marginal, and likened to a variety of untamed beasts. In the other he is not only more docile but productive as well. It is this latter category of animal metaphor that is especially characteristic of medieval descriptions of peasants. While to some extent all rebels (including townsmen and nobles) could be described as ravening beasts, the peasant in conditions of peace was uniquely likened to the tractable, useful domestic animals he used in his labors.

PRODUCTIVITY

Peasants could be held to resemble useful rather than threatening animals, in keeping with their acknowledged role in feeding the higher orders of society. The peasants might inhabit a space conceived and represented as isolated and remote, but as the conventional models of society emphasized the necessity of their labor for the survival of the clergy and nobility they could hardly be consistently presented as distant or irrelevant. They might be regarded in the manner of domestic animals, as both bestial and necessary.

In this sense the image of the peasant as domesticated animal functioned as a sign of productive lowliness but additionally implied the need for a degree of coercion. As with all useful farm animals, the peasant could not be relied on to work of his own volition. A medieval proverb likened the rustic, the ass, and the nut, for all must be beaten in order to produce anything.[23] Rustics, according to another rhymed saying, are best when weeping, worst when laughing.[24] A French proverb current in the medieval and early modern periods held that the only result of treating a peasant well ("anointing" him) was that he would sting (or prick) you; sting him and he will behave well.[25] In these examples the rustic is like an animal that only responds when goaded; ornery but ultimately compliant and certainly useful. Yet another medieval commonplace, this time a riddle, exemplifies this docile haplessness with the question "what do peasants most earnestly pray for?" The answer is that the lords may have a good supply of fine horses, for otherwise they will ride the peasants instead.[26]

More hostile opinion might regard peasants as only barely tamable. According the fourteenth-century Catalan Franciscan writer Francesc Eiximenis, servile peasants are like cruel and savage beasts who require beating and starving to compel their submission.[27] As with Gower's *Vox clamantis,* rebellious peasants were often likened to animals that broke the bonds of their coerced utility to run wild. In the late Middle Ages the Swiss epitomized impudent rusticity, and it was asserted that their success could have been prevented had they been supervised more strictly. A poem from the era of Appenzell's revolt against the Abbey of Saint Gall (the opening of the fifteenth century) says that peasants should be bled occasionally to get more work out of them.[28] The humorist Heinrich Bebel, in a poem written nearly a century later, recommended that the rebellious Swiss peasants be punished, just as a willow tree is trimmed with a knife to grow more vigorously.[29] These are not precisely animal metaphors but reflect the same view that peasants require harsh treatment to fulfill their productive role.

Representing peasants as animals could thus denote a general lowliness, or evoke images of dangerous, wild rage, or finally symbolize a utility achieved with the aid of coercion. In most instances the bestial nature of the peasant is comical or luridly exaggerated. For the most part we are not dealing with attempts at accurate description. One of the chief differences between medieval and modern presentations of subordination is the latter's tendency to make biological or other putatively scientific formulations of racial inferiority. Medieval satiric statements about peasants cannot be regarded as sociologically or scientifically "serious." At the same time, scholars of colonialism and slavery have shown the social implications of comical and satiric depictions magnified by their very improbability, repetition, and exaggeration. Presenting peasants as animals functioned as a more compelling version of Aristotelian natural slavery—the idea that some people are by nature best fit for mindless toil and subordination. The version was more compelling because it avoided the question of reconciling natural slavery with fundamental (Christian) equality by reiterating the ugliness, stupidity, and coarse materiality of peasants whose appropriateness for rural labor was most graphically underscored by their resemblance to farm animals, even to the very soil itself.

The peasant represented as animal is part of a general tendency to regard peasants in terms of gross physicality. It is above all the male peasants who are given a curiously asexual body. The *fabliaux* in particular (but medieval literature in general) emphasize the sluggish sexual drive of male peasants who are much more oriented toward the gastrointestinal side of bodily urges. They love to eat coarse food, sleep, and scratch, and are comfortable with (even fond of) excrement. Lacking courtesy, the peasant is incapable of love, and couples in the fashion of beasts according to the French *History of Julius Caesar.* His activity is no more dignified (or threatening) than that of rutting animals.[30] Knights and clergy are driven by sexual passion and their objects of (predatory) desire are sometimes young peasant women who may be socially inappropriate but physically suitable, even alluring in contrast to their lumpen male peers. Boorish materiality and the grotesque or bestial body belong to male peasants while females are rendered as desirable and even rather clever if greedy and eager. Only with the fourteenth century do female rustics come to be at least occasionally depicted in coarse and grotesque terms similar to those employed for males.[31]

Male peasants are not threatening except as dangerous mobs in insurrections.[32] Singly they do not pose any sort of danger (which differentiates medieval images from those of many subordinate groups of other historical epochs). Not only is the peasant by definition militarily inept compared to the knight, but his lowly nature makes him peculiarly passive and tractable if plodding and unwilling (once again like a domestic animal). That rustics can be bought and sold like cattle is one of the persistent forms of denoting servile status, which is the clearest index of social subordination. Robert of Courçon distinguished three kinds of serfs (*servi*), the lowest of which (found supposedly in Apulia and Sicily) can be bought and sold like sheep and cattle.[33] In the fourteenth century Ferry, lord of Rocourt (in the Swiss Jura region) answered the complaints of a village worthy by reminding him that he was his serf and that Ferry, if he wished, could take him by the foot and sell him in the market.[34] Judges on the London Eyre of 1244 distinguished the right of lords to punish their villeins or sell them "like oxen and cows" from the right to kill or maim them, which belonged to the king.[35]

SERVITUDE AND HUMANITY

Materiality, corporality, a bestial nature, lack of aggressiveness (both military and sexual) and servile condition were joined aspects of a lower nature attributed to peasants, particularly to male peasants. They were docile if well controlled, but dangerous en masse. Servitude, although it never affected the universality of the medieval peasantry, was a particular emblem of hapless productivity. Servitude could be associated with punishment for sin or the appropriate condition for those of a lower order of competence or mental acuity. Building on a vulgarized legacy of Augustine and Isidore of Seville, Spanish writers of the late Middle Ages frequently linked sin, servitude, and bestial character.[36]

Subordination to another's arbitrary will and the ownership of one person by another demonstrated graphically what was implicit in the social condition of all peasant tenants, whether legally free or not: exploitation and constraint. Servitude represented a telling distillation of injustice, not necessarily or exclusively because of its direct economic impact but because bondage placed serfs below a certain threshold of freedom that defined human status before God. Either this was appropriate to their (necessarily subhuman) nature, or a violation of a certain minimal human dignity. The rhetorical force of Christian equality was not that it implied social equality but that it did require a certain liberty consistent with status as a human being, or at least so argued late medieval peasants and their spokesmen.

Christ's sacrifice had freed all from the bonds of servitude. While this servitude was often conceived as subservience to sin and not as a constraint of literal freedom, there was ample precedent for arguing that while servitude might not matter in God's eyes, it was a violation of a natural liberty not permanently obscured by the Fall or other events meriting divine chastisement. In a passage that would frequently be cited in later centuries, Gregory the Great wrote that the Incarnation had restored to humanity its earlier liberty and released it from the chains of servitude.[37] It was a good deed to free slaves, Gregory asserted, who were men born free by nature but subjugated by the law of nations.

This was hardly a call to abolition, but it did make Christ's sacrifice the guarantee of an equal human likeness, at least among Christians. The notion of similitude not only symbolized but legally granted by Christ appears in many medieval guises. Adam of Eynsham, for example, denounced the Forest Laws of Henry II of England by contrasting the inappropriate protection of animals (who should be available for use by all) with the cruel treatment of human beings: "In revenge for irrational wild animals, which ought by natural law to be available to all in common, he [the king] had either punished by death or cruelly mutilated in their limbs human beings, who employ reason, were saved by the same blood of Christ and share the same nature in equality."[38] The contrast between human beings and animals was used to reinforce assertions of human equality. There are two places in

Genesis in which human dignity and power are defined by control over animals. Genesis 1:26 begins with God's statement, "Let us make man in our image and likeness," followed by the conferral of dominion over the creatures of earth, sea, and sky. Genesis 9 opens with God's command to Noah and his offspring to increase and multiply, to subdue the denizens of the earth. The mark of being an animal is to be dominated by humans and put to various uses. Servitude thus by definition tends toward treating humans like animals in violation of their created and redeemed nature. Another text of Gregory the Great invokes Genesis 9 to contrast the divinely sanctioned rule of humanity over animals with the unjust domination of one man by another. God commanded that animals be ruled by humanity and tamed to productive uses, not that human beings be subordinated to one another.[39] This would become a theme repeated by Carolingian writers[40] and a commonplace for the denunciation of slavery and serfdom in the high Middle Ages. A letter of the emperor Conrad II (ca. 1027) condemned the sale of slaves or serfs (*mancipia*) as if they were beasts, a violation of canon law. Similar language appears in legislation of the Synod of Westminster in 1102 and in the *Chronica Bohemorum* (early twelfth century) of Cosmas of Prague.[41] Thomassin von Zerclaria (a Friulian poet writing in German) lamented the enserfment of free men who are thus treated like cattle.[42] Stephen Langton, whose biblical commentaries repeatedly attack the oppression of the poor by the powerful, referred to Gregory's distinction between domination over animals and humans in stating that God does not sanction the latter which violates human equality.[43] Two laws passed by the Great Council of Ragusa (Dubrovnik) in 1416 and 1466 invoked God's creation of man in His image and likeness to protest against the slave trade by which human beings were treated like animals.[44]

None of this means that there was an effective political opinion advocating the abolition of either slavery or serfdom, much less that such sentiment as there was in that direction had much immediate effect. What is evident, however, is that the idea of humans treated as if they were animals had a certain moral force as a denunciation of subjugation. In a host of medieval peasant rebellions the assertion of equality was coupled with a condemnation of arbitrary seigneurial domination, especially of serfdom. As far back as the Norman peasants' rebellion at the end of the tenth century the peasants are supposed to have proclaimed that they were men, just like their lords, formed in the same way, with hearts as large and equally capable of feeling pain.[45] John Ball's famous Blackheath sermon at the height of the English Rising of 1381 condemns servitude as a violation of God's intent at Creation.[46] A prologue to a document reporting the organization of servile peasant syndicates in mid-fifteenth-century Catalonia begins by invoking

Gregory's letter to the bishop of Syracuse on Christ's sacrifice and liberation from servitude.[47]

The point at which the contradiction between human status and treatment as an animal becomes clearly a peasant statement (not merely attributed to them) is with the German Peasant War of 1525. With the invention of printing and the proliferation of short pamphlets outlining local demands, the remonstrances of servile tenants were couched in a form that has been preserved. Serfs of the abbey of Ochsenhausen in Upper Swabia protested in a manifesto against being "sold like cattle and calves," arguing that "we all have one lord, that is God in heaven."[48] The tenants of the prince-archbishop of Salzburg complained that servitude violated the Gospel and amounted to a claim to lead men around by the nose, like cattle "only even more tyrannically."[49] Peasants of the abbey of Kempten in Bavaria who were barely able to hold on to free status listed the oppressive practices of the monastery and summarized their treatment as worse than that meted out to serfs or dogs.[50]

PEASANTS AND MONSTERS

None of this is intended to argue that the Middle Ages was a particularly tolerant period, or to deny that the prevailing image of peasants was of contemptible beings tending toward the subhuman. Peasants were objects of derision as well as occasionally fear. Insofar as they were productive, their nature and utility were likened to those of plodding domestic animals. As rebels they were regarded as dangerous savage beasts. In addition iconographic signs of otherness were transmitted from one outcast group to another, so that on various occasions peasants were portrayed as black, or as grotesquely misshapen (like the monstrous races), or likened to infidels.[51] Serfs in particular might be regarded as a "race" affected by Noah's curse against his son Ham, in preference to Africans who were also candidates for this distinction. Cain was commonly thought to have been the first peasant, but at the same time as early as Beowulf, semihuman monsters were his progeny and the mysterious "Mark of Cain" was depicted as horns growing out of his head.

Despite such crossing and mixing of images of otherness, different groups were associated with particular kinds of unfavorable typology. Stupidity, excrement, toil were attributes of peasants not shared with other despised groups, just as a certain negative vocabulary was employed uniquely to typify Jews. Animals might serve as metaphors for all manner of persons (including as complimentary ones in the case of the great, such as Albert the Bear or Richard Lionheart), but the border between human and nonhuman was drawn with especial reference to two outcast (or potentially out-cast) groups: peasants and the monstrous races. The former were more clear-ly likened to beasts while the latter were malformed but less in the direction of animals than as variations on the human: one-legged people who shaded themselves from the tropical sun with their single large foot (Sciopods); those with no head, but faces built into their chests (Blemmyae), people with immense ears drooping to their ankles (Panotii); others with no mouths who were nourished by the smell of apples (Astomi) . . . The one great exception was formed by the dog-headed people (Cynocephali), thought to be unusually intelligent, whom even Marco Polo (rather cautious about the monstrous races) believed to inhabit regions near where he traveled (al-though he confessed he had not seen them himself).[52]

Both peasants and monstrous races were viewed alternatively as human and nonhuman. I have already mentioned this oscillation in the various stories of knights coming upon frightening solitary forest rustics who are revealed as human not so much by any change in perceived shape as by conversation. The monstrous races, on the other hand, tended not to speak.[53] They might live in societies, often cultivating valuable commodities (nota-bly spices), but they were marked off by their form and by nakedness (they are seldom shown as wearing clothes other than perhaps a few skins), and muteness. Yet they too were portrayed in an indeterminate manner that played with human and nonhuman imagery. There are certain well-known examples of their being accepted as human beings. At the entrance to the nave of the basilica of Vézelay, the tympanum sculpture shows apostles sent out to the farthest reaches of the earth where the Pygmies, Cynocephali, and long-eared people dwell. These strange nations are still sufficiently human to receive the Word of God.[54]

HUMAN EXEMPLAR OR SUBHUMAN SUBORDINATE

Images of humanity and animality were fluid rather than fixed according to a consistent and clear taxonomy. A reiterated statement of difference alter-nated with its disavowal, an obsessive but inconsistent focus on the separa-tion between cultivated and barbarous was accompanied by a disfavored but persistent refrain of similarity. The peasant might pose a conceptual or moral problem in reconciling full humanity (status as a Christian) with exploitation, and indeed the oscillation between bestial and human was part of a larger apparent ambivalence in which favorable and unfavorable depic-tions coexisted and interlaced. Peasants were virtuous toilers to be pitied and at the same time fit for labor; imbued with materialism, ignorance, and greed and practitioners of a simple, virtuous life; they were beloved by God but at the same time inheritors of Noah's curse against Ham; risible but pious; alien and exemplary.

Such contradictions are not unique to the medieval peasant image. In late nineteenth-century Russia, for example, conventional topoi included the sturdy, devout representative of the Nation's soul, the impoverished, ignorant rustic, and the grasping *kulak*. These made up a set of not completely incompatible responses to a rediscovery of rural life by writers after the 1861 Emancipation.[55] Opinion about the peasantry was not so much uncertain or contradictory as diffused across a range of possibilities that could coexist or be fit together.

Hugo von Trimberg, a didactic German poet active around 1300, shows in the course of his long poem *Der Renner* almost the entire repertoire of peasant images including animal similes. Throughout the poem, which concerns the vices of different orders, Hugo laments the violence meted out to the unfortunate rural population by lords who are acclaimed as men of honor while boasting of their misdeeds. Hugo remarks that even a "wild heathen" would pity a dog who was as ill-treated as are the peasants by those claiming to be Christians. Once again, as we have seen before, the opposition human/animal is closely (and with bitter paradox) related to that between Christian and non-Christian. Hugo is confident that wickedness will, nevertheless, receive ultimate retribution in the next life where the nobles will burn and the poor who have meekly accepted their lot on earth will find little difficulty in entering paradise.[56]

In the same poem, however, Hugo shows the peasants as debased. He introduces the story of a supposed first-person encounter with peasants by declaring that they are a stubborn lot who would gladly serve the devil were they not held in check by the harsh oversight of their lords.[57] Hugo recalls a scene that he saw when riding through a benighted village of peasants lying about idly ("as is their custom"), with the women "searching like animals" for lice in the hair of their men.[58] Hugo gets into a debate with the peasants over why they are unfree while their oppressors prosper. Hugo explains peasant servitude by telling the story of Noah's curse on Ham, convincing the rustics (with an ease that does nothing to enhance verisimilitude) that their lack of freedom is just. Ham is the ancestor of serfs along with witches and heretics. Yet, Hugo continues, earthly freedom is not all it's cracked up to be, for it does not last. These poor rustics, cursed though they are in this world, will find the gates of heaven open to them, while those who profit from their labor will find entrance barred.[59]

The course of sacred and earthly history makes coherent the varying presentation of peasants. Peasants are accursed in the past, oppressed in the present, and blessed in the future. Their ignorant, animal nature, along with Ham's punishment, merits subordination but their sinfulness is expiated by suffering. It goes without saying that Hugo's sanctimonious teachings are designed to encourage passivity and excuse oppression by referring to a conveniently distant reckoning. Nevertheless, this massive collection of conventional arguments also exhibits points that could be appropriated to denounce seigneurial oppression, serfdom, and inhumanity in more vivid and immediate terms.

With the tumultuous fourteenth century an era of relatively frequent and serious peasant rebellions began. In this setting it became less feasible to hold together the various favorable and unfavorable attitudes. From the Black Death of 1348 to the German Peasants' War of 1525 the peasants are depicted as either bestial or sanctified; as either dangerous or the only virtuous class; as either amenable only to coercion or unjustly oppressed. The period sees both the most savage denunciations (like that of Gower), the most contemptuous satires (like the plays and poems involving the prankster Neidhart, the noble "enemy of the peasants"), and at the same time the most strident condemnations of servitude and the cult of the pious rustic (the latter particularly intense before and during the early years of the German Reformation). The vocabulary of peasant description does not change dramatically but its intensity is greater and the extremes predominate over mediating ideas such as the unfolding of God's intentions or the supposition of mutual service among social orders.

The representation of peasants as animals does not therefore predominate in the late Middle Ages but becomes more strident. Wild savagery is more feared while complaisant domesticity is less confidently assumed. Lamentations over treating rustics as animals take on greater force and significance as the possibility of insurrection using such arguments becomes a reality. The traditional ways of talking about peasants do not give way before a radically new imagery but are marshaled after 1350 in ways that clash more irreconcilably and with more immediate social impact.

PEASANTS AND THE MEDIEVAL "OTHER"

Ultimately the elaboration of a complex of representation of which bestial imagery formed a part degraded the medieval peasantry if only on account of their subject-position as objects of their superiors' discussions. Certainly they were perceived as different and subordinate in relation to the powerful, not as autonomous actors. Yet unlike Muslims, Jews, or others of alien religion or minority status or distant place of habitation, peasants could not always or completely be regarded as bestial, or even as alien. It is not particularly helpful to apply a totalizing conception of "the other" in relation to the Middle Ages, one in which Jews, Saracens, peasants, sexual transgressors, and lepers are interchangeably excluded. Not only does this fetishize the perception of alterity[60] as a concept independent of differentiation in reality, but it reinforces the dominant culture's definition of the ideal by referring everything to it, losing sight of the divisions among "others" (Jews and Muslims in Iberia, for example). A process of "othering" has, at different times and in different places, rendered familiar strangers as dangerous, inferior, or degenerate. Otherness has been invented by being structured as radically different from an anxiously defended (if unexamined) "normal."[61] For the Middle Ages, however, one must distinguish those geographically outside the orbit of European life, notably the monstrous races or the dimly perceived inhabitants of India, Ethiopia, or sub-Saharan Africa. The former were the purest example of an invented other. Religiously alien peoples (Jews, Muslims, heretics), were imagined along different axes depending on physical proximity, perceived danger, or degree of social subordination. They might be familiar but objects of fears of contagion or subversion. Lepers were at the same time radically different by reason of their disease and yet by their origin similar to those who segregated them. All these people were in some sense part of the divine plan but also troubling; objects of a sometimes playful, sometimes paranoid imagining.

When considering medieval ideas about peasants (or women as well), we are dealing with perception of populations so numerous as to be incapable of literal marginalization. They were at most "proximate others" by reason not only of closeness but of their secular necessity.[62] They were not just part of some mysterious intention of God's that would be revealed in the fullness of time; they were required for the immediate survival of even the most socially exalted. The "nondifference" of peasants was also reinforced by the fact that they were not slaves, nor infidels, nor, in fact, of a strikingly different physical appearance. Part of the point of negative images depicting them as misshapen, pagan, or docile was to counteract their apparent similarity, to demonstrate that they were natural subordinates, fit by nature (in the Aristotelian sense) for subjugation. This was difficult to maintain for the reasons outlined earlier, and thus discourse about peasants shifted among foci of unfavorable alterity (the peasant as savage or beast), similarity (the peasant as human and equal), and favorable dissimilarity (the peasant as more pious, as fulfilling God's commands). Regarding women and peasants, there was a constant shifting of seemingly contradictory images. For women these images might vary according to beauty and defilement; misogyny and adoration; sexuality and virginity. Women and peasants shared an image of physicality but with the difference that while the female body was sexual, that of the peasant was bestial.

The dominant culture of any society, including the medieval, does not always classify those whom it regards as different with easy confidence. Some "others" are less different and must be dealt with by a proliferation of negative stereotypes. In that very proliferation, however, the internal consistency of vision and purpose is strained and its complexity contains within it its own contestation.[63] Reiterated assertion of peasants' animal nature implicitly brought into play the question of their humanity. The contrast between the treatment to be meted out to animals and to humans according to Genesis contradicted what was observed to be the exploited labor of peasants. As with Carlo Levi's recollection, the mark of peasant inclusion in medieval society, their Christian belief, was an implicit attack on mistreatment that rendered them not only unequal but degraded in violation of a basic similitude, even, one might say, of rights appertaining to the human condition.

NOTES

1. Liana Vardi, "Imagining the Harvest in Early Modern Europe," *American Historical Review* 101 (1996): 1356–97.

2. Eugen Weber, *Peasants into Frenchmen: The Modernization of Rural France, 1870–1914* (Stanford, Calif.: Stanford University Press, 1976).

3. Jean de la Bruyère, *Les caractères ou les moeurs de ce siècle* (Paris: Imprimerie Nationale, 1962), no. 128 (IV), p. 339.

4. Carlo Levi, *Christ Stopped at Eboli: The Story of a Year,* trans. Frances Frenaye, 2d ed. (New York: Farrar, Strauss and Giroux, 1963), p. 3.

5. Herwig Ebner, "Der Bauer in der mittelalterlichen historiographie," in *Bäuerliche Sachkultur des Spätmittelalters,* Österr. Akad. Wiss., Phil.-Hist. Kl., Sitz. 439 (Vienna: Vandenhoeck & Ruprecht, 1984), p. 95. An earlier Latin version is "Rusticus est quasi bos, nisi quod sua cornua desunt," in Hans Walther, ed., *Proverbia sententiaeque latinitatis medii aevi: Lateinische Sprichwörter und Sentenzen des Mittelalters in alphabetischer Anordnung* (Göttingen, 1966), no. 27026, p. 641.

6. The eminent Catalan historian Dr. Josep Maria Pons i Guri pointed this out to me some years ago.

7. I have discussed these and other ideas of the peasantry in the Middle Ages in a book published about a year after the conference at which this paper was originally given, *Images of the Medieval Peasant* (Stanford, Calif.: Stanford University Press, 1999).

8. Edmond Faral, ed., "Des vilains ou des XXII manieres de vilain," *Romania* 48 (1922): 243–64.

9. A Munich manuscript probably by Georg Prenperger, a graduate of the University of Vienna, in *Parodistische Texte: Beispiele zur lateinischen Parodie im Mittelalter,* ed. Paul Lehmann (Munich: Drei Masken Verlag, 1923), no. 7, pp. 21–22.

10. Ronald E. Pepin, ed. and trans., *Scorn for the World: Bernard of Cluny's De Contemptu Mundi,* Medieval Texts and Studies 8 (East Lansing, Mich.: Colleagues Press, 1991), book 2, vv. 257–59, p. 90; "Alphabeto disposto contra i villani," in *Carmina medii aevi* (Florence: Libreria Dante, 1883), p. 27; "De natura rusticorum," ibid., p. 37.

11. Cit. Marie-Thérèse de Medeiros, *Jacques et chroniqueurs: Une étude comparée de récits contemporains relatant la Jacquerie de 1358* (Paris: Henri Champion, 1979), p. 15.

12. Pietro Torelli, ed., *L'Archivo Capitolare della Cattedral di Mantova fino alla caduta dei Bonacolsi* (Verona: A. Mondadori, 1924), p. 63. I owe this information to the kind advice of Duane Osheim.

13. Johann Alton, ed., *Li romans de Claris et Laris,* Bibliothek des litterarischen Vereins in Stuttgart 169 (Tübingen: Litterarischer Verein in Stuttgart, 1884), vv. 8371–84, pp. 226–27.

14. Chrétien de Troyes, *Le chevalier au lion (Yvain),* ed. Mario Roques (Paris: Henri Champion, 1967), vv. 286–305, pp. 9–10. For this and other examples from French romances see Micheline de Combarieu, "Image et représentation du vilain dans les chansons de geste (et dans quelques autres textes médiévaux," *Senefiance* 5 (1978): 13–14.

15. On the forest as a strange alternate world to the court, see Jacques Le Goff, "Le désert-forêt dans l'Occident médiéval," and "Lévi-Strauss en Brocéliande: Esquisse pour une analyse d'un roman courtois," in *L'imaginaire médiéval* (Paris: Gallimard, 1985), pp. 59–75, 151–87. The forest was also the habitat of the wild man, a savage without clothes or dressed in animal pelts, a human who had reverted to a state of animal nature but who (like the forest rustics) was disturbing rather than dangerous, armed with a crude and ineffective club. See Richard Bernheimer, *Wild Men in the Middle Ages: A Study in Art, Sentiment, and Demonology* (Cambridge, Mass.: Harvard University Press, 1952).

16. *Historia Gaufredi, Ducis Normannorum et Comites Andegavorum,* in *Chroniques des comtes d'Anjou et des seigneurs d'Amboise,* ed. Louis Halphen and René Poupardin (Paris: August Picard, 1913), p. 184; Rigord, *Gesta Philippi* I.3, in *Oeuvres de Rigord et de Guillaume le Breton, historiens de Philippe-Auguste,* vol. 1, ed. H. François Delaborde (Paris: Librairie Renouard, 1882), pp. 10–11. D. D. R. Owen, "The Prince and the Churl: The Traumatic

Experience of Philip Augustus," *Journal of Medieval History* 18 (1992): 141–44, argues that this story is derived from literature, specifically *Yvain*.

17. Felix Hemmerli, *De nobilitate et rusticitate dialogus* (Strasbourg: Johann Prüss, ca. 1497), c. 1, f. 1r. On Hemmerli and this book, see Frank Hieronymous, "Felix Hemmerli und Sebastian Brant, oder Zürich und die Eidgenossen—Basel, die Eidgenossen und das Reich: Engagierte Literatur und Politik im 15. Jahrhundert," in *Für Christoph Vischer, Direktor der Basler Universitätsbibliothek* (Basel: Universitäts-Bibliothek, 1973), pp. 21–57.

18. For Froissart and other historians' accounts of murder, rape, and cruelty, see Medeiros, *Jacques et chroniqueurs,* pp. 25–67.

19. Günther Franz, ed., *Quellen zur Geschichte des deutschen Bauernstandes im Mittelalter* (Darmstadt: Wissenschaftliche Buchgesellschaft, 1974), no. 117, p. 312.

20. John Brownbill, ed., "The Ledger-Book of Vale Royal Abbey," in *Lancashire and Cheshire Record Society* 68 (1914): 37–42.

21. Edgar Bonjour et al., *A Short History of Switzerland* (Oxford: Oxford University Press, 1952), p. 106.

22. John Gower, *Vox clamantis,* ed. G. C. Macaulay, vol. 4 of *The Complete Works of John Gower* (Oxford: Oxford University Press, 1902), book 1, pp. 20–81.

23. Walther, *Proverbia,* 4, no. 27016, p. 640: "Rusticus ac asinus, nux, hec tria connumerata, / Non faciunt fructum, fuerint nisi combaculata."

24. Ibid., no. 26997, p. 637: "Rusticus gens est optima flens et pessima ridens."

25. "Oignez vilain, il vous poindra; poignez vilain il vous oindra." G. G. Coulton, *The Medieval Village* (Cambridge, 1925; reprint ed., New York: Harper and Row, 1960), p. 234. It also appears with slight differences in Rabelais's *Gargantua,* ch. 22. A Latin version is in Hemmerli, *De nobilitate et rusticitate* c. 32, f. 124r.

26. Hilde Hügli, *Der deutsche Bauer im Mittelalter dargestellt nach den deutschen literarischen Quellen vom 11.–15. Jahrhundert* (Berne: P. Haupt, 1929), p. 3.

27. Francesc Eiximenis, *Lo Crèstia,* book 12, excerpted in Jill Webster, ed., *Francesc Eiximenis: La societat catalana al segle XIV* (Barcelona: Edicions 62, 1967), p. 59.

28. Traugott Schiess, ed., *Reimchronik des Appenzellerkrieges (1400–1404),* Mitteilungen zur vaterländischen Geschichte, vol. 35 (Saint Gall: Fehr'sche Buch, 1913), vv. 1496–98.

29. In Theodor Lorentzen, ed., "Zwei Flugschriften aus der Zeit Maximilians I," vv. 373–77, *Neue Heidelberger Jahrbücher* 17 (1913): 178.

30. A. Longfors, ed., "Li histoire de Julius César," *Romania* 56 (1930): 367: "Volentei d'amer ki en vilain se met estrinner le fais ausi comme une

beste salvage, ne il poet son corage aploiier a nule cortoisie ne a nul bonté, ains est ensi comme rage, quant vilains s'entremet d'amer."

31. William Paden, ed. and trans., *The Medieval Pastourelle*, 2 vols. (New York: Garland Press, 1981), especially nos. 31, 43, 44, 148, 149; Kathryn Gravdal, *Ravishing Maidens: Writing Rape in Medieval French Literature and Law* (Philadelphia: University of Pennsylvania Press, 1991); Paul Freedman, "Baleful and Winsome *Serranas*," in *Letters and Society in Fifteenth-Century Spain: Studies Presented to P. E. Russell on His Eightieth Birthday,* ed. Alan Deyermond and Jeremy Lawrence (Llangrannog: Dolphin Book Company, 1993), 17–27.

32. In German literature, especially in the Neidhart poems, the rustic men are violent and carry weapons that are above their station (swords in particular). Their violence, however, is directed against each other. Their drunken, murderous brawls underscore their savage and stupid nature and their inappropriate pretensions to social advancement.

33. John W. Baldwin, *Masters, Princes, and Merchants,* 2 vols. (Princeton, N.J.: Princeton University Press, 1970), 1:237–38, 2:172.

34. Joseph Trouillat, ed., *Monuments de l'histoire de l'ancien évêché de Bâle,* vol. 5 (Porrentruy, 1867), p. 886: "et s'il me plaisait je te pourroye prendre par le pied et te mener vendre au marché."

35. D. A. Carpenter, "English Peasants in Politics, 1258–1267," *Past & Present,* no. 136 (1992), reprinted in Carpenter, *The Reign of Henry III* (London: Hambledon Press, 1996), p. 344 of reprint.

36. Adeline Rucquoi, "Mancilla y limpieza: La obsesión por el pecado en Castilla a fines del siglo XV," in *Os "Ultimos fins" na cultura ibérica dos sécs. (XV–XVIII)* (Porto: Revista de faculdade de Letras-Linguas e Literaturas— Anexo VIII, 1997), pp. 125–26.

37. Gregory, *Registrum epistolarum* VI.12, Corpus Christianorum 140, vol. 1, p. 380.

38. H. E. Salter, ed., "Vision of the Monk of Eynsham," in *Eynsham Cartulary,* vol. 2 Oxford Historical Society, vol. 51 (Oxford: Clarendon Press, 1908), c. 41, p. 348. I owe this reference to Robert Bartlett of the University of St. Andrews.

39. Gregory, *Moralia in Job* XXI.15.22, Corpus Christianorum 143A, p. 1082. Cf. Augustine, *De civitate Dei* XIX. 15, whence this contrast derives. In Augustine, however, domination means the power of the state, something of less intrinsic interest to Gregory by reason of the weakness of public authority in his time. On the contrasts between Augustine and Gregory on servitude, see Robert Markus, introduction to part III, "Beginnings," in *The Cambridge History of Medieval Political Thought c. 350–c. 1450,* ed. J. H. Burns (Cambridge: Cambridge University Press, 1988), p. 121;

Vincenzo Recchia, *Gregorio magno e la società agricola* (Rome: Studium, 1978), pp. 118–20; Wolfgang Stürner, *Peccatum und Potestas: Der Sündenfall und die Entstehung der herrscherlichen Gewalt im mittelalterlichen Staatsdenken* (Sigmaringen: Jan Thorbecke Verlag, 1987), pp. 85–94.

40. For which see Piero A. Milani, *La schiavitù nel pensiero politico dai Greci al basso medio evo* (Milan, 1972), pp. 356–57; Alexander Ignor, *Über das allgemeine Rechtsdenken Eikes von Repgow* (Paderborn: Schöningh, 1984), pp. 234–37.

41. Hartmut Hoffmann, "Kirche und Sklaverei im frühen Mittelalter," *Deutsches Archiv für Erforschung des Mittelalters* 42 (1986): 1–6; *Councils and Synods with Other Documents Relating to the English Church,* vol. 1, pt. 2 (Oxford: Oxford University Press, 1981), no. 113, c. 28, p. 678.

42. Thomassin von Zerclaere, *Der Welsche Gast,* ed. F. W. von Kreis, vol. 1 (Göppingen: Kümmerli Verlag, 1984), vv. 8513–21, p. 293.

43. Paris, Bibliothèque Nationale, MS lat. 255, f. 5r, ed. Gilbert Dahan, in "L'exégèse de *Genèse* 1, 26 dans les commentaires du XII siècle," *Revue des études Augustiniennes* 38 (1992): 151.

44. Bariša Krekić, "L'abolition de l'esclavage à Dubrovnik (Raguse) au XVe siècle—mythe ou réalité?" *Byzantinische Forschungen* 12 (1987): 309–17.

45. Wace, *Le Roman de Rou de Wace,* ed. A. J. Holden, vol. 1 (Paris: A. & J. Picard, 1970), vv. 867–70, p. 193: "Nus sumes humes cum il sunt, / tels membres avum cum il unt / e autresi granz cors avum / et autretan suffrir poum." This has sometimes been dismissed as merely an imaginary reconstruction as Wace was writing long after the events. On its validity as a reflection of persistent peasant ideas, see Otto Gerhard Oexle, "Die Kultur der Rebellion: Schwureinung und Verschwörung im früh- und hochmittelalterlichen Okzident," in *Ordnung und Aufruhr im Mittelalter: Historische und juristische Studien zur Rebellion,* ed. Marie Theres Fögen (Frankfurt am Main: Vittorio Klostermann, 1995), pp. 122–24; idem, "Gilde und Kommune: Über die Entstehung von 'Einung' und 'Gemeinde' als Grundformen des Zusammenlebens in Europa," in *Theorien kommunaler Ordnung in Europa,* ed. Peter Blickle (Munich: R. Oldenbourg, 1996), pp. 78–81.

46. As reported by Thomas Walsingham, *Historia Anglicana,* ed. Henry Thomas Riley, Rolls Series 28, pt. 1, vol. 2 (London, 1864), p. 33; and Walsingham, *Chronicon Angliae,* ed. Edward Maunde Thompson, Rolls Series, vol. 64 (London: Longman, 1874), p. 321.

47. Girona, Arxiu Històric de l'Ajuntament, Secció XXV.2, Llibres manuscrits de tema divers, lligall 1, MS 8, f. 1r, ed. Paul Freedman, in *The Origins of Peasant Servitude in Medieval Catalonia* (Cambridge: Cambridge University Press, 1991), p. 224.

48. Cit. Horst Buszello, *Der deutsche Bauernkrieg von 1525 als politische Bewegung* (Berlin: Schöningh, 1969), p. 17: "nit wie die kye und kölber verkouft werden, dieweil wir alle nur ein herren, das ist got den herrn hymel, habe."

49. Günther Franz, ed., *Quellen zur Geschichte des Bauernkrieges in Deutschland* (Munich: R. Oldenbourg, 1963), no. 94, p. 301: "Zu den 8. [i.e. the eighth article of their grievance list] haben sich Geistlich und Weltlich frävenlich wider God aufgeworfen, und sich trotzt gesetzt wider das Ewangeliumb, und haben sich des Aigentumb angezogen, das allain Got mit Aigentumb zugehört, und die Menschen fur aigen under sich wellen biegen und schmuckhen und bei der Nesen in ir Geltnetz wellen ziegen . . . so wellen si mit arment Leudten Gwalt haven als ainer uber sein Vieh und noch vil tiranischer. . . . "

50. Ibid., no. 27, p. 129: "damit sich die Prelaten understanden haben und auch geton, unser Vordern, auch uns, die neulich an das gotzhaus in kaufweis oder ander Weg kopmen, davon genötigt, getrangt und vergwaltigt, unsern Bestant herter und erger gemacht, dann die Knecht und Hund seien. . . . "

51. Ruth Mellinkoff, *Outcasts: Signs of Otherness in Northern European Art of the Late Middle Ages,* 2 vols. (Berkeley, Calif.: University of California Press, 1993).

52. John Block Friedman, *The Monstrous Races in Medieval Art and Thought* (Cambridge, Mass.: Harvard University Press, 1981; reprint ed., Syracuse, N.Y.: Syracuse University Press, 2000). One finds descriptions of monstrous peoples in medieval bestiaries, especially those composed in England. Debra Hassig, *Medieval Bestiaries: Text, Image, Ideology* (Cambridge: Cambridge University Press, 1995), pp. 172–73.

53. Although the Donestre claim to speak the language of strangers they encounter and say they know his relatives before killing the unlucky traveler. Friedman, *Monstrous Races,* p. 15.

54. Émile Mâle, *L'art religieux du XIIe siècle en France: Étude sur les origines de l'iconographie du moyen âge* (Paris: Armand Colin, 1947), pp. 326–32.

55. Cathy A. Frierson, *Peasant Icons: Representations of Rural People in Late Nineteenth-Century Russia* (New York: Oxford University Press, 1993); Andrew Donskov, *The Changing Image of the Peasant in Nineteenth-Century Russian Drama* (Helsinki: Suomalainen Tiedeakatemia, 1972).

56. Hugo von Trimberg, *Der Renner,* ed. Gustav Ehrismann, vol. 1, Bibliothek des litterarischen Vereins in Stuttgart, vol. 247 (Tübingen: Litterarischer Verein in Stuttgart, 1908), vv. 843–45, p. 34; 1453–59, p. 60; 2220–28, pp. 92–93; 3405–23, pp. 140–41; 3807–10, p. 157; 6930–47, pp. 289–90.

57. Ibid., vv. 1309–14, pp. 54–55.

58. Ibid., vv. 1315–20, p. 55: In einer dorf kam ich geriten, / Dâ lâgen gebûr nâch iren siten / An irm gemache ûf irn wammen. / Zuo irn houbten sâzen ir ammen, / Die mit flîze tierlich suochten / Der si lützel hin nâch geruochten.

59. Ibid., vv. 1321–1456, pp. 55–60.

60. The expression "fetishization of alterity" appears in Nicholas Thomas, *Colonialism's Culture: Anthropology, Travel, and Government* (Princeton, N.J.: Princeton University Press, 1994), p. 159. I deal with the themes treated here in "The Medieval 'Other,' the Middle Ages as 'Other,' in *Marvels, Monsters and Miracles: Studies in the Medieval and Early Modern Imagination*, ed. Timothy S. Jones and David Sprunger (Kalamazoo, 2001), pp. 1–24.

61. See, e.g., Edward Said, *Orientalism* (New York: Pantheon Books, 1979); Mark Bassin, "Inventing Siberia: Visions of the Russian East in the Early Nineteenth Century," *American Historical Review* 96 (1991): 763–94; Allen W. Batteau, *The Invention of Appalachia* (Tucson, Ariz.: University of Arizona Press, 1990); Larry Wolf, *Inventing Eastern Europe: The Map of Civilization in the Mind of the Enlightenment* (Stanford, Calif.: Stanford University Press, 1994); Calvin Martin, ed., *The American Indian and the Problem of History* (New York: Oxford University Press, 1987).

62. The term "proximate other" is used by Jonathan Dollimore, *Sexual Dissidence: Augustine to Wilde, Freud to Foucault* (Oxford: Clarendon Press, 1991), p. 135, in reference to Augustine's view of the Manicheans.

63. Homi K. Bhabha, "Difference, Discrimination and the Discourse of Colonialism," in *The Politics of Theory: Proceedings of the Essex Conference on the Sociology of Literature, July 1982,* ed. Francis Barker et al. (Colchester: University of Essex, 1988), pp. 194–211, especially pp. 204–5. See also his articles "The Other Question—The Stereotype and Colonial Discourse," *Screen* 24 (November–December 1983): 18–36; "Of Mimicry and Man: The Ambivalence of Colonial Discourse," *October* 28 (1984): 317–25; "Signs Taken for Wonders: Questions of Ambivalence and Authority under a Tree outside Delhi, May 1817," *Critical Inquiry* 12 (autumn 1985): 144–65. The last three articles have been reprinted in Bhabha, *The Location of Culture* (London: Routledge, 1994), pp. 66–84, 85–92, 102–22.

3

Separating the Men from the Goats

Masculinity, Civilization, and Identity Formation in the Medieval University

Ruth Mazo Karras

Medieval society was one of collectivities in which identity came from membership in particular groups. Many of these groups—knights, monks, apprentices, guildspeople—underwent particular initiation ceremonies that marked their selection or separation from the rest of society.[1] In knighthood, for example, the ritual of dubbing admitted one into a military elite. For men of the aristocracy, it also marked a coming of age, the attainment of manhood. The entrance into a university, into the elite intellectual world, also marked acceptance into a masculine subculture. The ritual process of initiation into that subculture reveals a great deal about medieval ideas of what it meant to be a man—as distinguished from a boy, from a woman, and also from a beast.

Rituals of initiation into university life appear in only a few sources; the most detailed depiction comes in a book of Latin dialogues for the use of students at German universities in the late fifteenth century. The *Manuale Scholarium* was presumably intended for students whose Latin was not up to the standard they would need at the universities, where not only all instruction but also all conversation among students was to be in Latin.[2] Historians have taken the dialogues as illustrative of actual situations in which students might find themselves, and the appropriate linguistic responses to those situations.[3] This text, however, is more than an antiquarian's dream of vignettes of everyday life at the university. Particularly in its depiction of an initiation ceremony for freshmen, it provides insight into the meaning of a university education for those not destined to go on to be great scholars. In today's debates over the role of universities in North American society, where legislators who want to improve their constituents' employment opportunities at the least cost are pitted against those who speak from the ivory tower for the life of the mind without considering the needs of the world outside, it is useful to be reminded that these issues are not new. In the age in which the European university began, intellectual inquiry was only peripherally relevant to many or most undergraduate students, who were concerned with where the education would get them.[4] This particular text indicates the role of university education in the civilizing process and the creation of an elite masculine identity, crucial features of what education could do for the average student.

The classic studies on initiation rituals, by Arnold van Gennep and Mircea Eliade, offer typologies that are helpful in analyzing the ritual from the *Manuale Scholarium.* For van Gennep an initiation ceremony is just one example of a "rite of passage," an important event in one's life marked by special rituals and having a wide social significance. Although they often do not coincide with biological puberty, initiation rituals constitute a sort of social puberty: they mark the separation from the asexual category of child and the incorporation into the group of adult men and women.[5] The rite of initiation is often quite different for men and for women. Many societies need such a ritual for men more than for women, since for women marriage fulfills the same functions. Men must derive their identity from other adult men rather than from their household status.[6] For women, menarche is a biological indicator of maturity and marriageability (although these may need a complementary social recognition as well), while men, lacking such a clear indicator, must prove their maturity and manhood by undergoing various tests.[7]

For women, too, marriage often separates them from the natal family, whereas men may need a special ritual to separate them from the mother who raised them. This ritual can involve giving them a status above that of women; in many societies the initiation means not just becoming an *adult* male, but an adult *male.* The distinction between a man and a woman is more important than that between a man and a boy.[8] Various components of male initiation rituals in different societies have been interpreted as rejection or domination of the feminine.[9] David Gilmore, an anthropologist who has focused on the construction of masculinity, denies that "male initiations are uniformly or even primarily concerned with inculcating male dominance." He suggests instead that manhood acts as a social barrier against human enemies, forces of nature, time, and human weaknesses that endanger group life.[10] Yet if some of these dangers—notably forces of nature and human weakness—are identified with the feminine, then achieving manhood must mean triumphing over womanishness. The process of initiation for young men often, if not always, involves the creation of a binary opposition between masculinity and femininity.

Rites of passage like puberty rituals are society-wide, applying to all men (or all women) of a certain age within the culture. Mircea Eliade identifies

other kinds of initiation in addition to those that apply to everyone: those
that bring the initiate into a secret society or brotherhood, and shamanistic
initiations, which bring their subjects into a particular vocation.[11] In all
forms, the initiate dies and is reborn as a new man (Eliade discusses men
almost exclusively), with special knowledge and spiritual power: "Initiatory
death signifies the end at once of childhood, of ignorance, and of the profane condition."[12] Entrance into the medieval university was clearly not a
rite of passage that applied to all men of a certain age group. It falls
between Eliade's two other categories. The university certainly was an exclusive, if not a secret, society within medieval culture more generally. But
since medieval students were considered members of the clergy (even if they
had not taken orders), and since the universities were among other things
vocational schools for future clergymen, entrance into the university could
be seen as a step on the road to special spiritual powers, as with Eliade's
shamanistic initiations.

The third major anthropological theorist who has dealt with initiation
rituals, Victor Turner, focuses on the bonding that emerges from the initiation, which he calls *communitas*. *Communitas* is obviously of the utmost
importance for secret societies or fraternities, as well as the community of
students at the medieval university, and is much the same sort of phenomenon that is discussed today as "male bonding." For Turner, this bonding,
which is more fraternal than hierarchical, is created through various means
which include ritual humiliation: "In the liminal phase of Ndembu rites of
passage, and in similar rites the world over, communitas is engendered by
ritual humiliation, stripping of signs and insignia of preliminary status,
ritual leveling, and ordeals and tests of various kinds, intended to show that
'man thou art dust!'"[13]

When anthropologists have turned to study initiation rituals in contemporary Western society, they have tended to focus not on rituals common to
all members of a society or a given subculture, but rather on particular,
exclusive groups. It should not be surprising that one of these groups is the
college fraternity: it fulfills Eliade's description of a secret society, and it is
also relatively accessible to anthropologists, who can find native informants
right on their own campuses. Studies of fraternities are relevant to a consideration of medieval initiation rituals in that they involve young men at
approximately the same stage of life, in approximately the same social
situation (at an educational institution, possibly away from home for the
first time). Medieval students may on average have been slightly younger
than modern ones, but not much—the average age of university entrance
may have been around seventeen, though many students were younger—
and in any case people assumed adult responsibilities at a younger age in

that era.[14] Without suggesting some essential component of the masculine psyche that makes young men in groups behave in certain ways no matter what the historical context, we can still compare the rituals of modern fraternities and medieval student groups to identify differences based on the historical frameworks.

Descriptions of modern fraternity initiations give varying accounts of what constitutes manhood and brotherhood. One study based on fieldwork in the late 1950s describes the process of separation from the community outside the fraternity through the heavy time requirements placed on pledges; the deliberate disorientation of the pledges during the transition phase; the cutting of the pledges' hair to create equality and to remove an association with the past—a purification as well as a disorientation; the reintegration into the new ritual system and reconfirmation of the hierarchical social structure of the fraternity.[15] Gender issues are entirely absent in this analysis. The author never even specifies whether the (unnamed) campus is all male or coeducational. There is also very little emphasis on masculinity in the hazing of the pledges: occasionally they are referred to as "girls" but the main focus does not seem to be on what it means to become a man.[16] And there is no mention at all of sexual prowess as a standard of manhood. This lack of emphasis, which may be due to the fact that the fraternity members knew they were being observed, stands in stark contrast to other accounts, for example, Larry Colton's memoir of his membership in Pi Kappa Alpha fraternity at the University of California at Berkeley in the mid-1960s. There, pledges were constantly referred to as "cunts" and challenged to be "man enough" to join the fraternity. Manhood was measured by the ability to withstand physical torture, humiliation, and large amounts of alcohol, and also by the pledges' sexual history and current behavior.[17] The emphasis on sex also emerges in accounts of gang rapes that have taken place in fraternities in recent years. This behavior takes male bonding to its extreme: men prove their manhood through drinking and sex, and their brotherhood through drinking and raping together. Peggy Reeves Sanday's account of fraternity gang rape places the practice squarely within the context of the fraternities' other customs. According to Sanday, the fraternity initiations she describes are rituals in which the pledges cleanse themselves of effeminacy. The pledges must kill the inner woman and deny all femininity within them; this is done "by first stressing sexual differences and then representing these differences as hierarchical: part of the same psychic process, manhood and brotherhood are represented as infinitely superior to the despised and dirty feminine. The ritual inducts pledges into the brotherhood by first producing and then resolving anxiety about masculinity."[18]

The bonding as brothers risks a homoeroticism that must be denied through the aggressive assertion of heterosexuality.

The sexual practices of contemporary fraternity men cannot, of course, be extrapolated back into the Middle Ages. More directly relevant to the medieval experience of initiation rituals and the construction of masculinity is the process that Sanday describes. Young men come to a university: they are in a new place, not sure what to expect, worried that they do not belong. They need to become members of a group or community. To become members they must deny their previous identity through a process of ritual humiliation. Having achieved this denial, they can begin to construct their new—adult, masculine—identity. In contemporary fraternities this is done through the rejection of the feminine. As we shall see, in the medieval university it was accomplished through a rejection of the bestial and uncivilized, though the bestial still carried with it overtones of femininity.

For most medieval students, who did not pursue higher degrees, the university was a place to acquire skills, credentials, and connections that would help them in their career paths, whether within the church or without. The time spent at the university acculturated them into a world of shared experience that set them off from the uneducated perhaps even more than their actual learning. This was even more true of students at the German universities of the later Middle Ages than it was, for example, of Paris in its thirteenth-century heyday. The German universities were beginning to become finishing schools for the sons of the nobility; they were also part of the expected path for the sons of petty knights, small merchants, or prosperous artisans as well as the wealthy. In effect, the students were there to learn a system of behavior as well as a body of knowledge.

The types of student behavior prohibited in the statutes of the medieval universities indicate what modes of life students were learning. In effect, they were learning from their peers to live like the elites they hoped to join. They wore fashionable clothing rather than prescribed academic dress, carried and used weapons, drank, gambled, and consorted with prostitutes.[19] Carrying weapons, although it was not a feature only of aristocratic society in the later Middle Ages, fit in with a pseudochivalric ethos. The need to demonstrate one's masculinity through fighting might seem incongruous in a population where so many were clergy or presumed to be preparing for a life in the church. However, that circumstance may have been exactly what made students so ready to defend their honor by force. Someone who by reason of his tonsure, or likely future tonsure, might be expected not to fight back might be seen as fair game for frauds or insults. Students therefore had to show their willingness to stand up for themselves manfully. Heterosexual activity may in part have been motivated by the same factors.

These student behaviors, which can be seen as imitations of aristocratic masculinity, coexisted uneasily with another ideal of masculinity, that of the lettered man whose education brought with it wisdom and moderation. At the same time as they functioned as finishing schools for students who would not enter holy orders, the universities were also vocational schools for the clergy and professional schools for scholars. The initiation ritual of the *depositio* as presented in the *Manuale Scholarium* mediates between these different ideas of masculinity, symbolically stripping the initiate of his animalistic nature, which might express itself in the pursuits of drinking, whoring, and fighting, and yet at the same time concluding with a feast that comports well with the aristocratic virtue of largesse.

The readiness to gamble and to spend on clothing and on banquets signifies, above all, that one can afford to do so. Largesse was also considered a virtue within the university context. This largesse was often displayed by individuals' providing (voluntarily or not) feasts for their colleagues, often on celebratory occasions marking milestones in a university education.

The first milestone was entrance into the university. The new student or *beanus* was often made to provide a feast for other students.[20] At Orleans in 1367, for example, the authorities were very concerned because this practice was impoverishing many students, who had only a little money laboriously acquired by their parents and relatives. These students were being bullied into providing banquets for their fellows, and led to the tavern "like sheep to the slaughter."[21] For the students involved, it was a question of demonstrating one's suitability for membership in the community through one's largesse. A student might also be expected or required to provide a feast for his colleagues, examiners, or the whole "nation" (at Paris and other universities, an organization of students and masters coming from the same geographical region) when he "determined" as a bachelor (achieved his degree by taking the leading role in a public disputation) or when he "incepted" as a master (gave his first lecture) or took up an office in the nation.[22]

Both of these features—hazing of the freshman or *beanus,* and the use of a feast to mark (or to pay for) one's entrance into the community of scholars—are found in the statutes of the German universities. For example, according to a decree of the Heidelberg arts faculty in 1419, a bachelor who had just been examined for his license was not to invite anyone to a bath or a feast after the bath, except the dean and his fellow examiners, because "in such excessive and abundant banquets poor men are greatly harmed."[23] Inviting the examiners, however, seems to have been routine, and the bathhouse as venue might imply that the examinee hired the services of prostitutes as well. There was a similar provision at Vienna, requiring the bachelor to spend not more than thirty pence for bath and feast.[24]

Although financial hazing of new entrants was prevalent at the German universities, it was not the only form. The 1447 statutes of Erfurt required that "from a *beanus* for the removal [*depositio*] of his *beanium* no more than a third of a Rhenish florin shall be exacted, unless permission to spend more has been obtained from the rector of the University and the Secret Council."[25] Presumably such permission could be obtained in the case of a wealthier student. The use of *beanium* as a noun, representing the status of freshman as a thing that could be removed by a specific act or ceremony, indicates that being a *beanus* was not just a question of newness but a matter of having some taint from which one had to be purified. Hazing could also take the form of taunting or other harassment. At Vienna in 1385 students were prohibited from exacting money from or insulting the *beani*; at Leipzig they were told not to harass them during the procession of Corpus Christi. Other university and college regulations provided a penalty for students who threw urine or feces at *beani* or otherwise physically molested them.[26] Clearly the ritual humiliation aspect of initiation was present here.

The most detailed account we have of the initiation of a *beanus* is from the *Manuale Scholarium*. The relation of this account to social practice, however, is not unproblematic. The *Manuale Scholarium* was probably first published in Heidelberg, sometime in the 1480s; there were seven editions in various cities before the end of the fifteenth century. It consists of eighteen dialogues between two students, Bartoldus and Camillus, about various aspects of student life. Because the titles of many of the chapters begin with "How students talk about . . . ," commentators have taken the *Manuale* as a guide to the kind of everyday Latin a student would need to know. The learning of Latin, indeed, was a major part of what set university men off from other people in the late Middle Ages; it was not only the language of scholarship, but also a sign of membership in a particular elite.[27] The *Manuale* also has been taken as a general guide to student life.[28] Some aspects of it can be substantiated from other sources: the giving of gifts to examiners (which was, of course, prohibited), the disputations, the regulations about clothing. It is still not entirely clear, however, whether it was meant, or can be taken, as a direct reflection of practice, or whether it is in part tongue-in-cheek, depicting stereotypes that have some truth to them but are nevertheless stylized or exaggerated.

The authorship of the *Manuale* as we have it is not known. Most of the work, however, also appears in a book by Paul Schneevogel (Paulus Niavis) of Leipzig. Scholars at first suggested that Schneevogel had simply plagiarized the work, claiming it as his own; more recent work, however, gives priority to Schneevogel and considers the *Manuale* a revised version of his book.[29] Schneevogel's work was entitled "Conversational Latin for New Students," and if the work was in fact originally written for this purpose, it probably bears the same relation to social practice as a tourist phrasebook does today—close enough to make it useful, but not a reliable description. It seems most likely that the book was originally written at Leipzig, but then reworked for a Heidelberg audience, and as it stands probably refers to practices that would have been recognizable to students at most German universities, even if they did not correspond in precise detail to the practices at any one. The *Manuale* covers a wide range of topics: matriculation, the initiation ceremony, lectures, the clash between the philosophical schools of the *via antiqua* and the *via moderna,* the law faculty, the beauties of nature, meals, student quarrels, examinations, the requirement of speaking Latin, the disposal of chamberpots, proper academic dress, disputations, lending money, news from home, women and love, jugglers and traveling players, inviting one's masters to the baths or feasts.

The section that concerns us here is the description of the *depositio cornuum* or removal of the initiate's horns. One of the two students comments to the other about a horrible stink in the room: "there's either been a corpse rotting here, or a goat, filthiest of all beasts." They find it to be a horrible monster: "for this beast is horned, has ears like an ox, and his teeth, sticking out in both directions from his jaw, threaten to bite like a wild boar. He has a nose curved like an owl's beak, and red and bleary eyes threatening rage." They then discover that the monster is actually a *beanus.* When they offer him wine and he attempts to drink, they call him venomous and say that he "ought to drink water, muddy water, at the brook with the cattle." They then speak of how his mother would be sad if she knew how he was being treated, and accuse him of weeping when he hears his mother mentioned. They address him: "O *beanus,* o ass, o stinking goat, o smelly female goat, o toad, o zero, o figure of nothing, o you nothing at all! May the devil shit all over you and piss on your stomach and feet!" They discuss cutting off his horns, pulling out his teeth, cutting his beard and nose hairs; one student goes to get implements, and returns with a salve as well, made from goat excrement. They saw off the horns, pull out the teeth, and shave the beard using water with fragrant herbs picked from the garden by the outlet of the privy. They threaten to hang him by a rope in the privy. They then force him to confess to a variety of crimes, from theft to rape to perjury. As "penance" for these offenses, they order him to buy them a generous dinner with fine wine. They all then wish him luck; he has become a member of the community.[30]

To what extent was this ritual of deposition actually practiced? It is well attested from the sixteenth century on, as a more or less official ritual of the

German universities.[31] The initiate wore a hat with horns which were sawn off, had false teeth pulled, had his head shaved, and underwent other indignities. It is not so clear what was actually practiced in the later medieval period. Heidelberg records from 1454 contain a list of students who "put off [*deposuerunt*] their *beanium*."[32] This phrase, however, may not refer specifically to the removal of the horns, because the same phrase is used as in Erfurt in the statute limiting the amount a *beanus* could be made to pay. It could mean simply "removal of freshman-ness" rather than "removal of horns." There are two other texts from Erfurt, however, which when read in conjunction with the *Manuale* seem to support the existence of a practice similar to that described there. One is Goswin Kempgyn of Neuss's *Trivita Studentium,* written at Erfurt sometime in the mid-fifteenth century. This text is a long poem describing various aspects of student life and study. In the one manuscript that has survived, it is heavily glossed, so even where the poem itself is cryptic, the glosses explain what is happening to the *beanus.* The whole ritual is called the *vexatio beanum* (harassment of the *beanus*). The *beanus* is to be transformed by the use of ragged clothing, basin, and blade, and to be bathed. He is advised to bear the ritual patiently rather than fight it.[33] There is no reference to horns, but the shaving and bathing are similar, and the use of excrement is implicit in references to the buttocks and farting.[34]

The other text is a pamphlet from 1494, the *Monopolium der Schweinezunft* by Johannes Schram.[35] This parody of a quodlibetal disputation discussed the *beanus* as follows:

> Of *beani,* whether they can be received in our society, I decree: they must be cleansed of their *beanium* before they are received. And the way they must be cleansed is clear from the third part of Alexander, distinction 23ff., *on horned animals,* line *beasts,* verse *full of stench*; *A sea, a wave, a body of water purge forth that which makes a shameful sound, and feminine filth; these likewise are good for a beanus, honey, liquid, water, wine (there's some good Latin), the drinking of which pleases the one being purified and the one helping.* Cups, *gantz volle* [completely full], drinking, *das sie werden tolle* [so they get crazy], because the *depositio* alone is not enough, but that there be a feast for his colleagues, of good wine (according to others, good beer), which I prove thus. . . .[36]

Clearly the feast itself is connected with the purging of the *beanus's* taint and accompanies, rather than constitutes, the *depositio.*

As to what exactly is the taint that must be purged, the *Manuale* is our best clue. There we must look for exactly what sort of transition the *beanus* is in fact making. The *beanus* is in a liminal state between the status of unlearned child and that of university student, but what are the features that distinguish those statuses?

One thing that is happening to the *beanus* is the transition from an animal—an especially bestial one—into a human. This transition represents the civilizing process: the bringing of the rude, unlearned, rough new entrant within the pale of acceptable society. The unlearned man is compared to a human beast. Indeed, such an image of bestiality corresponds well to medieval literary depictions of peasants. The image of the uneducated person as bestial is found in the writings of university men throughout the high and late Middle Ages.[37] Jacques Le Goff notes with reference to this particular text:

> Thus the future intellectual abandoned his original condition, which strongly resembled the images of the peasant, the country bumpkin found in the satirical literature of the time. From bestiality to humanity, from rusticity to urbanity, these ceremonies, in which, degraded and practically emptied of its original content, the old primitive essence appeared, recall that the intellectual had been extracted from a rural environment, from an agrarian civilization, from a rude, uncivilized life on the land.[38]

But it was not an abstract or essential medieval intellectual who was being cleansed of the taint of bestiality or rusticity; it was students in fifteenth-century German universities. And, in fact, a comparison with the treatment of peasants in fifteenth-century German literature reveals that the connection of this ritual with rusticity is not nearly as direct as one might expect.

Peasants were depicted in late medieval German literature as stupid, boorish, violent, and with an affinity for excrement, but they were not particularly depicted as bestial. Violence was a more important theme in depictions of peasants than animal nature.[39] Peasants were criticized for laziness and for ambitions beyond their station, but these criticisms did not for the most part use animal imagery. In the Shrovetide plays that were performed in a number of towns, peasants are shown as unrestrained in sex, excretion, and gluttony.[40] It is precisely this unrestrained behavior that the university student is being asked to give up as he becomes a member of the learned community. Yet, although peasants are indeed shown as foolish, immoral, and bestial in their appetites, they are not often described as bestial in appearance or directly compared to animals. They do appear likened to animals in the stories of the Neidhart tradition, a collection of tales which appeared in a variety of forms in late medieval Germany.[41] In the Neidhart Fuchs chapbook, the peasants are compared to bears, cranes, swine, wild boars, oxen, and dogs. Yet even here the comparison is behavioral; they are not grotesque as in some earlier French literature.[42]

Although the representation of the *beanus* as a horned beast does not resonate with particular texts of fifteenth-century German literature representing peasants, the taint of rusticity still remains as part of the pollution from which the *beanus* must be cleansed. Even if fifteenth-century German peasants are not depicted as goats, they are shown as filthy and hypersexual, characteristics connected with the *beanus* (as well as with Jews and women).

The connection of the *beanus* with rusticity was largely independent of the actual demographics of the medieval university. A study of the social origins of university students in medieval Heidelberg shows that although there was a high percentage (ranging up to 45 percent in one year) of *pauperes,* or students whose income was low enough that they were exempt from matriculation fees, these were not mainly rural dwellers. Only 11 percent of all students in a sample between 1386 and 1450 were from villages. And not all of these, of course, would be poor or even uncultured; they were the sons of the village elite, although they still might be considered *rustici* simply because of their rural origins.[43]

Only a small segment of the university population in fifteenth-century Germany, then, came from rural origins. Nevertheless, the *beanus* may have been considered a rustic in a figurative rather than a literal sense, simply because he had not yet entered into the community of the educated. The learning of Latin, in particular, was taken in medieval universities to distinguish between rustics and others: a statute of the Collège de Foix at the University of Toulouse in 1429, for example, spoke of the "rudeness, swineherdishness, and viciousness" of the vernacular, which "plowmen, swineherds, and rural dwellers" speak.[44] Even so, peasants or rural dwellers were a small enough segment of the university population, and the relation of the goat imagery to depictions of peasants is indirect enough, to suggest that a rejection of rusticity is not all that is going on in the initiation ritual of the *depositio.*

If we focus on the goat, "filthiest of beasts," it becomes apparent that the ritual is connected with sexuality and abjection as well as rusticity. The goat is the animal mentioned most prominently in the *Manuale*; it is also the one that is characterized by horns and beard, the features which must be removed. Goat excrement also appears prominently. The general function in the text of excrement (which is not all goat excrement) is to connect the initiate with filth. But goat excrement was also thought to have medicinal properties. According to Albertus Magnus, "the fat of a goat, mixed with the excrement of a goat, rubbed on gout, eases the pain; the excrement of female goats, burned, mixed with vinegar or a mixture of vinegar and honey, rubbed in vigorously, cures baldness."[45] Vincent of Beauvais, in his magisterial compilation *Speculum Naturale*, gives more recipes involving goat excrement, which he says is efficacious for wasp stings, uterine flux, snake-bite, scrofula, hemorrhage, baldness, excoriation, burns, gout, arthritis, and abscesses.[46] Both baldness and gout are characteristic of men rather than women; baldness is a sign of maturity and gout of luxurious living, both presumably to be obtained in the future by the prospective student.[47] Yet, in the name of healing, and following commonly accepted healing practice, the initiators in the *Manuale* were going to smear the initiate with feces. A Heidelberg prohibition from 1466 indicates that feces were used in hazing *beani*.[48]

The goat was connected in medieval culture not only with physical but also with spiritual filth. Goats appear in the Old Testament, especially in Leviticus, as sin-offerings. They are sacrificed for the sins of the people, or sent out into the wilderness with the sins of the people upon them (scape-goats).[49] Old Testament images of sacrifice to redeem sin were interpreted as types of Christ, and the goat was discussed in this connection by Augustine, Hrabanus Maurus, Rupert of Deutz, and others.[50] Even when the New Testament directly contrasts the sacrifice of Christ with that of an animal— "Neither by the blood of goats and calves, but by his own blood he entered in once into the holy place, having obtained eternal redemption for us" (Heb. 9:12)—the goat was still identified as a type of Christ.[51] More often, however, medieval traditions about goats drew more on another biblical theme, that of Christ as the shepherd separating the sheep from the goats (Matt. 25:32), than on the goat as a type of Christ. Many commentators made the direct connection between the goats and sinners and between the sheep and saints. The sheep on the right hand and goats on the left became a theme in early Christian art. But the sin here connected with the goat was not just any sin, but the sins of the flesh and the impurity of the body.[52]

The connection of the goat with the sins of the flesh is also found in the bestiary tradition. Bestiaries described various animals and gave moral explanations for their characteristics; they were intended not just to convey knowledge about nature but also to edify. Many of the Latin and vernacular bestiaries were more or less direct translations from the Greek Physiologus, which did not include the goat, but some supplemented this with information from elsewhere, notably from Isidore of Seville, the sixth/seventh-century encylopedist. Isidore had this to say about the goat: "The male goat [*hircus*] is a lascivious animal, and wanton, and always eager for sexual intercourse, which looks sideways because of libidinousness, from which it gets its name: for *hirqui* are the corners of the eyes, according to Suetonius. Its nature is so hot that its blood alone will dissolve the stone adamant, which neither fire nor iron will vanquish." Isidore also discussed the *caper* and *capra* (another word for male and female goat), the *haedus* (kid), and wild goats (*agrestes caprae* or *capreae*) which live on the heights of mountains and have especially good vision.[53] The goat's sharp eyes are taken in some bestiary texts to symbolize the all-seeing God, and the wild goat's discernment of good herbs on mountains is like that of priests who seek out Jesus to cure people. Some bestiary illustrations show a goat pasturing on the mountains, or looking into the distance, but others depict the lascivious male goat, bearded and with long horns.[54] One text quotes a reference to male goats in Psalms and interprets: "The he-goats are those who follow the depravities of the devil and clothe themselves in the shaggy hide of vice."[55] Another interprets the blood that dissolves adamant as corruption of the law of God.[56]

The goat's connection with the libido is also found outside the bestiary tradition. One of the most extreme examples is *Moriuht,* an eleventh-century Latin poem by Walter of Rouen, about an extremely libidinous Irishman who is constantly referred to as a *caper* (and his wife as a *capra*). The modern editor of this poem suggests that its connection of goats with filth, odor, and sex is drawn from classical sources.[57] In medieval art, the personification of *Luxuria* (Lust), one of the seven deadly sins, is often shown riding on a goat.[58] Albertus Magnus thought enough of the sexual power of goats to claim that "whoever eats two goats' testicles and has intercourse, from the surplus of the digestion of this meal will engender a male child, unless there is an impediment in the woman with whom he has intercourse."[59]

The goat, especially as a symbol of sin, was also associated with the Jew. Jews were sometimes depicted with horns. The direct link was with the Devil rather than the goat, but the diabolical horned Jew was sometimes shown together with a goat whose horns were identical to his. Since the goat was the Devil's chosen animal, Jews were often depicted riding goats or with goat-like beards. The odor attributed to Jews in the Middle Ages further links them to the *beanus* of the dialogue.[60] It is not likely that the *Manuale's* intent was to portray the *beanus* as a Jew. However, the association with the Jew would have resonated for medieval readers, and would have identified the *beanus* with the imagined character of the Jew as filthy, depraved, and nonhuman.

The sexual aspect of the goat, and its odor, are both clearly present in the *Manuale* dialogue. The aroma that Camillus smells brings a goat immediately to his mind, and he calls the *beanus* an *olens capra,* echoing the way classical sources describe the *hircus,* but making the *beanus* into a female rather than a male goat. Part of the *beanus's* pre-initiate status, his not knowing how to behave properly or his lack of civilization, is his libido as well as his smell.

One possible reading of the *Manuale* text is that the *beanus* is being feminized, rather than cleansed of the feminine. The cutting off of the horns, the shaving of the beard, and the transformation of the odor into a sweet smell might point in this direction. Given the status hierarchy of the university, and the lack of actual women, the new students, the youngest members, could be effectively cast in the feminine role (with possible homoerotic implications). However, while perfumes and unguents might be connected with women or effeminacy, strong odors could also be connected with women, and often were in medieval misogynous discourse. The horns, too, are not distinctively masculine—the female goats raised in northwestern Europe in the Middle Ages also had horns. Nor can the cutting off of the horns be a simple castration symbol. Horns, of course, were a sign of cuckoldry; their removal might indicate that the *beanus* was no longer to be a figure of ridicule. The language of the ritual clearly points to a cleansing of the feminine, not a feminizing of the *beanus*. The Erfurt mock quodlibet, which refers to "feminine filth" (*lutum femineum*) as that which must be purged along with the foul odor, makes this connection as well.[61]

Rather than feminizing, the ritual was initiating the student into an alternative form of masculinity. It rejected the bestiality of uncontrolled sexuality. Yet it is not likely that a student-initiated ritual would be attempting to turn the prospective student into an asexual celibate. The authorities at medieval universities might have preferred that their students have nothing to do with women, and several of the other dialogues in the *Manuale* suggest that this ought to be the case, but it is clear enough from other sorts of records that this was never accepted by the students themselves. Rather, the ritual would seem to be taking away not the initiate's sexuality, but his uncontrolled and indiscriminate sexual impulses. He is now to be civilized, a gentleman.[62]

For those who did come from an aristocratic background, and were not intended for a life in the church, the *depositio* might also perform the function of making the entrance into the intellectual world acceptable. In making explicit the rejection of the feminine, the ritual in effect denied that study or Latinity was effeminate, that it was incompatible with knighthood and honor. If the uneducated man was like a female goat, then to enter the university was not to deny one's masculinity but to affirm it.

The civilized student might be sexually active but not lascivious and wanton, which were the characteristics both of women and of animals. Many medieval medical scholars, after all, recommended moderate coitus as productive of good health for men; it was the Aristotelian idea of balance and moderation rather than the Christian idea of chastity that controlled their work.[63] Rational and controlled sexual desire was associated with humans, as opposed to irrational, lustful animals.[64] Uncontrolled, animal lasciviousness was also associated in many medieval discourses with femininity; the initiate here is becoming not only human, but masculine.[65] The masculinity is one that mediates between the church's demand of celibacy (not often honored) and total sexual abandon. University students might emulate aristocratic practices in taking their pleasure where they could find it, but they were not to be controlled by it.

The rejection of the feminine along with the animal resonates with contemporary fraternity practice. Fraternity boys become men through rejection of the feminine. Pledges are humiliated by being called "girls," "pussies," "cunts"; by surviving the hazing they prove they are men (not women). The medieval student was proving he was a man (not an animal). But the medieval student, in rejecting animality, also rejected feminine weakness, and indeed modern fraternity initiations also cast the pledges as animals who need to be humanized.[66]

Both medieval and modern initiations also share an emphasis on separation from the mother. Bartoldus refers to the *beanus* as too "softly reared" for the harsh treatment they are giving him: "What if his mother, who loves him alone, should know this? Oh how many tears she would weep, how her heart would feel saddened! . . . Hey, look at his face. He's not weeping, is he? Certainly his eyes are wet. When he heard his mother mentioned, he was moved. . . ."[67] Compare this to Sanday's account, in which the pledges are called "mama's boys," and told: "Listen up, girls. . . . All your life you've been a bunch of nerds. You always went home from school to your mom, and she cooked for you, did your wash, made your beds, and told you what to wear. . . . We're going to cleanse the weak, dependent pussy out of you, and maybe then you won't look so wretched."[68] The idea of independence would not be expressed the same way in the medieval context—many of the students would be expected to have servants, even at the university—but the parallel remains in the cleansing of the weak and feminine.

The medieval university was a men-only system. The world of power for which it was supposed to prepare its graduates was a world without women. Where the modern ritual may be intended to reassure young men who are insecure about their masculinity by providing tests for them to pass and a confirmation that they have cleansed the feminine (and the homoerotic) from their identity, there was less need for this in the medieval system. That system was already so gendered that the exclusively masculine nature of the university was not in question. The rejection of the feminine is therefore much less explicit in the medieval ritual, but it still lurks behind this text. Women are already excluded from the university setting, but the masculine members of the university community still have to expunge the feminine from within themselves.

The student entering the university was becoming a man. What sort of man? This question is partly one of social status, or status-linked behavior: he was to act not like a rustic, but like a gentleman. It was partly a question of adherence to certain standards of propriety. He was to follow the advice of his rational mind and not his animalistic desires. To follow those desires would make him not only unsuitable for education, but in fact like a woman. The question of whether women had rational souls was open for debate in this period; following Aristotle, they were held to be much weaker than men, and more prey to their emotions.[69] The student was to be of a higher sort.

Despite a greater presence of women in late medieval universities than in earlier (as servants, and even, in Germany, as wives of masters)[70] misogynistic views were still prevalent. The *Manuale* repeats a number of misogynist commonplaces. Bartoldus has seen a particular girl in church, for whom he is aflame with love; Camillus tells him that she is poisonous because she is menstruating. Camillus is going to a dance; Bartoldus dissuades him, arguing that it is better to stay home and study than associate with women, for "the roses seem to blossom on the cheek and there is all that is beauty on the surface, but inside there is an ulcer, full of madness, and foulness, and poison." He also refuses to accompany his friend to a party, even though the women there will be decent as well as beautiful, because "in one hour you are bound to be so inflamed that for a fortnight you'll have no kind of appetite for study."[71] Women are distracting as well as dangerous. Bartoldus falls in love with the daughter of a judge, who sends him a ring as a gift; Camillus warns him against becoming entrapped, as she is already pregnant by another and looking for someone on whom to father her child. The common stereotype of women as fickle and lustful rears its head once again.

Medieval students would have had little opportunity to interact with women as social equals. Even if prohibitions against bringing women into the colleges were frequently disregarded, it would not be the respectable women of the town who would be brought into students' rooms in this manner, but rather prostitutes, who were ubiquitous in university towns.[72] Students would, of course, have occasion to do business with other women—landladies or retailers—as well as with prostitutes. But these would generally not be women of their own social class. The *Manuale,* along with other medieval misogynist texts, seems dedicated to maintaining women as the social "other." A man might consort with them but they could not be his peers; women of his own class, potential marriage partners, were to be discouraged. This attitude toward women would have had an effect on the student's postuniversity career. And it was perhaps the informal education in appropriate masculine and civilized behavior, given in an all-male environment, rather than the content of the curriculum, that would have most shaped his behavior. In this, too, medieval student society resembled the contemporary university fraternity.

This initiation ritual marks not only a stage in life, or a stage in one's vocation or career, but an assertion of identity, and an identity that is specifically masculine, since women are by definition excluded. The ceremony itself creates a cultured, civilized, elite if not aristocratic masculine identity. The initiate is incorporated into a society of the shaven and bathed, the sweet-smelling, in other words the society of those who can afford a comfortable life and are ready to assume the privileges that go with it. It is also a society of those who can control their sexual impulses. They may still carouse with their companions, as the feast at the end of the ritual indicates, but they share higher goals as well.

The *depositio* marked a student's entry into the university, not his graduation from it. It therefore constituted no specific transition into a particular career. But it did mark the beginnings of the student's formation as an educated man, and all the social cachet that went along with it. He was marked as the right kind of person, whatever his actual academic accomplishments. He could emulate some aristocratic practices, but he was more than a knight because he was educated. Simply the fact of being a university man, regardless of what he knew or could do, was important in the medieval context, as it is often important today. And the text from Heidelberg reveals to us what kind of man that was: constructed through a rite of passage as a member of an elite group who could moderate their animal natures and live like gentlemen. By transcending the bestial and feminine, the medieval university student could become a man.

NOTES

I thank William Chester Jordan, the director of the Davis Center, and the audience, especially Peter Brown, Sharon Farmer, Mary Fissell, Jón Haukur Ingimundarson, Ken Mills, John Murrin, and Mary Henninger-Voss, for their suggestions.

1. See, e.g., Maurice Keen, *Chivalry* (New Haven, Conn.: Yale University Press, 1984), pp. 64–82; Benjamin R. McRee, "Unity or Division? The

Social Meaning of Guild Ceremony in Urban Communities," in *City and Spectacle in Medieval Europe,* ed. Barbara A. Hanawalt and Kathryn L. Reyerson (Minneapolis: University of Minnesota Press, 1994), pp. 189–207.

2. The *Manuale Scholarium* is edited in Friedrich Zarncke, *Die deutschen Universitäten im Mittelalter* (Leipzig: T. D. Weigel, 1857), pp. 1–48.

3. Hastings Rashdall, *The Universities of Europe in the Middle Ages,* ed. F. M. Powicke and A. B. Emden, 2d ed., vol. 3 (Oxford: Clarendon Press, 1936), p. 378 n. 3.

4. Alan B. Cobban, "Reflections on the Role of Medieval Universities in Contemporary Society," in *Intellectual Life in the Middle Ages: Essays Presented to Margaret Gibson,* ed. Lesley Smith and Benedicta Ward (London: Hambledon Press, 1992), pp. 227–41; Stephen C. Ferruolo, "'Quid dant artes nisi luctum?' Learning, Ambition, and Careers in the Medieval University," *History of Education Quarterly* 28 (1988): 1–22.

5. Arnold van Gennep, *The Rites of Passage,* trans. Monika B. Vizedom and Gabriella L. Caffee (Chicago: University of Chicago Press, 1960), pp. 65–68.

6. T. O. Beidelman, "Containing Time: Rites of Passage and Moral Space or Bachelard among the Kaguru, 1957–1966," *Anthropos* 86 (1991): 453; Marie-Paule Ferry, "Mariage des femmes et initation des hommes: Beliyan et Bedik du Sénégal oriental," *Journal des Africanistes* 55 (1985): 75–83.

7. James L. Brain, "Male Menstruation in History and Anthropology," *Journal of Psychohistory* 15 (1988): 13 (although his argument that all forms of bloodletting in men are imitations of menstruation is pushing the evidence a bit far).

8. Jean-Claude Muller, *La Calebasse Sacrée: Initiations Rukuba (Nigéria central)* (Montreal: Presses Universitaires, 1989), pp. 206–9; William M. Schneider and Mary Jo Schneider, "Selako Male Initiation," *Ethnology* 30 (1991): 285–88.

9. Filip De Boeck, "Of Bushbucks without Horns: Male and Female Initiation among the Aluund of Southwest Zaïre," *Journal des Africanistes* 61 (1991): 56–57; Gilbert Herdt, "Transitional Objects in Sambia Initiation," *Ethos* 15 (1987): 46.

10. David D. Gilmore, *Manhood in the Making: Cultural Concepts of Masculinity* (New Haven, Conn.: Yale University Press, 1990), pp. 168, 226.

11. Mircea Eliade, *Rites and Symbols of Initiation: The Mysteries of Birth and Rebirth,* trans. Willard R. Trask (New York: Harper & Row, 1958), p. 2.

12. Ibid., pp. x, xii.

13. Victor Turner, *Dramas, Fields, and Metaphors: Symbolic Action in Human Society* (Ithaca, N.Y.: Cornell University Press, 1974), p. 53.

14. Although the statutory minimum age at many universities was fourteen, entrance at that age does not seem to have been typical. There are only a few places for which there are good data, but at New College, Oxford, in the fifteenth century, the average age at entrance was seventeen and a half years. At Oxford in the sixteenth century the median age was seventeen, and two-thirds of undergraduates entered between the ages of sixteen and eighteen. At Wittenberg in the mid-sixteenth century the typical age of matriculation was seventeen. T. A. R. Evans, "The Number, Origins, and Careers of Scholars," in *History of the University of Oxford*, ed. T. Aston, vol. 2 (Oxford: Clarendon Press, 1992), pp. 499–500; Owen and Miriam Gingerich, "Matriculation Ages in Sixteenth-Century Wittenberg," *History of Universities* 6 (1986–87): 135–37.

15. Thomas A. Leemon, *The Rites of Passage in a Student Culture: A Study of the Dynamics of Transition* (New York: Teachers College Press, 1972).

16. "What do you think this is, a girl scout camp?" Ibid., p. 120; also pp. 152, 153.

17. Larry Colton, *Goat Brothers* (New York: Doubleday, 1993), pp. 3–185.

18. Peggy Reeves Sanday, *Fraternity Gang Rape: Sex, Brotherhood, and Privilege on Campus* (New York: New York University Press, 1990), p. 171.

19. Léo Moulin, *La vie des étudiants au moyen âge* (Paris: Bibliothèque Albin Michel de l'histoire, 1991), is the best general account. For the regulations from fifteenth-century German universities: Rudolf Kink, *Geschichte der kaiserlichen Universität Wien*, 2 vols. (Vienna: Carl Gerold & Sohn, 1854), vol. 2; J. C. Hermann Weissenborn, ed., *Acten der Erfurter Universität*, vol. 1 (Halle: Otto Hendel, 1881); H. Ott and J. M. Fletcher, eds., *The Medieval Statutes of the Faculty of Arts of the University of Freiburg im Breisgau*, Texts and Studies in the History of Mediaeval Education, vol. 10 (Notre Dame: Mediaeval Institute, 1964); Friedrich Zarncke, *Die Statutenbücher der Universität Leipzig* (Leipzig: S. Hirzel, 1861); Eduard Winkelmann, *Urkundenbuch der Universität Heidelberg* (Heidelberg: Winter, 1886).

20. The word *bejanus* or *beanus* first appears in France and is thought to derive from *bec-jaune*. Early modern German texts explained the term as an acronym: Beanus Est Animal Nesciens Vitam Studiosorum, "A *beanus* is an animal that does not know the life of the scholarly." Wilhelm Fabricius, *Die Akademische Deposition* (Frankfurt am Main: L. Lichtenberg, 1895), p. 4. This is, of course, a false etymology. Several people have asked me whether the "beanies" worn by freshmen at some U.S. universities earlier in the twentieth century could have any possible relation to "beanus," but the *Oxford English Dictionary*, 2d ed., derives "beanie" from "bean" as slang for "head."

21. Marcel Fournier, *Les Statuts et privilèges des universités françaises depuis leur fondation jusqu'en 1789*, vol. 1 (Paris: Larose et Forcel, 1890), pp. 125–

26; see also Heinrich Denifle and Emile Chatelain, *Chartularium Universitatis Parisiensium,* vol. 2 (Paris: Delalain, 1891), pp. 523–24.

22. Examples abound in *Auctarium chartularii universitatis Parisiensis,* vol. 1: *Liber Procuratorum Nationis Anglicanae (Alemanniae) in Universitate Parisiensi 1333–1406,* ed. Heinrich Denifle and Emile Chatelain, 2d ed. (Paris: Didier, 1937).

23. Winkelmann, *Urkundenbuch,* p. 117. On the sociability of baths see Georges Duby and Philippe Braunstein, "The Emergence of the Individual," in *A History of Private Life,* vol. 2: *Revelations of the Medieval World,* ed. Georges Duby, trans. Arthur Goldhammer (Cambridge, Mass.: Harvard University Press, 1988), pp. 600–610.

24. Kink, *Geschichte der kaiserlichen Universität Wien,* 1:55 (1427).

25. Weissenborn, *Acten der Erfurter Universität,* p. 18. There are earlier (fragmentary) statutes from the 1370s or 1380s or perhaps after 1395 that do not include this provision, which may thus be new in the mid-fifteenth century.

26. Kink, *Geschichte der kaiserlichen Universität Wien,* 2:77; Zarncke, *Die Statutenbücher,* pp. 111, 102; Winkelmann, *Urkundenbuch,* p. 183.

27. Walter Ong, "Latin Language Study as a Renaissance Puberty Rite," in *Rhetoric, Romance, and Technology: Studies in the Interaction of Expression and Culture* (Ithaca, N.Y.: Cornell University Press, 1971), pp. 115–19.

28. For the ways different scholars have used it, see the introduction to the English translation by Robert Seybolt, *The Manuale Scholarium: An Original Account of Life in the Mediaeval University* (Cambridge, Mass.: Harvard University Press, 1921), pp. 9–12. More recent scholarship has treated it in much the same way.

29. Gerhard Ritter, "Über den Quellenwert und Verfasser des sogennanten 'Heidelberger Gesprächbüchleins für Studenten' (manuale scholarium, um 1490)," *Zeitschrift für die Geschichte des Oberrheins,* n.s. 38 (1923): 4–32; Gerhard Streckenbach, "Paulus Niavis, 'Latinum ydeoma pro novellis studentibus'—ein Gesprächbüchlein aus dem letzten Viertel des 15. Jahrhunderts," *Mittellateinisches Jahrbuch* 6 (1970): 152–91, 7 (1971): 187–251.

30. Zarncke, *Die deutschen Universitäten,* p. 6.

31. Fabricius, *Die Akademische Deposition,* pp. 41–69; Johann Friedrich Hantz, *Geschichte der Universität Heidelberg,* vol. 1 (Mannheim: J. Schneider, 1862), p. 86. Tools for the *depositio,* including knives and pliers, are depicted in Rud. Kittel, *Die Universität Leipzig und ihre Stellung im Kulturleben* (Dresden: Heligsche Verlagsanstalt, 1924). Luther gave a spiritual interpretation of the *depositio* in one of his *Tischreden* (vol. 4, no. 4714, cited in Almuth Märker, *Geschichte der Universität Erfurt 1392–1816* [Weimar: Bôhlau, 1993], p. 31).

32. Gustav Toepke, ed., *Die Matrikel der Universität Heidelberg*, vol. 1 (Heidelberg: Carl Winter, 1884; reprint ed., Nendeln: Kraus Reprint, 1976), p. 278.

33. Michael Bernhard, *Goswin Kempgyn de Nussia Trivita Studentium: Eine Einführung in das Universitätsstudium aus dem 15. Jahrhundert*, Münchener Beiträge zur Mediävistik und Renaissance-Forschung, vol. 26 (Munich: Arbeo-Gesellschaft, 1976), pp. 61–62.

34. Shaving also appears in the records of New College, Oxford, from 1400; it was apparently a "vile and horrible" ritual inflicted upon new masters of arts the night before their inception. *Statutes of the Colleges of Oxford*, vol. 1 (Oxford: J. H. Parker, 1853), New College, p. 47.

35. Johannes Schram of Dachau, as he is identified in the pamphlet, matriculated at Erfurt in 1490 and became a Master of Arts in 1494. The matriculation is in Weissenborn, *Acten*, p. 435, and the list of masters is in Erich Kleineidam, *Universitas Studii Erffordensis: Überblick über der Universität Erfurt im Mittelalter, 1392–1521*, vol. 1 (Leipzig: St. Benno–Verlag, 1964), p. 386.

36. Johannes Schram, *Monopolium der Schweinezunft*, in Zarncke, *Die deutschen Universitäten*, p. 111.

37. Alexander Murray, *Reason and Society in the Middle Ages* (Oxford: Clarendon Press, 1978), pp. 237–44.

38. Jacques Le Goff, *Intellectuals in the Middle Ages*, trans. Teresa Lavender Fagan (Cambridge, Mass.: Blackwell, 1992), p. 80.

39. I rely here on Paul Freedman, *Images of the Medieval Peasant* (Stanford, Calif.: Stanford University Press, 1999). I am grateful to Professor Freedman for making a portion of the manuscript available to me in advance of publication. See also the essay by Paul Freedman in this volume.

40. John E. Tailby, "Peasants in Fifteenth-Century *Fastnachtspiele* from Nuremberg: The Problems of Their Identification and the Significance of their Presentation," *Daphnis* 4 (1975): 178. See also Hagen Bastian, *Mummenschanz: Sinneslust and Gefühlsbeherrschung im Fastnachtspiel des 15. Jahurhunderts* (Frankfurt: Syndikat, 1983), p. 72; Samuel Kinser, "Presentation and Representation: Carnival at Nuremberg, 1450–1550," *Representations* 13 (1986): 8; James A. Parente, Jr., "Empowering Readers: Humanism, Politics, and Money in Early Modern German Drama," in *The Harvest of Humanism in Central Europe: Essays in Honor of Lewis W. Spitz*, ed. Manfred P. Fleisher (St. Louis: Concordia, 1992), p. 270.

41. Eckehard Simon, *Neidhart von Reuental* (Boston: Twayne, 1975).

42. Freedman, *Images*, pp. 135–36, 140.

43. Christoph Fuchs, *Dives, Pauper, Nobilis, Magister, Frater, Clericus: Sozialgeschichtliche Untersuchungen über Heidelberger Universitätsbesucher des Spätmittelalters (1386–1450)*, pp. 17, 75–76.

44. Fournier, *Statuts et privilèges,* 1:828.

45. Albertus Magnus, *De Animalibus Libri XXVI,* ed. Hermann Stadler, Beiträge zur Geschichte der Philosophie des Mittelalters, Texte und Untersuchungen, vols. 15–16 (Münster in Westfalen: Aschendorff, 1916), 22.2.1, p. 1369.

46. Vincent of Beauvais, *Speculum Naturale* (Nuremberg: Anton Koberger, 1485), 19:31, 124r.

47. This use of excrement for male ailments contrasts sharply with Hippocratic writings which associate excrement with the ailments of women. Heinrich von Staden, "Women and Dirt," *Helios* 19 (1992): 7–30.

48. Winkelmann, *Urkundenbuch,* p. 183. Or perhaps their use was merely threatened or implied. Present-day fraternity initiation rituals (although with their emphasis on alcohol, they tend to focus on vomiting more than on excreting) sometimes involve making the initiate believe that he is eating feces and drinking urine, when this is not actually the case. The purpose, according to Sanday, is to build trust and teach the initiate to obey unquestioningly. Sanday, *Fraternity Gang Rape,* pp. 160, 169; Colton, *Goat Brothers,* p. 48.

49. Lev. 4:23, 16:15, 16:21–22.

50. L. Wehrhahn-Stauch, "Bock," in *Lexikon der christlichen Ikonographie* (Rome: Herder, 1968), p. 314.

51. *Glossa Ordinaria* to Heb. 9:13, in J. P. Migne, ed., *Patrologiae cursus completus, Series latina,* vol. 114 (Paris: Migne, 1879), p. 658: "Hircus Christum significat, per similitudinem carnis peccati."

52. Wehrhahn-Stauch, "Bock," pp. 314–15.

53. Isidore of Seville, *Etymologies,* book 6, ed. Jacques André (Paris: Les Belles Lettres, 1986), 1:13–15, pp. 46–49.

54. Florence McCulloch, *Medieval Latin and French Bestiaries* (Chapel Hill: University of North Carolina Press, 1962), pp. 121–23; Robert Reinsch, ed., *Le Bestiare: Das Thierbuch des normannischen Dichters Guillaume le Clerc,* Altfranzösische Bibliothek, vol. 14 (Leipzig, 1892; reprint ed., New York: AMS Press, 1973), p. 298.

55. Richard Barber, trans., *Bestiary* (Woodbridge: Boydell Press, 1993), p. 83.

56. Emmanuel Walberg, ed., *Le Bestiare de Philippe de Thaün* (Lund: Hj. Möller, 1900), p. 105.

57. Walter of Rouen, *Moriuht: A Norman Latin Poem from the Early Eleventh Century,* ed. Christopher J. McDonough (Toronto: Pontifical Institute, 1995), p. 130. I thank Jan Ziolkowski for this reference.

58. William M. Voelkle, "Moran Manuscript M. 1001: The Seven Deadly Sins and the Seven Evil Ones," in *Monsters and Demons in the Ancient and*

Medieval Worlds, ed. Anne E. Farkas, Prudence O. Harper, and Evelyn B. Harrison (Mainz: Philipp von Zabern, 1987), p. 106; Wehrhahn-Stauch, "Bock," p. 16; Beryl Rowland, *Blind Beasts: Chaucer's Animal World* (Kent, Ohio: Kent State University Press, 1971), p. 19.

59. Albertus Magnus, *De Animalibus Libri XXVI,* 22:2:1, p. 1369.

60. Joshua Trachtenberg, *The Devil and the Jew: The Medieval Conception of the Jew and Its Relation to Modern Antisemitism* (Philadelphia: Jewish Publication Society, 1961), pp. 46–47.

61. Zarncke, *Die deutschen Universitäten,* p. 111.

62. I am not suggesting that the "civilizing process" going on in this initiation ritual is the same thing described by Norbert Elias: *The Civilizing Process,* vol. 1: *The History of Manners,* trans. Edmund Jephcott (New York: Urizen Books, 1978); vol. 2, *Power and Civility,* trans. Edmund Jephcott (New York: Pantheon, 1982). Elias is talking about the civilizing process on a societal rather than on an individual level. Elias suggests that "civilized" behavior became important at the time of the Renaissance and the rise of the state, as a centralized monopoly on violence replaced a system in which the individual nobleman could basically do as he pleased. But the story here about university initiation has little directly to do with state power.

63. John W. Baldwin, *The Language of Sex: Five Voices from Northern France Around 1200* (Chicago: University of Chicago Press, 1994), pp. 184–86; Joan Cadden, *Meanings of Sex Difference in the Middle Ages: Medicine, Science, and Culture* (Cambridge: Cambridge University Press, 1993), pp. 273–76; Danielle Jacquart and Claude Thomasset, *Sexuality and Medicine in the Middle Ages,* trans. Matthew Adamson (Princeton, N.J.: Princeton University Press, 1988), p. 136.

64. Joyce E. Salisbury, *The Beast Within: Animals in the Middle Ages* (New York: Routledge, 1994), pp. 78–80.

65. The literature on the connection of femininity and lasciviousness is vast. I have discussed it in various places, including "Gendered Sin and Misogyny in John of Bromyard's 'Summa Predicantium,'" *Traditio* 47 (1992): 233–57. See also R. Howard Bloch, *Medieval Misogyny and the Invention of Western Romantic Love* (Chicago: University of Chicago Press, 1991). Salisbury, *The Beast Within,* 155–58, discusses the association of women with animals.

66. At Colton's fraternity, pledges were known as "goats" and members of one's pledge class were one's "goat brothers." Colton recounts being harangued: "You're a fucking goat, that's what! A *goat*! You're the dumbest species on earth . . . " Colton, *Goat Brothers,* p. 42. Richard Ford reported of his Michigan State Sigma Chi pledge class in 1963: "You had to bray like

a donkey, buzz like a fly, bleat like a goat, be scorned, scourged, ridiculed, and insulted until they let you join them." Richard Ford, "Rules of the House," *Esquire,* June 1986, p. 234.

67. Zarncke, *Die deutschen Universitäten,* p. 6.

68. Sanday, *Fraternity Gang Rape,* 167. This was followed by the actual "cleansing," which involved anointing each pledge's scrotum with Ben-Gay.

69. Prudence Emily Allen, *The Concept of Woman: The Aristotelian Revolution 750 B.C.–A.D. 1250* (Montreal: Eden Press, 1985).

70. J. M. Fletcher, "Wealth and Poverty in the Medieval German Universities," in *Europe in the Late Middle Ages,* ed. J. R. Hale, J. R. L. Highfield, and B. Smalley (Evanston, Ill.: Northwestern University Press, 1965), pp. 418–19. See John M. Fletcher and Christopher A. Upton, "'Monastic Enclave' or 'Open Society'? A Consideration of the Role of Women in the Life of an Oxford College in the Early Tudor Period," *History of Education* 16 (1987): 1–9, for discussion of the roles of women within the university.

71. Zarncke, *Die deutschen Universitäten,* pp. 35–41.

72. See, e.g., Große Fürstenkolleg, Leipzig, in Zarncke, *Statutenbücher,* p. 196; Johannes Kerer, *Statuta Collegii Sapientiae: The Statutes of the Collegium Sapientiae in Freiburg University. Freiburg, Breisgau, 1497,* ed. Josef Hermann Beckmann (Lindau: Jan Thorbecke, 1957), pp. 28, 38. For prostitutes and students generally, see Ruth Mazo Karras, "Sharing Wine, Women, and Song: Masculine Identity Formation in the Medieval European Universities," in *Becoming Male in the Middle Ages,* ed. Jeffrey Jerome Cohen and Bonnie Wheeler (New York: Garland, 1997), pp. 187–202.

PART TWO

WITCHCRAFT, BESTIALITY, AND VERMIN IN EARLY MODERN EUROPE AND AMERICA

4

Imagining Vermin in Early Modern England

Mary E. Fissell

Vermin. To us the word connotes icky, dirty, nasty, disease-bearing animals who are out of place, invaders of human territory. Vermin are animals whom it is largely acceptable to kill. We can purchase an array of devices, from "roach motels" to smoke bombs, in order to do the job. "Vermin," of course, is not a timeless category. It has a history. In the seventeenth century, birds and animals whom we now consider rare or beautiful—kingfishers, herons, ospreys, and otters—were labeled vermin, and methods were developed to kill them. The ways in which these animals were imagined and represented suggest that, as well as being a threat to material survival, these animals were problematic because they called into question some of the social relations which humans had built around themselves and animals.

Three related characteristics were crucial to the category "vermin" in the later seventeenth and early eighteenth centuries. First, vermin poached human food, often items which were ready for human consumption; vermin ate things in which humans had already invested considerable time and effort. The second characteristic of vermin was their cleverness, displayed in the many ways in which they succeeded in devouring humans' food. These beasts were smart. While humans outweighed them by factors of tens or thousands, humans could not be assured that their superior strength was sufficient to eliminate these pests. Instead, humans built elaborate traps and concocted special poisons in order to lure these animals to their deaths. Finally, vermin possessed the ability to manipulate symbols, and even language itself. In fables, vermin were masters of discourse, while in household guides, vermin responded to symbols manipulated by humans. Because they could communicate, vermin were better able to plot together to raid human larders, and to avoid capture by humans. The communal actions they undertook at times made a disturbing mirror image of human society.

As with all animals, vermin were composed of a mix of projections, fantasies, identifications, and real flesh-and-blood creatures with their own agendas and goals.[1] Vermin threatened the always tenuous balance between ease and hardship, satiety and starvation, enough and not-enough. At the same time, they were imagined as animals who sometimes displayed a mastery of certain human forms and customs, a mastery which made humans uneasy. I do not want to cast vermin as boundary-problems in the way that Mary Douglas characterizes the abominations of Leviticus or the pangolin.[2] Instead, I want to historicize vermin, both as material beings and as a symbolic category rich in meanings specific to Restoration England.

In other words, I take from Douglas and other structuralists the idea that animals are both natural and cultural objects. Categories of animals can function as a means through which a particular social group articulates its sense of itself. Robert Darnton's essay on the Great Cat Massacre takes structuralist insights a step further by attempting to historicize a particular incident, the killing of cats by a group of Parisian printers, journeymen, and apprentices.[3] Darnton combines an analysis of the specific economic structures of the print trade with a much more general interpretation of the significance of cats in early modern Europe. I wish to analyze a category of early modern animals at a higher level of resolution than Darnton does by exploring the production of meanings by particular types of texts. Specific reading practices, instantiated within texts as well as in social customs, helped to produce an array of meanings about vermin that was historically specific.

The second historiographic intent of the paper is to question some of the inherently modernizing narratives now current about human and animal relations in the early modern period. Within discussions of English humans and animals, historians have tended to construct narratives around the rise of new sensibilities to animals, from animal-welfare movements to pet-keeping. Both Harriet Ritvo and Keith Thomas rely upon this type of transition in their major works, as does John Berger in his germinal essay, "Why Look at Animals?"[4] For Thomas, early modern views of animals might be said to be the dark side of the "world we have lost." *Man and the Natural World,* like his earlier *Religion and the Decline of Magic,* move, the reader from a customary, highly symbolic, small-scale world to one characterized as rational, mechanistic, and recognizably modern. In each work, what is left behind can be described with a certain nostalgia—the varied names country folk used to call the kinds of wildlife around them, for instance—but by the end of the book, the reader breathes a certain sigh of relief that burning witches or baiting bulls is a thing of the past. My exploration of vermin does not fit particularly well into such a modernizing narrative. Perhaps we do not become nicer, gentler, kinder people toward rats and moles. Any excursion to the mousetrap section of one's local supermarket reminds us that we kill mice in ways as brutal as any in the seventeenth century. What is different, it seems to me, is the ways in which we imagine what vermin are and can do. The early modern texts I have analyzed portray vermin as direct competitors with humans for resources. Dirt and disgust are not mentioned. Instead, these small animals are the enemy, poaching human food rather than decently eating animal food.

Vermin were defined legally in Elizabethan and Henrician statutes which authorized parishes to provide payments for the killing of vermin injurious to grain. The statutes can be understood as a response to an economic crisis characterized by a growing population and rising grain prices. While the Henrician statute focused closely on birds that ate grain or spoiled fruit trees, the Elizabethan one also included foxes, stoats, weasels, hedgehogs, and a host of other "four-footed beasts" who damaged or ate human food.[5] The willingness of a parish to pay bounties for certain animals' heads helped to define vermin in practice, although much more archival work is needed to analyze the function of these acts on a local level.[6]

Legal status and local procedures provide one framework for understanding vermin, but by the later seventeenth century, English men and women had access to a range of books which discussed animals, and vermin in particular. Specifically, I focus on books which were cheap and easy to read, which historians have called "cheap print." From the 1640s onwards, thousands and thousands of these books were produced, often by specialized publishers and printers.[7] These works both constructed and responded to a growing audience of readers; conservative estimates suggest that half of all English men and a quarter of all English women could read by 1700. Most of the books I discuss in this paper cost 1s. 6d. or less, and shorter pamphlets were often priced at a few pence each.[8]

In what follows, I explore both didactic and nondidactic works. The production of "how-to" books boomed, on topics from cookery to navigation to beekeeping to curing venereal disease. Such topics had long been addressed in print, but what makes the later seventeenth century distinctive is the numbers of titles available, the sheer quantity of books produced, and the conscious rhetorical framing of many books as easy, popular, or open to all.[9] The production of books we might consider "fiction," namely fables, chapbooks, and joke books, also increased in the later seventeenth century.

The didactic and fictional works I address have important commonalities despite their generic differences. First, each adopts a form composed of very brief narratives which demonstrate a moral or a suggested behavior. For example, Aesop's Fables contain moral tales we still recognize, such as the wolf in sheep's clothing. Jokes are also little stories with multiple, even conflicting messages. Even "how-to" books can be interpreted as series of narratives. For instance, *The Experienc'd Fowler* explains, "To drive away Weasles. Take a living Hedge Weasle, cut his Tail short, and it beeing a Hee, his Stones [i.e., testicles] out, turn him loose, and the very sight of him will fright all that come near him, to seek habitations elsewhere."[10]

Thus, both fictional and didactic works rely upon a series of very brief narratives. These tiny stories create texts full of contradictions and complexities, but they also invite readers to partake of a book in small pieces rather than presenting a unified or hierarchical model of knowledge. These books made of tiny fragments made cheap print accessible even to beginning readers, making elements of a printed book similar to the more ephemeral ballads and chapbooks which bridged oral and print cultural forms.

Second, I consider didactic and fictional works together because they were produced and advertised by the same publishers. For example, John Harris advertised fourteen "useful" books in his 1688 vermin-killing manual. These include a children's catechism priced at eightpence, six works of practical divinity (ranging in cost from one to three shillings), two popular medical works at sixpence and three shillings, two historical works, a fortune teller, a joke book, and a work of fiction at one shilling apiece.[11] Some works might be didactic in one context and entertaining in another. For example, Aesop's fables were read for pleasure, but they were also used as schoolbooks, instructing boys in rhetoric and Latin. On a humbler level, Aesop's fables appeared as copybooks—instructional works on handwriting.[12]

FOOD

First and foremost, cheap-print vermin were defined in relation to human food. In 1688, *A Necessary Family-Book* emphasized the ways in which vermin ate human food.[13] Foxes, this work advised, killed one thousand lambs, two thousand poultry, and four thousand pairs of rabbits every year. These numbers are meant to convey the magnitude of the fox's offense; no one could have calculated such figures accurately.[14] The section of the book on waterbirds reiterates the fact that vermin are those birds which eat human food: "The Herne [heron] destroys much young Fish"; coot or moorhen "are great destroyers of Fish." Worse yet, the cormorant "is a great destroyer of Fish also, he useth fresh Waters, and will dive under the water and take Fish of three or four Years growth."[15] In other words, the cormorant takes fish that are of a size to be eaten by humans.

In fiction, vermin eat human food constantly. In one version of the fable "The Country Mouse and the City Mouse," human foods are lovingly detailed. The country mouse serves up beans and peas, cheese parings and bacon rind, and a black pudding sprinkled with sugar. This may be rural fare, but it includes sugar, an imported luxury commodity manufactured for humans. The city mouse promises her cousin more sophisticated foods—a venison pasty and sugar and sack. Venison was a socially specific human food since deer hunting was supposed to be restricted to the aristocracy. However, illicit venison could be found for sale in markets, and recipes in cookbooks explained how to make counterfeit venison.[16] When the country mouse is scared by dogs, she leaves, telling her cousin, "I'le ne're to eat quelquechose, and high rogouts strive."[17] Both "quelquechose" and "rogouts" are French words first introduced into English cookery books in the early seventeenth century. The first was often rendered "kickshaw" in English, and quickly both came to be used pejoratively to describe over-fancy foreign food. Undoubtedly, many an English barn full of grain was ravaged by mice, but in these stories, mice eat food specifically prepared for human tables.

Hunger and food, greed and satiety, want and plenty—all of these recur in different genres of cheap print. In the seventeenth century, England saw the last of its subsistence crises, as defined by demographers. Large-scale famine no longer threatened the land, but bad harvests recurred, and people went hungry while subsisting on whatever they could find. So too, memory of famine or hard times probably lasted long after actual famines had become a thing of the past.[18] However, I do not want to reduce themes in cheap print wholly to a material base. Rather, my aim is to understand what connotations human food, and the eating of it by animals, might have carried in the later seventeenth century.

Books on vermin-killing often noted that vermin died because they ate "greedily." Again and again, texts describe how "they will greedily eat it, and it quickly killeth them" or "the Mice will greedily eat of it, and it is present death to them" or "the Moulds [moles] will greedily eat of it, and it certainly kills them."[19] In vermin-killing manuals, "greed" may be used to displace any anxieties about killing vermin. It is as though the vermin invite their own deaths, because of their greedy behavior. Bugs are not described as "greedy," nor are waterbirds. Only the four-footed beasts are greedy. Cheap-print books which discuss food, cookery, and manners suggest that various techniques were employed to discourage or manage manifestations of human greed. As James Serpell notes, anthropomorphism has a dark side in which some animals are portrayed in highly negative human terms, thus justifying their extermination.[20] When vermin were called "greedy," in other words, that description carried with it a set of associations which created distance between vermin and human society. That distance was produced, in part, by means of jokes about greed, and instructions for carving meat, while the depiction of vermin as non-food animals in the same texts simultaneously undermined some of that carefully built distance.

In joke books, tensions between greed and politeness are frequently invoked. Sometimes, the joke is against a glutton: "One that was a great Eater, sitting down to Supper, complained that he had lost his Stomach. 'Well,' says a merry Fellow that was there, 'If a Poor Man has found it, he will be utterly undone.'"[21] In another joke, desire for food serves as a way to shame a hostess. A large dish of broth, with a small mutton chop in the middle of it, is put on the table. The guest begins to unbutton his doublet; when asked why, he replies "I mean to swim through this sea of Pottage, to that Island of Meat."[22] Here the issue is not greed per se. Instead, a critique of hospitality is performed through a gesture satirizing the desire for meat.

Jokes and stories are not univocal about greed, although it is usually portrayed as a very human failing. For example,

> A sharping scholar of King's Colledg in Oxford, being in the Kitchin, and seeing the Cook take up a Plumb-pudding out of the Pot, watching his opportunity, while the Cook's back was turn'd; he whipt up the Pudding into his own Chamber: which the Cook presently missing, runs up into the Scholars Chamber, and searched all about for it, but could not find it; the Scholar swore it was not in his Chambers (though the Cook smelt it) for he had ingeniously hung it out of his Window, which when the Cook was gone, he pull'd in, and eat as ingeniously.[23]

This combination of greed and cunning is itself reminiscent of descriptions of vermin. Although the scholar succeeds in this joke, he is not presented as admirable—the word "sharping" is pejorative. I suspect that this joke may derive from earlier ones about priests and monks, whose fondness for food and drink was a well-known stereotype.

Eating with a group of people involved a code of behavior and manners which, among other things, mediated between naked hunger and its satisfaction.[24] In particular, the elaborate art of carving meat was central to the display of good manners. The physical skill of cutting up parts of dead animals and the social one of allocating pieces of meat to guests appropriately revealed the host's finesse. The guests' careful recognition of social hierarchy, highlighted by who got what piece of the animal, enabled them to enact their own representation of that hierarchy. As such, an elaborate meal was a theater piece, a display of food and courtesy in which eating was embedded within cultural forms. Books of cheap print both popularized these standards of behavior, and made fun of them. Vermin, on the other hand, ate indiscriminately, without attention to hierarchy or manners. In fables, for example, vermin are not usually portrayed as sitting down to a meal together. The country mouse's dinner for her city cousin is quite unusual, and when the situation is reversed, the city mouse is often depicted eating her dainty food off the floor.

A work such as *Youth's Behaviour* (seventh edition 1661) laid out the basics of courtesy: "Take not thy repast like a glutton." "Eat not with cheeks full, and with full mouth." "Smell not to thy meat, and if thou holdest thy nose to it, set it not afterwards before another."[25] These precepts were not original; they were taken from Erasmus's *De Civilitate Morum Puerilium,* first translated and published in English in 1532, one of the foundational European works on manners or civility. *Youth's Behaviour* also includes a discussion of the complicated social relations of serving and proffering meats. If you are entertaining a guest, it is proper for you to serve them, even to dishes that are close to them. "But if one be invited by another, it is better to attend until that the master or other do carve him meat, than that he take it himself."[26]

At this time, "meat" could mean any sort of victual (as in "meat and drink"). However, in this text, it is clear that "meat" means animal parts, and that it is the focus of desire. "Cast not thine eyes upon the trenchers of others, and fix them not wishly upon the meat on the table." "One ought sometimes look off the meat, yet without gazing to and fro . . . or on the meat which is before others."[27] The importance of manners to distinguish human eating of animals from animal eating of animals is made clear, again in words taken from Erasmus: "Suck no bones at least in such wise that one may hear it. . . . Gnaw them not, nor tear the flesh with thy teeth, as dogs do, but make use of thy knife."[28] In books such as these, meat is the center of the meal, and it provides the greatest test of politeness.

Books on housewifery or cooking also emphasize the art of carving meat. The best-selling Hannah Woolley directs:

> If any Gentleman who attends the Table, be employed or commanded to cut up any Fowl or Pig, or anything else whatsoever, it is requisite that he have a clean napkin upon his Arm. . . . [he should remove the meat to be carved from the main dining table] till he hath made it ready for his Superiors to eat, and neatly and handsomly to carve it. . . . the neatest Carvers never touch any Meat but with the Knife and Fork; he must be very nimble, lest the Meat cool too much. . . . [29]

Much more specific instructions on carving were the basis of *The Genteel House-Keeper's Pastime,* first issued in 1671 (see figure 1). Various kinds of

CARVING CARDS.

Sold by J. Moxon At the Atlas in Warwick lane And at the three Bells in Ludgate street

1. Setting the scene for carving. Wrapper, *The Genteel House-Keeper's Pastime.* (George Peabody Library, Milton S. Eisenhower Library, Baltimore.)

meat are conspicuously displayed on the table. The format of instruction is unusual: a small pamphlet accompanies a deck of playing cards (see figures 2–4). The deck of cards sold for one shilling, and the accompanying pamphlet for sixpence.[30] The pamphlet explains how to carve, and provides suggestions for accompanying sauces. Some cuts of meat, such as the boar's head or the goose, are represented as clearly recognizable animal parts, while others, such as the venison pasty, are almost wholly transformed into works of art. In all cases, however, the elaborate carving methods transform the animal part into a food item. Notice, for example, the delicacy with which the boar's head must be cut, with a tiny portion carved out at the lines marked "1 and 2."

Instructions on carving also appeared in the very cheapest books. A twenty-one-page *Art of Courtship,* for example, included amorous dialogues, model compliments for courtship, and guides to the significance of moles and the interpretation of dreams.[31] Its title page also promised "rules for carving of Flesh, Fish, Fowl, and cutting up Pastry: Also to distinguish the best Piec-

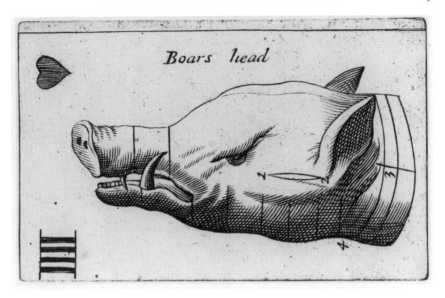

2. Boar's head. From *The Genteel House-Keeper's Pastime*. (George Peabody Library, Milton S. Eisenhower Library, Baltimore.)

3. Sir Loyn of Beef. From *The Genteel House-Keeper's Pastime*. (George Peabody Library, Milton S. Eisenhower Library, Baltimore.)

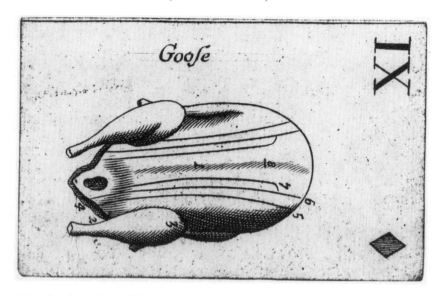

4. Rere that Goose. From *The Genteel House-Keeper's Pastime.* (George Peabody Library, Milton S. Eisenhower Library, Baltimore.)

es, and decently to serve a Table after the most Modish and Courtly manner." And, in two small pages, the book provides those instructions, including the fact that pigs' ears are "by ladies accounted best."[32] "Pastry" here meant meat pies, the proper carving of which formed a whole suit of the deck of playing cards mentioned above (see figure 5).

Carving and table manners delineated an elaborate and highly articulated social hierarchy, and defined civility as a triumph of politeness over greed, or manners over mouth. Vermin, who ate greedily and went to their deaths, illustrated the potential consequences of the uninhibited pursuit of bodily pleasures. Cheap print's emphasis upon the rituals of carving meat functioned in relation to vermin in a second way. Not only were vermin uncouth eaters who devoured their meat without any ceremony. Vermin were also animals who were never transformed into meat. Like humans, they ate meat but were never eaten themselves, at least within the purview of cheap print. While many vermin lived with humans in their houses, there was no place at, on, or under the dinner table for them, as meat or as meat eaters.

There is a range of potential reasons for the inedibility of vermin, but none is fully convincing. One reason may have been the dietary prohibitions in the Old Testament. As Leviticus had it, in the King James Version: "And whatsoever goeth upon his paws, among all manner of beasts that go on all

5. Border that Pasty. From *The Genteel House-Keeper's Pastime.* (George Peabody Library, Milton S. Eisenhower Library, Baltimore.)

four, those are unclean unto you: whoso toucheth their carcase shall be unclean until the even" (11:27). Specific types of vermin were also mentioned by name: "These shall also be unclean unto you among the creeping things that creep upon the earth; the weasel, and the mouse, and the tortoise after his kind, and the ferret, and the chameleon, and the lizard, and the snail, and the mole" (11:29–30). However, these biblical injunctions cannot be the sole reason that early modern texts do not represent vermin as edible, for in the same chapter of Leviticus, other animals were also forbidden, among them staples of English meat eating, such as pigs, "conies," and hares (11:5–7).[33] It might be argued that vermin were too small to make a meal, or that their flesh was too strong-tasting. However, cookbooks of the period include recipes for very small animals, such as infant rabbits, and there are recipes to conceal the strong taste of certain meats.

In contrast, water vermin could be eaten without a twinge. Although Leviticus forbade the consumption of herons, cormorants, and swans (reserved for royalty in early modern England), cookbooks provide instructions for their cooking and carving. The same bird could be vermin in one context, and dinner in another, and the methods for catching sporting and verminous birds were the same. Elaborate nets trapped birds on or near the water, whether they were to be killed for food or for the safety of fish. In other words, it is verminous four-footed animals, not verminous birds, that are represented as not transformable into human food; birds could shed their verminous identities and become meat without difficulty.

The larger topic of food taboos or avoidances, such as religious prohibitions of the consumption of specific animals, has been analyzed in a variety of disciplines. Anthropologists generalize that boundary animals, those animals who violate a particular culture's ordering of animal types by displaying characteristics of multiple categories, are rarely eaten. Others suggest that carnivorous animals are rarely eaten, perhaps because of an unspoken fear that such animals might have consumed human flesh. However, anthropologists also claim that every item that is food in one culture is the subject of avoidance in another, and vice versa.[34] Thus, the answer to the question, "why not eat vermin?" seems complex and even contradictory. I suspect that in the hardscrabble world of rural England, such small beasts probably were eaten. But in cheap print, four-footed vermin are always the eaters, never the eaten. Rather than seeking a structural explanation for the inedibility of vermin, here I can only suggest that, in early modern England, inedibility was part and parcel of the definition of vermin.

Finally, food and eating had important religious and moral connotations utterly unknown to vermin. Cheap-print books often stressed moderation in food and drink, for intertwined religious and health reasons. A *Rich Treasure, the Knowledge whereof is Useful, Profitable, Pleasant and Delightful* (1698), included remedies for the diseases of sheep, frugal ways to cut out a shift from the least possible fabric, directions for raising conies and pigeons, advice on the interpretation of dreams, and so on. A section on health counsels moderation in food and drink, which "will furnish Religious Persons with such a way and manner of Living, that they may with more ease, Cheerfulness and Alacrity, apply themselves to the Service of the Great God."[35] This text instructs the reader to determine how much food is appropriate for him or her on a daily basis. Although every person's individual constitution would dictate the specifics, about thirteen or fourteen ounces of food per day was suggested for the elderly and sedentary.[36]

Thus, vermin were in part defined by their consumption of human food. This transgression was materially and symbolically significant. The depredations of vermin left people hungry. Symbolically, vermin attacks on human food can be understood as representing a threat to human civility. The elaborate apparatuses of carving, dining, and godly moderation separated humans from animals, but vermin showed that a taste for human food need not be associated with human social norms. Finally, the irreducibility of vermin to meat made them an odd category. In the scripturally defined functionalist understanding of animals which predominated in early modern England, vermin were not useful to humans, but they lived with them, as did domestic animals, and stole their food.[37]

CUNNING AND TRICKERY

Greed was also often connected with cunning, the second characteristic of vermin. The classic medieval French tale of Reynard the Fox, as presented in chapbook form, illustrates the multiple connections between the two.[38] Reynard, known throughout Europe for his cunning, here uses his wits and other animals' greed to trick his way out of trouble. Various animals complain to the lion king that Reynard has eaten their relatives. When the king summons Reynard to court, he first sends a bear. Reynard sets a trap which lures the bear with honey and then closes around the bear's head. Next is sent a cat, who is trapped in a noose in a henhouse. The farmer had constructed the noose to catch Reynard, but the fox uses the cat's desire for mice to trap it instead. When Reynard finally appears, he pleads his case at the gallows by telling a complicated tale about treasure, conspiracy, and betrayal. The king saves Reynard from execution by hanging, and turns on those animals who betrayed him. Not coincidentally, they are some of the very same animals who had originally complained about Reynard.

The farmer in Reynard's tale could have learned how to set his trap from any one of a number of vermin-killing manuals, which often specify a noose for foxes (see figure 6). In these books, no other animal is dispatched by hanging, a uniquely human method of judicial killing. Other similar traps which catch an animal by the neck and kill it are referred to as snares, and are not visually represented as noose-like (see figure 7). Only foxes, whose cunning can outweigh even their desire for food, are killed as if they are human criminals. In the eighteenth century, gamekeepers in England began to construct so-called gamekeepers' gibbets, still employed in England to this day. The keeper will hang a number of animal pests, and leave their bodies hanging as a warning to other animals of that type. In other words, these are intended to be terrifying and edifying public spectacles, as were public executions in early modern England. The only difference is that their intended audience is composed of animals, not people.[39]

Foxes are unique in European literature, but they are also exemplars of the worst characteristics of vermin. The fox was represented as the most cunning animal (rather as we think of rats today), but cunning was also characteristic of all four-footed vermin. Therefore traps and tricks were recommended in vermin-killing manuals. The fierce drag-hook was de-

6. A Whip or Spring-Trap for the Fox. From *A Necessary Family-Book.*

7. A snare for birds. From *The Compleat English and French Vermin-killer.* (Folger Shakespeare Library, Washington, D.C.)

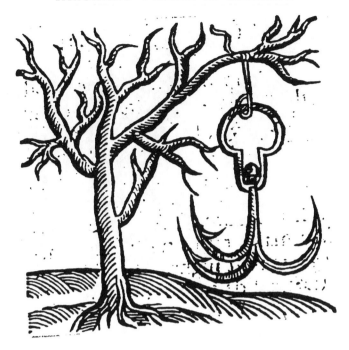

8. The Drag-hook to take the Fox. From *A Necessary Family-Book*. (Folger Shakespeare Library, Washington, D.C.)

scribed as an "engine" which could destroy many foxes (see figure 8). Polecats, buzzards, and kites might be trapped in deadfalls (see figure 9). *The Compleat English and French Vermin-killer* notes that traps for rats and mice are so well known that it need only describe one type.[40] To catch a fox, one manual recommended laying a false trail with a sheep's paunch after carefully rubbing one's shoes with it, so that the fox "may not scent your swetty Feet." After laying the trail, the human climbs a tree and waits for the fox with a gun.[41] Humans, in other words, needed to employ both specific technologies and their wits to catch vermin.

In fiction, vermin were sufficiently cunning to use tricks and traps themselves, as in the story of Reynard. A mouse battling a frog, for example, is described as follows: "The crafty Mouse, lurking under the Grass, sets upon the Frog by Ambuscado."[42] A rat bites an ox, but hides in a hole, and mocks the ox for failing to find him.[43] In the same collection, a weasel grown too old to hunt hides in a pile of meal, and devours every mouse who comes there to eat (see figure 10). The moral is: "Where virtue fails, make use of Policy."[44] A fox lures an ape who has been elected as king of the beasts,

9. The Dead-fall for Polecats. From *A Necessary Family-Book*. (Folger Shakespeare Library, Washington, D.C.)

telling him that there is buried treasure nearby, which (according to contemporaneous English law) belongs to the crown. The ape goes where directed, and falls into a trap set by the fox (see figure 11).[45] The trap in the illustration is one similar to those in vermin-killing guides (see figure 12). Many further stories could be told about the trickery and cunning of vermin, especially of foxes, but these examples have displayed the basic tropes, many of which date back to the Middle Ages and before.[46]

These stories are only the most obvious example of the ways in which trickery was utterly bound up with the category of vermin. Vermin-killing manuals also imply that tricking vermin was not so very different from tricking other human beings. While such a claim might seem far-fetched,

10. Of the Old Weasel, and the Mice. From W. D., *Aesop's Fables.*

11. The ape trapped by the fox. From W. D., *Aesop's Fables.*

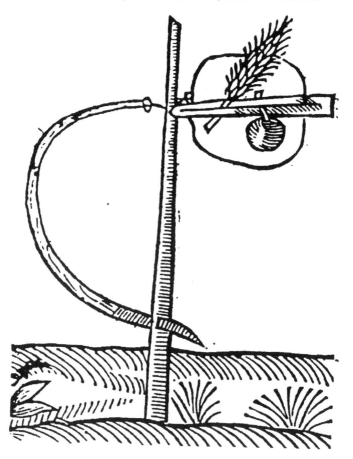

12. A bird trap. From *A Necessary Family-Book.* (Folger Shakespeare Library, Washington, D.C.)

A Necessary Family-Book, which opens with diagrams of vermin traps, concludes with a long section on magic tricks, entitled "Natural and Artificial Conclusions, both Pleasant and Profitable." This part of the book starts with a description of how to catch kites and ravens alive, typical of the preceding section on vermin-killing. However, the next trick is entitled, "To make a Cat Piss out a Fire." It starts with a "merry fellow" who came into an ale house in cold weather, and found a miserable fire. He proclaimed that he could make the hostess's cat piss out the flames, and "watching his opportunity" he did just that, thereby making his opinion of the inadequacy of the fire quite apparent.[47] Structurally, this trick resembles the joke about the man who faults his hostess's hospitality by threatening to swim through the pottage to get the chop. Other tricks follow, including such classics as figuring out what number a person is thinking of, or making a sixpence fall through a solid table, or conveying money secretly from one hand to the other. Other "natural and artificial conclusions" are of a practical nature: how to preserve cherries, pears, and nuts; how to know the hour of the day by hand and fingers (a sort of do-it-yourself sundial); how to know if the wine has been watered; how to keep fleas off dogs.

This hodgepodge array is not at all unusual; its origins lie in books of secrets.[48] The link between vermin-killing and books of secrets is quite direct in some manuals. *The Vermin-killer* (1680), from which the *Necessary Family-Book* draws much of its advice on vermin, includes citations for the methods recommended, although these are not included in the derivative text. Such citations make a virtual roster of the (often suppositious) authors of books of secrets. Medieval and early modern authors such as Cornelius Agrippa, Albertus Magnus, and Mizaldus rub shoulders with ancients such as Pliny.[49] The key that linked vermin-killing, magical tricks, and recipes for preserving pears was not domestic management. Rather, each represents a manipulation of the natural world through human cunning. Legerdemain involved fooling the audience; vermin-killing required fooling the animals; and preserving fruit involved fooling the natural process of decay. As a number of historians have pointed out, books of secrets were closely tied to the seventeenth-century passion for demonstrations of the wonders of the natural world fostered by virtuosi. "Science" and "secrets" were wholly intermingled.[50]

SYMBOLS AND LANGUAGES

There is another element to the relationship between vermin and trickery. Tricks are often linked, not only to the manipulation of the natural world, but also to language itself. Language enables both humans and vermin to play tricks on others. For example, one book describes a trick that involves putting a piece of string on the floor, and getting someone to bet that he will be able to jump over that piece of string. In the imagined alehouse of the text, there is always a taker. Then the trickster moves the piece of string to the corner where the wall meets the floor, and the bettor cannot jump through the wall over the piece of string, and so loses his money. It is both the linguistic ambiguity involved in "this piece of string" and the manipulation of the structures of the material world that make the joke work.[51]

In addition to facilitating trickery, language enables quick-witted humans and vermin to get themselves out of trouble. For example, in a joke set in Charles the Bald's French court, a short Scotsman behaves quite rudely. Two tall scholars have come to dine, and the king sets a dish with two large and one small fish between the Scotsman and the scholars. The Scotsman promptly serves the two scholars the small fish, and puts the two big ones on his own plate. When reprimanded by the king, the Scotsman points to himself, and says, "Here are two great and one small fish"; pointing across the table, he says, "And there are two great and one little."[52] Just as in the case of the man who starts unbuttoning his doublet to swim toward the chop, clever words may absolve one from the social sin of greed. However, language does not always suffice. In a fable, a young man steals a piece of meat from a cookshop and quietly hands it to his companion. When questioned by the cook, the first man insists that he does not have the meat, and the second that he has not stolen the meat. Each is truthful within the narrow meanings of his words. But the cook is not fooled. Although he cannot recover his property, he reminds the thieves that God knows what truly took place, implying a punishment far more consequential than any the cook might inflict.[53]

Vermin were also masters of language, able to talk their way out of trouble again and again. In a fable by the "Young Aesop," a crafty fox wants to trouble a young coney. He is unsuccessful, and so appeals to the lion, king of the beasts, for a warrant. The hapless coney is brought to court; both the lawyers, for the prosecution and the defense, are foxes. "And strait two Foxes plead the cause, and so he's judg'd to dye." The moral to this unhappy tale is spelled out: "Might generally overcomes Right."[54] Foxes' cunning made them perfect for the role of lawyers, whose task was to manipulate language. Another children's book included an old proverb that also underlined the ways in which foxes use language to trick, "When the Fox preaches, beware the Geese."[55] Even the story of Reynard hinges upon linguistic ability. It is only by telling the king a long and complicated story about treasure and betrayal that Reynard transforms himself from villain to hero, and escapes execution.

In Aesop's fables, foxes have linguistic abilities that dogs lack, even though dogs resemble foxes. In one tale, a sheepdog savages one of his master's sheep. The master threatens to kill him, but the dog tells him that it was a wolf who did the killing. But the farmer is not taken in by the dog's speech, and kills it forthwith.[56] In a fable which closely resembles the one about the two thieves in a cookshop, a dog steals a piece of meat from a butcher. However, the dog cannot use language to escape. On the contrary, the dog is caught because all the dogs bark uncontrollably as they quarrel about the distribution of the meat.[57] The "language" of dogs, barking, betrays them rather than enabling them to get away with the crime.

Vermin used language, a system of signs, to deceive and to trick. In many fables, vermin are also expert readers of signs, interpreting the material world in order to avoid being tricked themselves. In one such, the lion king is ill, and invites all of the animals to visit him, just as visiting the sick was a cardinal virtue in early modern England. The fox, however, refuses to go. When summoned specifically by the lion, the fox offers to pray for the lion's health, but will not visit. This refusal is explained as follows: "she was terrified with the footsteps: which indeed sith they were all towards the lions den, none returning back, it was a sign that many beasts had entred in, but that none had come forth."[58] Sherlock Holmes could not ask for better readings of footprints. Of all the animals, only this fox noticed and correctly interpreted these marks. In contrast, one of the animals most similar to the fox, the dog, lacks the ability to read symbols. A fable explains how a biting dog is outfitted with a bell by its master, to warn people of its whereabouts. The dog, however, cannot read the sign correctly, and assumes that the bell is given to him as "an ornament for his goodness," until another dog explains to him that the bell is actually a mark of disgrace.[59]

While vermin in fiction can use human language, those represented in vermin-killing manuals do not. However, there are hints that humans thought that the vermin whom they encountered in their daily lives were capable of interpreting symbols. One of the *Vermin-killer*'s recommendations for getting rid of rats and mice is violent and symbolic: "Take the Head of a Rat or Mouse, pull the Skin from of it, and cary the Head where the Mice and Rats come, and they will be immediately gone from thence, Running altogether as if they were bewitched, and come no more."[60] Here is the domestic version of the gamekeeper's gibbet. Mice and rats are presumed to be able to abstract from a skinned head to their own safety, or lack thereof. The display of the tiny head reminds one of contemporaneous human executions for treason, when Londoners routinely saw the heads of the executed stuck on pikes as dreadful warnings.[61]

A related method, used to rid one's house of flies, reveals the differing capacities of insect versus four-footed vermin to read symbols. Here, the reader is directed to make an image of a fly on a plate of copper, brass, or tin, and an image of Pisces on the obverse. As the plate is made, the reader is to chant "This is the image which doth clean rid all Flies forever." When completed, the image is to be buried in the center of the house.[62] This practice relies upon sympathetic magic. There is no suggestion that the flies will actually see their image in the plate. Rather, the charm spoken and the power of extranatural invocations of the zodiac will eliminate the flies without the flies understanding what has happened to them. Mice and rats flee "as if bewitched," but the flies leave because they are in fact bewitched, in some sense.

In another example, rats, mice, or moles respond to the cries of one of their own kind who has been immured in a clay pot stuck over the fire. The *Vermin-Killer* explains what happens next: "all the rats and Mice in the house, hearing the Cry of those in the Pot, will run immediately to the Place, where the Pot standeth on the Fire, as if they did intend by force to deliver the rats and Mice in the Pot." Once they are gathered together, the human can kill them all in one place.[63] Here, the humans use animals' identification with one of their own kind as a trick to kill them. The trick only works, however, if these animals understand the distress encoded in the animal's cry, and recognize what kind of animal is in distress. A mole's cries, for example, will only gather moles together, not rats and mice as well. A variation of this technique was recommended in a later vermin-killing manual: one should beat or cut a rat or a mouse, and then let him go. His cries will scare all the rest of his kind away.[64]

This last example suggests another aspect to vermin's ability to under-stand and manipulate symbols, or language. The ability to communicate enables these animals to act corporatively. Vermin can be described as as-sembling in human-like formations; as the *Vermin-Killer* says, "all the rats and Mice will make their Appearance, as if it were to be an Assembly of an Army."[65] Mice are described as "in Council" or a "Committee."[66] These animals adopt human social forms—the assembly of an army, the meeting of a committee. In contrast, a group of fleas drawn to a bowl of goat's blood is described in animal terms: "all the Flies [fleas] will come into it, like a swarm of bees."[67] In *The Fables of Young Aesop,* mice are portrayed as able to understand each other in "The Friendship of Mice." A mouse loses his footing and falls into a water barrel in a deserted house. He is saved from drowning by his fellow mice who make a long chain with their bodies, upon which he climbs out of danger (see figure 13).[68] In another fable, mice talk amongst themselves and succeed in evading a cat. Until the mice band together, the cat has caught many of them. Once together, however, they realize that if they stay up above floor level, the cat cannot reach them. (see figure 14). The cat tries a countermove, pretending to be dead, but the mouse cooperative is not fooled. One mouse playfully addresses the cat while warning the rest of the mice: "Ho Friend, if I knew for certain that thou wert the Cat, I would not come down."[69] Not only can mice employ human language, they can use it in sophisticated ways, teasing the cat while alerting their fellows.

I have suggested that various kinds of four-footed vermin were imagined to have linguistic powers of some kind. Whether discoursing of dinners or

13. The Friendship of Mice. From *The Fables of Young Aesop.*

14. Of the Mice and the Cat. From W. D., *Aesop's Fables.*

reading the sign of a skinned head, these animals could use and manipulate words and signs. Aside from the potential unease generated by animals who appeared to have human skills of language, this feature of vermin may have had another disquieting aspect. Humans themselves used a grid of language to array the natural world, and particularly the animals with whom they dealt regularly.[70] Here I focus on two such languages: those of hunting and carving. They are, of course, related—animals killed in a hunt would be served up as an ornament to a dinner. Participation in hunting was increasingly limited to the upper classes, but the cheap-print literature of the later seventeenth century offers its readers access to that gentlemanly world.

For example, *The School of Recreation,* published in 1696, discusses a full range of gentlemanly talents and skills. Hunting, riding, racing, hawking, tennis, bowling, fowling, and angling are all demystified, as are cockfighting and military maneuvers. The book opens with the topic of hunting, because, as the author explains, "it challenges the sublim Epithets of Royal, Artificial, Manly and Warlike, for its Stateliness, Cunning, and Indurance."[71] It is difficult to imagine how a book could successfully instruct one to stay on a horse, or follow a hound, and like others of its type, this text does not take up those challenges. Instead, the author declares, "I reckon it the most necessary part of the Hunter to understand the Names, Degrees, Ages and Seasons of the aforesaid different beasts of Forest or Venery, Chase, and Warren." What follows is an elaboration of the naming practices of hunting. For example, in its first year, a hart is called a hind-calf, then a knobber, a brock, a staggard, a stag and finally a hart, year by year. Such names were tricky; badgers were also commonly referred to as brocks. A buck followed a similar succession of names: a fawn, a pricket, a sorrel, a sore, a buck of the first head, and finally a great buck.[72] This emphasis upon naming is utterly typical of books on hunting.

And so it is with cookery. Once the hunted animal or bird was brought to the kitchen, it underwent another linguistic framing. As discussed above, carving was one of the actions which transformed nature (a dead animal) into culture (meat which becomes a means of enacting social difference). To this day, carving retains a certain mystique, as a kind of specialized social skill. However, we no longer use an elaborate vocabulary to distinguish each animal from another. Carving a turkey, a chicken, a capon, or even a goose, follows the same general pattern. Once you know how to do one, usually you can carve all the rest.

In the seventeenth century, however, cheap print makes each individual animal separate and distinct, and offers both a specialized language and a set of techniques to demarcate one type of animal from the next. As discussed above, the playing cards called *The Genteel House-keepers Pastime* provided animal-by-animal diagrams of carving as well as the terms used to distinguish them. Here, a capon, turkey, hen, and pullet are all different, linguistically and practically. In many books which lack illustrations, it is only the language of carving which provides this level of distinction. Hannah Woolley and a host of other cookery writers enjoined their readers to say, "allay a pheasant," "break a deer," "mince that plover," "rear that goose," "sauce a capon," "spaul that hen," etc..[73] Not all forms of meat which needed to be carved had their own specific terms. The hierarchy of meats, and of the animals from whence they came, was articulated through these words. In the set of playing cards, mackerel, carp, turbot, and sole lack specific words to describe their carving, although other fishes had them. The only item of pastry which takes a specific term is the venison pasty, that most aristocratic of meats. Almost all of the face cards (i.e., king, queen, knave) depict meats that take a specific carving word, while those which do not have such terms are usually found amongst the twos, threes, and fours of the suits.

In books of hunting and cookery, using the correct name for an animal or meat was crucial to social success, and cheap-print books were careful to explain these specialized languages to their readers. We cannot know if readers of these texts enjoyed a kind of imagined emulation of their betters, or actually put these instructions into practice, but in either case, using the right word was essential. On a humbler level, rural people employed extensive naming practices. Keith Thomas reminds us that each type of bird had its own human-like name, such as Jenny Wren, Robin Redbreast, or Will Wagtail.[74] Thus language itself serves to order the motley world of animals. Vermin, who appear to have access to the tools which make that order, seem potentially disruptive of the categories made by humans to contain animals.

SOME CONCLUDING THOUGHTS

I have argued that four-footed vermin were imagined in early modern England according to three characteristics: they ate human food; they were cunning; and they understood symbols. Each of these three, of course, was also characteristic of humans. The very same books which advise one on tricking vermin with traps instruct one on how to avoid being tricked into buying unsatisfactory meat by a poulterer. A full analysis of the relationships among cheap-print and other types of sources, such as diaries, city ordinances, and the like, will require a much larger study. Here I can only draw some preliminary conclusions about cheap-print and its constructions of relationships between humans and animals. First, various types of cheap-print sources used here each have their own generic peculiarities. Playing cards, for instance, adopt different rhetorical forms than do chapbooks, although playing cards depicting Aesop's fables mix those categories. Each genre has its own trajectory, which needs further explication. However, many of these genres share certain features, perhaps because of the large quantities in which they were produced. The publishers of these works needed to make them appealing and accessible to those readers who lacked the rhetorical and linguistic skills required by more elaborate works.

In particular, I have focused on the ways in which many of these texts are made up of small stories, tiny units whose themes might cohere, but which do not make up a hierarchically structured text. Readers of the cheap editions of Aesop, or of vermin books, or texts on legerdemain, or joke books, could open the book at any point and jump in, without having to start at the beginning and work their way through.[75] The advice-oriented books, from *The Art of Courtship* to the works of Hannah Woolley, function similarly. A reader might dip into a section on carving, or on interpreting the significance of moles on the face, without having to read any other part of the book. Illustrations in these works function in a related manner: they provide a summing up of a particular story. Look again, for example, at figure 6. Not only do we see how to make a trap that will catch a fox—we see the outcome of this particular narrative, namely, the successful capture of the fox. The brevity of the written narrative is caught in an iconographic freeze-frame, reminiscent of a range of other contemporaneous images.[76]

There is another crucial feature to these texts, aside from their nonhierarchical aspect. All of the texts are highly didactic in nature. While we do not usually think of joke books as producing moral messages, these books can be read as a long series of tiny playlets, each producing laughter and an example of a social interaction, be it one to copy or one to avoid. Similarly, the sections of cheap-print books on legerdemain enact tiny dramas about how to be the center of attention in the alehouse, or how to impress people with what appear to be highly developed mathematical skills. However, these small narratives cannot be read in a wholly unitary way. Although I have drawn out certain themes, some of these are produced by means of their contestation rather than their straightforward articulation. For example, the joke about the two scholars and the two tiny fish works in multiple ways: it shows an example of discourtesy that one should not emulate, it points towards a general principle about meat at meals, it hints that the French do not know how to set a good table, it suggests that the Scots are a canny race, and it implies that a quick wit may absolve one of rudeness. At the same time, it makes fun of the social precepts which govern the gratification of a very basic desire, that of hunger.

While I have tried to suggest that the modernizing narratives which structure most of the historical discussions of animals do not account for vermin particularly well, there is one striking discontinuity between the early modern and modern periods. Early modern cheap print of the type I analyze here does not link vermin with dirt or disgust. Dirt, in Mary Douglas's famous definition, is matter out of place. It is easy to see how small creeping animals—matter which moves into the wrong places on its own four feet—might be dirty.[77] Perhaps it is only in the nineteenth century that English vermin acquire (or reacquire?) these connotations of dirt and disgust. Christopher Herbert has analyzed Henry Mayhew's use of the figure of the rat in Mayhew's best-selling *London Labour and the London Poor* of 1861–62, showing how rats symbolize filth and dirt. Mayhew's rats, like the early modern vermin discussed above, are preternaturally smart, and seem to be able to communicate with each other in frightening ways. However, Mayhew's rats have an "evil glamour" according to Herbert, and function in the text as taboo objects, powerfully attractive and repulsive simultaneously. As such, they are emblems of filth, of out-of-control working-class sexuality, of vice and disease. Mayhew writes about a celebrated rat catcher as if he were possessed of the occult powers inherent in the dangerous taboo animal whom he alone can control. With a frisson of horror, Mayhew tells us that this rat catcher, unbeknownst to his wife, has eaten cooked rats with pleasure—he claims that they were moist as rabbits.[78] The way in which Mayhew employs this detail to produce horror brings us back to a characteristic aspect of vermin recognizable in early modern texts, namely that they are not eaten. However, the early modern texts I have analyzed here do not produce horror or disgust; they simply ignore vermin as a category of meat. Nor are vermin characterized by links to filth, to sexuality, to the potentially polluting aspects of the working classes. Any such argument from silence remains open to potential revision, but the texts I examine here simply do not treat vermin as disgusting or dirty.

In part, such a lack may be related to the material specificities of early modern English life. Perhaps disgust is something of a luxury, only possible when adequate means are available to barricade oneself from the source of potential contamination.[79] A parallel case might be found in Naomi Rogers's analysis of the American transformation of the household fly from innocent, even amusing, domestic animal to disgusting germ-laden menace in the later nineteenth century.[80] While Rogers rightly points to the role of germ theory in reconstructing the meanings of the fly, it is also the case that the transformation took place at a moment when middle-class Americans were pursuing what Nancy Tomes has called "the private side of public health."[81] Men and women made use of a wide range of commercial products to fortify their homes against dirt and disease, a project easily adapted to germ theory when it became widely known.

Rather than dirt and disgust, early modern representations emphasize those aspects of vermin which are the most threatening to the human social fabric. Vermin's consumption of human food threatens social integrity in two ways. First, their greed implies that there might not be enough food for all, and that social mechanisms, such as the Assize of Bread (the fixing of bread prices), might not be sufficient to remedy the split between those who have enough to eat, and those who do not. Second, vermin's taste for fancy human food, gobbled without human manners, hints that the social bonds established around a dinner table by means of manners may not be sufficient to restrain appetites so that there will be food for all. Even at an ample table, humans do not consume equal portions. Instead, food is used to display social hierarchy. However, that very hierarchy is supposed to guarantee that no one at the table goes hungry. Noble banquets routinely served much more food than could be consumed, and gave the leftovers to the poor. However, this style of household and banqueting had fallen into decline in the later seventeenth century.[82]

Similarly, vermin's reliance on cunning and trickery questions the functioning of human society. The obverse of trickery is trust. Are people what they represent themselves to be? Joke books are full of deceptions, as are books on legerdemain. While cheap-print books were providing detailed instructions on cosmetics and beauty, moralists were inveighing against the seemingly new custom of giving servants the cast-off clothes of their masters. They worried that a person's clothing no longer located him or her correctly in a hierarchy. Similarly, writers argued for better regulation of charity, arguing that benevolent people were imposed upon by rogues who misrepresented their worthiness for aid. It was by means of linguistic skills— the skill of their narratives—that the beggars were able to gain money not rightfully theirs. The issue was not only that such money went to the wrong people, but that the reciprocal relations of obligation and deference which were supposed to govern the interactions of rich and poor were thereby harmed.

These suggestions are of a sort that cannot be concretely linked to vermin-killing manuals. However, as suggested above, animals are always composed of projections, fantasies, identifications—and of real material beings with their own ideas and practices. By highlighting some aspects of vermin that troubled early modern people, we begin to see what kinds of changes require historical explanation. Both "fact" and "fiction" written about vermin can help us to analyze how the realms of imagination have their own histories, enacted in material worlds as well as in fantasies.

NOTES

This paper was written while I was a fellow at the Shelby Cullom Davis Center for Historical Studies at Princeton University; I am grateful to the center for generous financial support, and to its director William Chester Jordan and my fellow fellows for intellectual comradeship. My thanks to those who read and commented on earlier versions of the paper: Kathleen Crowther-Heyck, Laura Gowing, Mary Henninger-Voss, Maryanne Kowalewski, Pamela Long, Gregg Mitman, John Murrin, and James Serpell; and to Tamara Griggs for superb research assistance.

1. Steve Baker, *Picturing the Beast. Animals, Identity, and Representation* (Manchester: Manchester University Press, 1993); Tim Ingold, ed., *What Is an Animal?* (London: Unwin Hyman, 1988); R. G. Willis, ed., *Signifying Animals: Human Meaning in the Natural World* (London: Unwin Hyman, 1990).

2. Mary Douglas, *Purity and Danger: An Analysis of Concepts of Pollution and Taboo* (New York: Frederick A. Prager, 1966), see esp. pp. 41–57, 159–79. See also Susan Leigh Star and James Griesemer, "Institutional Ecology, 'Translations,' and Boundary Objects: Amateurs and Professionals in Berkeley's Museum of Vertebrate Zoology, 1907–1939," *Social Studies of Science* 19 (1989): 387–420, which focuses upon animals, geographic regions, etc., which functioned as objects that could be used or exploited by more than one professional group.

3. Robert Darnton, "Workers Revolt: The Great Cat Massacre of the Rue Saint-Séverin," in *The Great Cat Massacre and Other Episodes in French Cultural History* (1984; New York: Vintage Books, 1985), pp. 75–104. My fascination with the tensions between an account such as Darnton's and a poststructuralist analysis focusing on the ways in which texts produce meaning is, in part, shaped by Roger Chartier, "Texts, Symbols, and Frenchness," *Journal of Modern History* 57 (1985): 682–95, and Darnton's reply, "The Symbolic Element in History," ibid., 58 (1986): 218–34, as well as Dominick LaCapra, "Chartier, Darnton, and the Great Symbol Massacre," and James Fernandez, "Historians Tell Tales: Of Cartesian Cats and Gallic Cockfights," ibid., 60 (1988): 95–112, 113–27. See also Harold Mah, "Suppressing the Text: The Metaphysics of Ethnographic History in Darnton's Great Cat Massacre," *History Workshop Journal* 31 (1991): 1–20.

4. Harriet Ritvo, *The Animal Estate. The English and Other Creatures in the Victorian Age* (Cambridge, Mass.: Harvard University Press, 1987); John Berger, "Why Look at Animals?" in *About Looking* (New York: Pantheon

Books, 1980), pp.1–26; Keith Thomas, *Man and the Natural World: Changing Attitudes in England 1500–1800* (London: Penguin Books, 1984).

5. For a transcript of the Elizabethan statute, see "Destruction of Birds and Vermin," *The East Anglian* 3 (1869): 275–79. Animals mentioned by name in the act include magpies, rooks, crows, choughs, pine martens, "fursketts" (furze-cats, or hares), "mouldkites" (I assume a type of predatory bird), buzzards, "shags" (crested cormorants), ringtails, osprey, "woodwalls" (green woodpeckers), jays, kites, kingfishers, bullfinches, "grays" (badgers), "fitchetts" (a kind of polecat), polecats, weasels, stoats, "fayrbodes" (probably a type of wild cat), wildcats, otters, hedgehogs, rats, mice, and moles. The act protects herons, shovelers, and swans. In the eighteenth and nineteenth centuries, parishes paid bounties for thousands of sparrows and sparrow eggs. See also T. N. Brushfield, "On the Destruction of Vermin in Rural Parishes," *Report & Transactions of the Devonshire Association for the Advancement of Science, Literature and Art* 29 (1887); J. S. Elliott, *Bedfordshire Vermin Payments* (Luton: The City Museum, 1936); J. W. Millard, "Destruction of Parish Vermin in the Sixteenth Century at Bedingfield," *The East Anglian,* n.s. 2 (1887–88): 328–29; P. J. Dillon and E. L. Jones, "Trevor Falla's Vermin Transcripts for Devon," *The Devon Historian* 33 (October 1986): 15–19 (many thanks to Maryanne Kowalewski for this last reference). I have not yet been able to consult Charles Oldham, "Payments for 'Vermin' by Some Hertfordshire Churchwardens," *Transactions of the Hertfordshire Natural History Society and Field Club* 19: 79ff.

The phrase "four-footed beasts" is very roughly equivalent to our category "mammals"; it is used repeatedly in pre-Linnean discussions, as in Edward Topsell's *Historie of Foure-Footed Beasts* (1607).

6. E. L. Jones argues that the period of the Restoration saw an increase in campaigns against raptors and corvids (kites, buzzards, ravens, and the like, who preyed on small poultry or infant lambs or dead sheep) and bullfinches and jays who harmed fruit trees. E. L. Jones, "The Bird Pests of British Agriculture in Recent Centuries," *Agricultural History Review* 20 (1972): 107–25; see esp. pp. 110–14. However, he bases his arguments largely upon the essays by N. F. Ticehurst, "On the Former Abundance of Kites, Buzzard, and Raven in Kent," *British Birds* 14 (1920): 34–37; and "Rewards for Vermin Killing Paid by the Churchwardens of Tenterden, 1626 to 1712," *Hastings and East Sussex Naturalist* 5 (1935): 69–82. Much further work is needed on such accounts before generalizations can be made about the changing status of particular species.

7. On cheap print, see Margaret Spufford, *Small Books and Pleasant Histories: Popular Fiction and Its Readership in Seventeenth-Century England* (Cambridge: Cambridge University Press, 1981); Tessa Watt, *Cheap Print and*

Popular Piety (Cambridge: Cambridge University Press, 1991). For a brief introduction to the growing literature on reading and readership, see Andrew Bennett, *Readers and Reading* (London: Longman, 1995).

8. The cost of books is determined in one of three ways: some books include the price, printed on the title page. Other prices are listed in publishers' advertisements. Finally, some prices can be obtained from Robert Clavel, *A Catalogue of All the Books printed in England since the dreadful fire of London in 1666 to the end of Michaelmas term, 1672* (London: printed by R. Simmons for Robert Clavel, in Cross-key Court in Little-britain, 1673; facsimile ed., Farnborough, Hants.: Gregg Press, 1965. Unfortunately Clavel's later catalogues lack prices.

9. Didactic books have not usually been analyzed as a category in and of themselves. Rather, historians have focused on specific topics, such as medicine or conduct. For a discussion of late medieval and early modern how-to books that moves beyond specific categories, see Richard Hoffman, *Fishers' Craft and Lettered Art* (Toronto: University of Toronto Press, 1997), especially the last two chapters.

10. J. S., *The Experienc'd Fowler: Or, the Gentleman, Citizen, and Country-Man's Pleasant and Profitable Recreation* (London: Printed for Jo. Sprint, at the Blue Bell, and G. Conyers, at the Ring in Little Britain, 1697), p. 146. An edition of this work was advertised by Conyers for sixpence. in the early 1720s; see *The Compleat English and French Vermin-Killer,* (London: Printed for G. Conyers, at the Ring in Little Brittain, [1721?], price one shilling), p. 67, for the advertisement.

11. *A Necessary Family-Book, Both for the City & Country, In Two Parts* (London: printed for John Harris, at the Harrow against the Church in the Poultry, 1688). Price sixpence.

12. "Aesop's fables" is not a stable entity—many different fables have been included in various collections linked with the name Aesop. In England, Aesop became a standard schoolbook; a contract survives from 1631 for producing twelve thousand copies of a schoolbook Aesop over the course of three years. See David G. Hale, "Aesop in Renaissance England," *The Library,* 5th ser., 27 (1972): 116–25; more generally see Ben E. Perry, *Studies in the Text History of the Life and Fables of Aesop,* Philological Monographs, no. 7 (Haverford, Pa.: American Philological Association, 1936). By the later seventeenth century, a number of different versions were in print, ranging from the "W. D." version—which cost between one shlling in the *Compleat English and French Vermin-Killer* advertisement, and two shillings in Clavel, *Catalogue*; Clavel lists schoolbook editions of Aesop from one to two shillings, p. 103—to the more expensive engraved Barlow and Ogilby versions (Clavel lists Barlow at eight shillings in 1672, p. 30).

Aesop's fables were also used in copybooks such as John Bickham, *Fables and other Short Poems; Collected from the most celebrated English Authors. The Whole curiously Engrav'd, for the practice & Amusement of Young Gentlemen & Ladies, in the Art of Writing,* (London: Printed and sold by Thos. Cobb [who Married ye Widow of Mr. John Cluer] at ye Printing Office in Bow Church Yard, London, where may be had Copy-Books of Round-Hand, with Copys at ye Top to write after, [1731]). George Bickham, this work's engraver, produced a number of other copy books as well as manuals on drawing. This book is thirty-two pages long; I have not yet been able to determine its cost. See Sir Ambrose Heal, *The English Writing Masters and Their Copy-Books, 1570–1800: A Biographical Dictionary and Bibliography* (Cambridge: Cambridge University Press, 1931).

Finally, a series of broadsides used Aesop as a means to political critique; see Annabel Patterson, *Fables of Power: Aesopian Writing and Political History* (Durham, N.C.: Duke University Press, 1991) for a discussion of the political meanings ascribed to the fables and to the life of Aesop himself, often included with the fables. See also Jane E. Lewis, *The English Fable: Aesop and Literary Culture, 1651–1740* (Cambridge: Cambridge University Press, 1996).

On a more general level, J. Paul Hunter has argued that the structures and readership of didactic works were crucial to the development of that preeminent form of fiction, the novel. J. Paul Hunter, *Before Novels: The Cultural Contexts of Eighteenth-Century English Fiction* (New York: Norton, 1990).

13. *Necessary Family-Book,* p. 7. Vermin have been associated with food in a variety of ways in the past. See, for instance, Marie-Christine Pouchelle, *The Body and Surgery in the Middle Ages,* trans. Rosemary Morris (London: Polity Press, 1990), pp. 170–73, for a discussion of vermin (worms and other creeping things) as consumers of the human body. Thanks to Sue Lederer for this reference.

14. For comparison, it was estimated that in 1726, 100,000 beeves, 100,000 calves, and 600,000 sheep were slaughtered for human consumption in London. Thomas, *Man and the Natural World,* p. 26.

15. *Necessary Family-Book,* pp. 7, 41, 44, 45.

16. C. Anne Wilson, *Food and Drink in Britain* (London: Constable, 1973), pp. 108–10.

17. *Aesop Naturaliz'd and Expos'd to the Publick View* (Cambridge: Printed by John Hayes, for Edward Hall Bookseller there, 1697), p. 46.

18. John Walter and Keith Wrightson, "Dearth and the Social Order in Early Modern England," *Past and Present,* no. 71 (1976): 22–42; Andrew Appleby, *Famine in Tudor and Stuart England* (Stanford, Calif.: Stanford

University Press, 1978); idem, "Grain Prices and Subsistence Crises in England and France, 1590–1740," *Journal of Economic History* 39 (1979): 865–87. Work on food riots in the eighteenth century suggests that absence of famine by no means implied a lack of anxiety about food and starvation. John Bohstedt, *Riots and Community Politics in England and Wales, 1790–1810* (Cambridge, Mass.: Harvard University Press, 1983); E. P. Thompson, "The Moral Economy of the English Crowd in the Eighteenth Century," *Past and Present,* no. 50 (1971): 76–136.

19. *Necessary Family-Book,* pp. 17, 38. W. W. [probably William Wadham], *The Vermin-Killer, being a very necessary family book, containing Exact Rules and Directions for the Artificiall killing and destroying of all manner of Vermin, &c.* (London: Printed for Samuel Lee at the Feathers near the Post-Office in Lombard-Street, 1680), p. 10. The former is based upon the latter, but there are items in each which are not duplicated in the other. By the 1750s, another version of this text no longer describes vermin as eating greedily. See *The Vermin-killer: Being a Compleat and Necessary Family-Book* (London: Printed and sold by W. Owen, at Homer's Head, near Temple Bar, [1755?], price sixpence).

20. James Serpell, *In the Company of Animals* (Cambridge: Cambridge University Press, 1985), p. 198.

21. H. C., *England's Jests Refin'd and Improv'd, being a Choice Collection of the Merriest Jests, Smartest Repartees, Wittiest Sayings, and most notable Bulls, yet extant* (London: Printed for John Harris at the Harrow in the Poultry, 1693, price one shilling), p. 40. For an introduction to the history of jokes, see Jan Bremmer and Herman Roodenburg, eds., *A Cultural History of Humour* (Oxford: Polity Press, 1997).

22. *England's Jests,* p. 46.

23. Ibid., p. 10.

24. Norbert Elias, *The Civilizing Process,* vol. 1: *The History of Manners* (1939; reprint ed., Oxford: Basil Blackwell, 1982); Stephen Mennell, *All Manner of Food* (Oxford: Basil Blackwell, 1985). For a different analysis of the ritual aspects of a meal, see Mary Douglas, "Deciphering a Meal," *Daedalus* 101 (1972): 61–81, and on meat in particular, see Nick Fiddes, *Meat: A Natural Symbol* (London: Routledge, 1991).

25. Francis Hawkins, *Youth's Behaviour, or Decencie in Conversation Amongst Men,* 7th ed. (London: Printed for W. Lee, and are to be sold at the Turks-head, in Fleet-street near Ram-Alley, 1661).

26. Ibid., p. 31.

27. Ibid., pp. 32–33.

28. Ibid., p. 34.

29. Hannah Woolley, *The Queen-like Closet: or Rich Cabinet, Stored with all manner of Rare Receipts for Preserving, Candying, and Cookery. Very Pleasant and*

Beneficial to all Ingenious Persons of the Female Sex, 5th ed. (London: Printed for R. Chiswel at the Rose and Crown in St. Paul's Church yard, and T. Sawbridge at the Three Flower-de-Luces in Little-Britain, 1684), p. 258.

30. *The Genteel house-keepers pastime, or, The mode of carving at the table represented in a pack of playing cards by which together with the instructions in this book any ordinary capacity may easily learn how to cut up or carve in mode all the most usual dishes of flesh, fish, fowl, and baked meats . . . set forth by the best masters in the faculty of carving and published for publick use* (London: Printed for J. Moxon, 1693). Notice how carving is elevated by the claim that the work is based on the "best masters in the faculty," as if carving were analogous to law or medicine. A number of sets of educational playing cards were manufactured in late seventeenth-century England, and this deck appears to have been aimed at the cheaper end of the market. Other decks were also available in colored or colored-and-gilt versions for three or five shillings, but the *Pastime* was not advertised in such different versions, although it was reprinted in 1693 and 1717.

31. *The Art of courtship, or, The School of delight containing amorous dialogues, complemental expressions, poems, letters and discourses upon sundry occasions relating to love and business . . . and rules for carving flesh, fish, fowl . . .* (London: Printed by I. M. for I. Back, 1686).

32. Ibid., f. B1v.

33. Conies are rabbits; well into the eighteenth century, "rabbit" meant an infant rabbit. They were commonly bred and raised for eating.

34. Douglas, *Purity and Danger,* for example. For a discussion of a number of such food avoidances over a wide geographical range, see Frederick J. Simoons, *Eat Not This Flesh: Food Avoidances from Prehistory to the Present,* 2d rev. ed. (Madison: University of Wisconsin Press, 1994). A recent study is suggestive of more historicized ways to understand animals who are not eaten in particular cultures: Claudine Fabre-Vassas, *The Singular Beast: Jews, Christians, and the Pig,* trans. Carol Volk (New York: Columbia University Press, 1997).

35. *A Rich Treasure, the Knowledge whereof is Useful, Profitable, Pleasant and Delightful* (London: Printed for Geo. Conyers, at the Ring in Little Britain, price one shilling), pp. 108–9. A manuscript date of publication (1698) has been added to the Huntington's copy of the work. I suspect that the section on diet derives from the works of Thomas Tryon, also published by Conyers. On Tryon, and the links between vegetarianism and specific religious groups, see Thomas, *Man and the Natural World,* pp. 289–97.

36. *A Rich Treasure,* p. 114.

37. See Thomas, *Man and the Natural World,* pp. 17–41, 51–64.

38. *The most pleasant history of Reynard the fox,* Entered according to order (London: Printed for J. Conyers, and are to be sold by J. Blare at the Looking-glass on London-Bridge, [1700?]). According to Wing, this twenty-three-page version is a free adaptation and translation of: "Le roman de Renart," in prose, attributed to John Shirley (fl. 1680–1702), who published a version in heroic verse in 1681 with a slightly different title.

39. Serpell, *In the Company of Animals,* p. 200. Such displays of animals are perhaps also linked to the medieval and early modern trials of animals accused of crimes. See E. P. Evans, *The Criminal Prosecution and Capital Punishment of Animals* (1906; reprint ed., Union, N.J.: Lawbook Exchange, 1998); Esther Cohen, "Law, Folklore and Animal Lore," *Past and Present,* no. 110 (1986): 6–37. Thanks to Sue Woodson for this last reference.

40. *Compleat English and French Vermin-killer,* p. 1. This incorporates some of the earlier vermin-killing manuals I discuss, but adds a considerable proportion of new material. The diary of an early eighteenth-century gentry farmer refers to at least four types of mouse or rat trap, and he consults with neighbors and the blacksmith about new designs for traps. He is even solicited by a woman selling a new type of trap, which he rejects as a fraud. Nicholas Blundell, *The Great Diurnall of Nicholas Blundell,* ed. J. J. Bagley, *The Record Society of Lancaster and Cheshire* 110 (1968), 112 (1970), 114 (1972), 112: 29, 38, 46, 222, 274, 277; 114: 8, 89, 225, 235.

41. *Compleat English and French Vermin-killer,* p. 60.

42. W. D., *Aesop's Fables with their Morals in Prose and Verse,* 12th ed. (London: Printed for Frances Egglesfield, and are to be sold by Randal Taylor at Stationers Hall, 1691), p. 4. Ultimately, both are eaten by a kite. This is one of the fables rewritten specifically in language meant to evoke the English Civil War; its moral is, "In like manner it happneth to factious Citizens, who being inflamed with a desire of rule, whilst they contend among themselves to be made Magistrates, do put their Estates, and also their Lives very often in danger."

43. Ibid., p. 160.

44. Ibid., p. 102.

45. Ibid., p. 231.

46. Joyce E. Salisbury, *The Beast Within: Animals in the Middle Ages* (London: Routledge, 1994), see esp. pp. 122–24 on the medieval Reynard the Fox.

47. *Necessary Family-Book,* p. 61.

48. William Eamon, *Science and the Secrets of Nature* (Princeton, N.J.: Princeton University Press, 1994), is the most recent comprehensive treatment of such works.

49. Most of the tricks in the *Necessary Family-Book* are taken from John White's book of secrets, *A Rich Cabinet, with variety of inventions* ([London:] printed for William Gilbertson at the signe of the Bible without Newgate in Giltspur-street, 1651). This is the first edition; a number of expanded editions were published in the latter half of the seventeenth century and on into the eighteenth century. See Eamon, *Science and the Secrets of Nature,* pp. 307–8.

50. The term "science" is anachronistic here. On these links, see Eamon, *Secrets of Nature*; Pamela O. Long, "Power, Patronage, and the Authorship of 'Ars': From Mechanical Know-How to Mechanical Knowledge in the Last Scribal Age," *Isis* 88 (1997): 1–41.

51. The same joke appears in *A Rich Treasure,* p. 51, except that a long tobacco pipe is used instead of a piece of string.

52. *England's Jests,* pp. 14–15.

53. W. D., *Aesop's Fables,* p. 72.

54. B. H., *The Fables of Young Aesop, with their Morals,* 2d ed. (London: Printed and sold by Benj. Harris, at the coruer [*sic*] of Grace-Church-Street, next Cornhill, 1698), p. 66. It is assumed that "B. H." was Benjamin Harris, a vehement Baptist and small publisher. My thanks to Andrea Immel, curator of the Cotsen Collection of Children's Books, for calling my attention to this work.

55. T. H., *A Guide for the Child and Youth* (London: Printed by J. Roberts, for the Company of Stationers, 1732), f. 9r.

56. *Aesop Explain'd,* p. 41.

57. *Young Aesop,* p. 74.

58. W. D., *Aesop's Fables,* p. 67.

59. Ibid., p. 135. So too, a dog drowning in a well misreads a farmer's gestures. The farmer wants to rescue the dog, but the dog thinks that the man will push him in further, so the dog bites the man. The man then abandons the dog to drowning. Ibid., p. 279.

60. *Vermin-killer* (1680), pp. 4–5.

61. There is some evidence that similar practices were employed to ensure that parishes did not pay bounties for the same animals twice; bounty heads were sometimes displayed publicly in the churchyard. For evidence of this practice, see Elliott, *Bedfordshire Vermin Payments,* p. 10; the law stipulated that the heads be "burned consumed or cut in sunder." Moles, too, responded to symbolic acts of destruction. One book recommended putting a dead mole "into a common Haunt" and all the other moles will "absolutely forsake it." *Compleat English and French Vermin-killer,* p. 10.

62. *A thousand more notable things: or, modern curiosities. Viz. Divers physical receipts. Monthly observations in gardening, . . . To prevent diseases in children. Directions for all midwives, . . . By G. Johnson,* Part II (London: Sold [by

George Conyers] at the Ring in Little-Britain, [1706?]), p.11. The only extant copy of this work that I have found is British Library, 1480.a.10.

63. *Vermin-killer* (1680), pp. 6–7, 8–9.

64. *Compleat English and French Vermin-killer,* p. 4. This same entry continues, "Some takes them and fleas the Skin off their Heads, and that does the same," linking these two methods of symbolic action.

65. *Vermin-killer* (1680), p. 6.

66. W. D., *Aesop's Fables,* p. 288.

67. *Vermin-killer* (1680), p. 28.

68. *Young Aesop,* p. 54.

69. W. D., *Aesop's Fables,* p. 230.

70. Edmund Leach, "Anthropological Aspects of Language: Animal Categories and Verbal Abuse," in *New Directions in the Study of Language,* ed. E. M. Leeneberg (Cambridge, Mass.: MIT Press, 1964).

71. R. H. [Robert Howlett], *The School of Recreation: or a Guide to the Most Ingenious Exercises of Hunting. Riding. Racing. Fireworks. Military Discipline. The Science of Defence* . . . (London: printed for H. Rhodes, at the Star, the Corner of Bride-Lane, Fleet-street, 1696), p.1.

72. Ibid., p. 2.

73. [Hannah Woolley], *The Accomplish'd Ladies Delight in preserving, Physick, Beautifying, and Cookery,* 5th ed. (London: Printed for Benjamin Harris, at the Stationers Arms and Anchor, in the Piazza, at the Royal-Exchange in Cornhil, 1685).

74. Thomas, *Man and the Natural World,* p. 82.

75. On the nonlinear quality of much early modern prose, see Michel de Certeau, *The Practice of Everyday Life,* trans. Steven F. Rendall (Berkeley: University of California Press, 1984), pp. 165–76; Lisa Jardine and Anthony Grafton, "'Studied for Action': How Gabriel Harvey Read his Livy," *Past and Present,* no. 129 (1990): 30–78; and Carlo Ginzburg, *The Cheese and the Worms: The Cosmos of a Sixteenth-Century Miller,* trans. John Tedeschi and Anne Tedeschi (Baltimore: Johns Hopkins University Press, 1980).

76. The most obvious example is the emblem book, usually aimed at a smaller, wealthier, and better-educated market than the works I study here.

77. See the texts from Leviticus above, in which such animals are specifically labeled "unclean."

78. Christopher Herbert, "Rat Worship and Taboo in Mayhew's London," *Representations* 23 (1988): 1–24.

79. For a wide-ranging discussion, see William Ian Miller, *The Anatomy of Disgust* (Cambridge, Mass.: Harvard University Press, 1997).

80. Naomi Rogers, "Germs with Legs: Flies, Disease, and the New Public Health," *Bulletin of the History of Medicine* 63 (1989): 599–617. Mayhew

specifically notes that "These winged tormentors are not, like most of our apterous enemies, calculated to excite disgust and nausea when we see or speak of them." Henry Mayhew, *London Labour and the London Poor: A Cyclopaedia of the Condition and Earnings of Those That Will Work, Those That Cannot Work, and Those That Will Not Work,* vol. 3 (London : Griffin, Bohn, and Company, 1861–62), p. 24.

81. Nancy J. Tomes, "The Private Side of Public Health," *Bulletin of the History of Medicine* 64 (1990): 509–39.

82. Felicity Heal, *Hospitality in Early Modern England* (Oxford: Clarendon Press, 1990).

5

"THINGS FEARFUL TO NAME"
BESTIALITY IN EARLY AMERICA

JOHN M. MURRIN

In the Old Testament, the Lord has no tolerance for either sodomy or bestiality.[1] He destroyed Sodom and Gomorrah with fire and brimstone and later empowered the people of Israel to slaughter the Benjaminites because of the sodomitical activities of the people of Gibeah. His command was unequivocal:[2] "If a man also lie with mankind as he lieth with a woman, both of them have committed an abomination: they shall surely be put to death. . . . And if a man lie with a beast, he shall surely be put to death; and ye shall slay the beast. And if a woman approach unto any beast, and lie down thereto, thou shalt kill the woman and the beast; they shall surely be put to death; their blood shall be upon them" (Lev. 20:13, 15–16). In the New Testament, Paul shared the same revulsion: "For this cause God gave them up unto vile affections: for even their women did change the natural use into that which is against nature: And likewise also the men, leaving the natural use of the women, burned in their lust one toward another, men with men working that which is unseemly. . . . " (Rom. 1:26–27). By the early modern era, virtually all Christian theologians shared Paul's condemnation of "unnatural" sexual acts, a category that became so widely used that it is still deeply embedded in the criminal codes of American state governments. And yet, despite these shared beliefs, Christian societies differed dramatically in the kinds of unnatural sexual acts that they chose to prosecute.

CONFLICTING EUROPEAN PRECEDENTS

To take two extremes from Protestant Europe, Sweden executed six or seven hundred people, mostly adolescent boys and young men, for bestiality, but hardly anyone for sodomy.[3] The Netherlands reversed these priorities. The

Dutch republic probably had only about ten bestiality prosecutions between 1630 and 1805, but when a partial collapse of the dikes coincided with the discovery of an extensive homosexual network in Amsterdam, Utrecht, and other cities, the Dutch put the two phenomena together in 1730 and 1731 and tried about 250 boys and young men for sodomy. Nearly all were convicted, of whom about two dozen were executed. They were strangled, then burnt at the stake, and then heavy weights were attached to the remains, which were "drowned" in the sea.[4]

English practice stood between Sweden's and the Netherlands's. Sodomy and bestiality became capital crimes under Henry VIII (about a century later than in Sweden), probably as part of his campaign to suppress the monasteries and confiscate their lands. But prosecutions for either were rare, though not as infrequent as bestiality trials in the Netherlands—only thirty for bestiality in five counties during the long reign of Elizabeth I, and only six for sodomy over much of England in the seventeenth century, four executions in London between 1709 and 1726, and four more trials in Surrey between 1660 and 1800. On the other hand, because conviction for either offense required proof of penetration, which was always difficult to provide, trials for attempted sodomy or attempted bestiality were much more common. They did not involve the death penalty, but the offenders were certainly considered infamous. A common sentence was an hour in the pillory, which could have fatal consequences.[5]

These trials were selective in another sense as well. Although one woman and her dog were hanged at Tyburn in 1679,[6] women were almost never tried for homosexual acts or for bestiality, largely because the requirement of penetration almost defined the offense as a male act. Protestant clergymen sometimes agitated for a broader definition of the crime, something more in keeping with the biblical mandates. But, for reasons that remain unclear, the lawcourts continued to insist on penetration. Female bestiality emerged in another context—with lethal results. When accused English witches confessed to sexual relations with the devil, he frequently assumed an animal's shape. No such confessions have yet been found in English America, but these fantasies crossed the ocean. Witch accusations in New England often involved a search, usually of the genitals, for familiars.[7]

In the American colonies, only two cases have emerged, both in New England, that involved women engaged in sexual play with one another. Their acts were treated as lewd and lascivious behavior, not as potential crimes against nature, even though one of the principal offenders, the servant Elizabeth Johnson, was also punished for the highly provocative offense of "stopping her ears with her hands when the Word of God was read."[8] Only two cases of female bestiality have come to light in the colonies. In 1702 the grand jury refused to indict one woman in Boston.[9] But in Monmouth County, New Jersey, Hannah Corkin was indicted for buggery in 1757 but convicted only of attempted buggery. Her offense must have been flagrant, however, for she received an exceptionally severe sentence—four whippings, each of twenty lashes, in four different towns in consecutive weeks.[10]

Trials for deviant sex reversed the patterns that prevailed in trials for witchcraft. According to both the Bible and early modern theology, men and women could commit either crime, but only men were actively suspected of sodomy or bestiality, while women were always the prime targets of witchcraft accusations. Men who fell under suspicion of witchcraft were usually related to a woman who was the chief suspect. But in any sexual relation with an animal, as the Swedish bestiality trials reveal, a man was seen doing the devil's work in a way that went beyond conventional sins. God had created an orderly nature with clear boundaries between humans and beasts. Satan, and the buggerers who served him, were challenging those boundaries and threatening to reduce everything to confusion. Swedish sources are rich in this imagery, but it also appears in New England. In New Haven Colony, when one man interrupted another buggering a cow, the accused claimed that he was merely milking her. "Yet it is the Devills Milking and would bring him to the gallows," his accuser replied.[11] People still believed, as we shall see in several dramatic North American cases, that sexual unions between humans and animals, and between different species of animals, could produce offspring.[12] In Sweden, the Swiss Canton of Fribourg, the Republic of Geneva, and New England, the active prosecution of witchcraft and bestiality rose and fell together. For both clergy and magistrates, at least in regimes strongly dedicated to godliness, the two crimes seemed closely related.[13] In the Netherlands, by contrast, the magistrates usually rejected clerical advice about both crimes. Bestiality was almost ignored. The last conviction for witchcraft occurred in 1595, and the last trial in 1610.[14]

Bestiality lowered a man to the level of a beast, but it also left something human in the animal. To eat a defiled animal thus involved the danger of cannibalism. The fear of human debasement ran deep enough to prevent men from milking cows. Women performed that chore. Any Swedish man who entered a barn that housed milk cows needed a superb excuse, or he would attract suspicion of bestial motives.[15] So strong was the sense of defilement from any copulation with animals that in Sweden it overrode the double standard of sexual behavior. Men would turn in other men for this offense, even though conviction usually meant death. The lack of sodomy trials in Sweden suggests that, for 150 years after 1630, bestiality seemed uniquely odious among crimes that men were likely to commit. In Sweden, as in New England, the active suppression of bestiality was accompanied by a major witch hunt aimed mostly at women, but in New England the campaign against bestiality lost its energy far sooner than in Sweden.[16]

BERMUDA AND THE WEST INDIES

I have never done any research in Bermudan or West Indian records, but five cases from the islands have come to my attention. In Bermuda in 1622 two men were executed, one for sodomizing a boy, the other for buggering a sow. According to several witnesses, "a Dung-hill Cocke . . . did continually haunt a Pigge" belonging to the buggerer's master. When that pig soon "languished and died," the cock turned its attention to the sow involved in the buggery case, and one of the cock's hens hatched a two-headed chick. Clearly bestiality threw all nature into upheaval in Bermuda.[17]

In October 1789 on the island of Dominica, a soldier named Sparrow, "the tallest straitest & cleanest Grenadier in the whole Regt.," was seen in full uniform by a thirteen-year-old girl buggering a turkey. Because the girl was too young to testify under oath, the bloodied turkey became the evidence against Sparrow. "The Turkey was killed her feathers plucked off & body thrown down the precipice. The soldier was dresst in her feathers and drummed out of the Regt. wt. the Rogue's March. . . . if the Girl had been of age he would have been hung." Sparrow tried to take ship for America, but when the captain learned who he was, he denied him passage. "Oh says the Capt. I am to carry a Cargo of Turkeys & if you go with me I am afraid that I'll lose the sell of them." Evidently the offense was so notorious that news of it could be expected to cross hundreds of miles of ocean, spread enthusiastically, no doubt, by the ship's crew. In 1792 on the Dutch island of Curaçao, two enslaved boys accused Juan Anthonij, a fellow slave, of buggering a she-ass. He was convicted, strangled at the stake, and then tied to the animal and thrown into a ferryboat that was sunk in the sea. In 1837, nearly half a century later, a former slave named Ben was condemned to death for bestiality on the island of St. Vincent, but the sentence was then reduced to hard labor for life. He was probably elderly. According to one report, "Breaks stones sometimes; is chiefly employed in cleaning the yard. . . ."[18]

Bestiality was probably rarer on the islands than the mainland, at least after the founding generation of indentured servants had moved on. Except in Jamaica, planters did not maintain much livestock because animals took valuable land away from sugarcane. And the sex ratio among African slaves, who rapidly became the chief labor source after 1645, was more evenly balanced than it was among servants in the Chesapeake colonies.[19]

THE SOUTHERN COLONIES

In the early decades of settlement in Virginia and Maryland, men outnumbered women by five or six to one. Often a settler's main source of wealth was his livestock. Male servants who had served their terms frequently teamed up with one another, living together in a small cabin while they worked and saved in an effort to acquire their own land. In this environment we would expect sodomy to be a frequent occurrence. And because men must have milked most of the cows, the danger of bestiality was ever present. New England, by contrast, was settled by families. Both sodomy and bestiality should have been comparatively rare events. And yet nearly all the trials for these two offenses, as for witchcraft, took place in New England, not in the southern colonies.[20]

In 1624 Virginia executed Richard Cornish (alias Williams), a ship captain, for forcibly sodomizing William Couse, one of his ship's boys, who testified that Cornish had put him "to payne in the fundement." Two men, Cornish's brother Jeffrey and one Edward Nevell, complained aboard a ship in far off Canadian waters that Richard Cornish *was hangd for a rascally boye wrongfully,"* and that *"he was put to death through a scurvie boys meanes, & no other came against him."* When Nevell returned to Virginia, the governor put him on trial for his words, and Nevell suffered the loss of both ears in the pillory and was sentenced to serve the colony for a year. Even this cruel example did not stifle the criticism. In February 1625/26, James Hickmote heard Peter Marten "Commendinge . . . *Cornish* for an excellent mariner and skillfull Artist." Thomas Hatch agreed, adding "that in his consyence he thought the said Cornishe was put to death wrongfully." Hickmote warned Hatch: *"you were best take heede w* you saye, you have a president {precedent} before your eyes the other dye, And it will cost you yo* eares yf you use such woordes."* Hatch defiantly replied, *"I care not for my eares, lett them hange me yf they will[.]"* The court ordered Hatch whipped from the fort to the gallows and back again and then to lose one of his ears. Surviving records do not explain whether these critics thought an innocent man had been convicted, or that Cornish should have been tried by jury, or that the penalty was excessive, or that the hierarchy of the maritime community would be hopelessly compromised if authorities started hanging ship captains upon the unsupported claims of cabin boys, whether or not a sexual encounter had taken place.[21]

No other sodomy case has yet surfaced in the court records of colonial Virginia, but some of the suicides look suspicious. In 1625 John Verone, a servant boy in a household of half a dozen males older than he, was kept at home doing women's work while the others went out to the fields. He took care of the kitchen, cleaned up, and fetched water. One wonders whether he was also the object of sexual advances from some or all of his housemates. If so, nobody was foolish enough to volunteer that information to the authorities, who showed up to take depositions after Verone hanged himself in the loft of the house around noon on a workday. In Surry County, which probably never had more than eight hundred people living there between 1650 and 1670, at least two servant boys hanged themselves and another was found dead with bruised thighs. None of these deaths led to a criminal prosecution. The implication is, I think, that no one tried to stamp out sexual relations between consenting males and that nonconsensual sex may have occurred more often than magistrates cared to recognize. In Maryland, where the court records are much fuller than in Virginia, no sodomy or bestiality trials have yet been found.[22]

Three bestiality cases survive in Virginia's lower court records. In 1644 in Northampton County on the Eastern Shore, Robert Wyard and his wife Ellinor were walking home from a neighbor's house between six and seven in the morning. While passing through the woods they happened upon Nathaniel Moore, one of the neighbor's servants, buggering "a little Black Calfe." They approached close enough to strike Moore with a stick, but instead Robert surprised him by shouting, "Villaine what are you doeing heare, hee made answeare nothing Resting the Calfe what should I doe." Robert replied, "villaine you lye you are Buggering the Calfe hee Answeared you lie." Then Ellinor interjected, "you lye for wee stoode lookeing on you." Robert warned him, "Villaine you have done inough to be hang'd." Moore replied, "doe your worst. I care not what you cann doe." While the Wyards noted the animal's markings, doubtless to identify it so that it too could be executed, Moore "untyed the Calfe and came leadeing the Calfe and bid [Robert] stand by and lett the Calfe come by." The Wyards informed the calf's owner what they had seen, reported the incident to the county court, and posted bond to prosecute the case before the General Court in Jamestown. Two points emerge from this encounter. The Wyards were genuinely shocked by what they saw, but Moore seemed far more defiant than ashamed of what he had done.[23]

A second case occurred in Lancaster County in 1712 when, on a Sunday morning in June, several people, including at least one woman, saw Robert Jones, a laborer, vigorously copulating with a mare. By then Virginia had become a community of conventional families, and, as the numerous depositions in the case indicate, the incident instantly became a major topic of local gossip, especially among women. When caught in the act, Jones claimed that he was merely trying to remove something ("spaniells") from the mare's back, but otherwise his voice does not come through in the records. The court spent some time trying to identify the mare, whose tail had been pulled or cut off between the incident and the court appearance. The owner, almost certainly, was trying to save the animal. Both Jones and the mare were bound over for trial in Williamsburg.[24]

In Augusta County in 1763, William Sharp accused William Jones of buggering a mare. The local justices were "of Opinion that he is Guilty of the Fact wherewith he stands Charged" and ordered him to stand trial in Williamsburg three months later.[25]

No records survive to indicate the final disposition of any of these cases, but in all of them the lower court was clearly establishing the basis for a capital trial. The only reason for sending the mare to Williamsburg in 1712 would have been to make it possible to slay the animal before Jones was hanged. Nobody claimed it had been bloodied and could thus be used as evidence. Quite possibly Virginia did hang the three men for bestiality, and since few of the higher court records survive, maybe more. On the other hand, the witnesses in each case would have had to travel considerable distances to convict the accused men and may just have dropped the matter. The 1644 incident occurred, for example, during a very dangerous Indian war. The total absence of bestiality trials in Maryland suggests that prosecutions for this offense must have been quite rare in the Chesapeake colonies.

What evidence we have from the Carolinas confirms this suspicion. North Carolina's higher court records are reasonably full, but hardly any criminal records have survived for South Carolina. In the extant records for both colonies, no one was actually prosecuted for sodomy. But John Clark, Esq., did sue two brothers, William and Edward Wynne, for damages when they told people that he had often tried to sodomize them and other young men. Because Clark was a justice of the peace who had served as a militia captain and assemblyman, he was determined to protect his reputation and probably hoped to intimidate the Wynnes into silence by suing them. But at the next court when the trial was supposed to take place, the Wynnes appeared, he did not, and he suffered a nonsuit. They probably found enough supporting witnesses to make a convincing case. Perhaps the most striking feature about this confrontation was its ambiguity. Clark's homosexual inclinations had not prevented him from rising to the top of North Carolina society. His reputation suffered irreparable loss only after he tried to force himself upon unwilling partners.[26]

In 1724 Thomas Handcock sued Solomon Hughes for trespass and assault for calling him "a Cow buggering Son of a bitch." But at the next court session Handcock announced that the two had reached an agreement, and he dropped the suit. Presumably Hughes apologized and probably paid Handcock to make the settlement.[27] Two prosecutions for bestiality were begun in the 1760s. John Everitt, a laborer, was accused of having "a venereal affair with . . . a Mare," and Robert Johnston, a hatter, faced the charge that he "did commit and perpetrate that detestable and abominable Crime of buggery (not to be named among Christians)" with a black cow. Apparently these cases never came to trial.[28]

The most sensational bestiality case in the southern colonies that has yet come to light occurred in South Carolina. In 1703 Francis Oldfield, an Indian trader, was unable to sleep one night. He heard a noise, got up, and looked in the room next to his in what was obviously a crude cabin. "By means of the light of the Moon shineing thro the holes and windows, And of a small fire on the floor, He plainly saw John Dixon . . . In the very act of Buggering a Brown Bitch, which . . . Bitch after . . . Dixon had done the Beastly act, Jumpt from of[f] the Cabin, and turning about lickt her privy parts." After Oldfield confided to a friend what he had seen, Dixon "earnestly intreated [him], never to reveal the thing." Oldfield "concealled it for some moneths l[o]nger; But could not be at ease in his minde still thinking itt his duty to Informe a majestrate with what he knew." He brought the matter before Thomas Nairne, Esq., one of the most prominent men in the colony. Nairne also got a deposition from the widow Jannet Tibbs, who claimed "That John Dixon . . . being at her hous and, as his custom is, discoursing Lewd Ribaldry with some of his companions, among other Beastly Expressions, was Instructing them how to Bugger a cat and in particular told them to tye her head in a Bag, and hold up her Taill." The widow "ordered s'd Dixon to Leave her house, and could never afterwards endure him."

Presumably Nairne took some judicial action against Dixon, but it was not fatal. Five years later, after Nairne and the governor had fought a huge public quarrel over Indian policy, the governor got depositions from Dixon and an equally disreputable friend, who swore that they had heard Nairne speak treason against Queen Anne. The governor imprisoned Nairne for at least five months. What we know about this case stems from Nairne's efforts to vindicate himself before British officials. Although some South Carolinians, such as Oldfield, the widow Tibbs, and probably Nairne, shared the conventional Christian loathing for all forms of bestiality, other colonists thought it amusing. Dixon suffered no permanent damage from Oldfield's accusations. And though also accused at least twice of trading without a license, he played a prominent role in the colony's Indian affairs for the next six years and was even involved in deciding which Indians would be enslaved and which remain free. Nairne finally won his release. In 1715, Nairne was tortured to death by Indians in the first days of the Yamasee War, begun by the Indians who feared that they would be the colony's next targets for enslavement. Dixon may have been killed at the same time. The Indian traders were the Yamasees' first targets, and Dixon's name disappears from the colony's Indian records after August 1714.[29]

THE MIDDLE COLONIES

In the Middle Atlantic colonies, nearly everything we know about homosexuality comes from private sources, not public records. The most important exceptions occurred in New Netherland. In 1646 the colony executed "Jan Creoli, a Negro" slave, for raping Manuel Congo, a ten-year-old African boy. Creoli also admitted that he had committed sodomy in the West Indies. In keeping with Dutch custom, Creoli was strangled and then burned at the stake. The court also ordered Congo tied to a stake with wood piled about him to witness the execution. After Creoli's sentence was carried out, Congo was beaten with rods and released. This sentence displayed the magistrates' fear and loathing of the offense. The court acknowledged "the innocence and youth of the boy" but felt obliged to punish him for being part of an abomination.[30] A year later Harmen Meyndertz van den Bogaert, famous in the colony for his journey though the Iroquois country in 1634–35, was accused of sodomizing his black servant Tobias and fled to the Mohawks for protection. Hans Vos followed him, seized him in an Indian warehouse that burned down during the struggle, and returned him to Fort Orange for trial. In early 1648 Van den Bogaert tried to escape across the icy North (Hudson) River, but drowned when the ice broke.[31] In 1660 Jan Quisthout van der Linde, a soldier, was stripped of his arms, his sword was broken, and he was tied in a sack and cast into the river to drown for sodomizing an orphan boy in his service. The boy was privately whipped and then bound to another master in a different community.[32] The Dutch horror of sodomy clearly carried over into New Netherland. In a colony with fewer than a thousand people in 1646 and just over six thousand by 1664, three executions, or attempted executions, were a lot for this offense.

The only official proceeding against sodomy in New Jersey that I know of occurred in Burlington County in 1745. The grand jury presented Jacob Johnson, a cordwainer, "for assaulting Hans Peter Creiz and committing sodomy with him . . . against his will and consent." Apparently the case never went to trial.[33]

The Quaker colonies of West New Jersey and Pennsylvania never even defined bestiality as a capital crime in the seventeenth century. West Jersey made murder and treason punishable by death, but only if so directed by the legislature in each case. The colony never passed a statute defining sodomy or bestiality as crimes. Pennsylvania provided whippings for both offenses, plus the forfeiture of one-third of the person's estate, and imprisonment for six months—or, for a second offense, for life.[34]

Complaints to the home government forced Pennsylvania to toughen its laws in 1700. Sodomy and bestiality became punishable by imprisonment for life, with a whipping every three months for the first year. A married man convicted of sodomy or bestiality would be castrated, whipped every three months for a year, and imprisoned for life, and the spouse of any person convicted of either crime could receive a divorce. When London objected to castration, that penalty was removed in 1706. Both crimes finally became capital offenses in 1718 when Pennsylvania adopted most of the English criminal code in exchange for concessions to Quakers on judicial oaths.[35] Under this law Thomas White was hanged for sodomy in 1748.[36] No one else was executed for either sodomy or bestiality in Pennsylvania or Delaware until John Ross was hanged for "buggery" in 1786, a year before the legislature removed sodomy and bestiality from the list of capital crimes.[37]

Private sources show a surprising degree of tolerance for male homosexual activity. The most striking incidents involve some of the leaders of the Great Awakening in New Jersey. Theodorus Jacobus Frelinghuysen, who became the most effective evangelical preacher of the Dutch Reformed Church in the colony, was accused of intimate sexual relations with his schoolmaster and associate, Jacobus Schuurman. Schuurman was charged, without any known rebuttal, "with attempting scandalous undertakings by night, upon the person of more than one man with whom he happened to sleep." He often slept with Frelinghuysen and, "both publicly and at home, often embraced him and kissed him." Frelinghuysen had already aroused controversy for denying Holy Communion to his ecclesiastical opponents because, he insisted, "they *must first* grow to maturity and make confession of their faith." They accused him of hypocrisy for continuing to give Communion to Schuurman. When challenged, Frelinghuysen insisted that it was "more necessary that Schuurman should be prayed for, than that he should be censured." The controversy traveled all the way to the Classis of Amsterdam, which did its best to reconcile the contending parties. Frelinghuysen quieted suspicion by taking a wife, and then Schuurman married her sister. The scandal did little to weaken Frelinghuysen's reputation. In the 1730s Gilbert Tennent, the most fiery preacher among New Jersey's evangelical Presbyterians, enthusiastically accepted him as a colleague in Christ. So did George Whitefield on his famous evangelical tour of the area in 1740.[38]

The College of New Jersey, which moved into Nassau Hall in Princeton in 1756, had been founded to institutionalize and perpetuate the revivals, and yet it soon attracted similar criticisms. Hannah Callender, a Philadelphian who passed through Princeton in 1759, "Walked around the college and the President's house. Good buildings for so young a country, placed on a well chosen spot of ground, with the command of the country around as far as the ken of sight," she observed in her diary, " . . . but whether the college will bring forth more good than hurt, time will demonstrate; seeing as I thought some trace of the monster vice have made their appearance even in so short a time as three years." Not a hint of this problem appears in any of the college's extant sources for the colonial era.[39] But three surviving diaries from 1786–87 do document the passionate relationship between James Gibson (A.B. 1787) and a young Philadelphia merchant, John Mifflin, a cousin of Thomas Mifflin, soon to become the first governor of Pennsylvania under the new state constitution of 1790. Gibson and Mifflin both kept diaries, as did Gibson's roommate, John Rhea Smith, who sometimes found it embarrassing to be in the same room with the other two. When Mifflin visited Princeton, Gibson got permission—presumably from President John Witherspoon or Vice President Samuel Stanhope Smith, arguably the most prestigious Presbyterian ministers in North America—to spend several nights sleeping with Mifflin in a tavern on Nassau Street.

The diaries reveal the intense passion of both young men but do not indicate whether the relationship became overtly sexual. Yet Mifflin did record an extraordinary dream. He and Gibson were in a small boat without oars or paddles moving down a high Philadelphia pier toward the most treacherous part of the Delaware River. Observers called from above to warn them of their peril. At the last moment, Mifflin leapt onto the pier and pulled Gibson up after him. Gibson was naked. As the two scrambled to find Gibson's clothes, Mifflin awoke. A culture saturated in Sigmund Freud can easily interpret the dream as fear of exposure, degradation, and shame because of their relationship. But Mifflin lived in the eighteenth century. He wondered only if the dream had been a premonition, whether he and Gibson would both be in a small boat and reenact the entire scene. Gibson graduated, married, and had a successful career.[40]

Homosexual inclinations did not necessarily undermine a man's reputation in the middle colonies. Nor did bestiality lead to death in the first half-century of English settlement. Only three cases have come to my attention. In East New Jersey in 1688, John Laine was acquitted of buggering a mare at Myles Foster's stable in Perth Amboy. There must have been strong grounds of suspicion because the court bound him to good behavior for one year. In Pennsylvania, a Chester County grand jury would not indict William Pusey for buggering a heifer in 1705.[41]

But in Burlington, West New Jersey, in 1692, Harry Negro, a "Servant" of Isaac Marriott, was seen buggering a cow by some girls. They summoned their mother, Mary Myers, who confirmed their story. After Harry finished the unspeakable act, she reported, "the Cow turned and looked after him." Harry pleaded not guilty. The jury heard testimony from the mother and one daughter, visited the site of the appalling deed, and found him guilty. "The Bench haveing Considered of the Sentence according to the Law," condemned him to hang. But then "Many of the Freeholders and Inhabitants [i.e., women?] of this County preferre a Petition to the Bench for Spareing the Negroes life, And to inflict other punishment upon him." The judges agreed to consider the request.

Nothing indicates the content of this petition. Did it point out that bestiality had not been defined as a capital crime in West New Jersey? What "Law" did the bench consider before passing sentence? An English statute? Or did the magistrates believe that New England law applied because the Jerseys had briefly been absorbed into the Dominion of New England in 1688–89? The petitioners may also have suggested that the Bible's stern standards ought not be applied to someone who had not been raised a Christian.

When the court again took up the case three months later, the sheriff reported that Harry could not be found. Someone had probably left the jail door open for him.[42] Harry, perhaps reflecting that he who loves and runs away may live to love—or kill—another day, then disappeared from West Jersey records. But a man with the same name ("Harrie" Negro) was tried for murder in East New Jersey in 1695 and found guilty of homicide in self-defense. The court then advised him to request a pardon.[43] We cannot be certain that they were the same man, but there could not have been many Africans named Harry Negro in New Jersey in the 1690s. The sources do not tell us what happened to the cow, although it too had been condemned. Unless Mary Myers had ascended far above the folklore of her day, she probably would have regarded its milk as contaminated. And yet we have to wonder. The West Jersey Concessions did specifically exempt animals, and anything else that happened to cause the death of a human, from judicial forfeiture, unless the animal itself was inherently dangerous to humans. Maybe the Quakers extended the same principle to bestiality. Perhaps the cow was spared.[44]

If the court really had no legal basis for imposing the death penalty, this fact suggests that Quakers, like other Englishmen, found bestiality revolting. Yet when the question became one of life or death, they could not execute this man. To Burlington's Quakers, bestiality evidently seemed much less revolting than the sexual molestation of a child. When Charles Sheepey was convicted of that offense in 1688, the court ordered him whipped for an hour through the streets of Burlington, kept in irons for three months, then whipped again and released from the irons. He was also sentenced to return to the next seven quarter courts and receive a two-hour whipping at each one, for a total of nine over a period of two years. Puritans would have imposed the biblical limit of thirty-nine lashes. Quakers did not, at least for this particular offense. Sheepey's sentence is the most severe punishment short of death that I have encountered in any set of colonial court records.[45]

Like Pennsylvania, New Jersey got tougher on "unnatural vice" in the eighteenth century. Salem County hanged Charles Conaway for bestiality in 1757. In 1774 John Taylor was also executed for this offense in Burlington, but since he had also been indicted for murder, the court probably had multiple reasons for hanging him. In several other cases, accusations failed to produce a trial, or the jury convicted the defendant of the lesser offense of attempted buggery. These men were whipped, not hanged.[46]

SODOMY IN EARLY NEW ENGLAND

By contrast, one man accused of bestiality in early New England had already argued explicitly that buggery was less repulsive than the molestation of a child. Unlike Harry Negro and Charles Sheepey in West New Jersey, he had been hanged.

Sodomy and bestiality in colonial New England have come under considerable scrutiny in the last quarter-century. Robert F. Oaks argued that homosexual relations must have been far more common than surviving legal records indicate and that, measured against the punishments meted out for buggery, the region was fairly tolerant of sodomy. Roger Thompson has replied that the region was a bastion of homophobic sentiment and that deviant sexual behavior was extremely rare. John Canup has also stressed the distinctive Puritan preoccupation with "the beast within" to account for the region's extraordinary horror of buggery.[47]

All of these scholars are making valid and important points. As in any society, many incidents of proscribed behavior never came to the attention of the authorities. But even if we multiply the known sodomy incidents by, shall we say, a factor of fifty, the number of participants would still be a tiny fraction of the total population, though probably not a trivial proportion of teenage boys. The ferocity of the rhetoric denouncing sodomy was indeed distinctive, and as Thompson points out, we have to wonder why the clergy and the magistrates worried so much about things that seldom happened. But then we have very little rhetoric at all from other colonies on this subject. New Englanders published sermons and even a few ponderous tomes of divinity or religious history. Other colonies did not. And yet if we set this rhetoric aside for a moment, the region's actual treatment of men or boys accused of sodomy was quite similar to what we have seen in other parts of colonial North America. Even the Puritans nearly always found a way to avoid executing the accused. The only two exceptions occurred in New Haven Colony, which was also the only New England colony to abolish jury trials.

In 1646 New Haven hanged William Plaine of Guilford, a married man who had committed sodomy with two men in England. In New England, "he had corrupted a great parte of the youth of Gilford by masturbation, which he had committed & provoked others to the like, above 100 tymes," reported John Winthrop; "& to some who questioned the lawfullnesse of suche a filthy practice, he did insinuate seedes of Atheism, questioning whither there were a God &c." Theophilus Eaton, the governor of New Haven, wrote to Winthrop on how to proceed in this case. The issue, no doubt was whether masturbation could be a capital crime. Winthrop agreed that this "monster in humaine shape . . . exceedinge all humane Rules, & examples that ever had been heard off" deserved to die, but remained vague about the biblical basis for executing him. Winthrop noted only his "frustratinge of the Ordinance of marriage & the hindringe the generation of mankinde." After the fact, New Haven adopted a law to cover the case. It declared that public masturbation, by "corrupting or tempting others to doe the like, . . . tends to the sin of Sodomy, if it be not one kind of it"; and "if the case considered with the aggravating circumstances, shall according to the mind of God revealed in his word require it, he shall be put to death, as the court of magistrates shall determine." In short, Plaine's crime was inciting others to sodomy.[48]

Unfortunately the New Haven Colony records do not survive for this case, or we would have a much fuller account of how many boys were involved with Plaine. But if these encounters happened more than a hundred times, they had been going on for months before any lad notified the authorities or some respectable resident interrupted one of the frolics. In the town of Guilford, many youths had sexual experiences for an extended period of time that godly adults knew nothing about.

Nine years later Thomas and Peter Richards interrupted John Knight and Peter Vincon, a servant boy, "Acting filthyness together," which the two brothers described in lurid detail. Vincon's testimony suggested that he had sometimes been a willing partner and on other occasions had resisted. On the day in question, Knight had said "shall we play" and Vincon had replied, "no play," but Knight "came to him" anyway. Partly because Knight had also tried to rape young Mary Clark several times, the court condemned him to death. Nothing in the record indicates that Vincon was punished, although he is described as of age, "fourteene yeares or somewhat more." This case is the only example of conventional sodomy that led to an execution in colonial New England, although Mingo, a slave in Charlestown, Massachusetts, was hanged for "forcible buggery" (sodomizing a young girl) in 1712. In 1755 at Lake George, a Massachusetts soldier named Bickerstaff received the then unprecedented sentence of one hundred lashes for "Profane swearing and a Sodomitical attempt." He was then drummed out of camp with a noose around his neck, a dramatic way of telling him that he deserved to die, and was kept in confinement for the rest of the campaign. But he was not executed.[49]

Puritan New England's first known encounter with the problem of sodomy occurred aboard the *Talbot* on its way to Salem in 1629. According to Rev. Francis Higginson, "This day we examined 5 beastly Sodomiticall boys, which confessed their wickedness not to bee named. The fact was so fowl we reserved them to bee punished by the governor when we came to New England, who afterward sent them backe to the [Massachusetts Bay] company to bee punished in ould England, as the crime deserved." Those over fourteen could have been hanged, but since five executions would almost have doubled the known total executed for sodomy in seventeenth-century England, we can be reasonably certain that they suffered some lesser punishment.[50]

Even New Haven Colony, the world's most severely Puritan society, learned to cope with youthful sex play among boys without resorting to the halter. At "A MEETING OF YE COURT EXTRAORDINARY" in March 1653, the magistrates examined six "youthes" who "had committed much wickedness in a filthy corrupting way one wth another." Their confessions "were of such a filthy nature as is not fitt to be made known in a publique way," but all six were publicly whipped. John Clarke, a servant who was probably older than the "youthes," was "charged by one of them for some filthy cariag," which he denied. When one of the other boys "in some measure cleered him" of that accusation, the court left his punishment to his master but warned Clarke "that if ever any such cariag came forth against him hereafter, the Court would call these miscariages upon him to minde againe."

The court feared, no doubt, that it might have another William Plaine on its hands. As this judgment indicates, hardly anyone accused of sodomy or any other serious crime in New Haven Colony ever received a complete acquittal.[51]

The most remarkable New England case was the whole adult life of Nicholas Sension of Wethersfield, Connecticut. He settled there around 1640, married a woman who then became a church member (he did not), and prospered. Quite often, he solicited sexual relations with other men. Once he even tried to seduce an unwilling bedmate while members of the Connecticut General Court were sleeping in the same room. The whole town seems to have known about his inclinations. He was reprimanded once in the 1640s and again in the 1660s, but people also liked him. Even a servant who resented and refused his sexual advances asked to remain in his service. Sension apparently established a long-term relationship with Nathaniel Pond, but after Pond was killed in Metacom's (King Philip's) War in 1675, Sension began once more to solicit sex from several young men. He was finally tried for sodomy in 1677, but the jury convicted him only of attempted sodomy. The court, dominated by magistrates from other communities who probably did not know Sension at all well, disfranchised him, ordered him to stand on the gallows with a noose around his neck, had him severely whipped, committed him to prison at the court's pleasure, and bound him to good behavior for a year. Had Sension lived about thirty miles southwest of Wethersfield in New Haven Colony, where there were no juries, he almost certainly would have been hanged, probably in the 1640s. The sentence, even though it could not be capital because of the jury verdict, reflects how one would expect a Puritan magistrate to respond to the foul crime of "going after strange flesh" (Jude 1:7). Far more remarkable is the community's toleration of Sension's behavior for nearly forty years. Two centuries before the category of "homosexual" was invented, many ordinary residents of Wethersfield were willing, historian Richard Godbeer has argued, "to treat sodomy as a condition rather than as an act; it became in their minds a habitual course of action that characterized some men throughout their lives."[52]

Like New Jersey, eighteenth-century New England had its own example of a clergyman, often accused of sodomy, yet accepted by most of his congregation. Stephen Gorton, minister to the Baptist congregation in New London, Connecticut, drew criticism for his homosexual inclinations from the 1720s into the 1750s. Several flagrant infractions prompted some church members to withdraw from the congregation, and in 1757 Gorton was suspended. Yet after he repented publicly for his sin, the congregation voted two to one to restore him to his pulpit. The women favored him by a margin of three to one, while the men split about evenly. But clearly these serious Christians believed that sodomy was a forgivable offense.[53]

BESTIALITY IN EARLY NEW ENGLAND

In New England for most of the seventeenth century, men who committed bestiality received no mercy. Those convicted of the act, as distinct from the attempt, were hanged. The court always allowed a fair amount of time between trial and execution so that the condemned man could have an opportunity to repent. God could forgive him. Humans dared not even try. "It is a *Crying* sin," explained Samuel Danforth; "it makes a clamorous noise in the ears of the holy God: it will not suffer God to rest in Heaven. . . . It defiles the Land; the Earth groans under the burthen of such Wickedness."[54]

The region experienced something close to a bestiality panic between 1640 and 1643. When the Great Migration finally ceased in 1641, New England probably had a higher percentage of young unmarried men than at any other point in the century. This group was much smaller than in colonies farther south. In Massachusetts the sex ratio (the number of men per one hundred women) was about 132 in 1641, at a time when it may still have exceeded 400 in Virginia. Yet young unmarried men, usually without known family attachments, provoked most of the cases of bestiality in the 1640s.[55]

In July 1640 Aaron Starke of Windsor was accused of buggering a heifer. A year earlier he had been whipped and fined, and the letter "R" was burned upon his cheek (for attempted rape?), for "the wrong done to Mary Holt . . . and when both are fit for that Condition to marry her." Instead, a month or two later she was whipped and banished for "vncleane practises" with John Bennett. Starke was still single when accused of bestiality. He "confesseth that he leaned crosse over the heifers Flanke, though at the first he denied that he came neere her, lastly he acknowledgeth that he had twice committed the acte wth the heifer but that shee was to narrowe." The court ordered a constable to keep him "wth locke and Chaine and hold him to hard labour & course diet" until summoned to trial. Nicholas Sension, the lifelong homosexual, was fined for not appearing to testify at this trial. One has to wonder how intimate the relationship was between these two men. The records of the next several courts have not survived, but Stark was not executed. Connecticut had not yet declared bestiality a capital crime, and the court may also have concluded that his confession amounted to no more than admission of the attempt, not the act. At any rate, Starke survived to be whipped for some other, unstated offense in 1643. He was also condemned to serve Captain John Mason during the pleasure of the court.[56]

Massachusetts began to experience similar trouble in the winter of 1640–41. "A wicked fellow, given up to bestiality, fearing to be taken by the hand of justice, fled to Long Island, and there was drowned," noted John Winthrop with equal measure of disgust and satisfaction. "He had confessed to some, that he was so given up to that abomination, that he never saw any beast go before him but he lusted after it." In December 1641 the General Court (the whole legislature) sentenced William Hatchet, an eighteen- or twenty-year-old servant in Salem, to be hanged for buggering a cow on the Lord's day. He had always been "a very stupid, idle, and ill-disposed boy, and would never regard the means of instruction, either in the church or family," Winthrop claimed. A woman too ill to attend public worship that day, while "looking out at her window, espied him in the very act; but being affrighted at it, and dwelling alone, she durst not call to him, but at night made it known" to a magistrate. Hatchet then "confessed the attempt and some entrance, but denied the completing of the fact." During the trial, "much scruple there was with many, because there was but one witness," whereas the Bible requires two for conviction of a capital crime. A majority voted to convict him on the strength of the woman's testimony and Hatchet's admission of some penetration, but when Governor Richard Bellingham could not overcome his own doubts and pronounce the sentence of death, the deputy governor, John Endicott, performed that function. The cow, of course, was condemned "to bee slayne & burnt or buried."

Only then did Hatchet confess "the full completing this foul fact, and attempting the like before." He became so penitent that his execution was postponed an extra week to let the grace of the Lord complete its work. "There is no doubt to be made but the Lord hath received his soul to his mercy," Winthrop affirmed. In March 1643 the Court of Assistants sentenced an Irish servant, Teagu Ocrimi, to stand at the place of execution with a halter around his neck and to be severely whipped "for a foule, & divilish attempt to bugger a cow of Mr. Makepeaces." The moral was sobering. "As people increased, so sin abounded, and especially the sin of uncleanness," concluded Winthrop, "and still the providence of God found them out."[57]

In neighboring Plymouth Colony, not long after Hatchet had been hanged in Massachusetts, someone saw Thomas Granger buggering a mare. His parents lived in Scituate, but this sixteen- or seventeen-year-old lad was a servant in a respectable household in Duxbury. During his examination, he confessed to having sex with "a mare, a cow, two goats, five sheep, two calves and a turkey." A large part of some poor farmer's flock of sheep had to be paraded before him so that he could identify which ones he had buggered and which could be spared. All of the defiled animals were slaughtered before his face on September 8, 1642, and then he was hanged. The animal carcasses were "cast into a great and large pit that was digged of purpose for them, and no use made of any part of them." Governor William Bradford wondered why "even sodomy and buggery (things fearful to name) have broke forth in this land oftener than once." The vigilance of churches and magistrates provided one answer. In populous old countries, such deeds "lie hid, as it were, in a wood or thicket and many horrible evils by that means are never seen nor known; whereas here they are, as it were, brought into the light and set in the plain field, or rather on a hill, made conspicuous to the view of all"—surely a less than inspirational application of John Winthrop's ideal of a city upon a hill![58]

In New Haven Colony, the exposure of abomination took an even more dramatic form when the Lord intervened directly to reveal the unspeakable wickedness of a lewd and irreverent servant. George Spencer, an ugly balding man with one "pearle" or false eye, had probably been whipped in Boston for receiving stolen goods, and had also been punished in New Haven for botching an attempt to escape to Virginia. He admitted that he had gained no spiritual benefit from the ministry of the famed John Davenport, that he had not said a single prayer during his five years in New England, and that he read the Bible only when ordered to do so by his master. In February 1642, Spencer's life took a cruel turn when a sow gave birth to a dead deformed piglet. The "monster" was completely bald and "had butt one eye in the midle of the face, and thatt large and open, like some blemished eye of a man." Out of its forehead "a thing of flesh grew forth and hung downe, itt was hollow, and like a mans instrumt of gen'ation."

The magistrates arrested Spencer and put him in prison. New Haven had not yet tried a capital crime. Spencer had observed enough of the colony's system of justice to know that the magistrates expected offenders to confess and repent. He had recently seen a man merely whipped for molesting a child, and as Spencer made clear, he thought that child molestation was a more disgusting crime than bestiality. Yet he denied his guilt until one magistrate "remembred him of thatt place of scripture, he thatt hideth his sin shall not prosper, butt he y[t] confesseth and forsaketh his sins shall finde mercie." Spencer then "answered he was sory and confessed he had done itt," only to learn that his confession would get him hanged and that mercy would come only from the Lord, not the Colony of New Haven. He retracted and repeated his confession several times in a desperate attempt to find a formula that would save his life. But on April 8, 1642, two months after the birth of the monster, the sow was put to the sword in front of the unrepentant Spencer, and he was hanged, "a terrible example of divine justice and wrath."[59]

The bestiality panic of 1641–43 passed, but the precedents remained. In late 1645 another New Haven sow gave birth to two deformed piglets that reminded observers of another servant whose name was, incredibly, Thomas Hogg. Although imprisoned for two or three months—longer than anyone else in the colony's history—Hogg refused to confess. The magistrates clearly believed he was guilty. They even brought him to the sow, made him fondle her, and noted that "immedyatly there appeared a working of lust in the sow" but not in another one that they also made him "scratch," and then asked him "what he thought of it, he said he saw a hand of God in it." Hogg wore a steel truss for his hernia, and because it kept cutting open his britches, his private parts had become rather too public. Apparently the deformed eyes of one piglet reminded observers of the hang of his scrotum, which far too many people had seen. But he never confessed, and without a second witness, the court did not hang him. It whipped him instead for general lewdness, which included at least one incident of masturbation.[60]

In 1647 a Connecticut jury found John Nubery, the seventeen-year-old son of a respectable settler, guilty of bestiality. Out "of horror of Conscience &c: to gloryfie God," he went before a magistrate and voluntarily confessed to several such attempts, "once to penetration but not to effution of seed." Connecticut hanged him, but as the elder Winthrop noted, "his Repentance & godly ende" were "very observable." This case, more clearly than any other, displays the Puritan hope that God would pardon an offence that humans could not forgive.[61]

By 1647 Massachusetts, Plymouth, New Haven, and Connecticut had each convicted and hanged one young man for bestiality. But then the pace fell off. New Haven hanged two more men. Walter Robinson, a fifteen-year-old boy who was seen by a sailor buggering a bitch in Milford, ran away when the sailor called to him that "he would be hanged," and finally admitted slight penetration of the animal, which was enough for the court to hang him in 1655.[62] Far more spectacular was the case of William Potter, one of the original founders of New Haven Colony, a member of John Davenport's church (it had the strictest admission procedures in all of New England), and a family man. A "weake infirme man," he was about sixty years old and had recently been exempted from the military watch because of his poor health. But his ailments did not impede his unusual sex life. In 1662, his teenaged son saw him buggering one of their sows and went to get his mother, who confirmed what father was doing. In what was clearly a lethal decision that they both understood, mother and son informed a magistrate. Confronted with two witnesses, Potter confessed. He admitted to a lifelong fondness for this activity beginning in England at about age ten. His wife had caught him some years earlier copulating with his bitch.

He had persuaded her not to tell the authorities and had even hanged the dog, apparently in a fit of remorse. This time he was, of course, condemned to die. In what remains the most awkward moment in any early American court record that I have read, Potter led his wife through his flocks, pointing out to her every animal that had been a sexual partner. On the day of his execution, a cow, two heifers, three sheep, and two sows all died with him. The case was so scandalous that Cotton Mather was still casting anathemas upon this "Hellish Hypocrite," *"Hell-Hound,"* and *"Bewitched Being"* thirty-seven years later.[63]

New Haven even detected an abomination when animals of different species grew amorous with one another. In 1655 Nicholas Bayley's dog tried to copulate with a sow. When a neighbor admonished Bayley to execute the dog, Bayley's wife retorted, "what would you have the poore creature doe, if he had not a bitch, he must have some thing." The court found this remark so shocking that it banished the depraved couple. It may be no coincidence that the Bayleys had also fallen under suspicion of witchcraft.[64]

Bestiality seemed so loathsome that even jokes about it were punishable. Young Jeremiah Johnson, the only person whose sense of humor emerges from the voluminous court records of New Haven colony and town, once overheard Edmund Dorman praying loudly in a swamp for a wife: "Lord thou knowest my necessity & canst supply it, Lord bend & bow her will & make her sensible of my condition." When someone later asked him for whom Dorman was praying, Johnson replied, "it may be his mare that God would make her seruiseable." Dorman, who married Hannah Hull three months later, sued Johnson for slander in September 1662. After several witnesses recounted other irreverent remarks that Johnson had made, the court warned him "that it was a fearefull thing to come to that height of sinning as to sit in ye seat of ye scorner," put off its decision for several months, and then imposed a good behavior bond of ten pounds on him, the only one I can recall seeing that had no time limit.[65]

Puritan missionaries even tried to impose their standards on the Indians. In January 1647 the first group of "praying Indians" agreed to abide by a set of laws that punished both adultery and bestiality with death. New England's priorities emerged quite clearly here. The code said nothing about sodomy, an offense that did occur among Indians, but instead prohibited bestiality among a people who had no large domesticated animals before the Europeans arrived and who had never shared the Christian prohibition of premarital sexual relations between men and women. Bestiality may have been unknown among the Indians.[66]

They did not remain ignorant for long. In 1656 two Indians informed Roger Williams, the founder of Rhode Island and at that time the president of the colony's Court of Trials, that they had seen Richard Chasmore of Pawtuxet, known locally as "Long Dick," buggering a heifer. One had seen him in the winter, the other in the spring. Williams tried to arrest Chasmore, but some men of Pawtuxet were able to protect him until he could flee to New Netherland. Pawtuxet was then on territory disputed between Rhode Island and Massachusetts. The escape so outraged Williams that he wrote to Governor Bellingham of Massachusetts and urged him to arrest Chasmore when he returned to Pawtuxet and bring him to trial in Boston. Chasmore's friends seemed willing to subject him to trial in Rhode Island. "I guesse ye bottome of ye Councell js," Williams explained, that the Chasmore faction expected "an easier doome with us where Indian Testimonie will not easily passe," although Williams had also heard that some men of Pawtuxet were beginning to believe the allegations against Chasmore "from his owne expressions."

Massachusetts did arrest Chasmore. But while the party was passing through Providence on its way to Boston, a group of local men, supported by an emergency Providence town meeting, liberated Chasmore who, however, agreed to stand trial in Newport in March 1657. Williams not only stepped down from the bench to prosecute Chasmore, but he also accused Chasmore's liberators and even threatened to send them to England for punishment by Oliver Cromwell's government. When no one was willing to testify for the prosecution in any of these cases, everyone went free. The Puritan horror of bestiality had finally encountered a stronger force in New England, the determination not to let the testimony of Indians condemn a white man to death. Williams understood those odds, which is no doubt why he tried Chasmore "upon a Comon fame of Buggarie" and not for the act itself, but the jury acquitted him anyway. No Indians testified in the case, but for the first time in New England records there is more than a hint that in at least one town, bestiality did not destroy a man's standing in his community.[67]

In the same year, 1657, the Massachusetts Court of Assistants not only dismissed the charge of bestiality that Ruben Cuppie made against Richard Pitfold but also whipped Cuppie for an irresponsible allegation that could have threatened the life of another. But in 1674 Massachusetts hanged Benjamin Goad of Roxbury, the seventeen-year-old son of godly parents, who was caught buggering a mare in an open field in the early afternoon of a sunny day. Goad did not fit the profile of an irresponsible and unattached servant, and the jury hesitated before convicting him, asking the bench to decide whether an initial admission and only one witness provided sufficient evidence to hang him. Others must also have thought that the penalty was too severe. "You pity his Youth and tender years," replied Samuel

Danforth in the only published New England sermon that focused specifically on bestiality, "but I pray pity the holy Law of God, which is shamefully violated; pity the glorious name of God, which is horribly profaned; pity the Land, which is fearfully polluted and defiled." Goad, he added, "was extremely addicted to Sloth and Idleness" and "lived in Disobedience to his Parents; in Lying, Stealing, Sabbath breaking, and was wont to flee away from Catechism." Yet the critics made their point in a quieter way. Goad became the last New England colonist to hang for bestiality.[68]

BESTIALITY AND WITCHCRAFT

In England, confessing witches often described their relations with the devil as acts of bestiality. In New England, Cotton Mather explained William Potter's lifelong bestiality as a form of Satanic possession. How close was the connection between bestiality and witchcraft? We have other clues.

Between 1642 and 1662 New England executed six men for bestiality. During nearly the same years, these colonies hanged thirteen women and two men for witchcraft. The bestiality trials began when the population of single servants was at its peak, but the witchcraft trials only started a few years later, when the region finally had enough postmenopausal women, who were always the prime suspects in New England, to attract a significant number of accusations. Nine of the executions (seven women and two of their husbands) were in Connecticut, four in Massachusetts, and two in New Haven. Hartford had a severe witch panic in 1662–63 when eleven people were tried, of whom four were executed and two escaped. The willingness of the courts to execute witches faltered when some people were convicted who simply did not match the stereotype of what a witch should be. In Massachusetts the deputies outvoted the magistrates to insist on the execution of Ann Hibben, a magistrate's widow, in 1656. The Hartford trials placed Judith Varlet, the niece of Peter Stuyvesant, in peril of her life, although she did survive. Between 1663 and the Salem outbreak in 1692, only one person was executed for witchcraft in New England—Goody Glover in Boston in 1688. During the same three decades, Benjamin Goad was the only man executed for bestiality.[69]

On the eve of the Salem trials, the totals stood at about two to one: sixteen executions for witchcraft (fourteen women and two men), and seven men for bestiality. The Salem outbreak was truly bizarre. There the testimony of lowly orphan girls acquired more credibility than that of respected church members, such as Rebecca Nurse and Mary Easty. No one who confessed was ever hanged, but all of those who were hanged insisted they were innocent. Had the Salem frenzy not occurred, the parallels between the earlier witch and bestiality prosecutions probably would have emerged long ago. Salem has diminished the significance of all of the early witch trials. But after Salem, no one else was executed for witchcraft in New England.[70]

After Benjamin Goad, no one else was executed for bestiality in colonial New England. Plymouth convicted Thomas Saddeler in 1681 but only had him whipped. In Maine, Benjamin Preble "utterly disownes" what the court called "a scandelous report ariseing from some publique fame of Buggery." But "severall evidences have been taken, although the treuth lyes darke & undiscovered, relating either to the Accusers or accused." The court let the matter drop. In Massachusetts, when John Barrett of Chelmsford was accused in 1674, the Middlesex County Court merely admonished him and never sent him to Boston for trial. Petty juries refused to convict Jack, a black "servant" in 1676, or John Lawrence of Sudbury a year later. Grand juries refused to indict Samuel Bayley of Weymouth in 1683 and Jonathan Gardiner of Roxbury in 1685. As Judge Samuel Sewall noted, there was only one witness against Gardiner. Thirty years later when a cow "brought forth a calf, which had so much of a human visage as to make the attentive spectators apprehensive that the poor animal had been impregnated by a beastly Negro," Cotton Mather did not launch a grim hunt for the human perpetrator. Instead he wrote up a description of the "monster" for the enlightenment of the Royal Society in London.[71]

In Connecticut a petty jury tried Simon Drake for buggering a cow in 1674 but found the accusation not "legally proved" although there was "great Ground of Suspition." The court released him. A year later a grand jury refused to indict John Sherwood of "some sodimeticall practices." Three later cases show that things had changed decisively. In 1697 John Arnoll (or Arnold) of Fairfield was caught in the act of buggering a mare by Phillip Lewis. Lewis reprimanded him and then returned with a friend, to whom Arnoll confessed that he was "very sorrowfull" for what he had done. Thirty years earlier this testimony would have satisfied the two-witness rule, and Arnoll would have hanged. Even though legal authorities were notified, he was not even brought to trial.[72]

In 1713 two interlocking Connecticut trials showed some of the ways that settlers linked bestiality and witchcraft in their own minds. While walking into the woods in Colchester one July day, Bethiah Taylor came upon Joseph Chapman copulating with a cow, "but she being afraid for her own Life dare not call to him but went immediatly . . . to Deacon Samuel Loomis" and asked his advice. He had little to offer, and when Chapman also showed up, she went home. Two or three weeks later Chapman came to her house, told her that he had been expecting a court summons upon her complaint, and threatened to sue her to protect his name if he was not brought to trial. One suspects that Taylor, having got nowhere talking with the deacon, had consulted her own friends. The story was spreading, probably among local women, and Chapman hoped he could bluff her into silence. But instead the authorities came to arrest him, and he fled and had to be pursued and captured.

Then, in a pretrial deposition, eighteen-year-old John Brown testified that two years earlier he had heard Goodwife Taylor call the wife of Thomas Brown (probably a relative of John) a witch who had turned herself into a cat to torment the Taylor children. Brown, no doubt, hoped to discredit Taylor's testimony. Someone who cried "Witch!" might also accuse a man of buggery. But Jonathan Lisburn, a fifty-year-old man, testified that three years earlier, in 1710, he had come upon Brown, then fifteen years old, buggering a mare. The "Sight being So amazing i did not Know what to doe wharfore i whent unto naibor pumry for advise," he reported. Pomeroy hesitated and then advised him to consult with a clergyman and "to discors with John to See if he colde no waiy Be made Senciable of his Sin." Bestiality was becoming forgivable. Lisburn took this advice and talked with the local minister and with Brown. When he asked Brown why he did such a thing, Brown replied "that he did not Know what was the mater he thought that he was Beweched . . . " In other words Chapman's defender was himself a buggerer willing to accuse others of witchcraft. Brown also escaped for a time, but the court clamped both men in irons, convicted them, and had them shamed on the gallows and whipped, but not hanged. Goody Taylor's testimony held up. In a Puritan society that offered no legal protection for personal confessions to a clergyman, even the minister was forced to testify in court about what Lisburn and Brown had told him.

In 1710 Brown had been detected in the act by a man, who kept the matter private among the two of them, a trusted neighbor, and a minister. Nobody alerted the legal authorities. In 1713 Chapman was interrupted by a woman, who also went first to a prominent member of the local church, but then the news got out, probably through the female gossip network, as in Virginia a year earlier. At a distance of nearly three centuries, we have to wonder how much Chapman and Brown knew about each other's buggery. Had it become, as in parts of England a century before, something that older boys showed to younger ones?[73]

By 1713 the double standard of sexual behavior had reasserted itself throughout the region. It had been in some jeopardy in the Puritan era, when courts had sometimes punished men more severely than women for the same act of fornication, and when quite a few men had pleaded guilty to sexual offenses and accepted their punishment. After 1700, almost without exception, men would not plead guilty to any sexual offense except making love to their own wives before their wedding day. Some husbands, just to avoid a small fine, pleaded not guilty to that charge as well, even though that plea left their wives, who had recently given birth, open to acute embarrassment. Juries nearly always sided with the men, not the women. As the 1713 bestiality convictions indicate, the double standard now extended to that crime as well. Brown and Chapman tried to protect each other.[74]

Benjamin Goad was hanged in 1674. Metacom's (King Philip's) War broke out in 1675, and New England spent most of the next four decades at war with neighboring Indians and, after 1689, New France. The massive mobilization of men for these wars created an ethic of male bonding powerful enough to overcome the disgust and loathing that the previous generation had felt for sodomy and bestiality. When men live together for a long time without women, some of them will turn to one another for sexual gratification.

No doubt some will also turn to the animal population. After 1713 occasional accusations of bestiality turn up in the court records of the New England colonies, but they simply reinforce the pattern already in place by 1713. When James Warren saw Gershom Thomas having sex with a heifer on a Sunday morning in 1746, Thomas's friends urged Warren to keep the matter private and even offered to pay him. When Mary Corey awoke one morning in 1743 and heard her husband Seth copulating with his bitch, she fled to a neighbor's house, while Seth sought out his brother as a mediator and, perhaps in contrition, executed the dog. Confronted by Joseph Hebard, who was probably Mary's father, Seth confessed that "I am a Deavl." Hebard "advised him to go Into some hole or Corner and Cast himself on ye Earth Before God and Beg of God that he would Brake his hart and humble him." The case went before a magistrate but never came to trial. Between 1713 and the Revolution, only two cases that I know of were actually tried. A Connecticut prosecution ended in acquittal in 1770 when three jurors outlasted the nine who favored conviction. A year later, when several people watched drunken John Sennet, a married New Hampshire man, bugger a mare on Boston Common, "in the Face of the Sun, in its Meridian Lustre," he was convicted only of attempted buggery in March 1772, was humiliated on the gallows, and whipped. In this area, as in so many others, New England looked a lot more like old England in the eighteenth century than it still resembled the city upon a hill once envisioned by John Winthrop.[75]

BESTIALITY, WITCHCRAFT, AND FORGIVENESS

Bestiality discredited men in the way that witchcraft discredited women. At least in New England, both began as unforgivable crimes that were becoming forgivable by the end of the seventeenth century. No one was executed for bestiality after Benjamin Goad in 1674. During the Salem witch trials, no one who confessed was executed. All nineteen of those hanged insisted they were innocent. In the eyes of the court, they remained unrepentant. But when Mary Lacey, Jr., confessed in court in July 1692 that she had actually worshipped Satan, a magistrate reassured her that "you may yet be delivered if god give you repentance." "I hope he will," she replied. She survived.[76] In all likelihood, acts of sodomy and bestiality were much rarer in New England than in other mainland colonies. Yet New England prosecuted both offenses, and witchcraft, far more vigorously than the other colonies except New Netherland with its singular horror of male sodomy.

Within New England, bestiality stigmatized young men, mostly teenagers, with the spectacular exception of sixty-year-old William Potter in New Haven. The panic of the early 1640s involved mostly male servants who had no relatives in New England. (The exception was Thomas Granger in Plymouth Colony, and even he was living in someone else's household.) After the mid-1640s, the accused were much more likely to come from respectable households, and the passion for executing them began to diminish. The offense usually involved an actual transgression against a real animal, except in the New Haven pig cases when deformed piglets provided the only tangible evidence.

Witchcraft, by contrast, stigmatized mostly older women, often grandmothers. When men were the accusers, the typical offenders were women past menopause, some of whom had acquired title to property and had no male heirs. When women were the primary accusers, as at Hartford in 1662–63 and Salem in 1692, elderly women remained the primary suspects, but more of them were church members with no lack of male heirs. And more men were accused, some of whom, such as Rev. George Burroughs, had acquired a reputation for abusing their wives and children. An accusation of witchcraft, unlike one of bestiality, usually did not involve a specific act. The crime was more in the imagination of the victim than in the deeds of the accused. Once spectral evidence became all but sufficient for conviction, the accused were left with no effective defense. Nobody could prove that her spectre had *not* tormented somebody.[77]

In the early American bestiality cases, women—who seldom spent time in the fields or forests—appear quite disproportionately as accusers. This pattern suggests that the double standard of sexual propriety probably protected most men from accusations by other men most of the time. Men must have witnessed this offense far more often than women, but they hardly ever pursued the matter into a court of law. Harry Negro's accusers in West Jersey were all women. At least one woman was involved in the Virginia cases of 1644 and 1712. A South Carolina woman testified against John Dixon. Even though Francis Oldfield finally brought Dixon before a magistrate, he agonized for months before taking that step. In New England the record does not indicate who denounced Thomas Granger in Plymouth, Benjamin Goad in Massachusetts, or Aaron Starke in Connecticut. God, or the piglets, denounced George Spencer and put Thomas Hogg's life in peril, while John Nubery denounced himself. But in the cases that have left adequate information about the accusers, women played an outsized role in New England as well. Only Walter Robinson of New Haven, denounced by a sailor, and John Arnoll of Connecticut were prosecuted by men. William Hatchet of Massachusetts, William Potter of New Haven, and Joseph Chapman of Connecticut were all turned in by women. The Chapman case, by exposing John Brown's earlier act of buggery, gives us a clear glimpse of men shielding other men from the law while also trying to reform the malefactor. Quite possibly, even in New England, the double standard operated effectively most of the time for most men when the offense involved sodomy or bestiality. Rather more slowly, men began to apply it once again to fornication as well.

The legal system offers indirect evidence for this hypothesis. Magistrates belonged to the social and cultural elite. Jurors were often ordinary farmers. All six men sentenced to death for sodomy in the seventeenth century—one in Virginia in 1624, three in New Netherland, and two in New Haven—were condemned without a jury trial. The only colonial jury known to have condemned anyone to die for this offense gave its verdict in Pennsylvania in 1748. By contrast, New England juries were willing to convict young men of bestiality at least until 1674. After 1674 no one was executed for bestiality in New England before the Revolution and only two men in New Jersey. If male sodomy was indeed more common than bestiality, this pattern suggests that ordinary men in New England found buggery a much more loathsome offense—until the accused turned out to be the son of a friend or acquaintance.

Another striking pattern was the inability of contemporaries to see animals as victims in bestiality cases. In insisting on penetration as a defining element of the crime, the courts allowed legal custom to override Scripture. But in destroying the animals involved in this offense, they allowed Scripture to override their own better sensibilities. In 1641 the Massachusetts Body of Liberties explicitly prohibited "any Tirrany or Crueltie towards any bruite Creature which are usuallie kept for mans use," and Quaker West New Jersey exempted animals from judicial forfeiture after a crime unless they were inherently dangerous. Yet courts in both colonies condemned animals to death after someone had buggered them. No one in the colonies took the initiative to intercede on behalf of such a victim the way a French convent and parish priest did in 1750 to prevent a court at Vanvres from condemning a she-ass to death. They bore "witness that she is in word and deed and in all her habits of life a most honest creature" who must have been an unwilling participant in the crime. The court agreed and set the animal free.[78]

EPILOGUE

In August 1799, a century and a quarter after the execution of Benjamin Goad, the Connecticut Superior Court condemned Gideon Washburn of Litchfield to hang for acts of bestiality committed over a five-year period with two cows, two mares, and a heifer. In October Washburn petitioned the legislature for a pardon or a postponement of the execution, which was scheduled to take place on his eighty-third birthday. He protested his inno-cence but also complained that the jury had violated the Puritan two-witness rule. Of the four witnesses against him, "*three* of them [had testified] each to *one* fact, and the other to *three* several facts, that no *two* witnesses testified of any *one* fact." Washburn's memory, but not his morals, harkened back to the Puritan era when the biblical two-witness rule had been en-forced. But under English common law, which was already beginning to prevail at the time of his birth, one witness was sufficient in a capital crime (except treason) if the jury found the testimony credible. Washburn's peti-tion provoked a furious debate. The original manuscript has orders and counterorders written all over the reverse side. The lower house voted to comply with his request for a pardon, but the upper house would agree to no more than a postponement until January 1800. Instead, he died in prison a few days before the scheduled hanging.[79]

Washburn was almost the prototype of the dirty old man, and yet people had obviously known about his inclinations for years before anybody brought his actions to the attention of the Superior Court. He became, I suspect, the victim of a Federalist political panic. Britain's Royal Navy, after the massive 1797 mutinies at Spithead and the Nore, resumed executions for sodomy as part of its campaign to root out radicalism. Federalist New England, which had just seen the first publication of John Winthrop's *Journal* by Noah Webster in 1790, went on a frenzy against the "Bavarian Illuminati" in the late 1790s. Their subversive activities, several prominent men warned, were undermining the morals of America. Washburn's lonely sexual acts, which had once seemed pathetic, suddenly became dangerous in the most solidly

Federalist state in the Union. In 1812, in a similar case in strongly Federalist Seneca County, New York, William Moulton, a fifty-eight-year-old veteran of the Revolutionary War and a prominent Democratic-Republican, was accused of buggering a bitch, which then delivered a litter of puppies that "had large heads, no hair on them nor tails, and on the side of their head they had small ears." Moulton denied the charge, which may have been no more than a political smear, although the depositions do convey a sense of both surprise and outrage. Whatever the result of the trial, Moulton lived through the ordeal.[80]

Occasional bestiality trials have occurred in the United States since then. In Reconstruction Virginia a black teenager, Austin Robertson, was sentenced to a year in the penitentiary for buggering a heifer, but that conviction was overturned on the grounds that penetration had not been proved and was probably impossible because Robertson was too short. As late as the 1950s, an Indiana man was convicted of bestiality with a chicken. He appealed on the grounds that a chicken was not a beast under Indiana law. The court agreed with him but upheld his conviction for sodomy.[81] Bestiality has never again become the abomination and obsession that it was, briefly, for seventeenth-century New Englanders.

NOTES

This paper was prepared for a joint meeting of the Shelby Cullom Davis Center and the Philadelphia (now McNeil) Center for Early American Studies, held at Princeton University, January 16, 1998. The author wishes to thank William Chester Jordan for his persistent encouragement of the project, Mary Fissell for her thoughtful formal commentary, and the numerous participants for their many helpful suggestions.

1. In this paper, unless otherwise indicated, I use "sodomy" to describe sexual relations between men, and "buggery" to mean relations between men and animals, even though actual usage, then and now, was and is much looser.

2. All biblical citations are to the "Authorized" or King James version.

3. Jonas Liliequist, "Peasants against Nature: Crossing the Boundaries between Man and Animal in Seventeenth- and Eighteenth-Century Sweden," *Focaal*, no. 13 (1990): 28–54, esp. pp. 29, 50 n. 5. This essay is the most thoughtful discussion of bestiality in the early modern era that I have seen. My thanks to James Serpell for calling it to my attention and for giving me a copy.

4. Simon Schama, *The Embarrassment of Riches: An Interpretation of Dutch Culture in the Golden Age* (New York: Knopf, 1987), pp. 601–6.

5. Keith Thomas, *Man and the Natural World: Changing Attitudes in England 1500–1800* (London: Allen Lane, 1983), p. 119; J. A. Sharpe, *Crime in Early Modern England, 1550–1750* (London: Longman, 1984), pp. 49, 54; J. S. Cockburn, "The Nature and Incidence of Crime in England, 1559–1625," in *Crime in England, 1550–1800,* ed. J. S. Cockburn (Princeton, N.J.: Princeton University Press, 1977), p. 58; J. M. Beattie, *Crime and the Courts in England, 1660–1800* (Princeton, N.J.: Princeton University Press, 1986), p. 432; Frank McLynn, *Crime and Punishment in Eighteenth-Century England* (London: Routledge, 1989), pp. 283–85. The four London executions grew out of concerted campaigns to shut down "molly houses," or homosexual brothels. See Randolph Trumbach, "London," in *Queen Sites: Gay Urban Histories Since 1600,* ed. David Higgs (London: Routledge, 1999), pp. 91, 95.

6. Thomas, *Man and the Natural World,* p. 98.

7. See, for example, the opinion of Rev. Charles Chauncy, 1642, in William Bradford, *Of Plymouth Plantation, 1620–1647,* ed. Samuel Eliot Morison (New York: Knopf, 1959), p. 410; Jim Sharpe, "The Devil in East Anglia: The Matthew Hopkins Trials Reconsidered," in *Witchcraft in Early Modern History: Studies in Culture and Belief,* ed. Jonathan Barry, Marianne Hester, and Gareth Roberts (Cambridge: Cambridge University Press, 1996), pp. 237–54.

8. George Francis Dow, ed., *Records and Files of the Quarterly Courts of Essex County* [Massachusetts], vol. 1: *1636–1656* (Salem, Mass.: The Essex Institute, 1911), p. 44 (the quotation is from Dow's summary of the case); Nathaniel B. Shurtleff and David Pulsifer, eds., *Records of the Colony of New Plymouth in New England,* 12 vols. (Boston: William White, 1855–61), 2:137. For a thoughtful discussion of both cases, see Richard Godbeer, "'The Cry of Sodom': Discourse, Intercourse, and Desire in Colonial New England," *William and Mary Quarterly,* 3d ser., 52 (1995): 268.

9. I recall seeing the accusation of female bestiality over twenty years ago in the manuscript records of the Court of General Sessions of the Peace for Suffolk County, Massachusetts, for somewhere around 1702. If I ever took a note on the case, I cannot now find it.

10. Henry Clay Reed, "Chapters in a History of Crime and Punishment in New Jersey" (Ph.D. diss., Princeton University, 1939), p. 462.

11. Liliequist, "Peasants against Nature," esp. pp. 33–39; trial of John Ferris, June 30, 1657, Records of New Haven Colony: General Court, May 1653 to Dec. 1664, pp. 145–46 (Connecticut State Library, Hartford).

12. See Winthrop D. Jordan, *White over Black: American Attitudes toward the Negro, 1550–1812* (Chapel Hill: University of North Carolina Press,

1968), pp. 28–32. For example, Willem Kieft, the director general of New Netherland, accused Everardus Bogardus, the Dutch Reformed minister of New Amsterdam, of committing a crime for declaring in a public sermon "that in Africa, in consequence of the excessive heat, different animals copulate together, whereby many monsters are generated. But in this temperate climate you [the preacher] knew not, you said, whence these monsters of men proceeded. They are the mighty but they ought to be made unmighty, who have many fathers. . . . " Even "Children," Kieft concluded, "can tell to whom you hereby allude." Kenneth Scott and Kenn Stryker-Rodda, eds., A. J. F. Van Laer, trans., *New York Historical Manuscripts: Dutch,* vol. 4: *Council Minutes, 1638–1649* (Baltimore: Genealogical Publishing Co., 1974), pp. 295–96. My thanks to Evan Haefeli for retrieving this citation for me.

13. See especially E. William Monter, *Witchcraft in France and Switzerland: The Borderlands during the Reformation* (Ithaca, N.Y.: Cornell University Press, 1976); Monter, "La sodomie à l'Epoque moderne en Suisse romande," *Annales: Economies—Sociétés—Civilisations* 29 (1974): 1023–33; and Bengt Ankarloo, "Sweden: The Mass Burnings (1668–1676)," in *Early Modern European Witchcraft: Centres and Peripheries,* ed. Bengt Ankarloo and Gustav Henningsen (Oxford: Clarendon Press, 1993), pp. 285–317.

14. J. H. Huizinga, *Dutch Civilisation in the Seventeenth Century and Other Essays* (New York: Harper and Row, 1969), pp. 59–60.

15. Liliequist, "Peasants against Nature," esp. pp. 39–40, 45–46. The dairy industry was just as highly gendered in England as in Sweden, but the skills that it required may have been a more powerful shaping factor than fear of bestiality. See Deborah Valenze, "The Art of Women and the Business of Men: Women's Work and the Dairy Industry c. 1740–1840," *Past and Present,* no. 130 (February 1991): 142–69. My thanks to Mary Fissell for this suggestion.

16. Ankarloo, "Sweden: The Mass Burnings (1668–1676)," and E. William Monter, "Scandinavian Witchcraft in Anglo-American Perspective," in Ankarloo and Henningsen, *Early Modern European Witchcraft,* pp. 285–317, 425–34.

17. Philip L. Barbour, ed., *The Complete Works of Captain John Smith (1580–1631),* vol. 2 (Chapel Hill: University of North Carolina Press, 1986), p. 387.

18. Jonathan Troup Journal, October 26 and 29, 1789, MS 2070, Department of Archives and Special Collections, University of Aberdeen, Scotland; [British] *House of Commons: Accounts and Papers* (1839), vol. 37, p. 708. My thanks to Roderick A. McDonald for calling these sources to my attention and for sending me copies of them. For the Dutch case, see the trial of

Juan Anthonij, black slave of Anna Sophia de Windt, widow of Dirk de Windt, Curaçao, August 23, 1792, Algemeen Rijksarchief, Staten-Generael 5814, The Hague. My thanks to Willem Klooster for sending me this case.

19. See generally Richard S. Dunn, *Sugar and Slaves: The Rise of the Planter Class in the English West Indies, 1624–1713* (Chapel Hill: University of North Carolina Press, 1972).

20. For the demography of the early Chesapeake colonies, see especially Edmund S. Morgan, *American Slavery, American Freedom: The Ordeal of Colonial Virginia* (New York: Norton, 1975), and the essays in Thad W. Tate and David L. Ammerman, eds., *The Chesapeake in the Seventeenth Century: Essays on Anglo-American Society* (Chapel Hill: University of North Carolina Press, 1979). For New England, perhaps the single most influential study has been Philip J. Greven, *Four Generations: Population, Land, and Family in Colonial Andover, Massachusetts* (Ithaca, N.Y.: Cornell University Press, 1970).

21. H. R. McIlwaine, ed., *Minutes of the Council and General Court of Colonial Virginia*, 2d ed. (Richmond: Virginia State Library, 1979), pp. 34, 42, 47, 81, 83, 85, 93 (emphasis in original). The first deposition (p. 34) gives Couse's age as twenty-nine, but all the other evidence treats him as a boy. Either the original clerk made a mistake, or the editor misread the manuscript. None of the official records mentions a jury, but they are incomplete.

22. Ibid., p. 53; Surry County, Orders, Deeds, Wills, 1645–1672 (transcript), pp. 18–19, 156, 162, Library of Virginia, Richmond. I have read nearly all of the surviving lower court trial records for seventeenth-century Maryland, published and unpublished, and the first two volumes of the published records of the Provincial Court, which tried cases involving the death penalty. No sodomy or bestiality cases appear in any of them, or in the index to the next ten volumes of the records of the Provincial Court (into the 1680s).

23. Susie M. Ames, ed., *County Court Records of Accomack-Northampton, Virginia, 1640–1645* (Charlottesville: University Press of Virginia, 1973), pp. 371–73, 376.

24. Lancaster County Court: Orders, etc., vol. 5 (1702–13), pp. 205–8, Library of Virginia, Richmond. My thanks to J. Jefferson Looney of the Library of Virginia for sending me photocopies of the depositions in this case. Kathleen M. Brown, *Good Wives, Nasty Wenches, and Anxious Patriarchs: Gender, Race, and Power in Colonial Virginia* (Chapel Hill: University of North Carolina Press, 1996), p. 301, first brought this case to my attention.

25. Augusta County, Order Book VIII, p. 97, Library of Virginia, Richmond. My thanks to Zbigniev Mazur for calling this case to my attention and providing me with a photocopy of the record.

26. William S. Price, Jr., et al., eds., *North Carolina Higher Court Minutes, 1709–1723* (Raleigh: The North Carolina State Department of Cultural

Resources, 1974), pp. 164–67, 173. Clark disappears from the court records after 1718, unless he was the John Clark, no longer "Esq." (i.e., no longer a justice) who was chosen to a jury in 1724 but who paid a fine rather than serve. Either reading suggests a man in disgrace. Robert J. Cain et al., eds., *North Carolina Higher Court Minutes, 1724–1730* (Raleigh: Department of Cultural Resources, Division of Archives and History, 1981), pp. 60, 65. These volumes are in *The Colonial Records of North Carolina,* 2d ser., vols. 5 and 6.

27. Ibid., 6:48–49, 92.

28. Donna J. Spindel, *Crime and Society in North Carolina, 1663–1776* (Baton Rouge: Louisiana State University Press, 1989), p. 51. In an e-mail exchange, Professor Spindel told me that she believes that she would have reported the results if these cases had actually been tried. But she did not check all of her notes to be certain.

29. Thomas Nairne to the earl of Sunderland, Charleston, S.C., October 16, 1708, and related depositions, petitions, and certificates, in Sunderland Collection, Box 1 (1704–10), Henry E. Huntington Library, San Marino, California. My thanks to Steven C. Bullock for sending me copies of his notes on these documents. For Dixon's later career, see W. L. McDowell, ed., *Journals of the Commissioners of the Indian Trade, September 20, 1710– August 29, 1718,* in *Colonial Records of South Carolina* (Columbia: South Carolina Archives Department, 1955), pp. 5, 7, 50, 51, 57, 59. See also Richard L. Haan, "'The Trade Do's not Flourish as Formerly': The Ecological Origins of the Yamasee War of 1715," *Ethnohistory* 28 (1981): 341–58.

30. Scott and Stryker-Rodda, *New York Historical Manuscripts: Dutch,* 4:326–28.

31. Charles T. Gehring and William A. Starna, eds., *A Journey into Mohawk and Oneida Country, 1634–1635: The Journal of Harmen Meyndertsz van den Bogaert* (Syracuse, N.Y.: Syracuse University Press, 1988), pp. xxii–xxiii. My thanks to Evan Haefeli for bringing this incident to my attention.

32. Edmund Bailey O'Callaghan, ed., *Calendar of Historical Manuscripts in the Office of the Secretary of State, Albany, N.Y.,* pt. 1: *Dutch Manuscripts, 1630–1664* (Albany, N.Y.: Weed, Parsons and Company, 1865), pp. 211, 213.

33. Court of General Quarter Sessions, Burlington County, Minute Book, 1739/40–1763, pp. 40, 41; MS Collection 36, Box C, New Jersey Archives, Trenton, contains the undated indictment. My thanks to Jean R. Soderlund, who came upon this case in her own research and passed this material along to me. Douglas Greenberg, in his *Crime and Law Enforcement in the Colony of New York, 1691–1776* (Ithaca, N.Y.: Cornell University Press, 1974), tabulated and computerized all known criminal offenses in provincial New York. He mentions no sodomy or bestiality trials.

34. Aaron Leaming and Jacob Spicer, eds., *The Grants, Concessions, and Original Constitutions of the Province of New Jersey, the Acts Passed during the Proprietary Governments, and other material Transactions before the Surrender thereof to Queen Anne* (1752), 2d ed. (Somerville, N.J.: Honeyman & Company, 1881), p. 404; Staughton George et al., eds., *Charter to William Penn, and Laws of the Province of Pennsylvania, Passed between the Years 1682 and 1700* (Harrisburg, Pa.: Lane S. Hart, State Printer, 1879), p. 110.

35. James T. Mitchell and Henry Flanders, eds., *The Statutes at Large of Pennsylvania from 1682 to 1801,* 18 vols. (Harrisburg, Pa.: Clarence M. Busch, State Printer, 1896–1908), 2:8, 183–84, 3:202.

36. According to J. Thomas Scharf and Thompson Westcott in their *History of Philadelphia, 1609–1884,* vol. 3 (Philadelphia: L. H. Everts and Company, 1884), p. 1827, White and Arthur Maginnis were both hanged in Philadelphia for sodomy in 1748. Such a double execution, if it was a punishment for a consensual sexual relationship between men, was probably a unique event in the history of the mainland colonies. I, at least, have encountered no others. But in all likelihood, it never happened. One Alexander Urie was executed in 1748 for murdering "Arthur McGinnes." Scharf and Westcott, apparently drawing on records of the Walnut Street Prison, probably conflated White's sodomy trial with the murder of Maginnis. No other evidence survives for White's trial or execution. My thanks to Susan Klepp for the Scharf-Westcott citation and for good advice about "unnatural vice" in eighteenth-century Pennsylvania, and to Jack D. Marietta (e-mail to the author, June 26, 1998) for the Urie-McGinnes case.

37. I do not know whether "buggery" in this case meant sodomy or bestiality. See Negley K. Teeters, "Public Executions in Pennsylvania, 1682 to 1834, with Annotated Lists of Persons Executed; and of Delays, Pardons, and Reprieves of Persons Sentenced to Death in Pennsylvania, 1682 to 1834," *Journal of the Lancaster County Historical Society* 64 (1960): 149. My thanks to Louis P. Masur for bringing this list to my attention. It is incomplete, however. Of the fifty-four executions listed in Scharf and Westcott, *History of Philadelphia,* 3:1826–27, fifteen are not on the Teeters list of ninety-four executions through 1775. Susan Klepp informs me that five men were convicted of "unnatural vice" between 1779 and 1815. Francis S. Fox has kindly sent me a copy of preliminary proceedings begun against Daniel Hughes for buggering a calf in Northampton County, Pennsylvania, on July 5, 1780, but apparently he never came to trial. Northampton County, Miscellaneous Papers, Box 1, August 10, 1780, in Fox to author, February 28, 1998.

38. Randall H. Balmer, *A Perfect Babble of Confusion: Dutch Religion and English Culture in the Middle Colonies* (New York: Oxford University Press,

1989), pp. 110–22. Balmer's most important source for this encounter is Joseph Anthony Loux, ed., *Boel's "Complaint" against Frelinghuisen* (Rensselaer, N.Y.: Hamilton Printing Co. for the Reformed Church Historical Society, 1979), which Princeton's Firestone Library does not have.

39. George Vaux, ed., "Extracts from the Diary of Hannah Callender," *Pennsylvania Magazine of History and Biography* 12 (1888): 436. At the time of Callender's visit, the college had no president. Jonathan Edwards had died in 1758. Samuel Davies, the Virginia revivalist, would not replace him until some months after Callender's visit of February 1759. With little adult supervision, some students may have been displaying affection for one another more openly than Callender thought seemly. My thanks to Brendan McConville for bringing this source to my attention.

40. Linda K. Salvucci, "James Gibson," in Ruth L. Woodward and Wesley Frank Craven, *Princetonians, 1784–1790: A Biographical Dictionary* (Princeton, N.J.: Princeton University Press, 1991), pp. 188–89; Journal of James Gibson, 1786, which is bound with Journal of "Leander" (Mifflin), Historical Society of Pennsylvania, microfilm copy at Princeton University Library; Journal of John R. Smith, 1786, Library of Congress, photocopy at Princeton University Library.

41. Preston W. Edsall, ed., *Journal of the Courts of Common Right and Chancery of East New Jersey, 1683–1702* (Philadelphia: American Legal History Society, 1937), p. 234; Dorothy Lapp, ed., *Records of the Courts of Chester County, Pennsylvania*, vol. 2 (Danboro, Pa.: R. T. Williams, 1972), pp. 143–44.

42. H. Clay Reed and George J. Miller, eds., *The Burlington Court Book: A Record of Quaker Jurisprudence in West New Jersey, 1680–1709* (Washington, D.C.: The American Historical Association, 1944), pp. 142–43, 148.

43. Edsall, *Journals of the Court of Common Right*, p. 285.

44. Leaming and Spicer, *Grants, Concessions, and Original Constitutions of New Jersey*, p. 404.

45. Read and Miller, *Burlington Court Book*, pp. 75–80.

46. Reed, "Crime and Punishment in New Jersey," pp. 461–63. I have not found any statutory basis for these New Jersey prosecutions.

47. Robert F. Oaks, "'Things Fearful to Name': Sodomy and Buggery in Seventeenth-Century New England," *Journal of Social History* 12 (1978–79): 268–81; Roger Thompson, *Sex in Middlesex: Popular Mores in a Massachusetts County, 1649–1699* (Amherst: The University of Massachusetts Press, 1986), esp. pp. 71–82; Thompson, "Attitudes towards Homosexuality in the Seventeenth-Century New England Colonies," *Journal of American Studies* 23 (1989): 40; John Canup, "'The Cry of Sodom Enquired Into': Bestiality and the Wilderness of Human Nature in Seventeenth-Century New England," *American Antiquarian Society, Proceedings* 98 (1988): 113–34. See also Bradley

Chapin, *Criminal Justice in Colonial America, 1606–1660* (Athens: The University of Georgia Press, 1983), which is very useful because it looks at more than New England. By contrast, Jonathan Goldberg, "Bradford's 'Ancient Members' and 'A Case of Buggery . . . Amongst Them,'" in *Nationalities and Sexualities,* ed. Andrew Parker et al. (London: Routledge, 1992), pp. 60–76, adds nothing important to the discussion.

48. Richard S. Dunn, James Savage, and Laetitia Yeandle, eds., *The Journal of John Winthrop, 1630–1649* (Cambridge, Mass.: The Belknap Press of Harvard University Press, 1996), p. 629; J. Hammond Trumbull, ed., *The True-Blue Laws of Connecticut and New-Haven* (Hartford, Conn.: American Publishing Co., 1879), p. 201. By contrast, when two married men and two younger men were caught in what seems to have been competitive masturbation on Long Island in May 1654, the town court of East Hampton, which was nominally under Connecticut's jurisdiction, declared that the offense was not "worthy of loss of life or limb." The magistrates had probably heard of the notorious William Plaine case and did not approve of New Haven's severity. *Records of the Town of East-Hampton, Long Island, Suffolk County, N.Y., with Other Ancient Documents of Historic Value,* vol. 1 (Sag-Harbor, N.Y.: John H. Hunt, 1887), p. 57. The quotation is a summary by the unnamed editor of the volume, who evidently regarded the actual documents as too lurid to publish.

49. Records of New Haven Colony: General Court, May 1653 to Dec. 1664, pp. 89–91, Connecticut State Library, Hartford; M. Halsey Thomas, ed., *The Diary of Samuel Sewall, 1674–1729,* 2 vols. (New York: Farrar, Straus and Giroux, 1973), 2:677, 678 (my thanks to Thomas Foster for informing me of the gender of Mingo's victim); Louis Effingham de Forest, ed., *The Journals and Papers of Seth Pomeroy, Sometime General in the Colonial Service* (New York: Society of Colonial Wars in the State of New York, 1926), p. 106. Thomas Foster has recently found two other eighteenth-century cases in Massachusetts. In 1714 Stephen Ropier was acquitted of sodomizing James Woodword, a boy. In 1740 Stephen Fessenden, a teacher, was acquitted of attempted sodomy with Thomas Brinley, a thirteen-year-old student. See Foster, "Locating Sodomy in Eighteenth-Century Massachusetts," paper presented at the Conference on Sexuality in Early America, sponsored by the Omohundro Institute of Early American History and Culture and the McNeil Center for Early American Studies, Philadelphia, June 1–3, 2001.

50. "Francis Higgeson's Journal," in *The Founding of Massachusetts,* ed. Stewart Mitchell (Boston: Massachusetts Historical Society, 1930), p. 71.

51. Franklin Bowditch Dexter, ed., *New Haven Town Records, 1649–1662* (New Haven, Conn.: New Haven Colony Historical Society, 1917), pp.

178–79. Because the boys are named in the record, the ages of at least some of them could probably be determined, but I have not tried to do that research. On the New Haven system of justice, which I have described elsewhere as inquisitorial rather than adversarial, see Gail Sussman Marcus, "'Due Execution of the Generall Rules of Righteousnesse': Criminal Procedure in New Haven Town and Colony, 1638–1658," and John M. Murrin, "Magistrates, Sinners, and a Precarious Liberty: Trial by Jury in Seventeenth-Century New England," in *Saints and Revolutionaries: Essays on Early American History,* ed. David Hall, John M. Murrin, and Thad W. Tate (New York: Norton, 1984), pp. 99–137, 152–206, esp. pp. 170–82.

52. Godbeer, "'The Cry of Sodom,'" pp. 259–86, esp. p. 283 (quotation). This outstanding essay also contains a list of all known sodomy prosecutions in colonial New England at pp. 285–86. Godbeer is mistaken about Sension's sentence, however, when he claims that he was not even whipped and was merely bound to good behavior (p. 260). See Norbert B. Lacy, "The Records of the Court of Assistants of Connecticut, 1665–1701," vol. 1 (M.A. thesis, Yale University, 1937), pp. 67–69. I have used the copy in the Connecticut State Library, Hartford.

53. Godbeer, "'The Cry of Sodom,'" pp. 277–79.

54. Samuel Danforth, *The Cry of Sodom Enqvired into; Upon Occasion of the Arraignment and Condemnation of Benjamin Goad, for his Prodigious Villany. Together with a Solemn Exhortation to Tremble at Gods Judgements, and to Abandon Youthful Lusts* (Cambridge, Mass.: Marmaduke Johnson, 1674), p. 8.

55. Virginia DeJohn Anderson, *New England's Generation: The Great Migration and the Formation of Society and Culture in the Seventeenth Century* (New York: Cambridge University Press, 1991), p. 223.

56. *Records of the Particular Court of Connecticut, 1639–1663* (Hartford: Connecticut Historical Society, 1928), pp. 3, 4, 13, 20; J. Hammond Trumbull, *The Public Records of the Colony of Connecticut,* 15 vols. (Hartford: Brown & Parsons, 1850–90), 1:77.

57. Winthrop, *Journal,* pp. 342–43, 374–76; Nathaniel B. Shurtleff, ed., *Records of the Governor and Company of the Massachusetts Bay in New England, 1628–1686,* 5 vols. in 6 (Boston: William White, 1853–54), 1:344; John Noble and John F. Cronin, eds., *Records of the Court of Assistants of the Colony of the Massachusetts Bay, 1630–1692,* 3 vols. (Boston: Suffolk County, 1901–28), 2:121.

58. Bradford, *Of Plymouth Plantation, 1620–1647,* pp. 320–22, 316–17. As Bradford makes clear, Governor Bellingham of Massachusetts had written him about the Hatchet case and other troublesome questions just before the Granger case arose.

59. Charles J. Hoadly, ed., *Records of the Colony and Plantation of New Haven, from 1638 to 1649* (Hartford, Conn.: Case, Tiffany, and Company, 1857), pp. 62–73.

60. Ibid., pp. 295–96. Hogg was successfully reabsorbed into the community. He was standing watch for the colony by 1648, took the standard oath of submission to the colony in 1654, and died insolvent, a ward of the town, sometime before the March 12, 1686, session of the New Haven County Court. Ibid., pp. 378, 140; New Haven County Court Records, 1666–1698, p. 159, Connecticut State Library, Hartford. In 1653 when a third monster piglet was born, the whole town of New Haven filed past to see if it resembled anyone in particular. It did not, and no one was accused. Dexter, *New Haven Town Records, 1649–1662*, pp. 158–59.

61. *Records of the Particular Court of Connecticut*, pp. 48, 49; Winthrop, *Journal*, p. 771.

62. Records of New Haven Colony: General Court, May 1653 to December 1654, pp. 85–87, Connecticut State Library, Hartford.

63. Charles J. Hoadly, ed., *Records of the Colony or Jurisdiction of New Haven, from May 1653 to the Union: Together with the New Haven Code of 1656* (Hartford, Conn.: Case, Tiffany, and Company, 1858), pp. 180, 440–43; Cotton Mather, *Pillars of Salt. An History of Some Criminals Executed in this Land; for Capital Crimes. With some of their Dying Speeches; Collected and Published, For the Warning of such as Live in Destructive Courses of Ungodliness . . .* (Boston: B. Green and J. Allen, 1699), reprinted in Daniel E. Williams, ed., *Pillars of Salt: An Anthology of Early American Criminal Narratives* (Madison, Wis.: Madison House, 1993), pp. 67–69.

64. Dexter, *New Haven Town Records, 1649–1662*, pp. 245–46; John Putnam Demos, *Entertaining Satan: Witchcraft and the Culture of Early New England* (New York: Oxford University Press, 1982), p. 403.

65. Franklin B. Dexter, ed., *New Haven Town Records, 1662–1684* (New Haven, Conn.: New Haven Colony Historical Society, 1919), pp. 7–8, 22–23.

66. Thomas Shepard, *The Clear Sun-shine of the Gospel Breaking Forth upon the Indians in New England* (London: R. Cotes for John Bellamy, 1648), in Massachusetts Historical Society, *Collections*, 3d ser., 4 (1834): 40. My thanks to David Silverman for bringing this reference to my attention. Indians were raising livestock by the 1660s. See Virginia DeJohn Anderson, "King Philip's Herds: Indians, Colonists, and the Problem of Livestock in Early New England," *William and Mary Quarterly*, 3d ser., 51 (1994): 601–24.

67. All of the documents in this case are assembled in Bradford Fuller Swan, *The Case of Richard Chasmore alias Long Dick* (Providence: Society of

Colonial Wars in the State of Rhode Island and Providence Plantations, 1944). See pp. 8 and 21 for the quotations. Williams was not reelected to the Court of Trials for the coming year.

68. Noble and Cronig, *Records of the Court of Assistants of Massachusetts Bay,* 3:66–67; 1:10, 14; Thomas, *Diary of Samuel Sewall,* 1:4; Danforth, *Cry of Sodom,* esp. p. 8.

69. Nathaniel J. Sheidley first suggested to me, in a 1992 graduate seminar, that accusing a male of bestiality was the moral equivalent of accusing a woman of witchcraft. For a very useful list of New England witch trials, see Demos, *Entertaining Satan,* pp. 401–9. Demos lumps New Haven and Connecticut together. In my tabulation, the Basset and Knapp trials on p. 403 are included under New Haven. The scattered documentary evidence for the early trials is collected in David D. Hall, ed., *Witch-Hunting in Seventeenth-Century New England: A Documentary History, 1638–1692* (Boston: Northeastern University Press, 1991).

70. The best study of Salem is Bernard Rosenthal, *Salem Story: Reading the Witch Trials of 1692* (New York: Cambridge University Press, 1993).

71. Shurtleff and Pulsifer, *Records of the Colony of New Plymouth,* 6:74; Robert E. Moody, ed., *Province and Court Records of Maine,* vol. 3: *Province of Maine Records, 1680–1692* (Portland: Maine Historical Society, 1947), p. 199; Thompson, *Sex in Middlesex,* p. 73; Noble and Cronin, *Records of the Court of Assistants of Massachusetts Bay,* 1:74, 87–88, 251, 273, 281; Thomas, *Diary of Samuel Sewall,* 1:64; Cotton Mather to the Royal Society, July 3, 1716, in *Selected Letters of Cotton Mather,* ed. Kenneth Silverman (Baton Rouge: Louisiana State University Press, 1971), pp. 209–10.

72. Lacy, "Records of the Court of Assistants of Connecticut," 1:52–53, 60; Connecticut State Archives, Crimes and Misdemeanors, 1662–1789, 1st ser., vol. 1, p. 216, Connecticut State Library, Hartford.

73. For the depositions in this case, see Connecticut State Archives, Crimes and Misdemeanors, 1662–1789, 1st ser., vol. 2, pp. 68–89, Connecticut State Library, Hartford. For the sentence, I am indebted to Cornelia Dayton's notes on the case, which are based on the manuscript records of the Connecticut Superior Court.

74. The best study of the resurrection of the double standard in New England is Cornelia Hughes Dayton, *Women before the Bar: Gender, Law, and Society in Connecticut, 1639–1789* (Chapel Hill: University of North Carolina Press, 1995), esp. pp. 32, 161. Her research is primarily in the records of New Haven colony and county. My own research in the criminal court records of nine New England counties has convinced me that the phenomenon occurred throughout the region. Men stopped pleading guilty to sex-

ual offenses in the decade 1700–1710. Incest was almost the only sexual crime for which a jury would convict a man.

75. Cornelia Dayton has sent me her notes on five more bestiality allegations in New Haven County between 1716 and 1770. See *Rex* v. *Gershom Thomas,* August 1746, New Haven County Superior Court Files; and *Rex* v. *Seth Cory,* 1743, Windham County Superior Court Files, Box 171, both in Connecticut State Archives, Hartford. Only one of the five led to a prosecution. See the account of the split jury in the trial of Thomas Alderman of Simsbury for having sex with a sheep, in *Connecticut Journal,* September 21, 1770. For the Sennet case see *Boston Gazette,* September 2, 1771, and March 16, 1772. My thanks to Jeremy Stern for sending me the Sennet material.

76. Paul Boyer and Stephen Nissenbaum, eds., *The Salem Witchcraft Papers: Verbatim Transcripts of the Legal Documents of the Salem Witchcraft Outbreak of 1692,* vol. 2 (New York: Da Capo Press, 1977), p. 520.

77. Wendel D. Cracker has shown that the Salem court took the ministers' advice and refused to convict on spectral evidence alone. In effect the judges validated spectral evidence by accepting the kind of testimony about *maleficium* that they had been throwing out for thirty years. But cases that involved only spectral evidence did not come to trial. See his "Spectral Evidence, Non-Spectral Acts of Witchcraft, and Confession at Salem in 1692," *Historical Journal* 40 (1997): 331–58.

78. Edmund S. Morgan, ed., *Puritan Political Ideas, 1558–1794* (Indianapolis: Bobbs-Merrill, 1965), p. 197; Leaming and Spicer, *Grants, Concessions, and Original Constitutions of New Jersey,* p. 404; E. P. Evans, *The Criminal Prosecution and Capital Punishment of Animals* (New York: Dutton, 1906), pp. 150–51.

79. Connecticut State Archives, Crimes and Misdemeanors, 2d ser., vol. 2, pp. 87a, 87b, 87c, 88a, Connecticut State Library, Hartford (emphasis in original); Albert E. Van Dusen, ed., *The Public Records of the State of Connecticut,* vol. 9 (Hartford: Connecticut State Library, 1953), pp. 437–38. My thanks to Doron Ben-Atar for unearthing the actual story of Washburn's death.

80. Arthur Gilbert, "Buggery and the British Navy, 1700–1861," *Journal of Social History* 10 (1976): 72–98; Vernon Stauffer, *New England and the Bavarian Illuminati* (New York: Columbia University Press, 1918); John L. Brooke, "Ancient Lodges and Self-Created Societies: Voluntary Association and the Public Sphere in the Early Republic," in *Launching the "Extended Republic": The Federalist Era,* ed. Ronald Hoffman and Peter J. Albert (Charlottesville: University Press of Virginia, 1996), pp. 273–377; Neil Francis Byl, "William Moulton's Endless Revolution: Deep-Sea Mutiny and Frontier Politics in the Early American Republic" (graduate seminar paper,

History Department, Pennsylvania State University, 1997), esp. pp. 34–36. My thanks to William Pencak for sending me a copy of Byl's interesting essay.

81. Secretary of the Commonwealth, Executive Papers, Box 16, December 16–31, 1870, December 29 packet, Library of Virginia, Richmond. My thanks to Diane Sommerville for giving me copies of these documents. Gary Rowe showed me the Indiana case on the Internet.

6

Guardian Spirits or Demonic Pets
The Concept of the Witch's Familiar in Early Modern England, 1530–1712

James A. Serpell

The image of the witch was made up of different elements, some of which, like the peculiarly
English belief in animal familiars, remain largely unaccounted for.
—*Keith Thomas,* Religion and the Decline of Magic *(1971)*

On February 25, 1582, Thomas Rabbet, the eight-year-old, illegitimate son
of Ursula (Ursley) Kemp, a widow of St. Osyth in Essex, testified before
Brian Darcy, J.P., that his mother kept four spirits:

> . . . the one called Tyffin, the other Tyttey, the third Pygine, and the
> fourth Jacke: and being asked of what colours they were, saith that
> Tyttey is like a little grey cat, Tyffin is like a white lambe, Pygine is
> black like a toad, and Jacke is black like a cat. And hee saith, hee hath
> seen his mother at times to give them beere to drinke, and of a white
> Lofe or Cake to eat, and saith that in the night time the said spirites
> will come to his mother, and sucke blood of her upon her armes and
> other places of her body.

Two local women also came forward and testified that Ursula Kemp had
bewitched their children. Grace Thurlow, who happened to work for Justice
Darcy, claimed that her infant daughter had broken her neck falling out of
a cradle shortly after Thurlow rejected an offer from Kemp to nurse the
child while she went to work. Agnes Letherdale, following a dispute with
Kemp over some scouring sand, believed that the other woman had afflicted
her daughter with a "great swelling in the bottome of the belly, and other
privie partes" that resulted in the child's painful death.

The following day, apparently in response to a false promise of leniency from Darcy, Ursula Kemp confirmed her son's testimony by bursting into tears, falling on her knees, and confessing to the ownership of the same four spirits, "whereof two of them were hees and the other two were shees: the two hee-spirits were to punishe and kill unto death, and the other two shees were to punishe with lameness and other diseases of bodily harme, and also to destroy cattell." She also confessed to sending Tyttey, her cat familiar, to punish Thurlow's wife, and Pygine the toad to kill Letherdale's child, as well as numerous other acts of malefice. In the process, she incriminated a number of other women as coconspirators.

In the end, a total of fourteen women were indicted for witchcraft at St. Osyth, of which at least two, including Ursula Kemp, were hanged. Most of those who were brought to trial were accused of keeping and using familiar spirits that appeared in the likeness of small animals—cats, dogs, ferrets, toads, a lamb, and, in one case, "a red thing like a lion."[1]

Although it has its own distinctive elements, the description of the witches' familiars at St. Osyth is reasonably typical of accounts found throughout the English witch trial literature of the late sixteenth and seventeenth centuries. Although familiars rarely appeared as odd-looking people, the vast majority of those that were described manifested themselves as commonplace animals, usually creatures no bigger than a dog, and often much smaller, in the case of insects such as flies, bees, or moths. Occasionally, the same familiar could appear in a variety of guises. Elizabeth Francis's familiar "Sathan," a key figure in a famous 1566 trial, appeared first "in the likeness of a white spotted cat" but later transformed himself into a toad, and later still into a dog with horns on his head.[2]

Often referred to as "spirits" or "imps," familiars could be acquired from a variety of sources. Many were represented as gifts of the Devil, given in return for a promise of allegiance. Others, like "Sathan," were obtained from other witches, or passed around and shared between groups of witches, like some kind of useful household implement. Frequently, they just appeared out of nowhere, like stray cats, offering their services and demanding to be fed. Familiars also acquired a variety of interesting names, many suggestive of pet names. Sometimes these names were bestowed by the witches themselves, but in other cases the Devil assigned a name, or the familiar chose its own name. When communicating with its mistress on such matters, the familiar was occasionally said to speak "in a hollow voice."

In the overwhelming majority of trials, especially those in the south of England and the Home Counties, the familiar was represented as a relatively autonomous being whose function was to serve as the witch's magical agent or emissary in the performance of acts of *maleficium*; that is, harming other people, their livestock, or property by supernatural means. In return

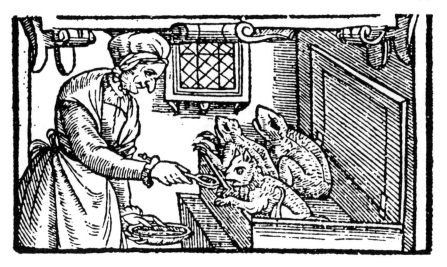

1. A witch keeping her familiars in a box and feeding them. From *A rehearsall both straung and true . . . at winsore . . . 1579.*

for these services, witches provided their familiars with shelter, often in boxes or pots lined with wool (see figure 1), and food—occasionally milk, oats, bread, cheese, cake or other scraps, but more usually blood sucked from reddish spots or swellings on the witch's own body. In many cases, teams of women were delegated the task of stripping and searching the accused for such telltale marks. During the peak of the English witch persecutions in the mid-seventeenth century, the quest for this kind of circumstantial evidence of the existence of familiars became an almost mandatory part of the judicial process.[3]

The origin of this "peculiarly English belief" in familiars is obscure. In his 1933 study, *Witchcraft and Demonianism,* C. L'Estrange Ewen conjectured that the idea originated in the pet-keeping habits of socially isolated women: "Scorned and shunned by their neighbours, the unhappy women were more inclined to make friends with animals as cat or dog, or more unusual pet, as chicken, ferret, rat, or toad. No doubt they were often heard talking to their favourites, and on the principle that birds of a feather flock together, the animals soon came to be looked upon as devils or familiars by the ignorant demonophobes."[4] In *Religion and the Decline of Magic,* Keith Thomas also acknowledged that many of these apparent familiars were probably companion animals, perhaps even "the only friends these lonely old women possessed."[5] Later, he went on to suggest that the identification of unconventional pets as witches' familiars was an example of the early modern propensity to regard pet-keeping itself as morally suspect because, like bestiality, it tended to blur the boundaries between animal and human.[6]

Although superficially plausible, these ideas linking belief in familiars with the phenomenon of pet-keeping raise a number of problematical questions; among them the fact that familiars are largely absent from all but a very few of the voluminous Continental narratives on the subject of witchcraft.[7] By 1566, the date of the first well-documented trial in England, periodic outbreaks of witch persecution had already been in progress for well over a century on the Continent of Europe. Yet it is difficult to find a single unequivocal reference to familiars of the English type in all of the Continental literature pertaining to witchcraft.[8] This is not to say, however, that animals played an insignificant part in Continental depictions of witchcraft. The Devil was widely reputed to appear to his disciples in the shape of an animal, usually a monstrous dog, cat, goat, or ram, and witches on the Continent made a habit of riding or flying to their Sabbats on the backs of demons disguised as animals (as well as on pitchforks and broomsticks) (figure 2). Continental witches were also credited with shape-shifting, the ability to transform both themselves and others into animals when occasion demanded (figure 3).[9] Two of these manifestations—the Devil appearing in animal form, and various instances of shape-shifting by witches—also made occasional appearances in the English trials.[10] But, despite the fact that England was unlikely to have had a monopoly on either pet-keeping or lonely old women, the notion of pet-like demons or spirits running malevolent errands in the guise of small animals seems to have gained little acceptance on the Continent, at least within official circles.

The possibility that the familiar was purely a product of the English judiciary's attempts to create a home-grown, legal definition of witchcraft also seems unlikely. Although a series of acts against witchcraft, conjuration, and sorcery were passed during the reigns of Henry VIII and Elizabeth I, none of the relevant legal statutes mentions anything resembling a familiar until the 1604 Act of James I, when it became a felony, punishable by death, to "consult, covenant with, entertain, employ, feed, or reward any evil and wicked Spirit, to or for any intent or purpose."[11] Familiars, however, appeared regularly in trial evidence and confessions from 1566 onward, so the concept was clearly well established in the popular imagination long before it acquired formal, legal recognition. Perhaps, as Keith Thomas implies, the English judiciary harbored more negative attitudes to pet-keeping than their Continental counterparts, and were therefore more likely to emphasize evidence of this nature. But if so, some explanation needs to be found for this peculiar cultural difference in judicial sensitivities.

2. A witches' Sabbat, with a witch shown riding on a demon in the form of a goat (Hans Balding Grien, Strasbourg, 1514).

3. Witches transforming into animals on their way to a Sabbat. From Ulrich Molitor, *Von den Unholden und Hexen* (Constance, 1489).

THE EVIDENCE

To address some of these questions, the present study examined the evidence concerning familiars as it is represented in both judicial and popular accounts of the period from 1530 to 1712, the earliest and latest dates for which familiars are recorded in trial evidence. For quantitative analyses, the study makes use of a computerized database containing contemporary accounts and official records of 322 English witch trials involving animal-related evidence. These data were obtained primarily from three comprehensive secondary sources—C. L'Estrange Ewen's two surveys of 1929 and 1933, and Macfarlane's 1970 study of the Essex witch trials[12]—with additional reference to primary source materials, mainly chapbooks or pamphlets, whenever appropriate. For each case, the year of the trial, the name and gender of the accused person, the geographical location, and the species, types, and names of the animals involved is recorded (if known), together with other relevant details of the case. The temporal distribution of these cases is illustrated in figure 4. Although there were many more witch-craft cases in England during this period than are represented here, the peaks and troughs in the frequency distribution closely parallel those ob-tained by Macfarlane for the temporal frequency of witchcraft indictments in the county of Essex.[13] Trials involving evidence of familiars are therefore not atypical, at least in terms of their temporal distribution. The compar-ison with Essex does, however, suggest that animal-related evidence was overrepresented in the 1645–46 prosecutions brought by the self-styled witch finders, Matthew Hopkins and John Stearne. As various authorities have pointed out, the extraordinary number of prosecutions initiated by Hopkins and Stearne, and the extreme methods they used for finding evi-dence and extracting confessions, have given them a unique position in the annals of English witch persecution.[14] For this reason, the material obtained from these trials is treated separately in the discussion that follows.

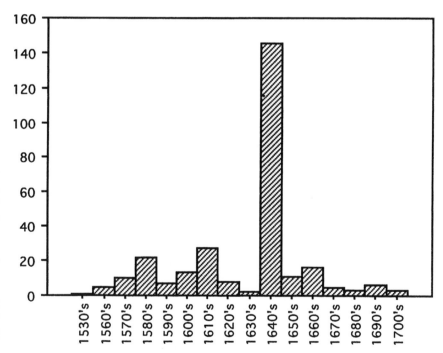

4. Distribution by decade of 322 witchcraft cases involving evidence of familiars or other "animal" manifestations. The peak during the 1640s is mainly due to the activities of the witch finders Matthew Hopkins and John Stearne.

Because of the sketchy nature of most of the assize records, it is virtually impossible to obtain an accurate estimate of the proportion of English witch trials that actually included evidence of the use of familiars, although Ewen's 1933 study, based on reasonably detailed depositions and testimonies, generates a figure of 60 percent (270 out of 450 cases), of which roughly half were brought by Hopkins and Stearne. The material contained in chapbooks or pamphlets—contemporary "eyewitness" accounts of witchcraft prosecutions whose titles suggest that they were written for the sensation-loving London literary market—tends to give an even higher figure. Macfarlane went to some pains to test the reliability of the pamphlets pertaining to the Essex trials by comparing them with appropriate assize records. On the basis of this he concluded that pamphlets were "a vital and reliable source, providing otherwise inaccessible material and correcting the somewhat narrow impression of witchcraft prosecutions provided by indictments."[15] Of the five pamphlets referred to by Macfarlane, all contain extensive references to witches' familiars.

DEMONIC PETS

The *Oxford English Dictionary* defines a pet as "any animal that is domesticated or tamed and kept as a favourite, or treated with indulgence and fondness." To what extent did the witches' familiars of the sixteenth and seventeenth centuries come close to fitting this definition? The practice of keeping animals purely for fun or companionship was certainly not unknown among the common people of England during this period. In his 1646 diatribe against the activities of Matthew Hopkins, the Rev. John Gaule, vicar of Great Staughton in Huntingdon, clearly alluded to pet-keeping among elderly women when he lamented that "Every old woman with a wrinkled face, a furred brow, a hairy lip, a gobber tooth, a squint eye, a squeaking voice, or a scolding tongue, having a rugged coat on her back, a skull cap on her head, a spindle in her hand, and a dog or cat by her side, is not only suspected, but pronounced for a witch."[16] Thomas Ady, another articulate critic of the witch craze, used the widespread existence of pet-keeping as grounds for dismissing testimonies concerning the keeping and feeding of so-called imps:

. . . for it is lawful to keep a Rat, or Mouse, or Dormouse, or any Creature tame, as to keep a tame Rabbit, or Bird; and one may be an Imp as well as another, and so may a Flea or Louse by the same reason; and so the Devil need not go far for a bodily shape to appear in, or to suck mens or womens flesh in; and if these were material Oathes, who

then may not be proved a Witch? and yet there was an honest woman
(so always formerly reputed) executed in *Cambridge* in the year 1645.
for keeping a tame Frogge in a Box for sport and Phantasie, which
Phantasie of keeping things tame of several species is both lawful and
common among very innocent and harmless people, as Mice, Dormice,
Grashoppers, Caterpillers, Snakes; yea a Gentleman, to please his Phantasie in trying conclusions, did once keep in a Box a Maggot that came
out of a Nut, till it grew to an incredible bigness.[17]

Some particularly well-known pets acquired reputations as familiars within
their own lifetimes. A white poodle called "Boye" belonging to Charles I's
flamboyant nephew, Prince Rupert, provides a much publicized case in point.
The prince used to sit Boye on the table beside him in Council meetings, as well
as kissing the dog from time to time during debates. During the Civil War,
Boye became a sort of Royalist mascot, a lucky charm who bounded along
beside the dashing young prince as he rode at the head of the Royalist army.
Among the Puritan Roundheads, Boye was viewed as the unnatural embodi-
ment of Royalist success, and soon rumors began to circulate that the dog was
a familiar with supernatural powers.[18] In a satirical pamphlet published in
1643, an unnamed Royalist writer played up to these Protestant superstitions
by attributing all sorts of occult powers to Boye, including prophesy, invisibil-
ity, the ability to find lost goods, the gift of tongues, and the capacity to render
himself and his master impenetrable to weapons.[19] Another good-humored pamphlet published in London in the same year used the device of a fictional
dialogue between Boye and an oafish Roundhead dog called Pepper to lampoon
the Protestant cause.[20] Unfortunately for the Royalists, the joke backfired the
following year when Boye was shot and killed at the battle of Marston Moor, a
landmark defeat for the Royalists, and a turning point of the war (figure 5). To
celebrate, an anonymous Puritan writer penned an extravagant work of doggerel
entitled *A Dog's Elegy or Rupert's Tears,* in which it was claimed that Boye was
killed by a "Valiant Souldier, who had skill in Necromancy":

> Sad Cavaliers, Rupert invites you all
> That doe survive, to his Dogs Funerall.
> Close-mourners are the Witch, Pope, & devill,
> That much lament yo'r later befallen evill.
>
> Lament poor Cavaliers, cry, howl and yelp
> For the great losse of your Malignant Whelp,
> Hee's dead! Hee's dead! No more alas can he
> Protect your Dammes, or get Victorie.[21]

DOGS ELEGY,
17

OR

RVPERT'S TEARS,

For the late Defeat given him at *Marston-*
moore, neer *York*, by the Three Renowned
Generalls; *Alexander Earl of* Leven, *Generall of the Scottish*
Forces, Fardinando *Lord* Fairefax, *and the Earle of* Man-
chefter *Generalls of the* English *Forces in the North.*

Where his beloved Dog, named *B O Y*, was killed by a Val-
liant Souldier, who had skill in *Necromancy.*

Likewise the strange breed of this Shagg'd Cavalier, *whelp'd of a Malignant*
Water-witch; *With all his Tricks, and Feats.*

Sad Cavaliers, *Rupert* invites you all ⎫ Close-mourners are the Witch, Pope,&devill,
That doe survive, to his Dogs Funerall. ⎭ That much lament yo'r late befallen evill.

Printed at *London*, for *G. B.* July 27. 1644.

5. *Dog's Elegy or Rupert's Tears.*

Attributing occult powers to famous pets was not, however, confined to England. According to a contemporary legend that survived for many centuries after his death, Cornelius Agrippa von Nettesheim (1486–1535), the eminent German astrologer, philosopher, and scholar, derived all of his occult knowledge from a dog called "Monsieur" who wore a collar decorated with magic symbols. When Agrippa lay dying, he is said to have removed the collar with the words: "depart, unhappy beast, the cause of eternal damnation"—at which Monsieur fled and drowned himself in the Saône.[22] In reality, according to Agrippa's own pupil, Johann Weyer, Monsieur was a thoroughly ordinary dog. "I cannot stop wondering" he wrote in 1563,

> . . . how people of high esteem can talk and write such unadulterated foolishness, unless it be just mean and empty blabber. I knew that black dog very well when I was in Bonn. It was a dog of moderate size and his name was *Monsieur*; quite frequently when Agrippa was out walking, I would accompany him leading the dog on a rope. It was a common, human dog and his master provided him with a companion, a bitch of the same colour and stature; he acquired her while I was there and gave her the name of *Mademoiselle*. As I see it, the cause for all this insane gossip was Agrippa's almost childish love for that dog, which is quite usual with some people.[23]

FAMILIAR TAXONOMY

Although familiars occurred in a variety of different forms, the range of species represented was limited, and may provide further clues concerning the origins of the concept. Analysis of trial evidence reveals that the largest single descriptive category of familiars is "Nondescript"; that is, cases where the familiars are simply not described (see figure 6). A typical example would be the 1645 trial of John Chambers in the village of Bramford in Suffolk in which the defendant eventually confessed to receiving three imps from the Devil, and using them to kill a bullock, a horse, and a child. No description of the familiars is offered, although we are told that two of their names were "Richard" and "John."[24] The most obvious explanation for this preponderance of undescribed familiars is that the courts' aggressive pursuit of evidence concerning familiars led some witnesses and defendants to fabricate evidence where none was otherwise forthcoming. Child testimonies often provided some of the more fanciful accounts.[25] The young son of Ellen Smythe, who was executed for witchcraft in 1579, testified that his mother kept three nondescript spirits: "Great Dicke, enclosed in a glass bottle:

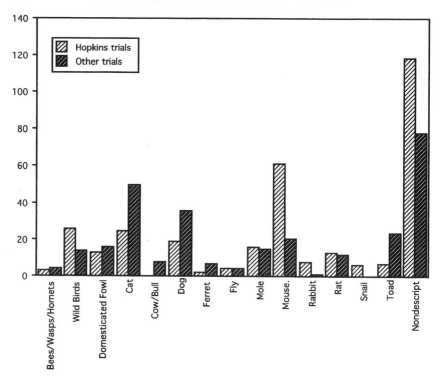

6. Frequency with which different "animals" are represented in trial evidence for the period 1530–1705. (Categories represented fewer then six times in total are omitted.)

Little Dicke in a leather bottle: and Willet in a wool pack."[26] When the bottles and pack were located and examined, however, "the spirits were vanished away."

The relative overrepresentation of nondescript familiars in the Hopkins and Stearne trials is also to be expected, given the evident zeal with which the witch finders gathered evidence of the possession and use of familiars. Although the use of physical torture as a means of extracting confessions from witchcraft suspects was not permitted under English common law, various forms of psychological coercion were widely employed. In addition to the frequent practice of "swimming" witches (if they sank, they were innocent), Hopkins is known to have employed sleep deprivation or "walking" as a means of wearing suspects down, and inducing them to confess. One of Francis Hutchinson's informants in the early eighteenth century stated that Hopkins and Stearne arrested a poor woman in Suffolk, and, by keeping her fasting and without sleep, induced her to confess that she had an imp called Nan. Concerned neighbors eventually drove the witch finders away, gave her something to eat, and allowed her to sleep. Afterwards she couldn't remember what she had confessed to, and said that the only thing she sometimes called Nan was one of her chickens. The unfortunate Parson Lowes of Brandeston in Suffolk, who confessed in 1645 to suckling three undescribed familiars, and sending them to sink a ship, was also, according to Hutchinson's sources, kept awake by running him backwards and forwards across the room until he was out of breath; "thus they did for several days and nights together, till he was weary of his life, and was scarce sensible of what he said or did."[27]

If "nondescript" familiars can be discounted, mice form the second largest category of imps, followed, in descending order, by cats, dogs, toads, wild birds, poultry, moles, and rats. As is evident from table 1, however, marked differences existed between the Hopkins and Stearne trials and the rest. In particular, mice and wild birds are overrepresented in the former, while cats, dogs, and toads are underrepresented.

Notwithstanding one commentator's claim that keeping tame rats and mice was common practice in seventeenth-century England,[28] the unusually high frequency of mice in the Hopkins trials may again be attributable to the unorthodox methods the witch finders employed to obtain evidence against those accused of witchcraft. Hopkins and Stearne made extensive use of "watching," a procedure that involved assigning people to observe the accused person throughout the day and night while incarcerated or under house arrest awaiting trial. The assumption behind this practice was that sooner or later the suspect would be visited by one or more hungry familiars seeking nourishment. No doubt mice and rats were the ubiquitous inhabitants of early modern jails and cottages, so it is unlikely that the "watchers" needed to wait long before seeing a rodent scuttling across the floor towards the accused. Thomas Ady, writing in 1655, considered evidence of rats or mice appearing or creeping under someone's clothes inadmissible for this reason: "foolish and senseless arguments, not grounded in the Word of God."[29] Unfortunately, the witch finders thought otherwise. A woman called Margaret Bayts of Framlingham in Suffolk was apparently incriminated by this method in August 1645. According to the account of her trial, she "was seen during a watching to be sucked by a thing in the likeness of a mouse that ran under her coats."[30] Similarly, a pamphlet from the same year records how the Devil appeared to Joan Williford of Faversham in Kent, initially in the shape of a little dog called "Bunne," but that he later reappeared to her twice in prison, and sucked her in the form of a mouse.[31] The practice of watching suspects in damp jails may also, perhaps, help to account for John Bysack's bizarre confession in 1645 that he had suckled six snail familiars named "Sydrake," "Jeffry," "Peter," "Ayleward," "Sacar," and "Pyman" for a period of twenty years.[32]

Livestock animals, apart from chickens, are conspicuous for their absence in trial accounts. Although "cows" occur at a low frequency in table 1, their presence can be wholly explained by a single case involving the dubious testimony of a child. In 1582, seven-year-old Agnes Dowsing testified that her mother, Annis Herd of Little Oakley in Essex, had "a box with six spirits like cows, as big as rats, with short horns that lie upon a bed of black and white wool." She then went on to say that her mother had given her a black and white cow called "Crowe," and her brother a red and white cow called "Donne," and that they were fed on straw and hay, and provided with water and beer to drink.[33] Happily, her mother was acquitted. This dearth of livestock is scarcely surprising. Identifying farm animals as familiars would have had the undesirable effect of potentially incriminating most of the farmers in England.

The removal of undescribed familiars from the original data set, together with most of the mice and rats, leaves us with an array of species more consistent with the *Oxford English Dictionary*'s definition of a pet. Cats and dogs now predominate numerically, followed by wild birds, toads, chickens, and moles. According to Keith Thomas, dogs, cats, and cage-birds were the most popular companion animals in the early modern period, just as they are to this day,[34] and chickens may also have been objects of affection, given that they were kept chiefly for their eggs rather than their meat. But what of moles and toads? Its burrowing habits, and prodigious appetite for worms and other invertebrates, renders the mole a difficult and unrewarding pet, to say the least. So its moderately frequent appearance as a familiar requires some other interpretation; perhaps related to superstitions deriving from the mole's earthy, subterranean affinity with graves, corpses, bodily corruption, and so on.[35]

The same may also be said of toads,[36] although toads are readily tamed, and were sometimes kept as pets. In a letter to Thomas Pennant dated June 18, 1768, the Rev. Gilbert White relates an anecdote concerning some ladies "of peculiar taste" who "took a fancy to a toad, which they nourished summer after summer, for many years, until he grew to a monstrous size, with the maggots which turn to flesh flies. The reptile used to come forth every evening from an hole under the garden-steps; and was taken up, after supper, on the table to be fed."[37] Pennant evidently responded with an account of a Devonshire household that kept a toad as a family pet for thirty-six years, despite local prejudices against these animals.[38]

TOADS, UGLY AND VENOMOUS

In addition to its companionable characteristics, a wealth of literature suggests that the toad occupied a special place in ideas concerning witchcraft and traditional healing throughout Europe during this period. Toad's blood and other secretions, together with henbane, belladonna, thorn apple, mandrake, and other "witch herbs," were among the staple ingredients of the proverbial witches' brews, potions, love philters, and hallucinogenic "flying ointments" supposedly concocted by witches and sorcerers during the Middle Ages.[39] Toads were also used to kill people.

According to one fourteenth-century chronicler, a sorceress in the employment of Queen Eleanor of Aquitaine sent vampire toads to suck the blood of Henry II's mistress, the Fair Rosamund.[40] In his *Materials towards a History of Witchcraft,* Henry Lea describes a case from Soissons in France in 1460, when someone called Yves Favins was approached by a poor woman who gave him a toad that she had been keeping in a pot. She then tells him "to baptize it and feed it on a consecrated wafer, which he did, giving it the name of John," following which the toad was killed and used to murder an entire family.[41] Jean Bodin in 1580 also makes passing reference to the practice of keeping toads in pots which he regarded as a suspicious circumstance, but not sufficient grounds for condemnation to death.[42] The diabolical association between toads and the consecrated Host resurfaced in the Normandy witch trials of the late sixteenth and early seventeenth centuries. Here, the typical victims of prosecution were male shepherds, and their magical spells were commonly thought to involve the use of toads and toad venom, together with fragments of stolen Eucharist.[43]

Toads featured prominently in some famous witchcraft prosecutions from the Basque region of France and Spain. The witches of Labourd in 1609 confessed to baptizing toads at their Sabbats, and dressing them in red or black velvet, with bells around their necks and feet. Witches danced with their toads, it was claimed, and children were given the task of tending entire crèches of toads while their owners attended the Sabbat. At Zugarramurdi in 1610 the witches confessed to receiving toads from the Devil as a sort of rite of initiation. The toads accompanied the witches to their meetings, and also provided them with a source of deadly poison. Ingredients for the witches' "flying ointment" were collected by whipping the toad with a switch until it swelled up, and took on a poisonous color. It was then squeezed under the witch's left foot until "excrement burst out of it at both ends." The resulting greenish-black fluid was carefully preserved in little bowls, and used as a salve.[44]

In Shakespeare's day, the association between toads, poison brews, and witchcraft was evidently common knowledge:

Toad, that under cold stone,
Days and nights hast thirty-one
Swelter'd venom sleeping got,
Boil thou first i' the charmed pot.[45]

In addition to numerous references to toad imps or familiars, evidence for the occult use of toads in England can be found in the *Examination* of the self-confessed Dorsetshire cunning man, John Walsh, who claimed in 1566 that witches keep toads which they give names to, and train to come when called: "Which Todes being called, the Witches strike with two withie Sperres on both sydes of y head, and saith to the Spirit their Pater Noster backward. . . . And when he is stricken, they commaunde the Tode to hurt such a man or woman as he would have hurted. Whereto if he swell, he will goo wher he is apointed. . . . "[46]

Like the later Basque testimonies, the account has a ring of authenticity to it, insofar as the description of toads swelling or puffing themselves up when struck on the head is entirely consistent with the defensive behavior of real toads. Further confirmation may perhaps be derived from a curious story published anonymously in the *Gentleman's Magazine* of 1832 concerning William Harvey, Charles I's personal physician, who is reputed to have investigated a local witch on the borders of Newmarket Heath in Suffolk. Claiming to be a wizard himself, Harvey gained the woman's confidence, and asked to see her familiar, whereupon she made a chuckling sound, and summoned a toad out from under a chest which she then fed from a saucer of milk.[47] Intrigued, Harvey persuaded the woman to leave her home on an errand, and, as soon as she was off the premises, seized the poor toad and summarily dissected it, thereby establishing that it in "no ways differed from other toades."[48]

The basis for much of this medieval and early modern toad lore probably lies in the pharmacological characteristics of toads and their by-products. The skin and glandular secretions of toads (genus: *Bufo*) have been the subject of a surprisingly extensive ethnopharmacological and biochemical literature, stemming largely from the notion that some of these substances have hallucinogenic properties that have been exploited for shamanistic purposes by Central and South American cultures since pre-Columbian times.[49] The topic also gained particular notoriety during the 1960s, 1970s, and 1980s following tabloid press reports of episodes of "toad licking" and "toad smoking" among America's recreational drug users. In response to these rumors, the Food and Drug Administration included bufotenine, a minor constituent of toad venom, in Schedule 1 of the Controlled Substances Act in 1967,[50] while possession of the species *Bufo marinus* became a criminal offense in the United States, subject to the same sanctions as possession of heroin and crack cocaine.[51] Ironically, and notwithstanding official belief in the societal hazards posed by illicit toad use, it appears that bufotenine has no mind-altering properties, and that the skin and glandular secretions of the majority of *Bufo* species, including *Bufo marinus* and the common toad of Europe, *Bufo bufo,* contain no hallucinogenic or psychedelic compounds. The only known exception to this rule is *Bufo alvarius,* the Sonoran desert toad, which secretes an extremely psychoactive derivative of bufotenine (5–MeO-DMT) that induces vivid hallucinations when smoked.[52]

Although bufotenine does not induce hallucinations, it does, along with several other compounds in toad skin, such as bufagenins and bufatoxins, exert powerful pharmacological effects on the heart and blood vessels, and on the peripheral vascular and nervous systems. These effects, comparable to those of the drug digitalis, are highly toxic, and can induce heart failure in humans and other animals at high doses. Medications based on toad venom have also a long history of use in Europe and Asia for the treatment of a wide variety of ailments including dropsy, heart failure, and nose bleeds, and as diuretics, expectorants, local anesthetics, and aphrodisiacs. Bufotenine and related compounds are also known to have antibacterial and antifungal properties.[53]

Toads are known to synthesize and make use of these biochemical agents as protection against predators and infections, actively secreting them from the paratoid glands on either side of the head when threatened or irritated. Medieval and early modern herbalists and cunning folk were evidently aware of the toxic and medicinal properties of these substances, and knew how to obtain them by striking toads with sticks until they puffed themselves up and exuded venom.

This common substrate of European toad lore does not, of course, exclude the possibility that some toad familiars were no more than pets, but it does suggest that toads in general belong in a separate category from cats, dogs, and birds, even if they were sometimes "treated with indulgence and fondness."

FAMILIAR (AND LESS FAMILIAR) NAMES

As Claude Lévi-Strauss once suggested, the kinds of names people give to animals are often an expression of their relation to human society.[54] As objects of economic production, cows and other livestock animals tend to be given descriptive, impersonal names. Pets, on the contrary, tend to acquire either personal "pet" names, or human names and nicknames. Many of the familiars described in witch trial records and pamphlets had names (see table 1) that may provide clues to the relationships that existed between them and their owners.

The earliest of these named familiars was "Sathan," the superannuated cat of Elizabeth Francis of Hatfield Peverill in Essex who was tried for witchcraft in 1566. According to her testimony, she acquired the familiar from her grandmother who urged her to "give her blood to Sathan (as she termed it), which she delivered her in the likeness of a white spotted cat." Elizabeth Francis made use of Sathan for sixteen years, according to her own confession, for the performance of various acts of malefice, before passing him on to another woman called Agnes Waterhouse whom he continued to serve for a further fifteen years. During this second period, his mistress kept him in a pot of wool but, "being moved by poverty" to use the wool, she prayed "in the name of the Father and of the Son and of the Holy Ghost that it would turn into a toad, and forthwith it was turned into a toad, and so [she] kept it in the pot without wool." Later still, according to the testimony of Agnes's daughter, Joan Waterhouse, Sathan also began appearing "in the likeness of an ill-favoured dog with horns on his head."[55]

Apart from a few notable exceptions, such as Rutterkin or Mamillion, subsequent familiars were rather less versatile than Sathan, and generally more prosaically named. As illustrated in the table under "Other Trials," most familiars tended to be given either standard (for the period) animal names, such as Pusse, Gibb, or Ball, or a reasonably consistent range of "diminutives": Jack, John, Bunne, Tibb, Minny, Will, Tom, Dick, Harry, Robin, Bess, Nan, and so on. Chicken familiars, like Lévi-Strauss's cows, were generally given either descriptive names—White, Blew, Calico—or imitative names that resembled the clucking of hens. In short, if toads, moles, mice, rats, and nondescript familiars are discounted, we are left with a collection of names that could readily be applied to animal companions.

As always, however, the Hopkins and Stearne trials are exceptional. Hopkins and Stearne displayed particular inventiveness when it came to the names of familiars. Hangman, Holt, Pease, and Germany were, one imagines, unconventional names for cats in the seventeenth century, as were Jarmara, Vinegar Tom, and Elimanzer for dogs, or Joweare and Naturall for mice. In his own 1647 account of the Essex witchcraft discoveries at Manningtree, Hopkins uses the exotic sounding names of the witches' familiars as further evidence of diabolical involvement, claiming that "no mortal could invent" names as bizarre as "Elemauzer, Pyewacket, Peck in the Crown, Griezel Greedigut, etc."[56] In fact, the evidence suggests that Hopkins may have invented them himself (see figure 7). According to the record of indictment of Elizabeth Clark of Manningtree, only four familiars were orig-

Table 1. Names Given to Familiars in the English Witch Trials

Hopkins & Stearne Trials	Other Trials
	Cats
Tomboy x 2, Hangman and Jacob, Holt, Newes, Tissy, Mouse, Besse, Pease, Germany	Sathan, Jill, Jenny, Titty, Jack x 2, Robin, Will, Tibb, Katt, Pusse, Gibbe, Puppet (alias Mammet), Giles, Dick, Jude, Bess, Inges, Fillie, Russoll, Bunne, Rutterkin, Mamillion
	Dogs
Jarmara, Vinegar Tom, James, Elimanzer, Pretty x 2, Lilly and Priscill, Grizzel and Greedigut	Sathan, Suckin, Tibb, Minny, Dandy, Ball, Tom, Robin, Dunsott, Bunne, George, Mamillion
	Toads
Richard and John	Sathan, Great Browning and Little Browning, Bonne, Pygine, Tom, Robin, Vizett
	Mice
Tibb, Joan, James, Prickeares x 3, Robin, Bird, Teates, Jack x 2, Rugge, Susan, Jockey; Touch, Pluck and Take, Joweare, John and Naturall; Littleman, Prettyman, and Daynty	Sweat (Sweet?), Rug, John and Robert, Will
	Rats
Tom, Will and Harry	Philip, Catche
	Moles
Tom, Nan, Jack and Will; Margaret, Amie and Susan; Wynowe, Jeso and Panu	Hisse Hisse, Tom, Pygine
	Poultry
Nan; Touch, Pluck and Take; Giles, Alice and Bess; Great Turkey and Little Turkey	Nan, Pluck, Catch, White, Blew (Blue?), Calico, Jack and Hardname
	Wild Birds
Robin, Harrie, Sparrow, Tom, Will x 2, Tibb; Tom, Robert and John	Tewhit (owl)
	Miscellaneous
Sydrake, Jeffrey, Peter, Aylewood, Sacar & Pyman (snails); Anthony and Blackfast, Sacke and Sugar (rabbits); Jake (hog); Frog (frog); Joan (spider); Newes (ferret); Jezebel (woman); Beelzebub and Trullibub (pieces of wood); Meribell, Jesus, Jockey, Sandy, Christ, Mounsier, Collyn, Dick, Tom, Kit, Will, Nan; Jackly and Pybold; Tit, Gray, Tray and Rob; Bess, Nan and Joan; Sis and Kate; Elemauzer, Pyewacket, Griezel, Greedigut, and Peck in the Crown (nondescript)	Bidd (ferret); Fancie (bear); Jack and Jill (frogs); Crowe and Bonne (cows); Grissil, Ball and Jack; Sothrens, Mercurie, Hercules and Jack; Jockey, Jack and Will; Great Dicke, Little Dick and Willet; Nicholas, Ned (nondescript)

Note: A few familiars appear more than once as different animals; "Sathan," for example, appears three times as cat, dog, and toad.

7. Frontispiece of Matthew Hopkins's *The Discovery of Witches* . . . 1647.

inally involved: "Holt" (a young white cat), "Vinegar Tom" (in the likeness of a greyhound), Jeremarye (a sandy-colored spaniel), and "Sacke and Sugar" (a black rabbit).[57] Reference to a white dog familiar called "Elimanzer" appeared in the confession of Ellen Clarke, another accused witch some three weeks later, but the other three names—Pyewacket, Peck in the Crown, and Griezel Greedigut—were published by Hopkins two years after the event when he also added the name of a ferret called "Newes."[58] In Stearne's account of the same trial published in 1648, the spaniel is named "Jermarah" and the cat is named "Lought," while the greyhound, rabbit, and ferret are mentioned but not named.[59] Both of these later accounts also added strange peculiarities to the animals that are not mentioned in the trial records. Hopkins, for example, described Jarmara as being "without any legs at all" whereas Stearne said that it had "legs not so long as a finger." The greyhound was described by Stearne as having "legs as long as a stag," while Hopkins claimed it had "the head of an ox" and that it abruptly transformed itself into the shape of a headless four-year-old child before vanishing at the door.

The witch finders also recycled some of these unlikely names. Mouse familiars called "Prickeares" appeared in three entirely separate Hopkins and Stearne trials, and, while Hopkins refers to "Griezel Greedigut" as the nondescript familiar of one of Elizabeth Clark's cronies in 1645, "Grizzell" and "Greedigut" are later named as the familiars of Jane Wallis of Keyston, Huntingdon, which appeared "in the shape of dogs with great bristles of hog's hair on their backs" in 1646.[60] Hopkins and Stearne were also more likely to find names for their miscellaneous or nondescript familiars—including snails and bits of wood—and these appellations more often had an exotic or fanciful quality.

VAMPIRE PETS

Perhaps the weirdest characteristic of familiars, and the strongest indication that they were other than mere pets, was their habit of drinking or sucking their owners' blood. In the introduction to his 1933 survey, Ewen seems content to give credence to the notion that early modern witches actually allowed their pets to drink their blood: "There is nothing incredible in the fact that human beings trained or permitted animals to suck or lick their blood, much more horrible forms of bestiality are known to the psycho-pathist and the criminal jurisprudent."[61] Such a literal interpretation of the evidence, however, seems unjustified.

An examination of the trial evidence in chronological sequence suggests that the whole idea of the blood-sucking familiar evolved from the older and simpler concept of rewarding, or sealing a pact with, a helpful spirit with a drop of one's own blood. As early as 1510, a teacher called John Steward, who was accused of conjuring spirits for the purpose of detecting buried treasure, denied giving his blood to spirits in the form of bumble bees.[62] John Walsh, the cunning man of Netherbury in Dorset, admitted in 1566 to employing a familiar that appeared to him in the form of either a dog or a pigeon, and which helped him to locate lost or stolen objects. Upon receiving this familiar he gave it "one drop of his blud, whych blud the Sprite did take away upon hys paw."[63] At her trial of the same date, Elizabeth Francis testified to rewarding "Sathan" with a drop of blood every time he did anything for her: "which she gave him by pricking herself, sometime in one place, and then in another, and where she pricked herself there remained a spot which was still to be seen."[64] At another well-publicized trial, of four witches at Windsor in 1579, one was accused of feeding a toad familiar with blood, "which she causeth to issue from her own flank"; another was said to have a black cat familiar called Jill, "and she daily feedeth it with milk, mingled with her own blood"; the third fed a kitten familiar called Jenny with "crumbs of bread and her own blood"; and the fourth fed her rat familiar, Philip, "with blood issuing from her right-hand wrist, the marks whereof evidently remain."[65]

By this stage, it seems to have become normal practice to search the accused for such marks. The jury of the Court Leet at Southampton in 1579 proposed that half a dozen honest matrons be found to strip a suspected witch and determine whether she had "eny bludie marke on hir bodie which is a common token to know all witches by." This, however, points to some confusion with the well-established Continental idea of the "Devil's mark," a special blemish with which Satan marked his disciples, and which could be recognized by its insensitivity to pain and its failure to bleed when pricked.[66]

The first recorded mention of bloodsucking familiars comes from Ursula Kemp's 1582 trial when she confesses to allowing her toad familiar, Pygine, to suck blood from a place on her thigh. From here on, however, the concept became increasingly stereotyped and exaggerated, and the search for bloody marks or spots began to expand to include lumps, boils, hernias, warts, excrescences, supernumerary nipples, or any accessory protuberance on the body that could be construed as the site of a familiar's recent gustatory attentions. The corpse of Alice Samuel, one of the notorious witches of Warboys, executed in 1593, was found to bear a lump of flesh resembling a teat about half an inch long "adjoining to so secret a place which it was not decent to be seen." Undeterred, however, by the constraints of decency, the jailer and his wife "made open show thereof onto divers that stood by. After this, the jailer's wife took the same teat in her hand, and seeming to strain it, there issued out at the first as if it had been beesenings (to use the jailer's word), which is a mixture of yellow milk and water: at the second time there came out in similitude as clear milk, and in the end very blood itself."[67]

Needless to say, these grotesque ideas and practices reached their nadir under the puritanical ministrations of Matthew Hopkins and John Stearne. Most of the witches they brought to trial—women, men and, in one case, a nine-year-old boy—confessed to suckling familiars several times a week from accessory teats, paps, or "bigs" on their bodies, often close to their "secret parts." Usually some form of appropriate blemish was detected following a strip search, but if not, it was simply assumed that the witch had been forewarned, and had cleverly concealed her "teat" from view. After being forced into early retirement by adverse public opinion, John Stearne published a long and tendentious defense of the witch finders' methods which included an extraordinarily detailed, seven-page anatomical guide to the differences between the witch's teat and "natural marks" such as flea bites, warts, wens, moles, rents, and hemorrhoids.[68] Fortunately, this contrived attempt to elevate witch-finding to the level of an exact science found relatively few adherents.

FAMILIARS AS HYBRID CREATURES

Judging from the historical record, the concept of the witch's familiar, as it developed in England during the sixteenth and seventeenth centuries, had complex origins, and cannot easily be explained in terms of a simple theory of misconstrued pet ownership. Rather, it represented a gradual conflation of several different ideas and phenomena, of which pet-keeping was only a component, albeit an important one.

Throughout Europe, a strong association between toads and witchcraft seems to have existed based on the pharmaceutical properties of these animals' secretions. The many descriptions of people nurturing toads, and naming them, suggests that toads may have been husbanded by witches, cunning folk, traditional healers, and so on, as sources of these "medicinal" compounds.

Belief in the spiritual origins of sickness and misfortune also appears to have been prevalent during this period. The tendency of English trial witnesses either to "invent" familiars when no pets were available to incriminate, or to attribute supernatural agency to the chance appearance of rats, mice, birds, snails, or insects in the vicinity of accused persons, reveals a widespread popular superstition regarding the existence of malevolent supernatural beings or "spirits" that assisted or represented witches in their magic, and preferentially adopted the physical form of animals while doing so. The fact that these beings were usually referred to as "imps" (literally "grafts") also indicates some ambiguity in the popular mind concerning whether such creatures existed independently of the witch, or were alien offshoots of her own persona.

Such ideas, according to anthropologists, are nearly universal among "shamanistic" cultures throughout the world.[69] For example, contemporary Mayan peoples living in the Mexican province of Chiapas believe that everybody possesses a "soul animal" (*chanul*) that exists independently of the body, and, in some senses, on a different, supernatural plane, but which is nevertheless indistinguishable from a real animal. These *chanul* are assigned to each person at birth by the celestial powers, and share reciprocally every stroke of fortune that their human counterparts experience. Most illness is thought to be the result of an injury inflicted upon a person's *chanul*, either deliberately by witchcraft, or by another person mistaking one's *chanul* for an ordinary animal and hurting or killing it. The only traditional remedy for such illnesses is to employ the services of a shaman who will use various rituals, and the influence of his own, more powerful soul animals, to discover the source of the affliction and counteract it. According to Mayan folklore, shamans and witches also possess the ability to adopt the material form of their *chanul* in order to gain access to the supernatural realm.[70]

In West Africa, the Banyang people of West Cameroon hold that people have the ability to transform themselves into, or to send out as extensions of themselves, "were-animals" (*babu*) which in this form are possessed of supernatural powers. Although occasional stories are told of people actually experiencing bodily transformations into animals, the Banyang usually speak of the were-animal as having a separate existence, mystically linked to, but materially independent of, the person who "owns" it as an attribute. Were-animals are also capable of performing acts of maleficent magic against other people, and whatever befalls the were-animal also befalls its "owner" wherever he or she happens to be.[71]

Shamanistic concepts such as these are clearly unique to the cultures and contexts in which they evolved, and are not intended to serve as models of European peasant ideology during the fifteenth, sixteenth, or seventeenth centuries. Nevertheless, these examples contain some striking echoes of medieval and early modern ideas related to shape-shifting, parallel injury, and spirits/souls adopting the form of animals, as well as suggesting a similar connection between witchcraft (or shamanism) and the use of an animal "alter ego" as a magical emissary. In the case of the Mayan *chanul*, it also demonstrates the remarkable tenacity of such beliefs, despite the coercive influence of nearly five centuries of Central American Christianization.[72]

Overlaid on this core of traditional beliefs and practices was the increasingly widespread habit of keeping animals such as dogs, cats, songbirds, ferrets, squirrels, hares, and so on, purely for companionship; a practice that was likely to have been more common among the older, less popular, and more antisocial members of rural English society at this time.[73]

Combined together and embellished with the occasional, imaginative fabrication, this coincidence of different historical factors produced a sort of composite or hybrid creature—the "imp" or "familiar"—a malignant, though otherwise commonplace, animal with supernatural powers that depended on the witch for care and nourishment in the same way that a pet is dependent on its owner, or a child is dependent on its parent. The comparison with a child seems particularly apt, since the familiar, as it came to be understood in the seventeenth century, was also a sort of demonic infant; not just dependent on the witch, but actually "nursing" from her in an obscenely distorted inversion of the normal mother-child relationship.[74] This image of the postmenopausal crone giving suck to her demonic animal companion— this grotesque mixing of animal and human categories, reproductive roles, and body fluids—was virtually tailor-made to provoke horror, revulsion, and sanctimonious outrage in the puritanical minds of early modern Englishmen. As many authors have noted, sixteenth- and seventeenth-century Protestants and Puritans were especially eager to suppress the growling of the "beast within,"[75] and any form of intimacy with domestic animals, whether sexual or maternal, was certain to be viewed as profoundly morally degrading, particularly when, in this case, it was combined with other lurid abominations, such as bloodsucking and diabolism.

Explaining the absence, or near absence, of familiars from Continental accounts of witches and their activities is in some ways more difficult. The habit of treating small animals "with indulgence and fondness" may simply have been less prevalent among the lower social orders of Continental Europe, and therefore numerically less likely to attract adverse attention from the authorities. Keith Thomas implies that pet-keeping proliferated more in England, and over a wider range of social strata, than it did elsewhere in Europe during the early modern period. However, he seems to base this claim largely on contemporary references to the excessive number of dogs that roamed England's streets and countryside.[76] Reliable comparative figures on the relative numbers of pets in England and elsewhere are simply nonexistent. Companion animals were considered to have little or no economic value as property at this time, and so tended to go unrecorded.[77]

A second possibility is that English prosecutors of witchcraft were more prejudicial and puritanical regarding the phenomenon of pet-keeping than their Continental counterparts, and were consequently more likely to view the activity as morally obnoxious. The problem with this conjecture is that, if we are to believe Keith Thomas, it leads to the paradoxical conclusion that pet-keeping proliferated to the greatest extent in the country where it was viewed with the greatest intolerance. In addition, we have Johann Weyer's observation of the public suspicions of witchcraft aroused by Agrippa von Nettesheim's "childish" affection for his dog, Monsieur. Not only does this reveal an isolated Continental instance of popular belief in an animal familiar, it also suggests that German antipathies regarding affection between people and animals were similar to English ones.

Alternatively, it is possible that the familiar failed to evolve on the Continent, at least as a judicial entity, because there was no niche for it within the official versions of witchcraft that emerged from the various episodes of European persecution. As several historians have pointed out, the model(s) of witchcraft that came to be accepted by ecclesiastical and judicial authorities on the European mainland was substantially different from the one that eventually became current in England.[78] From the fifteenth century onwards, Continental witchcraft was increasingly depicted as an organized, heretical religion or cult that existed in direct opposition to the established Church; a sort of sinister, inverted burlesque of Christianity.[79] Like witches everywhere, Continental witches used their occult powers to harm people, domestic animals, and other property, but they did this as instruments or servants of the Devil, to whom they surrendered themselves body and soul, just as good Christians surrendered themselves to God's will. As a token of Satanic allegiance, the Devil branded his disciples with the so-called "Devil's mark," and required them to gather together periodically to worship him at secret, nocturnal ceremonies known as Sabbats. During these ceremonies, the witches were said to perpetrate various abominable or obscene acts, such as kissing the Devil's posterior (figure 8), having sex with succubi, incubi, or Satan himself, sodomizing each other, engaging in cannibalistic feasts, saying the Lord's Prayer backwards, and spitting the Eucharist on the ground.[80] In England, by comparison, the witches were predominantly solitary. They did not join together to attend Sabbats, or worship Satan, and only rarely were they implicated in carnal relations with the Devil or his minions.

Both Norman Cohn and Richard Kieckhefer have argued, independently, that the English model of witchcraft was closer to the belief systems that existed at the popular level of European culture. In contrast, the official, "learned" or elite version that developed on the Continent was essentially a creation of the Inquisition whose agents were authorized to extract confessions under torture. To escape death and the pain of physical torture, most suspects freely admitted to anything suggested by the inquisitors, as well as readily divulging the names of their confederates. In this way, witches multiplied until substantial conspiracies eventually emerged, complete with all the trappings of a heretical religion.[81]

This elite conception of witchcraft did not erase the shamanistic animal-witch affiliation alluded to earlier. Rather it emphasized and elaborated different elements of that belief, in particular, shape-shifting—the notion of witches transforming themselves into animals in order to enter buildings or

8. Kissing the Devil's posterior. From Francesco Guazzo, *Compendium Maleficarum* (Milan, 1608).

travel to their Sabbats unnoticed—and the idea of Satan and his attendant demons assuming the guise of animals for similar purposes. As the story of Agrippa von Nettesheim's dog implies, the idea of the familiar spirit in animal form may have been just as prevalent at the level of popular culture on the Continent as it was in England. But such an introverted, individualistic concept had little chance of survival within the grandiose, orgiastic representation of witchcraft promulgated by the continental Church and judiciary. As Barbara Rosen has suggested: "The element of affection in the alliance, which, on the Continent, took the form of surrender and worship, and bestiality with demons, was in England expressed by the cosy, slightly perverted relationship of a lonely poverty-stricken women to her pet animal."[82]

CONCLUSION

Robin Briggs has recently argued for a common European substrate of popular witchcraft belief during the medieval and early modern periods.[83]

The survival of a coherent body of pre-Christian religious traditions in Europe during these periods has been difficult to demonstrate convincingly,[84] although evidence of the roles that animals played in European conceptions of witchcraft suggests that this common substrate included at least vestigial traces of shamanism. In particular, the apparent belief in the witch's (or shaman's) ability to shape-shift, or to perform magical acts by sending his or her spirit out of the body in the form of an animal, was quintessentially shamanistic.

Regional and local differences in sociopolitical, ecological, and judicial forces seem to have produced differences in how the information percolating up from this underlying substrate was filtered and interpreted by the prosecuting authorities. The different "animal" aspects of European witchcraft, including that of the English familiar, provide a striking illustration of the effects of this historical process.

NOTES

I wish to thank everybody at the Shelby Cullom Davis Center for Historical Studies, especially the director, William Chester Jordan, and my fellow fellows, Mary Fissell, Rob Meens, Gregg Mitman, and François Pouillon, for all of their kindness, encouragement, and good humor during my sojourn at Princeton. My special thanks are also due to Elizabeth Jackson for her help with research, and to Joyce Salisbury and Mary Henninger-Voss for their comments on an earlier draft of this paper.

1. *A true and just Recorde, of the Information, Examination and Confession of all the Witches, taken at St. Oses in the countie of Essex. . . . Written orderly, as the cases were tryed by evidence, by W. W.* (Imprinted in London at the three Cranes in a Vinetree by Thomas Dawson, 1582).

2. *The examination and confession of certaine Wytches at Chensford in the Countie of Essex before the Quenes majesties Judges, the XXVI daye of July Anno 1566,* reproduced in B. Rosen, *Witchcraft* (London: Edward Arnold, 1969), pp. 72–82.

3. C. L'E. Ewen, *Witchcraft and Demonianism* (London: Heath Cranton Ltd., 1933), pp. 155–64; B. Rosen, *Witchcraft* (London: Edward Arnold, 1969), pp. 30–32; K. Thomas, *Religion and the Decline of Magic* (London: Penguin Books, 1971), p. 446.

4. Ewen, *Witchcraft and Demonianism,* p. 69.

5. Thomas, *Religion and the Decline of Magic,* p. 525.

6. K. Thomas, *Man and the Natural World* (London: Allen Lane, 1983), pp. 39–40. This idea was also developed more fully in J. A. Serpell, *In the*

Company of Animals, 2d ed. (Cambridge: Cambridge University Press, 1996), pp. 158–59.

7. The "Continent" refers here primarily to Germany, France, Switzerland, Italy, and Spain. With respect to evidence of the use of familiars, it could also be said to include Scotland (see C. Larner, *Enemies of God* [Oxford: Basil Blackwell, 1981]).

8. Pope Innocent VIII's bull of 1485 makes no mention of familiars at all, and the 1487 *Malleus Maleficarum,* probably the most comprehensive and authoritative Continental text concerning the activities of witches, barely mentions them, apart from passing references to a witch in Basle who sent a familiar of indeterminate shape to afflict "an honest laborer" with leprosy, and another whose familiar accompanied her in the form of a raven to her place of execution, and prevented the wood from burning until it was driven off. The fanatical witch hunter Jean Bodin was virtually silent on the subject of familiars in his 1580 treatise *Demonomanie,* though he described the practice of keeping toads in pots as a suspicious circumstance, albeit not grounds for condemnation to death (cited in G. L. Kittredge, *Witchcraft in Old and New England* [New York: Russell & Russell, 1958, p. 182]). In his *Daemonolatreia* of 1595, Nicholas Remy of the Supreme Judicial Court of Nancy wrote of witches being visited in prison by familiars in the form of birds, crabs, hares, and mice, although, given the date, he may have acquired this information from English sources. He also claimed that witches were given the power to enter houses by means of their familiars. In the *Compendium Maleficarum* of 1608, Guazzo observed that newly initiated witches were each assigned personal demons who, in the form of goats, transported them to their Sabbats, but the description is suggestive of incubi and succubi rather than subordinate familiars.

9. N. Cohn, *Europe's Inner Demons* (New York: Basic Books, 1975), pp. 99–102.

10. Accounts of shape-shifting in England derive mainly from the northern counties of Yorkshire, Lancashire, and Northumberland, and usually refer to so-called "witch-hares," the preferred animal form adopted by witches when engaged in the theft of milk from their neighbors' cattle. The separation between this category of creatures and more typical animal familiars is somewhat ambiguous, however, since many folktales relate instances of witch-hares being pursued and wounded in one location while the witch herself is engaged in other activities elsewhere. In such cases, the witch invariably suffers an equivalent parallel injury, and is thus identified. Reference to parallel injury is extremely scarce in trial accounts of "typical" English familiars, although intimations of shape-shifting are occasionally encountered. In the notorious case of the Walkerne witch, Jane Wenham, in

1712, several witnesses not only testified to being visited and "tormented" by her cats, but also reported that one of these cats had the face of Jane Wenham (Ewen, *Witchcraft and Demonianism,* pp. 384–89).

11. The relevant section of the 1604 Act of Jas. I is reproduced in full in C. L'E. Ewen, *Witch Hunting and Witch Trials* (London: Heath Cranton Ltd., 1929), pp. 19–21.

12. Ewen, *Witch Hunting and Witch Trials*; Ewen, *Witchcraft and Demonianism*; R. Macfarlane, *Witchcraft in Tudor and Stuart England: A Regional and Comparative Study* (New York: Harper & Row, 1970).

13. Macfarlane, *Witchcraft in Tudor and Stuart England,* pp. 26–27.

14. W. Notestein, *A History of Witchcraft in England from 1558–1718* (Washington, D.C.: American Historical Association, 1911), pp. 164–205; Ewen, *Witchcraft and Demonianism,* pp. 254–61; Thomas, *Religion and the Decline of Magic,* pp. 536–45.

15. Macfarlane, *Witchcraft in Tudor and Stuart England,* p. 86.

16. Cited in Ewen, *Witchcraft and Demonianism,* p. 260.

17. Thomas Ady, *A Candle in the Dark: Shewing the Divine Cause of the Distractions of the Whole Nation of England, and of the Christian World* (London: Printed for Robert Ibb'tson dwelling in Smithfield neer Hosier Lane End, 1655), p. 135.

18. P. Dale-Green, *Dog* (London: Rupert Hart-Davis, 1966), p. 81–82.

19. Reproduced in part in K. M. Briggs, *Pale Hecate's Team* (London: Routledge and Kegan Paul, 1962), pp. 28–30.

20. *A Dialogue, or, Rather a Parley betweene Prince Rupert's Dogge whose name is Puddle, and Tobies Dog whose name is Pepper &c. . . .* (Printed at London for I. Smith, 1643), pp. 2–9.

21. *A Dog's Elegy or Rupert's Tears, For the late Defeat given him at Marston-moore, neer York . . .* (Printd at London for G. B. July 27, 1644), p. 3.

22. Dale-Green, *Dog,* p. 81.

23. The account is given in G. Zilboorg, *The Medical Man and the Witch in the Renaissance* (Baltimore: Johns Hopkins University Press, 1935), pp. 134–36.

24. Ewen, *Witch Hunting and Witch Trials,* p. 294.

25. The tendency in witchcraft cases for children to give wildly imaginative testimonies under cross-examination has been well documented in R. L. Sjöberg's study of child testimonies during an outbreak of witch hysteria in Sweden during the seventeenth century (*Journal of Child Psychology and Psychiatry* 36 [1995]: 1039–51). Robin Briggs reports a similar phenomenon in his study of the Lorraine witch persecutions, see *Witches and Neighbors* (New York: Viking, 1996), pp. 233–37.

26. *A Detection of damnable driftes, practized by three Witches arraigned at Chelmisforde in Essex . . . 1579.* Extracts in Ewen, *Witchcraft and Demonianism,* p. 150.

27. F. Hutchinson, *An historical essay concerning Witchcraft, with observations tending . . . to confute the vulgar errors about that point* (London: Printed for R. Knaplock at the Bishop's Head, and D. Midwinter, at the Three Crowns in St. Paul's Churchyard, 1718), p. 68.

28. Ady, *A Candle in the Dark,* p. 135.

29. Ibid.

30. Ewen, *Witchcraft and Demonianism,* p. 282.

31. *The Examination, Confession, Triall, and Execution, of Joane Williford, Joan Cariden, and Jane Hott* (London: Printed for J. G., October, 1645), p. 2.

32. J. Stearne, *A Confirmation and Discovery of Witch-Craft . . .* (London: Printed by William Wilson, dwelling in Little Saint Bartholomewes neere Smithfield, 1648), pp. 41–42.

33. *A True and just Record of the Information, Examination and Confession of all the Witches taken at St Oses . . . 1582,* pp. 161–2.

34. Thomas, *Man and the Natural World,* pp. 100–113; AVMA, *The Veterinary Service Market for Companion Animals* (Schaumberg, Ill.: American Veterinary Medical Association Information Center, 1992).

35. Moles could also be described as anomalous animals *sensu* Mary Douglas's theory of taboo in relation to animals that tend to cross categorical boundaries. In the case of the mole, these anomalous characteristics might include the fact that it is a mammal with fur that lives perpetually underground, and has no visible eyes or ears. See M. Douglas, *Purity and Danger* (New York: Routledge & Kegan Paul, 1966).

36. See especially M. E. Robbins, "The Truculent Toad in the Middle Ages," in *Animals in the Middle Ages,* ed. N. C. Flores (New York: Garland, 1996), pp. 25–47.

37. Gilbert White, *The Natural History of Selborne* (1768: reprint ed., London: J. M. Dent & Sons, 1949), p. 51.

38. Thomas, *Man and the Natural World,* pp. 110–11.

39. A. Allen, "Toads: The Biochemistry of the Witches' Cauldron," *History Today* 29 (1979): 265–68; R. Fletcher, "The Witches' Pharmacopoeia," *Bulletin of the Johns Hopkins Hospital,* no. 765 (1896): 147–56; M. J. Harner, "The Role of Hallucinogenic Plants in European Witchcraft," in *Hallucinogens and Shamanism,* ed. M. J. Harner (New York: Oxford University Press, 1973), pp. 125–50.

40. Ewen, *Witchcraft and Demonianism,* p. 73.

41. H. C. Lea, *A History of the Inquisition of the Middle Ages* (New York: Russell & Russell, 1958), p. 513.

42. The account is given in Kittredge, *Witchcraft in Old and New England,* p. 182.

43. W. Monter, "Toads and Eucharists: The Male Witches of Normandy, 1564–1660," *French Historical Studies* 20, no. 4 (1997): 563.

44. G. Henningson, *The Witches' Advocate: Basque Witchcraft and the Spanish Inquisition (1609–1614)* (Reno: University of Nevada Press, 1980), pp. 78–79.

45. *Macbeth* IV.1.

46. *The Examination of John Walsh, before Maister Thomas Williams . . .* (Imprynted at London by John Awdely dwelling in Little Britain Street without Aldersgate, 1566), pp. 8–11.

47. This is certainly the least plausible aspect of this account since toads are generally unresponsive to anything but live and mobile insect prey. It would be exceedingly difficult, if not impossible, to train one to "drink" milk from a saucer like a cat.

48. Notestein, *A History of Witchcraft in England from 1558–1718,* pp. 160–62.

49. W. Davis, *Shadows in the Sun* (New York: Island Press, 1998), pp. 203–38; P. T. Furst, "The Toad as Earth Mother: A Problem in Symbolism and Psychopharmacology," in *Hallucinogens and Culture,* ed. P. T. Furst (Novato, Calif.: Chandler & Sharp, 1976), pp. 158–82.

50. T. Lyttle, D. Goldstein, and J. Gartz, "Bufo Toads and Bufotenine: Fact and Fiction Surrounding an Alleged Psychedelic," *Journal of Psychoactive Drugs* 28, no. 3 (1996): 267–90.

51. Davis, *Shadows in the Sun,* p. 219.

52. W. Davis and A. T. Weil, "Identity of a New World Psychoactive Toad," *Ancient Mesoamerica* 3, no. 1 (1992): 51–59; Lyttle et al., "Bufo Toads and Bufotenine," pp. 273–74.

53. T. L. Barry, B. S. Petzinger, and S. W. Zito, "GC/MS Comparison of the West Indian Aphrodisiac 'Love Stone' to the Chinese Medication 'Chan Su': Bufotenine and Related Bufadienolides," *Forensic Science* 41, no. 6 (1996): 1068–73; Lyttle et al., "Bufo Toads and Bufotenine," p. 279.

54. C. Lévi-Strauss, *The Savage Mind* (London: Weidenfeld and Nicholson, 1966), pp. 205–7.

55. *The examination and confession of certaine Wytches at Chensford . . . 1566.*

56. *The Discovery of Witches in answer to severall queries lately delivered to the Judges of Assize for the County of Norfolk and now published by Matthew Hopkins. . . . 1647,* p. 2.

57. Ewen, *Witch Hunting and Witch Trials,* p. 22

58. Hopkins, *The Discovery of Witches* (1647), frontispiece.

59. Stearne, *A Confirmation and Discovery of Witch-Craft* (1648), pp. 14–16.

60. In fairness to Hopkins and Stearne, we should also allow for the possibility that these were standard names for pets in seventeenth-century England. Certainly, "Greedigut" is a singularly apt name for many dogs.

61. Ewen, *Witchcraft and Demonianism,* p. 74.

62. Ibid., pp. 142–43.

63. *The Examination of John Walsh . . . 1566.*

64. *The examination and confession of certaine Wytches at Chensford . . . 1566.*

65. *A Rehearsall both straung and true, of hainous and horrible actes committed by Elizabeth Stile, Alias Rockingham, Mother Dutton, Mother Devell, Mother Margaret, Fower notorious Witches, apprehended at winsore in the Countie of Barks. and at Abbington arraigned, condemned, and executed on the 26 daye of Februarie laste Anno. 1579.*

66. Ewen, *Witchcraft and Demonianism,* p. 75

67. *The most strange and admirable discoverie of the three witches of Warboys, arraigned, convicted and executed at the last Assizes at Hintingdon, for the bewitching of the five daughters of Robert Throckmorton Esquire, and divers other persons . . .* (London: Printed by the Widdowe Orwin for Thomas Man and John Winnington . . . 1593). Reprinted in Rosen, *Witchcraft,* pp. 239–97.

68. Stearne, *A Confirmation* (1648), pp. 43–49.

69. See especially: R. F. Benedict, "The Concept of the Guardian Spirit in North America," *Memoirs of the American Anthropological Association* 29 (1923): 3–93; A. I. Hallowell, "Bear Ceremonialism in the Northern Hemisphere," *American Anthropologist* 28, no. 1 (1926): 1–175; A. Hultkrantz, "On Belief in Non-Shamanic Guardian Spirits among the Saamis," in *Saami Religion,* ed. T. Ahlbäck (Abo, Finland: Donner Institute for Research in Religious and Cultural History, 1987), pp. 110–23; M. Mauss, *A General Theory of Magic,* trans. R. Brain (New York: Norton, 1975), pp. 33–39.

70. G. H. Gossen, "Animal Souls, Co-Essences, and Human Destiny in Mesoamerica," in *Monsters, Tricksters, and Sacred Cows: Animal Tales and American Identities,* ed. A. J. Arnold (Charlottesville: University Press of Virginia, 1996), pp. 80–107.

71. M. Ruel, "Were-Animals and the Introverted Witch," in *Witchcraft Confessions and Accusations,* ed. M. Douglas (London: Tavistock Publications, 1970), pp. 333–50.

72. Gossen, "Animal Souls," pp. 104–5.

73. Thomas, *Man and the Natural World,* pp. 100–210.

74. This theme has been elaborated recently by S. Clarke, *Thinking with Demons* (Oxford: Clarendon Press, 1997), p. 89; K. Newman, *Fashioning Femininity and English Renaissance Drama* (Chicago: Chicago University of Chicago Press, 1991), pp. 58–61. Although men or boys occasionally confessed to suckling familiars, the vast majority of trials and accusations involved women.

75. See especially J. Canup, "'The Cry of Sodom Enquired Into': Bestiality and the Wilderness of Human Nature in Seventeenth-Century New England," *Proceedings of the American Antiquarian Society* 98, no. 1 (1988): 113–34; Thomas, *Man and the Natural World,* pp. 17–50.

76. Thomas, *Man and the Natural World,* pp. 101–5.

77. Ibid., p. 112.

78. Ewen, *Witchcraft and Demonianism,* p. 71; Rosen, *Witchcraft,* pp. 30–32; Thomas, *Religion and the Decline of Magic,* p. 530; Cohn, *Europe's Inner Demons,* pp. 126–46.

79. Clarke, *Thinking with Demons,* passim.

80. Briggs, *Witches and Neighbors,* pp. 32–38; Ewen, *Witchcraft and Demonianism,* p. 71; Rosen, *Witchcraft,* pp. 30–32; Thomas, *Religion and the Decline of Magic,* p. 530; Cohn, *Europe's Inner Demons,* pp. 126–46.

81. Cohn, *Europe's Inner Demons,* pp. 126–46; R. Kieckhefer, *European Witch Trials: Their Foundations in Popular and Learned Culture, 1300–1500* (London: Routledge, 1976).

82. Rosen, *Witchcraft,* p. 32.

83. Briggs, *Witches and Neighbors,* passim.

84. Although see C. Ginzburg, *Ecstasies: Deciphering the Witches' Sabbath,* trans. R. Rosenthal (London: Hutchinson Radius, 1990); R. A. Horsley, "Further Reflections on Witchcraft and European Folk Religion," *History of Religions* 19, no. 1 (1979): 84–86; Mauss, *A General Theory of Magic,* pp. 35–37.

PART THREE

THE ANIMAL-HUMAN DIVIDE IN THE MODERN WORLD: PHILOSOPHICAL AND SCIENTIFIC APPROACHES

7

ON THE SEXUAL ASSAULT OF ANIMALS
A SOCIOLOGICAL VIEW

PIERS BEIRNE

> *O foul descent! that I who erst contended*
> *With Gods to sit the highest, am now constrain'd*
> *Into a Beast, and mixt with bestial slime,*
> *This essence to incarnate and imbrute.*
> —*Satan, in Milton's* Paradise Lost

In this paper I seek to contribute to an as yet unconstituted sociology of animal abuse, though my specific focus derives less from overtly theoretical labors directed to this end than from the practical needs of pedagogy. In trying to develop an undergraduate course on the sociology of animal abuse, I was immediately confronted with conveying to my students adequate responses to the deceptively simple question "what is animal abuse?" Class time devoted to the specter of such dramatic and well-publicized practices as factory farming, laboratory experimentation, trapping, circuses, and so on, would tend to stimulate among students, I believed, a visceral reaction rather than the desired goal of sustained inquiry about the nature of animal abuse.

It happened that, in casting a wide net for some heuristic device that would enable me to examine animal abuse in a pedagogic context, I stumbled upon two items relating to the crime of bestiality. Separated by three centuries and inhabiting vastly different cultural universes, these raised interesting questions about bestiality that forced me to rethink my understanding of it. One involved a censorious description of bestiality, the other a celebratory depiction of it.

The first of these items was a reference in Governor William Bradford's diary *Of Plymouth Plantation, 1620–1647.* Here, Bradford commented on the trial of one Thomas Granger for bestiality in 1642. According to Bradford, Granger, aged sixteen or seventeen, was indicted for "buggery with a mare, a cow, two goats, five sheep, two calves and a turkey."[1] Though he declined to enter into many of the details of the case, Bradford related that Granger, who had been accidentally discovered while engaging in "a lewd practice towards the mare," had freely admitted "the fact with that beast at that time"; and that he had also identified several sheep with whom he had been familiar. Under examination, Granger and another youth ("who had made some sodomitical attempts") had been asked how they first learned and came to "the knowledge and practice of such wickedness?" One of the pair confessed that he had long practiced it in England, where he had learned of it from others who kept cattle there. On these admissions Bradford reflected "[b]y which it appears how one wicked person may infect many, and what care all ought to have what servants they bring into their families."[2] Granger was found guilty and condemned to death. "A very sad spectacle it was," Bradford lamented, for "first the mare and then the cow and the rest of the lesser cattle were killed before his face, according to the law, Leviticus xx.15; and then he himself was executed."[3]

These entries in the governor's diary are interesting for several reasons, not least of which is that they betray the extensive ideological effects of Judeo-Christianity on attitudes towards human-animal sexual relations. Note, for example, that the "law" to which Bradford referred was not the prevailing English statute enacted under Henry VIII in 1533 but the Mosaic commandment contained in Leviticus (20:15): "if a man lieth with a beast, he shall surely be put to death: and ye shall slay the beast."[4] Several questions are prompted by Governor Bradford's musings. Why were the transgressions of the unfortunate Granger "accidentally discovered" and then reported to the authorities, while the "sodomitical attempts" of others were not? Are the circumstances of Granger's case representative of bestiality as a social practice or merely of those who are prosecuted for it?

At almost the same time as I came across Bradford's description of this case I was loaned a would-be erotic video provocatively entitled *Barnyard Love*. This crudely produced, undated German film graphically depicts numerous humans and other animals engaged in sexual acts. Among these are human males who engage in sexual intercourse with cows and hens and more often—given that heterosexual males are the film's chief audience—human females who have sexual intercourse with dogs, insert eels into their vaginas, and perform fellatio on dogs and horses.

Even from my amateurish perspective and despite the risks of anthropomorphism, I noticed how immensely varied were the filmed reactions of the different animals to attempted sexual union with and initiated by humans.

At one extreme, the dogs in *Barnyard Love* who were engaged in sexual activities with women seemed energetically to enjoy such human attention. To me, at least, it did not seem possible that such canine enthusiasm could be feigned by off-camera training designed to suppress more genuine emotions of grief and pain. At the opposite extreme, some animals, such as eels and hens, were obviously unwilling recipients of human sexual advances. None of my students would have much trouble, I thought, in identifying as animal abuse the case of one unfortunate hen who was literally fucked to death, which for her was doubtless a terrifying consequence of enforced sexual intercourse with a human male. Yet, in the case of large quadrupeds, such as the horses and cows depicted in the film, their reaction seemed closer to boredom or perhaps indifference than it did to pain or to bliss— eating, urinating, and defecating as they were during intercourse or while their genitalia were being manipulated. Indeed, it was unclear whether these larger animals were even aware of the prolonged sexual relations which humans had foisted on them. In their case, however, what I saw as animals' indifference might actually have been calculated detachment on their part and, despite the fact that we can probably never know it with much certainty, a coping strategy for numbing the pain inflicted on them by yet another of the myriad ways in which their lives are routinely invaded, inspected, and disposed of by humans.

Like the seventeenth-century case of Thomas Granger, the events depicted in films like *Barnyard Love* also raise interesting questions about the understanding of bestiality as a social practice. How should we approach bestiality: is it an outrageous and perhaps perverse act or, as the law's increasing tolerance of it suggests, a relatively benign form of social deviance? Why have sexual relations involving humans and animals been so vociferously and ubiquitously condemned and so little studied?

To these questions let me at once add how remarkable it is, given the intense levels of ideological and physical coercion that have been applied to bestiality, that the social sciences have almost completely ignored a social practice that is traditionally viewed with moral, judicial, and aesthetic outrage. One undoubted reason for this neglect is that to most of us bestiality is a disturbing form of sexual practice that invites hurried bewilderment rather than sustained intellectual inquiry. Thus, when, during his work on the medieval prosecution and capital punishment of animals, the historian E. P. Evans gruffly dismissed bestiality as "this disgusting crime," he was probably expressing not an idiosyncratic prejudice but an enduring sentiment that he shared with the great majority of his colleagues.[5] Indeed, in academic discourse the topic of bestiality tends to surface only in lectures on the evolution of criminal law given by professors who, with embarrassed chuckles, refer to the declining volume of bestiality prosecutions since the early nineteenth century in order to instantiate the secularized tolerance and the supposed rationality of Western law.[6] On the rare occasions when bestiality enters the literature of sociology and criminology it does so in a purely formal and shallow way, ancillary to other concerns; typical of these is a case in colonial New Haven involving a certain Thomas Hogg and a sow, referred to by Lawrence Friedman, who employs it only as a rhetorical device to deny the uniqueness of "somewhat exotic or outrageous examples of criminal behavior."[7] Moreover, while fictional and quasi-autobiographical accounts of bestiality occasionally appear in serious works of literature, like William Tester's *Darling*[8] and Peter Høeg's *The Woman and the Ape,*[9] accessible descriptions of it tend to be produced only by libertine presses and cinematographers as erotic commodities for consumption by a popular, albeit limited, audience.

In what follows I seek to introduce a view of bestiality which differs radically from both the anthropocentrism enshrined in the dogma of Judeo-Christianity and also from the pseudoliberal stance of tolerance fashionable today. I suggest, simply, that bestiality should be understood as sexual assault. However, first I must comment briefly on the evolution of different images of bestiality and the stated justifications for its censure.

"Among Christians a Crime Not to Be Named"

The cultural universe of bestiality is necessarily an anthropocentric one, though in many societies, past and present, it inhabits an ambiguous ideological terrain. On the one hand, it is exalted in mythic and folkloric traditions. Although they are not my concern here, it is worth noting that these favorable depictions of bestiality are often lodged in the sexual antics, the conquests, and the offspring of numerous gods, in the lineages of earthly monarchs and rulers, and in the texts of fairy stories and other morality tales. On the other hand, all known societies have likely applied some form of censure to human-animal sexual relations.[10] Moreover, the judicial accusation of bestiality occasionally blurs into, or is employed in concert with, other charges, such as witchcraft. Thus, some early medieval European accusations of witchcraft involved the claim that the defendant had partaken in a ritual salute of the Devil's backside, the *osculum infame* or obscene kiss.[11] In another case of unknown date, a certain Françoise Sécretain was burned alive because she had had carnal knowledge of domestic animals—a dog, a cat, and a cock—and because, she admitted, she was a witch and her animals were actually earthly forms of the devil.[12]

What we refer to as "bestiality" has been denominated variously in different places and times. Besides a hodgepodge of more or less polite colloquialisms, bestiality has also been termed "zoophilia," "zooerasty," "sodomy," and "buggery." The seventeenth-century English word "bestiality" derives from the Latin *bestialitas,* the latter being used in Aquinas's *Summa Theologica* severally to refer to primitive behavior, to human-animal sexual intercourse, and to the way in which animals copulate.[13] Until approximately the mid-nineteenth century, the term referred broadly to the beast-like, earthy, and savage qualities allegedly inhering in animals other than humans. Nowadays, "bestiality" tends exclusively to denote sexual relations between humans and animals. Usually, in law, it refers to sexual intercourse when a human penis or digit enters the vagina, anus, or cloaca of the animal. However, it often also entails any form of oral-genital contact, including those between women and animals and even, in psychiatry, fantasies about sex with animals.

Bestiality is sometimes classified as a crime against nature (*peccatio contra naturam*); in this it is a bedfellow of other crimes involving "pollution" such as sodomy, buggery, masturbation, and pedophilia. At other times, the terms "sodomy" and "buggery" are used interchangeably to describe bestiality, though they have also been employed to denote homosexuality. Each of these terms carries with it pejorative baggage that varies in its moral bases, in its intensity, and in the duration of its condemnation. Moreover, in some societies, such as in New England from the Puritan 1600s until the mid-nineteenth century, bestiality has been generally regarded with such trepidation that even the very mention of the word is censured. Accordingly, it is also referred to as "that unmentionable vice," or "a sin too fearful to be named," or "among Christians a crime not to be named."

Anthropocentrism and the Abominations of Leviticus

From its inception, Christianity applied austere standards and a strict discipline to those of its followers who violated its injunctions against the irremissible major sins of idolatry, the shedding of blood, and fornication, including bestiality.[14] In all cases, the prescribed penalty was death. The earliest and most influential justifications for censures of bestiality are the Mosaic commandments.[15] Deuteronomy, for example, declares "[c]ursed be he that lieth with any manner of beast" (27:21), while Exodus commands that "[w]hosoever lieth with a beast shall surely be put to death" (22:19)—the "whosoever" here referring to both men and women (Leviticus 20:15–16). Besides mandating death for humans, Leviticus also dictates that the offending animal be put to death, a practice that reached its zenith in certain late medieval European societies.[16] The precise intentions of those who originally condemned bestiality are probably not open to reclamation. However, over the ages three beliefs have persisted about its wrongfulness: it ruptures the natural, God-given order of the universe; it violates the procreative intent required of all sexual relations between Christians; and it produces monstrous offspring that are the work of the Devil.

Let us uncover each of these three beliefs in turn.

A Rupture of the "Natural" Order of the Universe

Prefaced by the general command, "Ye shall be holy: for I the Lord your God am holy," Leviticus declared: "Neither shalt thou lie with any beast to defile thyself therewith; neither shall any woman stand before a beast to lie down thereto: it is confusion" (18:23). This theme continues: "Ye shall keep my statutes. Thou shalt not let thy cattle gender with a diverse kind; thou shalt not sow thy field with mingled seed; neither shall a garment mingled of linen and woolen come upon thee." (19:19).

The rules that cattle should not "gender with a diverse kind" and that a field should not be sown "with mingled seed" lie at the heart of the Mosaic injunctions about bestiality.[17] On this same basis, the early Christian Church regarded copulation with a Jew as a form of bestiality and applied the penalty of death to it. So, too, from the time of Leviticus to that of seventeenth-century English moralists and beyond, bestiality has been regarded as sinful or criminal because it represents a rupture of the natural order of the universe, whose categories it is immoral to mix. Similarly, Governor Bradford recorded the opinions of three ministers given in 1642 about the acts of "unnatural vice" to be punished with death, among which were to be women who committed bestiality. Seeking affirmation in Leviticus, the ministers condemned bestiality, whether penetration had occurred or not, because it is "against the order of nature," "unnatural," and a "confusion."[18] Again, Richard Capel, a seventeenth-century Stuart moralist, argued that bestiality is the worst of sexual crimes because "it turns man into a very beast, makes a man a member of a brute creature."[19]

Violation of Procreative Intent

In matters of sexual relations "Be thou holy" means more than "Be thou separate," for Christian morality has long required that sexual intercourse flow not from pleasure or play but exclusively from a procreative intent. Bestiality has thus also been condemned because it is held to be a violation of the Christian rule that procreation is the sole purpose of sexual intercourse. Crimes against nature have therefore been proclaimed to be those in which the emission of seed is not accompanied by a procreative intent, as in masturbation, anal and oral sex, incest, adultery, rape, and bestiality.

Monstrous Offspring

Bestiality has also been condemned because of the offspring sexual unions between humans and animals are thought to produce or because of the evil that such offspring are held to signify or portend.[20] This particular condemnation has itself been part of a complex cultural framework that includes animism, paganism, and a fascination with monsters. Classical antiquity, for example, provides numerous seemingly nonjudgmental references to human-animal sexual relations, including stories where animals were thought to be in love with humans. Such cases are very prominent in *De natura animalium* (ca. 1800 B.P.), for example, the Roman historian and sophist Aelian's miscellany of facts about animals and humans, genuine or supposed, which he gleaned from Greek writers, including Aristotle. Drawing on material from and about Rome, Greece, India, Libya, and Egypt, Aelian documented how widespread was the belief in the actual offspring of animal-human unions ("creatures of composite nature"). As he wrote, "[m]any creatures are begotten with two faces and two breasts: some born of a cow have the foreparts of a man; others on the contrary spring up begotten of a man but with the head of a cow."[21] Although Aelian provided his readers with no clues as to how such offspring were regarded, they cannot always have been viewed with disfavor given his ubiquitous and often reverential references to creatures such as satyrs, centaurs, and minotaurs.

How easily the rigid boundaries between animals and humans can become blurred is recorded in a history of Ireland by the twelfth-century chronicler Giraldus of Wales. Without further comment he related how in the Glendalough mountains a cow gave birth to a man-calf, the fruit of a union between a man and a cow, the local folk "being especially addicted to such abominations."[22] Giraldus also reported how Irish men and women had sexual intercourse with cows, goats, and lions, and how the populace believed that such unions were occasionally fertile. Indeed, he pondered whether it is murder to kill the product of a man-cow union, for "[w]ho can disallow the claims of a creature which stands erect, laughs, and goes on two feet to belong to the human species?"[23] Similar superstitions appear in seventeenth-century New England, one case being related in the New Haven court records.[24] Moreover, the poetry of John Donne and the speeches and sermons of John Winthrop, Cotton Mather and his brother John, Samuel Danforth, and William Bradford, are infected with the fear that colonial agricultural society was a frontier existence not only beset with the internal dangers of alcohol, idleness, and lust but also surrounded by forests, wild animals, and savages.[25] Superstition combined with religious doctrine to assail bestiality and to portray its progeny as monsters resulting from the decay of civilization and the encroachment of the wilderness. Monstrous progeny were a visible reminder of how evil it was to transgress the God-given boundaries separating man from beast.[26]

NAMING BESTIALITY AS ANIMAL SEXUAL ASSAULT

The social control of the objects of such fears has been subject to great cultural variation in both style and volume. In some societies, the censure of bestiality has been accompanied by surprisingly few prosecutions. For example, despite the horror with which bestiality was viewed by Puritan zealots and legal writers in England and in colonial America,[27] it was rarely indicted and indictments were unlikely to result in convictions. In other societies, the number of convicts executed is staggering. Thus, in Sweden, from 1635 to 1778 there were as many as seven hundred executions for bestiality, and an even greater number of males was sentenced to flogging, church penalties, and public forced labor in chains.[28] Upon conviction, both human and animal were usually put to death, often by burning at the stake but occasionally by beheading or hanging, or blows to the head. The bodies of the condemned, both human and animal, were finally burned or butchered and buried together.[29]

If the penalties for bestiality and the entire range of unnatural acts had been strictly enforced, as Goodich has noted, then Europe and colonial America would have become vast penal institutions inhabited by populations restricted in diet and dress, excluded from church services, and condemned to a joyless life of fasts, prayers, and flagellation.[30] While the relative frequency with which bestiality was condemned in early modern societies partly reflects the greater contacts between humans and animals in rural societies, such public displays of atonement have largely been dispensed with in modern urban societies. It is far more efficient for the state to deal with bestiality behind closed doors, or even to ignore it, and for the local folk community either to ridicule those who engage in it or to ostracize them.

Indeed, since the mid-nineteenth century many "unnatural offences," including bestiality, have effectively been decriminalized. In the United States there is no federal bestiality statute and only twenty-seven of the fifty states now have such a statute.[31] Nowadays, a defendant will probably be charged with a misdemeanor like public indecency, breach of the peace, or cruelty to animals. Indeed, following the lead of Jeremy Bentham[32] and others, the social control of bestiality has formally passed from religion and criminal law to a psychiatric discourse at whose center lie diseased individuals who are often depicted as simpletons or imbeciles with psychopathic personalities and who allegedly sometimes also have aggressive and sadistic tendencies. However, at once subverting this psychiatrization and also echoing certain aspects of the spirit of decriminalization, there has gradually emerged a pseudoliberal tolerance of bestiality. This tendency implies that because bestiality is an interesting and vital part of almost every known culture it should not only be tolerated but even, within certain limits, celebrated.[33]

Are the decriminalization and the psychiatrization of bestiality and the drift to toleration of it signs of increasing civility and social progress? A superficial answer to this question is yes, if by it one means that censured humans are no longer brutalized by execution or by solitary confinement with hard labor. But that would be to look at bestiality solely from an anthropocentric position, which is just what the juridico-religious dogma surveyed here does.[34] Seldom, either in times past or now, do popular images of social control include recognition of the terror and the pain that judicial examination and execution inflict on animals convicted of sexual relations with humans. Neither in the Mosaic commandments nor in the records of past or present court proceedings, neither in the rantings of Puritan zealots nor in psychiatric testimony, is bestiality censured because of the harm that it inflicts on animals. But, especially in the case of smaller creatures like rabbits and hens, animals often suffer great pain and even death from human-animal sexual relations. While researchers have examined the physiological consequences of bestiality for humans,[35] they pay no such attention to the internal bleeding, the ruptured anal passages, the bruised vaginas, and the battered cloacas of animals, let alone to animals' psychological and emotional trauma. Such neglect of animal suffering mirrors the broader problem that, even when commentators admit the discursive relevance of animal abuse to the understanding of human societies, they do not perceive it, either theoretically or practically, as an object of study in its own right.

In principle, the attempt to understand bestiality as a form of animal abuse might profitably draw on the perspectives and insights of the three major tendencies that lie at the philosophical and theoretical heart of the animal protection community, namely, utilitarianism, liberal rights theory, and feminism. We might insist, following liberal rights theory for example, that if bestiality is engaged in with a mammal, then it is a harm inflicted on a moral patient entitled to the fundamental right of respectful treatment. But discursive support for this specific task is very difficult to find either in the writings of the animal protection community or in its day-to-day activities. Moreover, though in the last decade some of the most important contributions to the understanding of animal abuse have been made by feminism, except for brief statements by Carol Adams and Barbara Noske,[36] feminists have ignored the harmful effects of bestiality on animals. Departing from this curious silence, Adams insists that we should understand bestiality as forced sex with animals because sexual relationships of unequal power cannot be consensual.[37] In making this argument, and in asserting that all forms of masculinist oppression are linked, Adams thereby begins to claim the perspective of animals as a central concern of feminism.

I agree with Adams that, in seeking to replace anthropocentrism with an acknowledgment of the sentience of animals, we must start with the fact that in almost every situation humans and animals exist in a relation of potential or actual coercion. Whether as companions or as agricultural commodities, where they are thoroughly dependent on humans for food, shelter, and affection, or as creatures that roam free, where humans have the capacity to ensnare them and subject them to their will, animals' interaction with humans is always infused with the possibility of coercion. So it is with sex. Just as it is accurate to state that the sexual assault of women differs from normal sex because the former is sex obtained by physical, economic, psychological, or emotional coercion—any of which implies the impossibility of genuine consent—so, too, Adams's assertion that bestiality is always sexual coercion ("forced sex") is surely a correct description of most, if not all, human-animal sexual relations.

But I am not convinced that bestiality must entail sexual coercion simply because human-animal sexual relations always occur in a context of unequal power, however theorized. If unequal power is the definitive criterion, then sexual coercion would be an essential characteristic not only of intercourse between human adults and infants or children but of most adult heterosexual and even homosexual intercourse as well. Sexual coercion is not sex that occurs always and only in a context of unequal power, though on occasion, of course, situations of inequality imply coercion because for a variety of reasons the party with less power cannot freely dissent from participation. Ultimately, sexual coercion occurs whenever one party does not genuinely consent to sexual relations or does not have the ability to communicate consent to the other. Sometimes, one participant in a sexual encounter may appear to be consenting because s/he does not overtly resist, but that does not of course mean that genuine consent is present. For genuine consent to sexual relations to be present—somewhat to modify Box's formulation—

both participants must be conscious, fully informed, and positive in their desires.[38]

If genuine consent—defined in this way—is a necessary condition of sex between humans, then there is no good reason to suppose that it may be dispensed with in the case of sex between humans and other sentient animals. Bestiality involves sexual coercion because animals are incapable of genuinely saying "yes" or "no" to humans in ways that we can readily understand. A different way of putting this is to suggest that if it is true that we can never know what it is like to be an animal, as the philosopher Thomas Nagel has implied,[39] then presumably we will never know if animals are able to assent—in their terms—to human suggestions for sexual intimacy. Indeed, if we cannot know whether animals consent to our sexual overtures, then, when we tolerate human-animal sexual relations, we are as blameworthy as when we fail to condemn adults who have sexual relations with infants or with children or with other "moral patients"—to use Tom Regan's term[40]—who, for whatever reason, are unable to refuse participation. If it is proper to regard unwanted sexual advances to women, to infants, and to children as sexual assault, then, I suggest, sexual advances to animals should be viewed similarly.

Moreover, like infants, young children, and other "moral patients," animals are beings without an effective voice. Some animals, such as cows, hens, and other animals used in agriculture—including those I viewed in the film *Barnyard Love*—are not equipped to resist human sexual advances in any meaningful way owing to their docile and often human-bred natures. Other animals, in trying to resist human sexual advances, can certainly scratch, bite, growl, howl, hiss, and otherwise communicate protest about unwanted advances. But in most one-on-one situations an animal is incapable of enforcing her will to resist sexual assault, especially when a human is determined to effect his purpose. Moreover, animals are disadvantaged in yet another way, for when they are subjected to sexual coercion and to sexual assault, it is impossible for them to communicate the facts of their abuse to those who might give them aid.

In short, because bestiality is in certain key respects so similar to the sexual assault of women, children, and infants, I suggest that it should be named as *sexual assault*.

For many of the same reasons that, as it applies to humans, the concept of sexual assault is more widely applicable than that of rape, so, too, the sexual assault of animals comprises a wider range of actions than those found in dictionary definitions of bestiality or in notions embedded in popular culture, both of which tend to focus narrowly on penetration of the vagina, anus, or cloaca of an animal by a human penis. But if the concept

of the sexual assault of animals is not exhausted by penile or digital inser-
tion, then how wide should its scope be? Should it include touching, kissing, and fondling? If it is extended to fondling, for example, then to the
fondling of what, with what, and by whom? Given animals' inability to
communicate consent to human sexual overtures, I would like to establish—or at least to aim for—the general principle that *the sexual assault of
animals comprises all sexual advances by humans to animals and all sexual relations between them.* Admittedly, such a principle has inherent problems which
I cannot pretend to know how to solve. For example, how do we establish
a general rule for identifying actions that are physically identical to those
defined as sexual assault but which have a different intent? Consider the
following tale related to me by a colleague. "When I was a little girl I
didn't take my dog to bed—she was too big for that—but instead lay
regularly in her basket. I even sucked her nipples since I had seen her pups
do that. She allowed it and didn't prevent it, even though she wasn't suckling at the time. My mother, a doctor herself, was thank goodness not too
narrow-minded and left us alone in our tactile relationship."[41] This innocent
and affectionate suckling was probably not sexual in nature, it certainly was
not assaultive, and it doubtless caused the dog no harm.

Many actions like this can of course be either sexual or affective in
nature, depending on their social contexts or on the physiological responses
of the actors (for both humans and other animals, innocent, nonsexual physical touching and stroking slow the pulse and respiration and lower the
blood pressure, but quite the opposite responses are produced by sexual
arousal). But where, precisely, should a line of demarcation between them
be drawn? It is clear, to me at least, that the milking of a cow, for example,
has nothing to do with sexual assault. But how about electrically induced
ejaculation for insemination? Is this sexual assault? Simple or aggravated
assault? Neither?

In arguing that all sexual advances by humans to animals are assaultive,
I do not mean to dilute the severity of the condemnation of the sexual
assault of one human by another. However, I suspect that, for different
reasons, some feminists and most conservative opponents of the animal
protection community will wish to accuse me of just that. Such a response
assumes, wrongly I believe, not only that there is some anthropocentric
chain of moral claims and priorities wherein those of humans are necessarily
far above those of animals, but also that the interests of humans and animals
are incompatible. On the contrary, sexism and speciesism operate not in
opposition to each other but in tandem. Sexual assault of animals is typically—though not always—the product of a masculinity that sees women,
animals, and nature as objects that can be controlled, manipulated, and

exploited. Listen only to some of the sexist language that prepares the way for bodily sexual assault.[42] Much of this is voiced in speciesist terms. When a man describes women as "cows," "bitches," "(dumb) bunnies," "birds," "chicks," "foxes," "fresh meat," and their genitalia as "beavers" or "pussies," he uses derogatory language to distance himself emotionally from, and to elevate himself above, his prey by relegating them to a male-constructed category of "less than human" or, more importantly, "less than me." Reduced to this inferior status, both women and animals are thereby denied subjectivity by male predators who can then proceed to exploit and abuse them without guilt. Unchallenged, sexist and speciesist terms operate in concert to legitimize sexual assaults on women and animals.

TOWARDS A SOCIOLOGY OF ANIMAL SEXUAL ASSAULT

Thus far, in outlining and opposing conventional notions of bestiality, I have suggested their replacement with a concept of sexual assault. Although the sexual assault of animals often results from the same malicious masculinity and comprises the same harmful actions as those that constitute the sexual assault of one human by another, it is evidently not a unitary social practice but one with variable prevalence and differing social forms. Indeed, the documented range of animals involved in bestiality cases is quite diverse. This diversity encompasses companion animals, animals used in agriculture, and those used for labor. It includes mules, cows, sows, dogs, mares, ducks, sheep, goats, rabbits, hens, and others.

In what follows, I examine existing evidence about the prevalence of the sexual assault of animals and then construct a typology of its major forms. This is no easy task. For one thing, as will quickly become clear, it is often such a private act that the sociological dimensions of the sexual assault of animals are difficult to uncover. This problem is compounded by the longstanding historical fact that political, judicial, and religious authorities have exhibited a complex assortment of responses when confronted with it, including prosecuting it to the hilt, ignoring it altogether, and even frequently suppressing all mention of it.

Prevalence of Animal Sexual Assault

Evidence about the prevalence of the sexual assault of animals appears chiefly in three contexts: psychiatric studies, sexological surveys, and historical studies of court records. I examine each of these in turn.

Psychiatry

From the mid-nineteenth century onwards, the juridico-religious control of bestiality has given way to a medico-psychiatric discourse at whose center are deviants with a variety of mental and characterological defects. Indeed, the dominant images of bestiality and the scholarly pronouncements on its etiology and prevalence are not nowadays articulated in the outmoded theological rhetoric of demonic influences but in the deterministic straitjacket of mental abnormalities.

Following Richard von Krafft-Ebing's foundational text *Psychopathia Sexualis,* psychiatry has tended to extrapolate from individual case histories to comments about the causes of bestiality in general, among which the most prominent are psychopathological defects (or "zooerasty").[43] Recent psychiatric work regards bestiality as a sexual perversion that is largely practiced by young males who are often simpletons or imbeciles with psychopathic personalities and who sometimes also have aggressive and sadistic tendencies. Psychiatric researchers have even suggested that bestiality represents reaction against castration anxiety, that it might involve schizophrenia,[44] and that childhood traumata associated with it can lead to multiple personality disorder.[45] One study, which reports a remarkably high prevalence of bestiality in psychiatric in-patients, includes explanatory descriptions of bestiality as a heterosexual surrogate experience, as vested sadism, and as a reenactment of primal scenes.[46] Currently, the American Psychiatric Association classifies zoophilia as a form of paraphilic disorder.

In seeking to establish the claim that the human practitioners of bestiality are diseased and defective individuals, psychiatric studies are vulnerable to a number of theoretical and methodological objections, including their crude essentialism, their tendency to begin their investigations with a population that is already institutionalized, and their failure to compare their human subjects with adequate control groups. Indeed, Liliequist's comprehensive study of eighteenth-century bestiality prosecutions in Sweden found that some of the defendants "were idiots or not completely sensible, but not very many."[47] Moreover, the pronouncements of psychiatry about the supposed abnormality of the individuals who engage in bestiality have been contradicted somewhat by its offshoot and principal ally, namely, sexology, and to this we now turn.

Sexological Surveys

Where psychiatry proclaims the abnormality of the individual humans who engage in bestiality, sexology implicitly finds bestiality to be a relatively normal phenomenon because it is sometimes quite widely practiced. Where the former clothes those who engage in bestiality in the rhetoric of psychopathological defects, the latter depicts them as male victims of deficient social structures (i.e., adverse sex ratios). This affinity is most clear in the famous surveys of sexual behavior undertaken by Alfred Kinsey and his colleagues.[48] Here, bestiality is posited as an outlet for the satisfaction of biologically driven sexual urges and, despite sexology's posture of methodological and ethical neutrality, as an effect of low morality, great sexual desire, and lack of opportunity for "natural" (i.e. intraspecies heterosexual) indulgence.[49] These so-called causes are then attached to survey findings that bestiality is engaged in mainly by poor and often relatively uneducated young males in rural areas with nothing (or no one) better to do.

Sexologists have made a number of conflicting claims about the prevalence of bestiality. Krafft-Ebing originally suggested that it is resorted to by both men and women (with dogs only), that (with cows and horses) it is "none too infrequent," and that it is reported so rarely because it is such a secretive act.[50] Less circumspect is the claim of a study of twenty-one forms of paraphilic acts committed in Memphis and New York City by 561 sex offenders.[51] This reports that only 1.1 percent of all completed acts involve bestiality. Another study has compared the sexual outlet experiences of one hundred single Iowan male and male college students in 1974 and 1980.[52] It found that while the number of students who report having had sexual contact with an animal is very small, there was virtually no difference in either year in the incidence of this activity for males and females. According to Kinsey and his colleagues, about 8 percent of males have some sexual experience with animals, but a minimum of 40–50 percent of all "American farm boys" experience some form of sexual contact with animals, either with (17 percent) or without orgasm, in their preadolescent, adolescent and/or later histories, as do 5.1 percent of American females.[53]

Accompanying these astounding figures is the claim that "[s]uch data begin to show what the significance of animal intercourse might be if conditions were more favorable for such activity. . . . in certain Western areas of the United States, where animals are most readily available and social restraints on this matter are less stringent, we have secured incidence figures of as high as 65 per cent in some communities, and there are indications of still higher incidences in some other areas."[54]

But because Kinsey's research entirely lacked probability sampling, it erred in believing that valid generalizations about the prevalence of stigmatized sexual practices, including bestiality, could be made from the responses of the volunteers recruited to his survey. For example, there is little or no hard evidence with which to test in other agrarian and stock-farming societies his claim that bestiality is to a large extent a function of rural life's proximity to and familiarity with animals. In most Western societies—where the ownership of companion animals has dramatically increased and where, with the rise of factory farming, there has been a steady decline in the percentage of the human population living in agricultural areas or residing with farm animals inside their houses—it is not at all certain that it is farm animals who are nowadays the most common objects of experimentation by young male (or female) humans. Moreover, Kinsey's aggressive personal interviewing techniques ensured elevated levels of disclosure and reporting. For example, he explicitly warned interviewers to place the burden of denial on the respondent ("subject"): "The interviewer should not make it easy for a subject to deny his participation in any form of sexual activity. It is too easy to say no if he is simply asked whether he has ever engaged in any particular activity. We always assume that everyone has engaged in every type of activity. Consequently, we always begin by asking *when* they first engaged in such activity."[55]

Similarly, an investigation of the prevalence of bestiality among the mentally ill in California was based on a self-report questionnaire distributed to both an experimental group of twenty psychiatric in-patients and to two control groups, of which one comprised twenty medical in-patients, and the other twenty psychiatric staff.[56] Not only are these very weakly constituted control groups too small for results of any significance, but their concept of bestiality is operationalized as "both actual sexual contacts and sexual fantasy," a vague definition that does not lend itself to precise measurement.

In short, their reductionism and their poor methodological techniques imply that such studies can provide little or no reliable information about the prevalence of bestiality.

Socio-Legal Studies of Court Records

The exposure, investigation, and treatment of that juridico-psychiatric invention, the pathological bestialist, are not included among the several objects of a small socio-legal literature on the social control of bestiality. Although it has no common theoretical core and its authors seem usually to have labored in isolation from each other and in ignorance of each other's contributions, this emerging tradition has effectively proceeded from a social constructionist agenda. In sharper or broader focus, it has situated bestiality in the contexts both of changing attitudes to animals and to animal sexuality, and also of the diverse historical forms in and through which bestiality and "related offenses," such as masturbation and homosexuality, are censured. Often, it only touches briefly on bestiality, and this it does in the context of prior concerns like the social control of homosexuality and the medieval prosecution of animals. This emerging tradition is inhabited largely by historians, though it also includes a sprinkling of literary and legal scholarship.[57]

Two key features of the social control of bestiality can be detected in this fragmented literature. First, defendants in bestiality trials have overwhelmingly been young males from rural areas. Of these the majority seems to have been drawn from marginalized populations, especially the poor, non-natives, and heretics.[58] The social composition of bestiality defendants, in other words, is probably very similar to that of those typically charged with other crimes against public order or involving moral turpitude. Second, with the prominent exception of Sweden, criminal prosecution of bestiality has been a very rare event.[59] This has been demonstrated not only for France, Denmark, and the Netherlands but also, perhaps surprisingly, for such relatively inquisitorial societies as seventeenth-century England and colonial America.[60]

But my concern here is not to explain why the volume of bestiality prosecutions in most societies has generally been so small, interesting though that problem might be. Rather, I wish to explore what light the volume of bestiality prosecutions might throw on the prevalence of bestiality in a given culture. In the absence of such artifacts as self-report data and victimization surveys, can anything meaningful about the prevalence of bestiality be inferred from data on bestiality prosecutions?

The few scholars who have addressed this question have not tended to be shy in answering it in the affirmative, though none else have dared match the precision of a study of Austrian court proceedings from 1923 to 1965 which estimates that 1–2 percent of rural males occasionally have sexual contact with animals.[61] The historian J. A. Sharpe, for example, concludes that because of the rarity of bestiality prosecutions in seventeenth-century England and also because of the infrequent and stray nature of the references to the offence at that time, there was not a widespread indulgence of bestiality which failed to be reported there.[62] Drawing a different conclusion from the same sparsity of prosecutions, another study briefly touches upon the extent of bestiality in colonial America and of popular and judicial attitudes towards it. This surmises that in such a rural society "the act must have been common enough."[63] With a somewhat wider compass, Thompson finds that because cases of homosexuality, bestiality, or pedophilia in English and New England court records in the seventeenth century are "so uncommon as to be statistically insignificant," therefore "apart from masturbation, deviant sexual activity was exceedingly rare."[64] In the only in-depth study of bestiality prosecutions, Liliequist has suggested that the unparalleled indictment rate in Sweden from 1635 to 1754—which in some provinces was as high as 5–6 per 100,000 population—implies not only a very intolerant society but also one in which bestiality was widely practiced. He writes that the frequency of indictments in Sweden indicates, on the one hand, "a social network of control over and suspicion of male sexuality, a willingness and eagerness on the part of neighbors, masters, servants, and even family members to maintain the sanctions. On the other hand, there were persons who continued to find sexual gratification in bestiality in spite of the attitudes of disgust and repugnance and the risks of infamy, execution, or eternal damnation and association with the devil."[65]

Is it possible to unpack court records in such a way that we can detect the extent to which the social control of bestiality and the practice of it existed independently of each other? Though court records are often prisms through which we can apprehend the development of power relations, and though they might yield insight about particular histories of social control and about sexual tolerance or moral panics around bestiality, they cannot reflect the prevalence of bestiality with any accuracy. Whereas sexological surveys provide, or should provide, data on the admitted sexual practices of a randomly derived microcosm of the general population, court records reflect only the bureaucratic outcome of the interplay between some unknown volume of the population that engages in illegalities and the reporting, charging, and prosecuting of those unfortunates who have been caught. Quite independently of the prevalence of bestiality, the volume of formal complaints about it clearly depends on such factors as the countervailing power of religious zeal; the precariousness of political authority; whether the complainant has something to gain from the accused, like the recovery of despoiled or stolen property; the level of animosity between complainant and offender; the perceived likelihood that a complaint will be acted upon by political authorities; and the social character of interspecies relations. Moreover, like the regulation of other "unnatural offences," such as masturbation and homosexuality, the social control of bestiality has typically occurred through nonstate processes such as moral persuasion from the pulpit and socialization within the family. At a popular level, these mechanisms have no doubt been supplemented by tactics like derisive and hateful attacks on an offender voiced in the rhetoric of affronted manhood. Quite how these various tactics do or do not result in formal complaints by the citizenry to the authorities has yet to be investigated.

But complaints of bestiality are more likely to be made, for example, in situations where the complainant has something to gain from legal proceedings. Thus, in her study of criminal dispositions for bestiality in Queensland, Australia, between 1870 and 1949, Collins suggests that the volume of complaints may vary with the perception that bestiality is a property crime more than anything else.[66] Animal owners are more likely to complain that their animals have been sexually assaulted, in other words, not because the alleged offender has violated Christian precepts about the natural order of the universe but because their property has been damaged or despoiled.

Similarly, consider the nature of bestiality accusations in the 1950s among the Kaguru, a tribe of matrilineal Bantu cultivators living in a highland area of east-central Tanganyika. In the past, accusations of bestiality would have involved the serious charge of witchcraft, but in modern times they have invited only laughter and derision. Nowadays, the only justification for a public complaint is when an act of bestiality is seen to involve the breaking of a rule of property. This is so because the Kaguru consider the practice of sexual intercourse with another person's livestock—sheep and cows, especially—as an example of inappropriate use of personal property. Thus, in one case the local Kaguru court was told that a young male who attempted to mount his friend's sheep had enjoyed his friend's property without permission. The court found that had the youth enjoyed his own sheep, there would have been no case at all.[67]

Accusations of bestiality are also more likely to be made the greater the level of animosity between a complainant and an offender, such as when an informal complaint is used as an insult arising from an already existing feud. Thus, Scandinavian societies have a long history of using attributions of bestiality as insults. In *Njal's Saga,* Skarp-Hedin accuses Thorkel of sexual contact with a mare: "You would be better employed picking out of your teeth the bits of mare's arse you ate before you came here—your shepherd saw you at it, and was amazed at such disgusting behavior."[68] Personal animosity is also the obvious motive in a case reported in the ancient saga of *Ale-Hood.* "You didn't notice the fat stallion that Steingrim had till it was up your backside. That skinny mare you were on faltered under you . . . and I've never been able to make up my mind whether it was you or the mare that got it. Everybody could see how long you were stuck there, the stallion's legs had got such a grip on your cloak."[69]

Moreover, even after complaints of bestiality are brought before authorities, not all of them result in an entry in court records. While there may be a great many reasons for this, among the most powerful is the legal difficulty of proving an allegation of bestiality. In some jurisdictions a charge of bestiality could only proceed if penetration of the animal by the male organ could be proved. In England, for example, the great jurist Sir Edward Coke was adamant that penetration had to occur for a charge of

buggery to be successful.[70] This requirement must often have been a difficult one to satisfy, as is demonstrated in the case of William Spiller in
seventeenth-century Essex, where the accused was apparently saved by the
jury's strict adherence to this rule. "William Spiller, a yeoman's son of
Hatfield Broad Oak, was seen following a bullock in a close, having 'his
yarde in his hand stiffe standing,' but his explanation that he was prevented
from committing buggery because 'the Bullocke would not stand still'
apparently succeeded in obtaining an *ignoramus* for his indictment."[71]

Consider, too, the problem of witnessing what must often be an extremely
private act. In some jurisdictions at least two witnesses have been required for
conviction, one of which may include a confession by the accused. What happened if a confession was made under torture and then retracted? In 1673,
during examination before his trial, one Benjamin Goad of Roxbury, Massachusetts, admitted that he had committed "the unnatural and horrid act of bestiality" upon a mare.[72] Goad then retracted his admission and the court was
forced to consider whether the prisoner's "confession against himself" was sufficient to convict him. The court answered in the affirmative and, the mare
having first been "knocked on the head" in front of him, Goad was duly hanged.
Indeed, of the four bestiality indictments in the Massachusetts Colony during
the period 1673 to 1692, two resulted in acquittals, one may not even have
gone to trial, and only one resulted in a guilty verdict.

In summary, it is fair to say that the prospects for estimating the prevalence of bestiality from data lodged in court records are not auspicious.
The various subjective biases behind complaints to the authorities of cases
of bestiality mean that, in principle, the skewed recording of bestiality is no
different from that of all other crimes.

Typology of Animal Sexual Assault

> *Between the ages of 12 and 14, I used to fuck my horses.*
> *Every day I would wake up to feed the horses, clean the stalls, and fuck the mare.*
> *—Jeff Heiskell, lead singer of The Judybats*

In what follows I try to identify some key categories of a typology of the
forms of the sexual assault of animals, including: sexual fixation; commodification; adolescent sexual experimentation and gender socialization; and
aggravated cruelty. These four categories are structured in terms of both
differing human-animal social relationships and also the degree of harm
that abused animals suffer.

Sexual Fixation

This is the form of sexual assault that occurs when animals are the preferred sexual partners of humans. It is hard to believe that this was not the case when, for example, Thomas Granger was indicted for buggery with a veritable barnyard of animals in colonial New England in 1642.[73] Looked at from a somewhat different perspective, this must also have been true in eighteenth-century Sweden for those persons who continued to find sexual gratification in bestiality despite the very hostile and punitive social attitudes towards it.[74] In twentieth-century Australia, too, Collins has found that from the male participant's viewpoint, bestiality is often not a "replacement object" deriving from heterosexual starvation but a sexual practice sought after, often at great length, in its own right.[75] A rare description of sexual fixation with animals is provided by Krafft-Ebing, who designates it as "impulsive sodomy":

> A. was convicted of having committed masturbation and sodomy on dogs and rabbits. When twelve years old he saw how boys masturbated a dog. He imitated it, and thereafter he could not keep from abusing dogs, cats and rabbits in this vile manner. Much more frequently, however, he committed sodomy on female rabbits—the only animals that had a charm for him. At dusk he was accustomed to repair to his master's rabbit pen in order to gratify his vile desire. Rabbits with torn rectums were repeatedly found. . . . At the height of the attack there were sounds of bells, cold perspiration, trembling of the knees, and, finally, loss of resistive power, and impulsive performance of the perverse act. . . . A. stated that if called upon to choose between a woman and a female rabbit, he could make choice only of the latter.[76]

Sexual fixation with animals is probably the least common form of sexual assault of animals. Dekkers estimates that the percentage of humans who have sex *exclusively* with animals is far below 1 percent, though this figure lacks suitable evidence.[77] The psychological literature contains no adequate accounts of it, yet Adams asserts that there is a similarity in the respective worldviews of the zoophiliac, the rapist, and the child sexual abuser. "They all view the sex they have with their victims as consensual," she claims, "and they believe it benefits their sexual 'partners' as well as themselves."[78] Adams's claim is possibly correct. However, it will remain unsupported until a significant number of methodologically sensitive life histories have been completed on zoophiliacs. It is just as likely that "fixated humans" assault animals sexually not because they believe it benefits their sexual "partners" but because they enjoy inflicting pain on other creatures who, in this particular case, just happen to be animals because animals are more available to them than humans. Do they perhaps not start with animals and eventually "graduate" to humans?

Commodification

This is the predominant element in the sexual assaults of animals that are packaged as commodities for sale in a market. It often involves a twofold assault—one by a man on a woman who is assaulted and humiliated by being forced to have sex with an animal, the other on the animal who is coerced, without the possibility of giving genuine consent, into having sex with a human. Examples include live shows of women copulating with animals in bars and sex clubs or depictions of sexual assaults of animals in pornographic films such as *Barnyard Love* and *Deep Throat*. In the latter, for example, Linda Marchiano ("Linda Lovelace") is filmed having intercourse with a large dog resembling a German shepherd. During this act and for a long time after it, Marchiano herself "felt nothing but acute revulsion" and she agreed to be filmed in this two-hour episode only because her boyfriend and batterer threatened to kill her.[79]

Consider also the more problematic case of Deena the stripping chimpanzee. For one hundred dollars Deena and her trainer would appear at a social gathering, during which Deena would perform a striptease act for the partygoers. Is this sexual assault? Clearly, this case is one that combines commodification with aspects of sexual objectification. The chimp had been trained to perform like a human female stripper—a marketable action that it could not possibly have freely chosen to do, and whose social context it could not have fully understood. Though it is true that sexual abuse does not necessarily involve actual physical contact, perhaps this particular act should be understood less as sexual assault than as a violation of an animal's right to dignity, as Adams suggests.[80]

Adolescent Sexual Experimentation

This is probably the most prevalent social situation in which animals are sexually assaulted, as shown by quite disparate studies of seventeenth- and eighteenth-century Sweden and of mid-twentieth-century rural America.[81] However, precisely what the practice of adolescent sexual experimentation with animals represents symbolically and culturally, and how it contributes to gender socialization, vary from one social context to another.

Notwithstanding the problems involved in the interpretation of court records discussed earlier, in Liliequist's study of Sweden there was a remarkable occurrence of young Swedish boys below the age of fifteen charged with bestiality. Many were nine to thirteen years old, some even younger. He thus suggests that Sweden was a bestiality-prone society, though "the social, cultural, and psychological basis for this was not found in a general low grade of culture or dulled sensibilities, but in the socialization of boys."[82] While men oversaw horses and stables, and girls and women were responsible for looking after animals in the cowshed and the farmyard, and for milking, boys were responsible for herding them to and from pasture. Boyhood in seventeenth- and eighteenth-century Sweden therefore entailed very close relations with farm animals and offered the first view and knowledge of sexual relations as one animal mounted another. The herdsboys were "curious and excited explorers, eager to find out the secrets of sexuality belonging to adult and married life but present and visible in the life of farm animals."[83]

As adolescent sexual experimentation, sexual assault can be performed on animals either alone or with other adolescents who either watch or else participate. In a group context, some boys of necessity teach how it is done while others learn. It can be performed for a variety of reasons, including mere curiosity, cruelty, showing off for other boys, and acquiring the techniques of intercourse for later use on girls. For example, an anonymous colleague has told me that when she was doing anthropological fieldwork in rural Algeria, she and a coworker witnessed a very nervous young male (on the night before his wedding) "practicing" sexual intercourse with a donkey for the explicit purpose of not appearing hopelessly unskilled with his wife the following night. Presumably, too, there is some point towards the end of their adolescence when young males desist from experimental sexual activities with animals because such practices are regarded as unmanly or, perhaps, as perverse.

Aggravated Cruelty

It is reasonable to suppose, given their great predominance in sexual experimentation with animals, that young males also disproportionately engage in aggravated cruelty (i.e., a level of cruelty over and above that already presented in most such acts) during acts of sexual assault of animals. It is true that no specific pattern of aggravated cruelty has yet been uncovered among young males who engage in the sexual assault of animals, but this is so perhaps only because this category has not yet been properly researched. Psychologists have shown that children and adolescents who assault animals appear to be overwhelmingly young males of normal intelligence who are often sexually abused at home and whose family situations also often contain spousal abuse.[84]

Quite apart from the occurrence of cruelty during adolescent sexual experimentation, aggravated cruelty can be a major element in sexual assault in other ways. In mid-nineteenth-century England, for example, one case was reported in which two-foot-long knotted sticks were thrust into mares' wombs, which were then vigorously rent, and another in which the penises of cart horses and donkeys were cut off.[85] Multiple cases of such atrocities were confirmed in several English counties in 1993.[86] Similarly, in 1991 at a zoo in New Bedford, Massachusetts, a deer was found with fatal wounds that included a fractured jaw and extensive bleeding from the rectum and vagina.[87] Sometimes, aggravated cruelty against animals takes place in conjunction with the humiliation of women. This has been documented both in Nazi concentration camps and in the course of partner abuse.[88] In the latter, it can take the form of battering, which involves the use of animals for humiliation and sexual exploitation by batterers and/or marital rapists. Recent reports from Los Angeles "tell of a man who, after fights with his girlfriend, sought revenge by raping her pet chicken."[89] Moreover, if one allows that, like humans, animals are capable of experiencing nonphysical pain, then aggravated cruelty also occurs whenever sexual assault produces emotional or psychological pain and suffering.[90]

CONCLUSION

This paper has tried to replace anthropocentric censures of bestiality with a concept I term "animal sexual assault." My argument about the meaning and causes of the sexual assault of animals has derived largely from how the situation of animals as abused victims parallels that of women and, to some extent, that of infants and children. Specifically, bestiality should be understood as sexual assault because (1) human-animal sexual relations almost always involve coercion; (2) such practices often cause animals pain and even death; and (3) animals are unable either to communicate consent to us in a form that we can readily understand or to speak out about their abuse. Though space does not permit it here, this application of the concept of sexual assault to all human-animal sexual relations can doubtless be strengthened with the discursive support of utilitarianism and of liberal rights theory.

As I have proposed it, the concept of the sexual assault of animals clearly needs further elaboration. Key problems remain. For example, given the lack of studies of this form of sexual assault, my fourfold typology is quite provisional. Between the categories of aggravated cruelty and adolescent sexual experimentation, especially, there is obvious overlap. One must be able to distinguish, too, not only between the malicious masculinity behind aggravated cruelty and other situations of adolescent sexual experimentation and exploration, but also between the latter and innocent and affective fondling. Moreover, what is the social situation of females who assault animals sexually? Some difficulties seem to resist a clear answer—for example, is electrically induced ejaculation for insemination a form of sexual assault and, if so, is it an instance of commodification or of aggravated cruelty or both?

In advancing the notion that human-animal sexual relations are equivalent to sexual assault, I wish to add to neither the psychiatrization nor the criminalization of a practice which nowadays occupies a place at the outer margins of public and legal concern. But this leaves me in an uncomfortable position. If the sexual assault of an animal by a human is a harm that is objectionable for the same reasons as is an assault on one human by another—because it involves coercion, because it produces pain and suffering, and because it violates the rights of another being—then it would seem to constitute a sufficient condition for the censure of the human perpetrator. Clearly, we need to confront the nature of the censure that inevitably accompanies the relocation of bestiality as sexual assault. Should the censure involve criminalization? If so, of what severity? Should culpability be strict, or should the scales of justice depend on such factors as the moral significance of what was done, the degree of harm, and the species of animal assaulted?

Even if a cultural consensus could be established about the harmfulness of sexual assault—or any other form of animal abuse—for animals that are kept in confinement by humans, its effectiveness as a right would nevertheless be undermined by the rival cultural powers associated with the rights to private property and to privacy. Not coincidentally, it is of course precisely invocations of these rival rights that men use when they sexually abuse women and children. The right to privacy would undermine the detection and prosecution of sexual assault; the right to private property would be invoked to defend it. As Ted Benton has argued about the latter,[91] those who wish to ascribe rights to animals, including the right to respectful treatment, would eventually be forced to challenge the very existence of animals as private property.

NOTES

For their generous comments on this paper I am grateful to John Murrin, Rob Meens, James Serpell, and other members of the Shelby Cullom Davis Center seminar on "Animals and Human Society" at Princeton University.

1. William Bradford, *Of Plymouth Plantation, 1620–1647* (1650), ed. Samuel Eliot Morison (New York: Alfred A. Knopf, 1970), p. 320.

2. Ibid., p. 321.

3. Ibid., p. 320.

4. The earliest secular legislation on bestiality was probably enacted in Norway, where it was forbidden by the laws of *Gulathing* and *Fro stathing,* which punished it with castration and outlawry. On this see Laurence M. Larson, ed., *The Earliest Norwegian Laws* (New York: Columbia University Press, 1935), pp. 57, 252. In most European jurisdictions, once authority over cases of bestiality had passed, roughly speaking, from Church to state, bestiality became a capital offense. In Sweden it became a capital crime around 1400, though not until the eighteenth century did prosecutions for the offence peak there. On this see Jonas Liliequist, "Peasants against Nature: Crossing the Boundaries between Man and Animal in Seventeenth- and Eighteenth-Century Sweden," *Journal of the History of Sexuality* 1, no. 3 (1991): 393–423. In England, bestiality became a capital offence in 1533. Among the early English commentators on bestiality were the great legal authorities Sir William Blackstone and Sir Edward Coke. To Blackstone "the very mention of [the crime] is a disgrace to human nature" (cited in George Fletcher, *Rethinking Criminal Law* [Boston: Little, Brown, 1978], p. 383). To Coke—who followed St. Augustine's prescription that a sin by natural use, such as adultery or rape, is less shameful than one by unnatural use of "a member not granted for this"—bestiality was an instance of buggery which, in the seventeenth century, was held to be more serious than rape. "It is a detestable and abominable sin amongst Christians not to be named," Coke declared, "committed by carnal knowledge against the ordinance of the Creator, and order of nature, by mankind with mankind, or with brute beast, or by womankind with brute beast." Edward Coke, *The Third Part of the Institutes of the Laws of England,* vol. 3 (London: M. Flesher, 1642), p. 58.

5. Edward Payson Evans, *The Criminal Prosecution and Capital Punishment of Animals* (1906; reprint ed., London: Faber & Faber, 1987), p. 148.

6. An example of the comedic spin given to bestiality in the legal literature and among lawyers is the possibly apocryphal examination-in-chief in the English case of *Rex* v. *Cozins* (1834) (repeated in Graham Parker, "Is a Duck an Animal? An Exploration of Bestiality as a Crime," *Criminal Justice History* 7 [1986]: 96). George Gilbert had been charged with bestiality with a sheep. The act had been witnessed by a farm laborer, Albert Harris, who had been called as a witness for the Crown.

> *Prosecutor.* Mr. Harris, on the day in question, were you proceeding along a line adjacent to the farm of Mr. Clarke?
>
> *A.H.* I was.

Prosecutor. Would you describe for His Lordship what you saw.

A.H. Well, George Gilbert was standing in the doorway of the barn with a sheep.

Prosecutor. Yes, and what was he doing?

A.H. Well, he was messing around with the sheep.

Prosecutor. By that statement, are we to understand that the accused was having sexual intercourse with the sheep?

A.H. Er, yes.

Prosecutor. Mr. Harris, what did you do when you observed this shocking spectacle?

A.H. I said, "Morning, George."

7. Lawrence Friedman, *Crime and Punishment in American History* (New York: Basic Books, 1993), p. 1. See also Bradley Chapin, *Criminal Justice in Colonial America, 1606–1660* (Athens: University of Georgia Press, 1983), p. 127; Ronald M. Holmes, *Sex Crimes* (Newbury Park, Calif.: Sage, 1991), pp. 27–28.

8. William Tester, *Darling* (New York: Alfred A. Knopf, 1991).

9. Peter Høeg, *The Woman and the Ape* (New York: Farrar, Straus and Giroux, 1996).

10. In her classic study of the varieties of sexual deviance in 110 early societies, Brown found that bestiality was tabooed and punished in all societies (93 percent) about which information was available. Julia S. Brown, "A Comparative Study of Deviations from Sexual Mores," *American Sociological Review* 17, no. 2 (1952): 138.

11. Jeffrey Burton Russell, *A History of Witchcraft* (New York: Thames and Hudson, 1982), p. 63.

12. Gaston Dubois-Desaulle, *Bestiality: An Historical, Medical, Legal and Literary Study,* trans. A. F. N. (New York: Panurge Press, 1933), p. 58.

13. See further John Boswell, *Christianity, Social Tolerance, and Homosexuality* (Chicago: University of Chicago Press, 1980), p. 323 n. 69. Alternatively, "bestiality" might have derived from the Latin *animal,* which was originally translated into Middle English as *beste* or *beast* from the French *bête* which, in turn, probably derived from the Indo-European root for "that which is to be feared." See Andrée Collard with Joyce Contrucci, *Rape of the Wild* (Bloomington: Indiana University Press, 1989), p. 24.

14. John T. McNeill and Helena M. Gamer, *Medieval Handbooks of Penance* (New York: Columbia University Press, 1938), pp. 4–6.

15. Early censures of sexual offenses had two chief sources: formal conciliar decrees and penitentials. The conciliar decrees originated in the East, especially in the Byzantine Empire and in the Holy Land. Punishments for

violation of the decrees on bestiality were quite strict, e.g. the Ancyran Council (c. 314) decreed fifteen years of penance for those aged less than twenty, and twenty-five years for married persons aged twenty and over. The Celtic-inspired tradition of *libri poenitentiales*, which were systematizing handbooks of penance ("penitentials"), originated in sixth-century Wales and Ireland. Their chief aim was exposition of doctrine about the sacrament of penance and its administration. The penitentials combined elements of both sacrament and discipline; the latter typically consisted of fasting and, to a lesser extent, of self-scourging and of vigils that caused acute discomfort by loss of sleep. The medicine for the soul that these prescribed then spread to France, England, Italy, Spain, and Iceland. See Joyce E. Salisbury, *The Beast Within: Animals in the Middle Ages* (New York: Routledge, 1994), pp. 64–69.

16. Piers Beirne, "The Law Is an Ass: 'Reading' E. P. Evans' *The Medieval Prosecution and Capital Punishment of Animals,*" *Society and Animals* 2 no. 1 (1994): 27–46.

17. In her analysis of social pollution, Mary Douglas stressed that in the Mosaic rules holiness is exemplified by completeness, by keeping distinct the categories of divine creation, and by defining them precisely. Holiness therefore requires that individuals conform to the class to which they belong and different classes of things must therefore not be confused. *Purity and Danger: An Analysis of the Concepts of Pollution and Taboo* (London: ARK Paperbacks, 1984) pp. 53–54.

18. Bradford, *Of Plymouth Plantation,* pp. 404–12.

19. Quoted in Keith Thomas, *Man and the Natural World* (New York: Pantheon, 1983), p. 39.

20. Arnold J. Davidson, "The Horror of Monsters," in *The Boundaries of Humanity: Humans, Animals, Machines,* ed. James J. Sheehan and Morton Sosna (Berkeley: University of California Press, 1991): pp. 41–43.

21. Aelian, *On the Characteristics of Animals,* trans. A. F. Scholfield (Cambridge, Mass.: Harvard University Press, 1958), I.1, p. 21; XVI.3, p. 305.

22. Giraldus Cambrensis, *Historical Works,* ed. Thomas Wright (London: H. G. Bohn, 1863), p. 85.

23. Ibid.

24. In the 1641 New Haven case of George Spencer, John Wakeman's sow's litter contained a deformed piglet, which Wakeman brought to the Court for its consideration. According to the trial record,

[t]he monster was come to the full growth as the other pigs . . . but brought forth dead. It had no hair on the whole body, the skin was very tender, and of a reddish white color like a child's; the head was most strange, it had but one eye in the middle of the face, and that large and open, like some blemished eye of man; over the eye, in the

bottom of the forehead which was like a child's, a thing of flesh grew forth and hung down, it was a hollow, and like a man's instrument of generation. A nose, mouth and chin deformed, but not much unlike a child's, the neck and ears had also such resemblance. . . . Some hand of God appeared in an impression upon Goodwife Wakeman's spirit, sadly expecting, though she knew not why, some strange accident in that sow's pigging, and a strange impression was also upon many that saw the monster (therein guided by the near resemblance of the eye), that one George Spencer . . . had been actor in unnatural and abominable filthiness with the sow.

Records of the Colony and Plantation of New Haven (1641), ed. Charles J. Hoadly, vol. 1 (Hartford, Conn.: Case, Tiffany, 1857), pp. 62–63.

25. See Thomas, *Man and the Natural World,* pp. 38–41; and John Canup, "'The Cry of Sodom Enquired Into': Bestiality and the Wilderness of Human Nature in Seventeenth-Century New England," *American Antiquarian Society* 98, no. 1 (1988): 113–31.

26. On the changing fortunes of monsters in popular culture and on the influence of religion—especially Protestantism—and science in their rise and decline, see Paul Semonin, "Monsters in the Marketplace: The Exhibition of Human Oddities in Early Modern England," in *Freakery: Cultural Spectacles of the Extraordinary Body,* ed. Rosemarie Garland Thomson (New York: New York University Press, 1996), pp. 69–81.

27. J. A. Sharpe, *Crime in Seventeenth-Century England* (Cambridge: Cambridge University Press, 1983), pp. 65–66; Chapin, *Criminal Justice in Colonial America,* pp. 127–29.

28. Liliequist, "Peasants against Nature."

29. Halitgar's pseudo-Roman ninth-century penitential (c. 83) was even more specific about the fate of "polluted" animals: "[i]f a man has sinned with a goat or with a sheep or with any animal, no one shall eat its flesh or milk, but it shall be killed and given to the dog" (McNeill and Gamer, *Medieval Handbooks of Penance,* p. 313).

30. Michael Goodich, *The Unmentionable Vice: Homosexuality in the Later Medieval Period* (Santa Barbara, Calif.: Clio, 1979), pp. 66–67.

31. For a summary of the twenty-seven state bestiality statutes, see Richard A. Posner and Katherine B. Silbaugh, *A Guide to America's Sex Laws* (Chicago: University of Chicago Press, 1996), pp. 207–12. Most of these statutes focus on penetration; some distinguish among animals, birds, and fowls, and the language of several describes the forbidden act as "an abominable and detestable crime against nature." Recent cases involving bestiality in the United States include *State* v. *Bonynge,* 450 N.W. 2d 331 (Minn. App. 1990); and *People* v. *Carrier,* 254 N.W. 2d 35 (Mich. App. 1977).

Recent cases in England and Wales (where the maximum penalty is life imprisonment) include *Regina* v. *Pamela Jean P.* (1991), *Regina* v. *Tierney* (1990), *Regina* v. *Higson* (1984), and *Regina* v. *Williams* (1974). The facts in these latter cases are summarized in Bill Hebenton, Ken Pease, and Coretta Phillips, "Sentencing Offenders against Non-Human Animals," unpublished paper presented at the annual meeting of the American Society of Criminology, Chicago (1996).

32. In the course of his support of the decriminalization of sodomy in 1785, Bentham attacked the prosecution and punishment of acts of bestiality, arguing that the more they are permitted the more scope is allowed for malice or extortion to make use of them to effect its purpose upon the innocent. See Jeremy Bentham, "Essay on 'Paederasty,' Part 2," *Journal of Homosexuality* 4, no. 1 (1978): 91–107.

33. For example, see Midas Dekkers, *Dearest Pet: On Bestiality,* trans. Paul Vincent (London: Verso, 1994); and Marc Shell, *Children of the Earth: Literature, Politics and Nationhood* (New York: Oxford University Press, 1993), pp.148–75. On the Internet see "alt.sex.bestiality."

34. Indeed, relaxation in the social control of human behavior has not always been accompanied by an increase but, in some respects, by a decline in the level of juridical respect accorded animals. There has probably never been a general belief that the volition and intent of animals are of the same sort as those of humans, but some premodern legal authorities endowed them with the same legal capacities and obligations. The law occasionally created the fiction that animals were capable of understanding, responsibility, malice, and guilt. In the same way that a formal execution was regarded as the just desert of an animal convicted of bestiality or murder, so it was deemed only proper that animals enjoyed the right to a measure of due process, including the provision of defense attorneys and the presumption of innocence (Evans, *The Criminal Prosecution and Capital Punishment of Animals*; Beirne, "The Law Is an Ass"). For example, a she-ass was acquitted in the bestiality trial of Jacques Ferron in 1750, even though the human defendant was convicted and hanged; this verdict was influenced by the Curé Pintuel's testimony that because he had known the animal for four years and knew her to be virtuous, it was a case of rape rather than consensual relations. See Nicholas Sellers, "Criminal Prosecution of Animals," *The Shingle* 35 (1972): 183.

35. For example, C. Tournier, B. Croguennec, B. Pillegand, and R. Claude, "Ulcères rectaux par sodomisation animale," *La Nouvelle Presse Médicale* 10, no. 14 (1981): 1152.

36. Carol J. Adams, "Bestiality: the Unmentioned Abuse," *The Animals' Agenda* 15, no. 6 (1995): 29–31; and "Woman-Battering and Harm to

Animals," in *Animals and Women: Feminist Theoretical Explorations,* ed. Josephine Donovan and C. J. Adams (Durham, N.C.: Duke University Press, 1995), pp. 65–69. Barbara Noske, "Hoe Heet is een Ezelin?" *Opzij: Feministisch Maandblad* 21 (1993): 26. For a comprehensive bibliography of feminist approaches to human-animal interaction, see Josephine Donovan and Carol J. Adams, eds., *Animals and Women: Feminist Theoretical Explorations* (Durham, N.C.: Duke University Press, 1995), pp. 353–61.

37. Adams, "Bestiality: the Unmentioned Abuse."

38. Steven Box, *Power, Crime, and Mystification* (London: Tavistock, 1983), p. 124.

39. Thomas Nagel, "What Is It Like to Be a Bat?" *Philosophical Review* 83 (1974): 435–50.

40. Regan, *The Case for Animal Rights.*

41. Personal communication, September 20, 1996.

42. See further Joan Dunayer, "Sexist Words, Speciesist Roots," in Donovan and Adams, *Animals and Women,* pp. 11–31.

43. Richard von Krafft-Ebing, *Psychopathia Sexualis* . . . , trans. Franklin S. Klaf (1886; reprint ed., New York: Stein and Day, 1978), pp. 374–81.

44. M. U. Barnard, B. J. Clancy, and K. E. Krant, *Human Sexuality for Health Professionals* (Philadelphia: W. B. Saunders, 1978), pp. 210–11. See also E. A. Rappaport, "Zoophily and Zoerasty," *Psychoanalytical Quarterly* 37 (1968): 565–87.

45. Kate M. Hendrickson, Teresita McCarty, and Jean M. Goodwin, "Animal Alters: Case Reports," *Dissociation* 3, no. 4 (1990): 218–21.

46. W. A. Alvarez and J. P. Freinhar, "Prevalence Study of Bestiality (Zoophilia) in Psychiatric In-Patients, Medical In-Patients, and Psychiatric Staff," *International Journal of Psychosomatics* 38, nos. 1–4 (1991): 47.

47. Liliequist, "Peasants against Nature," p. 410.

48. Alfred C. Kinsey, Wardell B. Pomeroy, and Clyde E. Martin, *Sexual Behavior in the Human Male* (Philadelphia: W. B. Saunders, 1948); Alfred C. Kinsey, Wardell B. Pomeroy, Clyde E. Martin, and Paul H. Gebhard, *Sexual Behavior in the Human Female* (Philadelphia: W. B. Saunders, 1953).

49. However, some modern data suggest that urban men choose animals for sexual gratification and that bestiality cannot be explained by the sexological explanation of heterosexual sexual starvation. These data are reported in Anne-Marie Collins, "Woman or Beast? Bestiality in Queensland, 1870–1949," *Hecate* 17, no. 1 (1991): 37–38.

50. Krafft-Ebing, *Psychopathia Sexualis,* pp. 378–81.

51. G. G. Abel, J. V. Becker, M. Mittelman, J. Cunningham-Rathner, J. L. Rouleau, and W. D. Murphy, "Self-Reported Sex Crimes of Nonincarcerated Paraphiliacs," *Journal of Interpersonal Violence* 2, no. 1 (1987): 19.

52. M. D. Story, "A Comparison of University Student Experience with Various Sexual Outlets in 1974 and 1980," *Adolescence* 17, no. 68 (1982): 744, table 4.

53. Kinsey, Pomeroy and Martin, *Sexual Behavior in the Human Male,* p. 671; Kinsey, Pomeroy, Martin, and Gebhard, *Sexual Behavior in the Human Female,* p. 50.

54. Kinsey, Pomeroy, Martin, and Gebhard, *Sexual Behavior in the Human Female,* p. 671.

55. Kinsey, Pomeroy, and Martin, *Sexual Behavior in the Human Male,* p. 53. See also E. O. Laumann, J. H. Gagnon, R. T. Michael, and S. Michaels, *The Social Organization of Sexuality: Sexual Practices in the United States* (Chicago: University of Chicago Press, 1994), p. 290.

56. Alvarez and Freinhar, "Prevalence Study of Bestiality." See also K. T. Chee, "A Case of Bestiality," *Singapore Medical Journal* 15, no. 4 (1974): 287–88; and Barnard, Clancy, and Krantz, *Human Sexuality for Health Professionals,* pp. 210–11.

57. See James A. Brundage, *Law, Sex, and Christian Society in Medieval Europe* (Chicago: University of Chicago Press, 1987); Canup, "'The Cry of Sodom Enquired Into'"; Collins, "Woman or Beast? Bestiality in Queensland, 1870–1949"; Evans, *The Criminal Prosecution and Capital Punishment of Animals,* pp. 146–52; Eve Levin, *Sex and Society in the World of the Orthodox Slavs, 900–1700* (Ithaca, N.Y.: Cornell University Press, 1989); Liliequist, "Peasants against Nature"; E. W. Monter, "Sodomy and Heresy in Early Modern Switzerland," *Journal of Homosexuality* 6, no. 1/2 (1980): 41–55; E. W. Monter, *Frontiers of Heresy: the Spanish Inquisition from the Basque Lands to Sicily* (Cambridge: Cambridge University Press, 1990); R. F. Oaks, "'Things Fearful to Name': Sodomy and Buggery in Seventeenth-Century New England," *Journal of Social History* 12, no. 2 (1978): 268–81; R. F. Oaks, "Perceptions of Homosexuality by Justices of the Peace in Colonial Virginia," *Journal of Homosexuality* 1–2 (1979): 35–41; Salisbury, *The Beast Within*; and John Murrin, "'Things Fearful to Name': Bestiality in Early America," this volume. For literary scholarship, see Dekkers, *Dearest Pet.* For legal scholarship, see Parker, "Is a Duck an Animal?".

58. In seventeenth-century Switzerland and Spain, for example, those indicted were often heretics, Protestant victims of Catholic zeal, and vice versa. In Spanish Aragon, between 1570 and 1630, the accused were likely to be foreigners, particularly French men and African slaves. See Monter, "Sodomy and Heresy in Early Modern Switzerland"; Monter, *Frontiers of Heresy.* In Sweden, the great majority of those indicted (and executed) were either very young boys or else ordinary peasants, farm servants, soldiers, boatswains, craftsmen, and apprentices (Liliequist, "Peasants against Na-

ture," p. 410). So, too, of twenty-five bestiality defendants in Somerset in England between 1740 and 1850, eighteen were identified as laborers, one as a mason and laborer, and one as a carpenter. Polly Morris, "Sodomy and Male Honor: The Case of Somerset, 1740–1850," *Journal of Homosexuality* 16 (1989): 387. Similarly, in Queensland, Australia, of fifty-three criminal dispositions for bestiality between 1870 and 1949, the great majority of defendants were European laborers, though Chinese and aboriginal men were also accused (Collins, "Woman or Beast?" p. 37). Moreover, almost all those accused of the related offense of lycanthropy in sixteenth-century France were of the lowest social status—vagrants, beggars, shepherds, and peasants—some of them were not natives and many were women. Caroline Oates, "Metamorphosis and Lycanthropy in Franche-Comté, 1521–1643," in *Fragments for a History of the Human Body,* ed. Michel Fehrer (New York: Urzone), p. 326.

59. Consider England, for example: in *The Family, Sex and Marriage in England 1500–1800* (New York: Harper & Row, 1977), p. 519, Lawrence Stone has suggested that between 1558 and 1603 an Essex resident had more than a 25 percent chance of being accused of fornication, adultery, buggery, incest, bestiality, or bigamy, which suggests an image of Elizabethan society which was both sexually very lax and also highly inquisitorial, with a great readiness to denounce the transgressions of others. However, the chances of being indicted for bestiality were actually very slim; according to the assize records there were only eight cases in Essex in this period and only nine between 1620 and 1680; Kent had ten, Sussex five, Hertfordshire four, and Surrey three (Thomas, *Man and the Natural World,* p.119).

60. Liliequist, "Peasants against Nature," p. 396 n. 5.

61. The study is cited in Dekkers, *Dearest Pet,* p. 135.

62. Sharpe, *Crime in Seventeenth-Century England,* pp. 65–66. See also Morris, "Sodomy and Male Honor."

63. Chapin, *Criminal Justice in Colonial America,* p. 128. Yet, Chapin also documents that between 1606 and 1660 very few men were arraigned for bestiality and that, perhaps because common folk regarded it as a victimless crime, only four or five were actually hanged for it (ibid.). In fact, only two men were executed for bestiality in seventeenth-century Massachusetts and none for sodomy. See Roger Thompson, *Sex in Middlesex: Popular Mores in a Massachusetts County, 1649–1699* (Amherst: University of Massachusetts Press, 1986), p. 174. John Murrin writes only that "[i]n all likelihood, acts of sodomy and bestiality were much rarer in New England than in other mainland colonies" (above, p. 141).

64. Thompson, *Sex in Middlesex,* pp. 74–75. In early modern societies such as England, a lengthy delay was imposed on marriage after the onset

of puberty. After considerable debate amongst historians, it has been suggested that in England this frustrating youthful decade was handled in one of two ways. Either (a) the Puritan taboos against pollution and filthiness were effective in forcing adolescents to repress their sexual urges until marriage; indeed, Stone (*The Family, Sex and Marriage in England,* pp. 613–14) shows that at the height of Puritan control between 1590 and 1660 the rural illegitimacy ratio fell steadily to the astonishingly low point of half of 1 percent. Or (b) adolescents satisfied their sexual needs in ways other than intercourse, such as homosexuality, masturbation, bestiality, petting, coitus interruptus, anal or oral sex, and resort to prostitutes with a range of male or female partners. Yet, high rates of none of these deviant practices except prostitution supported by more than very fragmentary and inconclusive historical evidence (ibid., p. 616). In England, at least, it is likely that, though the general delay in marriage for young men to the age of twenty-six or more created an acute socio-sexual problem, this was largely deflected by successful Puritan ideology and partially relieved by a substantial increase in prostitution.

65. Ibid., p. 410.

66. Collins, "Woman or Beast?" p. 39.

67. T. O. Beidelman, "Kaguru Justice and the Concept of Legal Fictions," *Journal of African Law* 5, no. 1 (1961): 11–14.

68. Salisbury, *The Beast Within,* p. 94.

69. Ibid., p. 95.

70. Coke, *The Third Part of the Institutes of the Laws of England,* 3:58.

71. Sharpe, *Crime in Seventeenth-Century England,* pp. 65–66.

72. Hoadly, *Records of the Colony and Plantation of New Haven,* 1:10–11.

73. Bradford, *Of Plymouth Plantation,* p. 320.

74. Liliequist, "Peasants against Nature," p. 410.

75. Collins, "Woman or Beast?" pp. 40–41.

76. Krafft-Ebing, *Psychopathia Sexualis,* pp. 376–77.

77. Dekkers, *Dearest Pet,* p. 149

78. Adams, "Bestiality: The Unmentioned Abuse," p. 30.

79. Linda Lovelace with Mike McGrady, *Ordeal* (New York: Bell Publishing, 1980), pp. 107–14. See also Xaviera Hollander, *The Happy Hooker* (New York: Dell Publishing, 1972), p. 35.

80. Carol J. Adams, "Deena—the World's Only Stripping Chimp," *Animals' Voice Magazine* 3, no. 1 (1990): 72.

81. Liliequist, "Peasants against Nature"; Kinsey, Pomeroy, and Martin, *Sexual Behavior in the Human Male*; Kinsey, Pomeroy, Martin, and Gebhard, *Sexual Behavior in the Human Female.*

82. Liliequist, "Peasants against Nature," p. 414.

83. Ibid., p. 413.

84. Fernando Tapia, "Children Who Are Cruel to Animals," *Child Psychiatry and Human Development* 2, no. 2 (1971): 70–77; Alan R. Felthouse, "Childhood Cruelty to Cats, Dogs and Other Animals," *Bulletin of the American Academy of Psychiatry and Law* 9 (1981): 48–53. William N. Friedrich, Anthony J. Urquiza, and Robert L. Beilke, "Behavior Problems in Sexually Abused Young Children," *Journal of Pediatric Psychology* 11, no. 1 (1986): 47–57. See also Mic Hunter, *Abused Boys: The Neglected Victims of Sexual Abuse* (New York: Lexington, 1990), pp. 214–16.

85. John E. Archer, "A Fiendish Outrage? A Study of Animal Maiming: 1830–1870," *Agricultural History Review* 33, pt. 2 (1985): 152.

86. *The Times,* March 2, May 8, June 4, 1993.

87. *Standard Times,* July 26, 1991.

88. Sigmund Fleismann, *Bestiality: Sexual Intercourse Between Men and Women and Animals,* trans. Robert Harris (Baltimore: Medical Knowledge Press, 1968), pp. 50–71; Adams, "Woman-Battering and Harm to Animals," pp. 65–69.

89. Quoted in Holmes, *Sex Crimes,* p. 27.

90. Frank R. Ascione, "Children Who Are Cruel to Animals: A Review of Research and Implications for Developmental Psychopathology," *Anthrozoös* 6, no. 4 (1993): 226–46; Jeffrey Moussaieff Masson and Susan McCarthy, *When Elephants Weep: The Emotional Lives of Animals* (New York: Delacorte, 1995).

91. Ted Benton, *Natural Relations: Ecology, Animal Rights and Social Justice* (London: Verso, 1994), pp. 147–48.

8

THE FAMILIAR OTHER AND FERAL SELVES
LIFE AT THE HUMAN/ANIMAL BOUNDARY

H. PETER STEEVES

But man, proud man,
Dressed in a little brief authority,
Most ignorant of what he's most assured,
His glassy essence, like an angry ape,
Plays such fantastic tricks before high heaven
As make the angels weep.
—Measure for Measure

INTRODUCTION: AN EASY JOB

In September 1920, Reverend J. A. L. Singh set out into the Indian night to kill the *Manush-Bagha,* the man-ghost of the jungle.[1] The creature, it was said, had the body and limbs of a human, the face of a ghost. The villagers warned the reverend that it was a hideous beast—possibly not of this world—and that no one was safe in the jungle. Part human, part animal, part who-knows-what, but supernatural to be sure, it was a reason, they assured him, to travel in groups, to be sure to be home before dusk turned into night and the beast awakened, hungry.

Reverend Singh, more curious than frightened, suggested constructing a platform in a tree in order to have a vantage point from which to shoot the beast, but the villagers wanted no part of it. By early October, though, he had finally found someone to lead him to a place where there had been several sightings—to a white-ant mound near Godamuri, where the locals told stories of a creature that raced through the night, haunting the countryside. Singh and his party set up camp near the ant mound and began their vigil.

The short wait was soon rewarded. The first evening, three wolves tentatively made their way out of the ground, squeezing through the large holes in the mound. They were followed by two wolf cubs and, finally, by two white creatures—the man-ghosts—which Reverend Singh immediately recognized to be two female human children.

Singh persuaded the group to hold their fire as the wolf family disappeared into the jungle. Visibly shaken, the party disbanded and headed back to the village in spite of the reverend's assurance that he had solved the mystery and his pleas to remain and help excavate the mound. After the close encounter with the creatures no one, in fact, would stay with Reverend Singh, and he was forced to search for a new party of men from a tribe far away and unacquainted with the ghost story. One week later, he returned with his new group and began the dig, hoping to capture what he now believed to be the two feral children—human girls raised and cared for by the wolf family in the middle of the Indian wilderness.

With the first few strokes of the shovel, two male wolves emerged from the mound, ran past the diggers, and were enveloped by the jungle. Next, a female wolf appeared, and Singh knew right away that she would be the greatest obstacle to securing the children. Even as the party shouted and threatened her, she remained on the mound, baring her teeth and growling at the diggers. It soon became clear to everyone that she was prepared to make a stand—she was not going to abandon her home and her family so easily.

In his diaries, Reverend Singh explains:

I had a great mind to capture it, because I guessed from its whole bearing on the spot that it must have been the mother wolf, whose nature was so ferocious and affection so sublime. It struck me with wonder. I was simply amazed to think that an animal had such a noble feeling surpassing even that of mankind—the highest form of creation—to bestow all the love and affection of a fond and ideal mother on these peculiar beings, which surely had once been brought in . . . as food for the cubs. To permit them to live and be nurtured by them (wolves) in this fashion is divine. I failed to realize the import of the circumstances and became dumb and inert. In the meantime, the men pierced her through with arrows, and she fell dead. . . . After the mother wolf was killed, it was an easy job. . . . I threw one of the sheets on [the] ball of children and cubs and separated one from the other. . . . We gave the cubs to the diggers. . . . They went away happy and sold [them] in the Hat for a good price [while] . . . I took charge of the two human children.

Reverend Singh named the girls Kamala and Amala. Kamala was approximately eight years old and Amala was eighteen months. After their capture, the girls went to live with the reverend and his wife at their orphanage. But their time there was short. Amala lived less than a year; Kamala only nine. During her time with the Singhs, Kamala was studied and educated and civilized, though it seldom appeared that much of it stuck. She learned a few words, raced around on all fours, preferred the company of dogs to humans, and frightened the other orphans by prowling at night, sniffing and growling near their beds in the moonlight. She was unappreciated, though the center of attention, and unhappy, though finally once again among her own kind.

It is without question that when we study feral children we inevitably learn more about ourselves than our subject. There are more than fifty cases on record of feral children—human children raised in the wild by everything from bears and leopards to monkeys and birds. Our treatment of the adoptive animal parents is notorious—most find the fate of Amala and Kamala's mother and siblings. And the suffering and indignities that we inflict on the human children in the name of socializing and civilizing are equally embarrassing. The stories run from simple beatings and whippings (all in the name of "reinforcement training"), to the extreme cases such as the gazelle-boy, a human male raised by a family of gazelles, who, upon being captured, proved to possess the unnerving ability to leap great distances—jumping, nearly flying, through the air in the manner of his adoptive parents. His human benefactors, unable to persuade him to refrain from such activity and anxious to see him assimilated into human culture, considered their options and chose to cut the tendons in his legs, thereby inducing less gazelle-like behavior.[2]

Each story is different, intriguing in its own right. And each represents a crisis, not only for the way in which the children in these cases seem inevitably to be mishandled and brutalized as they are introduced to civilization, but because their very existence is a threat to our understanding of what it is to be human. The existence of feral children calls into question the firm boundary between human and animal, forcing us to reevaluate our understanding of ourselves and our world. A feral child is the human that is nearly an animal—the familiar that has nearly become the Other.

And the line of demarcation separating human from animal is eroded from another direction as well, as is evidenced by the myriad myths and stories of animals that are nearly human. Here the cases are not as well documented as those of feral children. It is possible that animals that are nearly human—the Bigfoot, the Sasquatch, the Yeti, etc.—do not exist at all. But the matter of their existence is not key here, for the fact that we acknowledge the possibility—even as myth—is telling. Indeed, even that which is more clearly fiction (werewolves and vampires, etc.) helps paint a picture of who we are and how we understand our humanity and the living world of which we are a part. In this way these stories of familiar Others and feral Selves—of humans that are nearly animals and animals that are nearly humans—ultimately challenge the boundaries of our communities in many ways, forcing us to ask questions of our collective identity and the ways in which we experience ourselves in the world.

Defining "Human": The Non-Physical Differences

Unaccomodated man is no more but such a poor, bare, forked animal as thou art.
—King Lear

Without giving the matter much thought, it seems clear what we mean by "human." Traditionally, the philosophical problem has been defining "person"—the moral individual. "Human" is usually considered to be easily defined, a matter of genetics or biology—at least a matter of science. "Person" is problematic both because it eludes a popularly accepted definition and because although there are things that are clearly people (e.g., you, the reader) and things that clearly are not (e.g., a hydrogen molecule), there are concrete examples of things about which our intuitions supposedly become murky (e.g., a fetus, a comatose patient).

Given this understanding of the problem, though, "human" must be similarly vague. A clear definition of "human" is not easily achieved, for here, too, there are creatures that are puzzling, existing in that nether region of uncertainty. We will be looking at these "problem" cases below. For now, let us concentrate on why the traditional boundary between human and animal is threatened when we try to define "human."

There are varieties of classical and ancient descriptions of humans that prove interesting. We know that Plato considered man the two-legged naked animal. Anaxagoras was entranced by human posture as well, and suggested that because we can stand upright on two legs we can better see our world and, more importantly, we can have free use of our hands, thus making us superior. Aristotle puts an interesting twist on Anaxagoras and suggests that it is our mental superiority that allows us to use our hands in creative ways, not vice versa. But it is Aristotle's notion of man as political and rational that has survived and remained most popular. A scholastic definition in this tradition is offered by Gunnar Broberg and proves an intriguing and worthwhile place to begin our inquiry in earnest:

> Man is a "substance." But so are the angels. So substance must be divided into corporeal and incorporeal. Man has "body," whereas the angels are incorporeal. But stone is also "body." So "body" must be divided into "living" and dead, that is, with or without a soul. Man is a living bodily substance, stone a lifeless one. But a plant also lives. Hence corporeal living substances must be divided into sentient and insentient. Man can feel, but the plant cannot. But a horse can also feel. So living, corporeal, sentient substances must be divided into "rational" and irrational. Only man is *rationalis*. . . . The series sets out the definition of man as *substantia corporea, vivens, sentiens, rationalis*— or, more concisely, *animal rationale*. It is a hierarchy with uncrossable boundaries.[3]

Apart from the presence of angels (which is another investigation altogether), one of the problems, of course, is defining "rationality." If it is to be equated with intelligence, awareness, or even problem-solving ability then it does little to separate human from animal. This problem—and the hierarchy created by the scholastic definition—is echoed in a thousand variations of the above argument, even those of the post-Darwinian age. Consider, for example and for a closer analysis, Charles Winick's definition from *The Dictionary of Anthropology*:

> *Man* . . . a hominid, namely Homo sapiens, who [makes] tools. . . . The word man is popularly used in a much more narrow manner than taxonomy would indicate, and its emotional connotations make it difficult to use in an objective manner. The major characteristics that distinguish man from monkeys, apes, and lemurs are the following: the nose's prominent bridge and well-developed tip, a median furrow in the upper lip, possession of the chin, . . . large brain (2½–3 times the size of the gorillas') . . . outrolling of the lips and visibility of the mucous membrane as a continuos red line, long life span, . . . symbolic expression, educability, and advanced culture.[4]

The fact that "Man" is used interchangeably with "human" is intriguing. As feminist writers properly point out, this is not simply a quirk of language but rather a linguistic manifestation of social conditions. It speaks to the marginalization of women—as if humanity can be described by excluding women and making reference only to men. Indeed, some have even suggested that since the word "human" contains the word "man" "it must be replaced (or respelled) if women are to have any hope of changing their social condition."[5]

The point of this, though, is not just to suggest how language and reality are interrelated but to illustrate that the "emotional connotations" of such words as "human" run deep. We would like to think that a firm, scientific, objective definition exists. In fact, even if we admit that such a notion as scientific objectivity is a comfortable fiction and that all language actually reflects a socially constructed reality, we would like to think that a word such as "human" is, in the relative scheme of things, *more* objective than some others. "Person" and "happiness" and "liberty" might seem a little vague, a little culturally dependent, but surely we can agree on what constitutes "humanity." After all, the word is a scientific term or at least a derivative of one. It is more like "manganese sulfate" or "microprocessor" than it is like "person" or "happiness."

Or so it would seem. Winick's definition struggles to provide an "objective" set of characteristics to distinguish human from other creatures, but the set proves suspect. First, it is important to note that Winick defines "human" by distinguishing humans from other creatures near the top of the assumed evolutionary ladder. Conjure up in your mind, he seems to be saying, that group of primate-monkey-ape-human-like creatures. Now, how can you tell the humans from the rest?

Already, it should be clear there is a problem. Before we even get to the set of characteristics peculiarly human, we see that this definition rests on a multitude of unarticulated assumptions. First, is it so obvious what characteristics constitute apes and monkeys and higher primates? These classifications must be clear before we can use them to define "human." Second, we should be aware that this type of definition is one that will allow us to pick out the real human from a group of creatures that are "human-like," but it does little to help us determine whether a creature in isolation is human. In the end we will presumably know how to tell a human from a gorilla, but such a relational definition will not help much in cases in which we are presented with a creature of unknown nature in isolation.

Let me be clearer on this problem because it is a fundamental one for the project at hand. Suppose we encounter a creature and we want to know if it is human.[6] Using the relational definition proposed by Winick, we would list its characteristics and then compare that list to a similar one of, for instance, gorilla characteristics. The argument goes that if we compare the nose, lip, chin, brain size, etc. of the creature, we should be close to determining whether it is human or not, but at most what we are determining is whether it is not very gorilla-like (or at least not very much like the "ideal" gorilla-type). Is "human" properly defined as "anything-that-is-go-rilla-like but has a larger brain, a more prominent nose, a longer life span, etc."? Something seems lacking.

But perhaps these specific characteristics, if scrutinized, do more work than one might suppose. Perhaps they can indeed define "human" and not simply separate humans from apes. Winick's definition, which is character-istic in the literature, lists two different types of distinguishing features. Not wanting to give in to any naïve dualism, we can still note that the first type is purely physical, and includes such notions as brain size, nose shape, lip formation, etc., while the second type is nonphysical and includes edu-cability, toolmaking know-how, symbolic expression, and cultural achieve-ments.

Unfortunately, the nonphysical characteristics are not very helpful, at least not without further explication. Educability is a large notion—large enough, surely, to include talking parrots, chimps who learn sign language, and even stupid-pet-trick-performing dogs. Indeed, the gazelles who raised the gazelle-boy in the wild seemed to have learned to interpret the boy's facial expressions to the same degree that the boy had learned the gazelles' ear-twitching language. Toolmaking, once thought to be the proud domain of "humans," is also an activity in which we now know other animals (that is, clearly nonhuman animals) indulge. Elephants have been known to use trees to scratch an itch. Some monkeys use stones to smash open nuts and seeds.[7] And other monkeys carefully choose tree limbs and methodically strip them of leaves and protruding stubs in order to fashion "dip sticks" to retrieve ants and other insects from holes in the ground and in stumps. This is not simply tool use, but toolmaking.

Also relevant to this question of tools is the fact that most creatures we now consider "human" are losing or have lost toolmaking abilities they might have had. Technology, often considered to be a tool, has clearly moved beyond the tool stage. It has become such that most "civilized" humans would have a hard time surviving for very long without their "civilizing" tools—thus causing us to question whether they serve us or, due to our dependence, we serve them. We have learned to push the right buttons on telephones and microwaves, but few of us could fashion tools that would help us survive if we were suddenly left without technology.[8]

The question of symbolic expression is similarly unhelpful in that al-though this is not a skill "humans" seem to be losing, it is clearly the case that a variety of animals use and understand symbols. From the gorilla/sign-language example, to the case of the research pigeons who used such con-cepts as "tree,"[9] non-"human" animals seem capable of a wide variety of abstractions. In fact, if what is truly meant by "symbolic expression" is "language," then it cannot be denied that animal languages abound. Whether at the subsonic level of elephants and whales, in the intricate language of birds,[10] or in the patterns of a dancing bee, information is constantly being transmitted around us. Sounds and movements represent objects and states of affairs, and to fail to call this "language" would be blind hubris.

Finally, there is the question of culture—once again, a difficult concept to pin down. Some wolves, we know, perform complex hunting ceremonies before they set out to the task. Ranking in chimp society is based neither on size nor strength but on the social status of one's parents. And dolphins, with their intricate social structures, are believed by many to possess a culture and a set of traditions particular to each school. Discussing the possibility of animals as sociocultural beings, Dutch philosopher Barbara Noske indicates that there is reason to believe that "culturally transmitted practices and ideas are part of a collective memory . . . [and] that dolphin traditions too are cultural in that they belong to the school as a whole, an entity which is greater than the sum of its individual parts."[11]

As a result, it would seem that the traditional nonphysical characteristics particular to humans do little to constitute a definition capable of distinguishing many species from each other. But what of the physical differences which supposedly define humanity?

DEFINING "HUMAN": THE PHYSICAL DIFFERENCES

He is only an animal, only sensible in the duller parts.
—Love's Labour's Lost

Often, human bodies are distinguished from animal bodies in a linguistically ad hoc manner. In English, humans have "hair" but animals have "fur." In Spanish, humans walk on "piernas" (legs) but animals walk on "patas." French animals smell with a "museau," but French humans use a "nez."[12] Surely, these body parts have more commonalities than differences, but the words serve to separate artificially.[13]

Unfortunately, the words themselves do little to help us *define* "human." In Spanish, for instance, a leg might be a *pierna* if it is human and a *pata* if it is nonhuman, but defining a human as having *piernas* rather than *patas* accomplishes nothing. These parts are named *after* one knows the type of creature with which one is dealing. Standing alone, the Spanish sentence "¿Con qué corre el?" ("What does he use to run?") cannot be answered unless one knows whether or not the subject is human. This testifies to the fact that the real difference is contrived. Legs are legs, but having a different word for a human leg separates humans (and serves to make us "special"). The word can only be used, then, after one has distinguished the human from the nonhuman.

The power of language to construct difference rather than mirror difference makes the task of determining particularly human physical traits difficult, but not necessarily impossible. Winick, recall, offered descriptions of a human nose, lip, chin, and brain based on shape, color, weight, etc. Are such differences the stuff of which a proper definition can be had?

The problem, once again, is the ad hoc nature of the list of qualities; and this problem, I maintain, is inevitable in any definition based on a list of characteristics.[14] The difficulty is in arguing for why this particular set of characteristics is key to being human. Curved lips and protruding chins are seen as important qualities, but why *these* qualities? The true problem becomes clear if we ask a distasteful yet enlightening question: why, someone might say, would we not include white skin as a particularly human trait? That is, humans, by definition, would have chins, furrowed lips, and fair skin, etc. The only possible response to such a question is that there are humans who aren't white—indeed, humans come in many colors—and therefore it would be wrong to include skin color as a determining factor. But now the problem should be evident, for how do we know that humans are not all white unless we already know who counts as a human? And this is cheating. If we are trying to define "human" we cannot say beforehand who is human and who is not, and therefore know what qualities seem to be common only to humans. It is as if we first divide up the world into humans and nonhumans, and then look to see what qualities the humans possess as a group that are not common to the creatures in the other group. Skin color won't work because humans have variously colored skin. Big brains might work, though, because all humans seem to have brains (on the average) larger than the creatures in the nonhuman group. Using this method we could then construct a list of qualities shared by humans and humans alone, but the question would remain: how did we know how to divide up the world initially? On what criteria did we base this initial categorization? It would seem that we had to know already who we wanted to count and who we didn't want to count before we started. Any definition achieved after this categorization is thus hopelessly ad hoc.

And there are other problems as well. Winick's insistence on *red* lips, for instance, seems curious. Surely this is neither a necessary nor sufficient condition for being human and it is questionable, really, whether the majority of "humans" actually have red lips. The question of a "well-developed tip" to the nose is equally suspect. Certainly, these are cultural ideals for (though perhaps not even common among) Europeans,[15] but this does not describe, for instance, the typical African face.

Realizing the significance of all of this, I will not take any more time to continue to develop the thesis of a cultural and racial bias in Winick's definition, but it is important to see the possibility of such bias and the ease with which such a "scientific" definition both reflects and more firmly establishes racial power structures in society. African humans, and "recent" African descendants,[16] are, by this definition, a little less human, a little closer to being animal. If we accept such a definition, we also tend to accept more easily such things as Charles Murray's claim that African Americans are less intelligent than whites,[17] and to accept the behavior of one of the LAPD officers who was involved in the Rodney King beating and who referred to a domestic violence call involving an African American family as a case of "gorillas in the mist." This defining business has serious implications for us all.

And what if Winick's definition were to be accepted? What if we ignored its ad hoc nature and the clear racial bias in this list of physical qualities needed to be truly human? *Is* this what we mean by truly human? Is being human to be understood as having a chin? I do not mean to diminish the role of physical structure in being human—indeed, the experience of body is something that must concern us throughout this project—but something seems lacking in such a definition: to be human is to be chinned.

Other approaches are similarly flawed. Philip Bock stresses the tool-making abilities of humans, but also offers a more historical-anthropological definition of human as "the favorite child of evolution."[18] Such genus-species attempts to straighten things out are interesting and have continuously grown in popularity since Darwin first suggested something similar in 1871.[19] According to such a family tree, apes and humans parted ways twenty to forty million years ago and have been evolving separately ever since. And you can thus tell a human by tracing its "bloodline."

Most scientists, it turns out, enjoy such a definition, and with increasing technology many feel that they can pinpoint the date at which humans first appeared with even greater accuracy. Physical anthropologist Chris Stringer uses advanced DNA analysis to supplement the standard tools of carbon dating and just plain digging in the dirt in order to suggest that early modern man appeared 30,000 years ago, probably in Africa.[20] A colleague of Stringer's further proposes that each branch of the genus *Homo* can claim a common mother—a single female who lived in Africa 200,000 years ago. All of this from DNA evidence.

The secular version of Eve is enticing. She pulls us all together—truly making us brothers and sisters. And she fits nicely into the scientific worldview as well, for even though it is hard to imagine that one real woman existed to whom we are all related, evolution seemingly demands that this must be the case. At a certain point some nonhuman animal fetus proved to be a random mutation, and Eve was born—the mother of all humanity.

One of the problems with such a story is that it is surely a crude telling of history. Evolution is a process, not an event, and modern humans probably "emerged" slowly—mutation by mutation. This is problematic because we are then left with a long period of time in which it is "clear" that the initial creatures are not human, it is "clear" that the end creatures are human, and it is completely *unclear* at what point humans actually appear and the nonhuman becomes the human.[21]

Perhaps someone might say, though, that a certain "branch" of the tree is the human branch, and since all of the creatures except for "us" have died off from that branch, is this not enough to constitute a definition of humanity?

Separating humans from other animals by means of branching evolution or DNA does not solve the problem of securing a definition. First, we must wonder how to cut the branch—i.e., how far back do we go to determine the start of "humans"? Pruning the nonhuman from the human once again seems an inherently arbitrary task and assumes that we already know what a human is. Second, there is the further assumption that these limbs (or DNA patterns) are easily distinguished—that we can draw an accurate picture of our family tree with each branch neatly placed, each DNA sequence understood and labeled. The truth is that scientists themselves continue to fight over the appropriate design of the tree and some are even questioning the validity of evolution's claim to be *the* one explanation of how the living world operates.[22] Indeed, assuming unerring knowledge of the "tree of evolution" as a given fundamentally begs several questions raised by the arguments presented here. As we will see, the problem that a Bigfoot creature raises is not just that his existence seems mysterious, almost the stuff of science fiction, but that he doesn't fit into our evolutionary schematism. Finally, the anthropological/genetic definition of "human" is lacking because it fails to reflect what we typically mean when we say "human." Defining "human" by means of distant hairy relatives or genetic tests capable of being run only by a few experts in our society is just as unfulfilling as defining "human" as a creature with a chin. There may be nothing inherently wrong with such a definition, but there is a strong sense that it fails to convey the essence of what (we think) we mean by "human."

The power of the anthropological approach, though, is the way in which it pulls us together, relating us to each other and attempting to define us as a group. But the secular Eve—that two-hundred-thousand-year-old African woman—can, at most, relate our bodies. The religious Eve,[23] on the other hand, relates us in immaterial ways, em*body*ing the "spirit" of our humanity. Perhaps what is needed is a mixture of these approaches. Can we give an account of a "fuller" humanity? Can we offer a history of the body and a history of the spirit capable of defining who we humans are?

Many communitarian theorists would maintain that they have accomplished just this. Authors such as Alastair MacIntyre, Michael Sandel, Stanley Hauerwas, and David Carr speak of narratives, stories, and traditions constituting our identity—constituting, even, our Selves.[24] Although these arguments are often at the level of individual communities and cultures, could they not be expanded to account for the constitution of all human communities and of all humans? Could telling a story about who "we" humans are—in body and spirit—actually serve to constitute this "we"?

An interesting difficulty with this solution is that if we look at our stories and our histories and even at our common goods, we discover that they do not constitute a community of humans, but rather a community of living beings of many different types. I call this a "Deep Community," and I have argued for it in some detail elsewhere.[25] The point is that the stories we tell do not separate humans from animals, but rather tie the living world together as one. Our stories are all interconnected, as are our goods. If one attempts to unweave these strands, they cannot stand alone.[26] I cannot tell the story of who I am without telling the story of the animals[27] around me: I am constituted, in part, by them. And the same is true at the level of the story of humanity.

But perhaps being human is best understood as being a particular character in the intertwining stories of the living world. Human characters have a certain physical presence and they play certain roles. The relationships humans have to other characters constitute what it means to be human, and the act of defining "human" thus becomes not an act of separating and distinguishing, but an act of recognizing the appropriate player in the context of the scene.

Such a definition is not very scientific. It is loose and open and admits the possibility of a constantly changing identity. And it is, I think, about the best we can hope for. The fact that what it means to be human changes with time and even with context places the traditional hierarchy and the traditional boundary between human and animal at risk. The strict dichotomies of human/animal, human/nonhuman, and us/them do not make sense in such a story. Yet we continue to think, speak, and act as if they do. And this is curious. What accounts for this chasm between the way in which we experience the world and the way in which we act in the world, between the experienced truth of who we are and the constructed fiction of who we think ourselves to be, between, most basically, phenomenology and praxis? This question will stay with us throughout this project as we now move to investigate what happens when the hierarchies collapse and the boundaries fail—what happens when we are faced with a crisis in our experience such that the familiar becomes the Other.

FERAL SELVES:
THE HUMAN THAT IS NEARLY ANIMAL

> *Come on, poor babe,*
> *Some powerful spirit instructs the kites and the ravens*
> *To be thy nurses! Wolves and bears, they say,*
> *Casting their savageness aside, have done*
> *Like offices of pity.*
> —A Winter's Tale

Feral children such as the wolf girls Kamala and Amala have formed part of our story for a long time. There are both mythical and factual cases, though the latter are becoming increasingly rare as "civilization" spreads across the land. The fact is, it is harder today for a child to remain hidden in the wilderness because there is, daily, less wilderness.

I begin by noting that although the feral children of myth play an important role in determining who we are, the factual cases are what I will focus on here. From Romulus and Remus to Tarzan, Mowgli, and the various heroes populating the dime-store novels of the genre which flourished in this country for the first half of the twentieth century, fiction has used the feral child to help us better understand ourselves and our society. The nonfictional cases, I maintain, serve much the same function in a different way. Still, it is common and not unwise to begin with some skepticism. Even our moments of skeptical inquiry say much about us.

In one tale of skepticism that is perhaps as fictional as the feral child it involves, we are told that Aristotle could admit the possibility of animals rearing humans, but insisted that each individual case needed his personal investigation. One medieval story suggests that Alexander the Great met and fell in love with a snake-girl—a human female who was said to have been "hatched" and cared for by snakes after being placed in a broken eggshell and abandoned by humans. Alexander lusted after the snake-girl and wanted her as his mistress, but his teacher, Aristotle, advised caution.

Placing a ring of snake venom around her, Aristotle sought to test the girl's origins. In the end, we are told, the fumes of the venom strangled her and the snake-girl died—a supposedly proud Aristotle nearby, thinking that he had proven that the girl could not have lived in the company of snakes.[28] Again, the fate of the feral child—real or mythical—is typically sealed upon his or her introduction into human society.

Our peculiar treatment of feral children is partially a direct result of our confusion over their, and more fundamentally our, nature. Surely there is a desire to see these children act in a more familiar manner—hence, the cutting of the gazelle-boy's tendons, the common desire to teach captured feral children to eat with utensils, the longing to coax them to speak, etc. In such cases there is an attempt to mold the habits, personality, and even the body of the child into something more recognizably human.

Indeed, the body plays an important role in our understanding here. Reverend Singh was especially bothered by the "corns on the knees and on the palm of the hand near the wrist which [Kamala and Amala] had developed from walking on all fours."[29] After scrubbing and treating the corns with boric acid, Reverend Singh cut the girls' hair and washed their bodies several times, struggling to remove layers and layers of "dirt." A transformation of the body had begun, but Singh soon discovered that it was in appearance only. The bodies of the girls were inherently different. In the following passage one should note the references to animals and to animal bodies as the ideal nonhuman body:

> They looked [like] human children again [but for the jawbones]. The jaws . . . had undergone some sort of change in the chewing of bones.
> . . . When they moved their jaws in chewing, the upper and lower jawbones appeared to part and close visibly, unlike human jaws. . . . They could sit on the ground squatting down, . . . but could not stand up at all. . . . Their eyes . . . had a peculiar blue glare, like that of a cat or dog, in the dark. At night . . . you saw only two blue lights sending forth rays in the dark. They could see better by night than by day. . . . They could detect the existence of . . . any object in the darkest place when and where human sight fails completely. . . . They had a powerful instinct and could smell meat or anything from a great distance like animals. . . . Their hands and arms were long, almost reaching to the knees. . . . The nails of the hand and foot were worn on the inside to a concave shape. . . . They used to eat or drink like dogs [and] could not walk like humans. They went on all fours [and] they used to sleep like pigs or dog pups, overlapping one another.[30]

1. Photographs of the "wolf girls" Kamala and Amala taken by Rev. J. A. L. Singh, 1920. *Left,* the girls asleep "overlapping one another," as Singh put it in his diary; *right,* one of the girls eating "as a dog lappeth." Reproduced by permission from Arnold Gesell, *Wolf Child and Human Child: Being a Narrative Interpretation of the Life History of Kamala, the Wolf Girl* (New York: Harper & Brothers, 1940), plates 5 and 6.

Indeed, the girls preferred to keep their bodies close in this manner, sometimes even when not sleeping. When Amala died, Kamala touched her face and clung to her body in the coffin. She cried two tears, and for the next six days sat in a corner, moving only to smell all of the places Amala had frequented. Left alone, though, Kamala soon began a strict regime designed by the Singhs to "help [her] use her body in human ways."[31]

The ease with which Reverend Singh separates animal traits from human traits in the girls should, at this point in our inquiry, stand out as clearly suspect. It is also important to note the degree to which the body is a social construct and the way in which this fact is evidenced by Singh's commentary. What accounts for the girls' bodies seeming so inhuman if, in fact, they were genetically human, the offspring of human parents? Singh, and most commentators, suggest a series of mutations—adaptations to the environment which erode the humanity of the body. In other words, what began as human has become animal. Chewing on bones, for instance, has warped the jaw, and walking on all fours has formed corns and calluses on the knees and wrists. Human wrists are smooth, and the assumption is that Kamala and Amala began with smooth wrists, and then adapted to walking like animals and were changed. *Restoring* their humanity involved reshaping the body.

The arms present a different problem. If, in fact, they were elongated, hanging to their knees, it is hard to explain how such a change—from "human" arms to more "simian" arms—took place. Would arms grow longer if we used them to walk? And what of the girls' eyes? Is a cat-like glare possible for human eyes in which the retina is typically thought to be incapable of reflecting light to any noticeable degree?[32] Mutations such as these cannot be accounted for by an appeal to simple adaptation without admitting that the body is naturally neither human nor animal but rather becomes whatever is most appropriate for the context. In a sense, this is what Darwinism is all about. The body, for Darwin, is an environmental construct, never stable, never finished. Evolution, though, is a slow process and will not admit the possibility of major change so quickly. Furthermore, evolutionary change is from generation to generation, not within one organism over a few years. An environmental construct is context-relative, but this answer will not explain Reverend Singh's observations and worries.

Perhaps a solution can be seen in Singh's observation that the girls had a "powerful instinct" that led them to smell over great distances "like animals." An instinct is curious because it strikes at the heart of Cartesian dualism—the way in which we supposedly exist as both body and mind. An instinct is psychological in nature; it dictates behavior. Yet it is precariously incarnate in that it is "built in" to a body—to a species-specific body. How could Kamala and Amala have a nonhuman instinct?

Suggesting, in this manner, that the body is a social construct is nothing new. Many feminist authors have written convincingly on the subject, and the sensory evidence surrounds us. Bodies are objectified and fought, dissected into pieces and admired, technologically modified and reinvented. The breast is surely a social creation. Fat is a social creation. Hair is a social creation. And this is more than a critique of Wonderbras, Jenny Craig, and Rogaine. It is an admission that what the body is (and what the body *should* be) is communally defined.[33] Being human is being a certain size and shape and smell, etc. It is not a matter of the body adapting to its surroundings but rather of the body being constructed to fit the society. And the same is true of animal bodies, which are usually, though not always, defined by their nonhuman characteristics.[34]

Instinct, arms, and eyes are certainly no exception, and the wolf-girls' failure to meet the human standard represents a crisis for us. Science is little help. By ancestor-definitions, the girls are human. By characteristic-definitions, they are animal. Their bodies are unfamiliar, yet like our own. Noske has suggested that feral children "not only have met the Other, they have almost become the Other."[35] Almost. Especially if we understand the animal Other to be a construct in the same sense as the human Self. But there is a crisis nonetheless. In fact, the great Swedish taxonomist Linnaeus (Carl von Linné)—of whom the Swedes still say "God created, and Linnaeus classified"—was so disturbed by feral children that he separated them on the pre-Darwinian biological tree as *Homo ferus.*

We are left to wonder if this is a legitimate distinction. Anthropological lineage was not enough to define humanity, for feral children surely are born from human parents. Perhaps Reverend Singh's insistence on the animal bodies Kamala and Amala had acquired was an attempt to understand their Otherness, and to reaffirm his own humanity. Perhaps Linnaeus's classification fulfills a similar need. What is clear is that the comfortable fiction of a human/animal dichotomy and the notion of a strict definition for "human" and "animal" are threatened by feral children.

At this point, though, we have only analyzed the body of the feral child and its implications for our notions of human and animal. Not wishing to degenerate into a full-blown dualism, we can still acknowledge that the crisis is not merely one of body. The behavior, psychology, and mental life of feral children also seem to call into question our concept of "human."

It is easy enough to suggest that what keeps feral children from being (fully) human is their lack of human education and culture. They neither use human language to communicate nor understand how humans interact with each other: years of living outside civilization have stripped them of their humanity. Perhaps, though, humanity is something that is not *taken* from feral children, but rather something that is never bestowed upon them. There is a variety of ways to argue such a point. One might say that feral children do not cast themselves as humans in their stories and thus never achieve human status. This is an interesting approach, but allow me to suggest another more phenomenological explanation beginning with the question: what if a child needs to be treated and attended to as human in order to be human?

I will only offer a brief sketch of this proposal here. What I have in mind is the notion that the burgeoning consciousness of the infant will not necessarily "develop" into human intentionality on its own, but rather requires the presence of a Significant Other who is human. Typically, the human Significant Other (very often the mother) attends to the infant as if he or she were human. This "gracious act of attention"[36] is thus responsible for "creating" a human-person—a new member of the community. The infant, as a consequence, develops senses of Self and Other *simultaneously.* It is not the case that an infant first has a sense of Self and then wonders if there really are other minds out there. He is not aware of his own Ego and then begins to investigate the world, seeing which objects act and look similar to the way he acts and looks, and thus which objects must be Others. Instead, the senses of Ego and Other arise as themes at the same time.

Now all of this is getting us involved in matters that are somewhat off-topic; but they are important, for it would seem that without the gracious act of attention coming from a human, the infant does not become human. Along the same lines, James Hart suggests that "[i]f the first Other is not a human person, the Other to the Other which I (i.e., the infant) can be is not a human person."[37] This would accomplish a great deal toward explaining the case of the feral child. Without a human Other to attend to the child *as human,* the child does not become human—which is not to say that feral children have no sense of Self or Other, but rather that such senses do not include "humanity." Amala and Kamala clearly did not have the intentional life of human beings. It is not just that their social skills, psychologies, and attitudes were nonhuman. Something deeper in the psychic life of the girls was different. The structures of their experience were not "human structures"—such structures could not arise and take shape in their burgeoning streams of consciousness without the presence of the human Other to cause them to take shape. How powerful, this gracious act of attention.

Indeed, if we imagine attending to nonhuman individuals such as dogs as if they were human, would it not be possible to "create" humanity? Anecdotal evidence abounds: the story of the pet dog "who thinks he is a member of the family—thinks he is human" is common. Perhaps there is at least some partial truth in such a claim, as a dog who is treated and attended to as human might be said to develop something of a "human" Self. Surely, there are physical limitations to and preconditions for such development, but the line between human and animal cannot be maintained with rigidity in the light of such evidence.

What does all this mean for our investigation into the concept of humanity? Humans, we know, are not defined genetically or anthropologically. Neither, though, are humans simply created through education and inculturation or through their participation in narratives and traditions. Humanity is in some respect the result of specific treatment within one's community. To have human experiences, one must be attended to as a human. To develop human intentionality one must be treated *as if* he or she already possessed such intentional structures. Being human is being treated by humans as human. This is the lesson of feral children who live in the murky region between Self and Other, human and animal—a region which we are slowly discovering is not one marked by strict boundaries.

FAMILIAR OTHERS:
THE ANIMAL THAT IS NEARLY HUMAN

A freckle whelp hag-born—not honored with
A human shape . . .
There would this monster make a man . . .
—The Tempest

Amala and Kamala—and dozens more like them—were real children. We have witnesses and photographs and documented accounts. Though feral children also live in myth and fiction, few dispute their reality.

Such is not the case with the creatures known as the Yeti, Sasquatch, Mono Grande, Bigfoot, etc. Although we have witnesses and photographs and documented accounts, few believe that such creatures are more than constructs of the imagination. This strong denial is interesting from a sociological perspective, but it also says much about our concepts of human and animal as well, for if such creatures exist, the boundary which we have been discussing would be even further eroded. However, it is not important—at least not for the particular task of this investigation—whether or not they do exist. Like most, I imagine that there are better explanations for the reported sightings than maintaining the existence of reclusive "monsters." I, too, am a slave to the scientific paradigm of the world. But I see no reason not to allow for the possibility of such creatures.

Regardless, this is not the crucial matter, for it is merely our experience of the possibility of such Others that I want to investigate. How do we make sense of our given humanity in a world where such creatures *might* exist? How do we know what is human and what is animal if we admit the possibility of a creature described as neither or as both? What do the stories of encounters—stories that are reported as truth—say about us and our understanding of the world? Let us first take up this last question, and, if the reader will indulge me, consider a story of one such encounter—a story chosen from thousands of others, mirroring, in many key respects, the archetypes and emotions found in similar stories told in nearly every culture and on every continent. Ours begins, romantically enough, with a European count and an archaeological quest.[38]

Count Pino Turolla is the stuff Indiana Jones's dreams are made of. Practicing archaeology as an adventure rather than an academic discipline, the Italian count began exploring the jungles of South America (and particularly the upper Amazon) in the early 1960s in an attempt to find traces of a pre-Columbian culture—a culture dating back much more than the conservative estimation of five thousand years—which he believes accounts for the common heritage of most indigenous peoples. Turolla has encountered puzzling artifacts—ancient stone figurines of elephants, camels, and other animals never thought to have walked the jungles and mountains of South America—but his most startling encounters have not been with objects but with animals. At least perhaps they were animals, for that is, after all, the whole question.

Known in various parts of the continent as *Los Monos Grandes* (the Giant Apes), Turolla speculates that the South American race of Bigfeet possesses a culture, uses tools, and perhaps provides the key to unlocking the mystery of the birth of South American civilization in general. He feels that the creatures are not human. Neither are they fully animal. And such a mysterious essence and lineage only adds to the intrigue—and the anxiety when they are near.

Late in 1970, Turolla had a particularly intriguing adventure—an encounter (there is no other word)—in the Guacamayo Range between Ecuador and Colombia. The land is the territory of the Aucas, an indigenous people who tell stories of beasts in the jungle and whose tribal shaman told Turolla and his assistant Oswaldo of a cave that might help them in their quest.

They left early in the morning, following the directions of the shaman, passing through a low, dark canyon. With each hour the foliage grew deeper, and by early afternoon the rain came so heavily that any sign of a trail disappeared. The two men stopped with their horses in an area they hoped was near the cave. They ate sardines, rested, and then continued their search on foot. At 3:30 P.M. they discovered the cave just as the shaman had described it. It was one hundred feet above them, and they began their ascent of the cliff wall with great anticipation.

When they finally reached the mouth they noticed something strange. The opening, it appeared, had been carved—constructed rather than naturally formed—in a trapezoidal shape with straight smooth lines. The entrance was smaller at the top than at the bottom, but it was still large and at least twenty feet high. The light fell into the cave for about fifty feet but it was clear that it was much deeper. Luckily, the men had their flashlights and thus decided to enter.

Passing from the light to the dark, the cave was silent. Not even the sound of the rain filled the space, and it now become apparent that what they had thought to be a cave was actually a tunnel. One hundred and fifty feet into the mountain, the rock walls became smooth. The flashlights strained to illuminate more of the passageway, but their bulbs were nearly overcome by the darkness. Pushing a few feet ahead, things began to change.

Dim tracks appeared in the dirt, heavy impressions along the ground. A thick scent filled the passageway, a smell of animals. And the tunnel forked, with a passage to the right leading off into shadows, taller and wider than the main tunnel straight ahead.

Oswaldo broke the silence and began muttering to himself. They could no longer see the sunlight or sense any trace of the outside world. Turolla took the lead, turning to the right, and with his hand touching the smooth wall he continued a slow walk deeper into the mountain.

They traveled another 250 feet and the passageway forked again. This time the main tunnel continued only a few more steps and emptied into a large chamber while a second tunnel split off to the left and again disappeared in the darkness. Turolla entered the chamber and Oswaldo followed. The ceiling was not visible—the flashlights could not illuminate the distant rock— and the men knew that they had reached a point to rest and collect their thoughts. Apprehensive, they smoked cigarettes and for the first time began talking about their experience. The anxiety slowly turned to calmness.

It was then that the screaming began. From high above them—and at the same instant from all around them—a shriek, a scream, a roar enveloped the men, bouncing off the walls of the cave and growing in intensity. They dropped their flashlights and cigarettes and backed toward the passageway through which they had entered a few minutes before. Oswaldo grabbed Turolla's arm just as a boulder fell from the ceiling, smashing into the ground where their cigarettes lay. Now several boulders began falling, as if someone were throwing them from high up in the cavern. The men were frozen—statues of fear—when across the beams of the still shining flashlights a large figure crossed. A creature—perhaps several—rushed toward the men. Turolla jumped, falling into the passageway and grabbing loose stones, perhaps with instinctive hopes of protecting himself. Oswaldo was still in the chamber, but the shadowy image of the huge creature rushing toward him had brought him to life and he screamed and fired his rifle out and up into the cavern. The roaring echoed, punctuated by the sound of the boulders as they fell to the floor, close now to where the flashlights lay and where Oswaldo stood. Turolla struggled to his feet and began running out, wishing for daylight. Oswaldo followed, aimlessly firing the last of his rounds behind him as he rushed through the passageway. The screaming continued; the pursuit continued. The men could feel the presence of the creatures behind them in relentless chase. It was unclear whether their hearts had stopped beating or whether they were beating so hard and fast that there were no separate beats to be felt. Their hands stretched before them in the darkness as they stumbled and ran through the tunnel—whatever was behind them was closing in.

And then the men reached the entrance to the cave, emerged into the light, and as suddenly as it had begun, the sound of the boulders and roars subsided. The creatures did not continue their chase beyond the mouth of the cave. To be safe, Turolla and Oswaldo hurried down the cliff to their horses and raced away. Turolla glanced at his watch and noted that it had been fifty-five minutes since they had first discovered the tunnel.

Nearly three hours later the men slowed their horses and ended their retreat. Oswaldo's dark hair was streaked with white and his eyes were filled with fear. Turolla realized that he still had hold of one of the loose rocks that he had grabbed after falling to the cavern floor, and when they stopped, he unclenched his fist and discovered that what had felt like a rock was actually a carved stone—an amulet in the shape of an ornamental ax with a face formed in the center.[39]

Later, Oswaldo finally showed signs of calming down as all night long Turolla told him stories of similar encounters he had had throughout the continent and even up into the United States and Canada. Together, they wondered aloud about the nature of the carved stone. The men neither slept nor ate, and at daybreak Oswaldo announced that he would accompany the count back to the cave if he so desired. The count, still recovering from the intense mixture of his own fear and amazement, agreed that they would return—another day.

Count Pino Turolla has made it his business to confront the familiar Other, but there are thousands more with tales of equally disturbing and intriguing isolated encounters. The majority of Native American cultures include stories of such creatures, and white settlers have been reporting sightings since they first arrived on the continent. Sasquatch, or Bigfoot as he has come to be known in the last few decades, is part of our story.

But how can we decide his nature? Is Bigfoot human, animal, or neither? What do such encounters tell us?

For some, the solution must be scientific, and many reputable (and disreputable) scientists have turned their attention to the subject in recent years. Indeed, when one begins to gather the literature and compile Bigfoot's bibliography what is most striking is the amount of scientific discussion on the subject as opposed to wild ramblings or simple descriptions of encounters. True, most scientists are eager to disprove the existence of Bigfoot. Some, though, are open to the possibility but skeptical of the reality. Their methods are curious and often entertaining. They study photographs and film[40] in order to uncover bone structure and joint mechanics ("Could this be a human in a costume? Could a human knee bend in such a way at this point in mid-stride? What are the similarities with an ape's body and movements?"). They investigate audio recordings of screams and roars thought to be of Bigfoot origin ("Could a human throat produce such a noise? What must the larynx look like to make this vibration and is such a shape a human-like shape?").[41] They speculate on the Bigfoot diet and sleeping habits; they catalog and make casts of Bigfoot prints; they even analyze hair and feces of "questionable" origin. The results are typically unsatisfactory and inconclusive—even given a sympathetic scientist.

In this spirit, anthropologist George W. Gill writes:

> [T]he following alternate hypotheses must be listed as the two possible explanations for our results:
>
> 1. That the most complex and sophisticated hoax in the history of anthropology has continued for centuries without being exposed;
>
> 2. That the most manlike (and largest) nonhuman primate on earth . . . remains undiscovered by modern science.
>
> Either conclusion appears totally preposterous in light of the problem-solving capability of modern science; yet, one of these two possible conclusions must be true.[42]

And investigators Kirlin and Hertel conclude: "Both typical human whistles and some abnormal types of whistles were found. . . . These whistles could either have been produced with some kind of a musical instrument or by the creature using only part of its vocal tract."[43] Finally, publisher and Bigfoot enthusiast John Green sums up the scientific controversy thus: "In short, if upright posture is what makes an animal a human, then the reports describe a human, but if it is his brain that distinguishes Homo sapiens from his animal relatives, then the Sasquatch is an animal, . . . nothing more."[44]

Inevitably, the scientific debate ends with such "wisdom": either it exists or it does not exist, and if it exists it is either human or nonhuman. The problem, as should now be familiar, is the degree of question-begging built in to the experiments. What is a "man-like nonhuman primate"? What is a "typical human whistle" as opposed to an abnormal whistle? And do we define "human" in terms of posture or brain size or neither? Green's use of the brain as the distinguishing factor is particularly intriguing, especially given that we have never had the opportunity to compare a human and a Bigfoot brain. We can only assume that Green is assuming that animal brains cause animals to live in the wild, while human brains are smarter, thus leading us to live in cities, surrounded by our technological cocoons. Since the Bigfoot is constantly roughing it, he must possess an animal brain. How startling the unquestioned presuppositions and assumptions at work here; how much they tell us about our constructed distinction between human and animal.

Species identity is another constant focus of the scientific debate, and the Bigfoot has been thought to be everything from the missing link to a distant cousin of Asian apes (and thus humans). Ultimately, appeals to species membership solve nothing in terms of separating human from animal or in terms of finding a home for Bigfoot. As we have already seen in our analysis of feral children, the fact that species is a social construct and not a "natural" classification is something philosophical analysis bears out. R. I. M. Dunbar argues, "The biological reality is that all classifications are artificial. They force a certain order onto the rather chaotic mess of the natural world. Species, as we describe them, are matters of convenience rather than biological reality."[45] On this point, however, there is no general agreement. The question of species simply will not go away. Let us return to it, then, one last time from the perspective of our investigations of the-animal-that-is-nearly-human.

Stephen R. L. Clark argues that species is a real phenomenon and that it is best understood as a successful breeding group: gorillas, for instance, constitute a species because they are linked by birth and because they interbreed. (The concept is similar to Kant's notion of a *Realgattung*—also defined as an interbreeding population.) There are three key elements here: (1) group membership being partially constituted by heredity; (2) the importance of restricted and successful interbreeding; and (3) the unimportance of physical similarity or other related traits. It is difficult to analyze each element separately since they are so interconnected, and we have already discussed the (un)importance of physical characteristics in our analysis of feral children. Consider, though, Clark's use of the metaphor of family in his discussion and defense of species:

> I am a member of the Clark family: but not because I resemble other Clarks, nor yet because there is a way that Clarks will naturally live that is unlike the way that others live. Even if Clarks were more inbred than they are (and so approximated the condition of a species) they need not always resemble each other. There might be atavisms, sports, changelings or disabled Clarks, but they would all be Clarks. . . . [46]

The point that this misses is that such an argument only works if we already assume a biological definition of family—assume, in essence, what Clark is trying to prove. "Family" can mean different things for different reasons. Were Clark to discover that he was adopted, would he no longer consider himself a member of the family? In what sense is Clark's mother truly a Clark since she is not related to any Clark ancestor, but instead joined the family through marriage? How will modern technologies such as surrogate motherhood and cloning change the definition of family and possible future Clarks? And why should we believe that there is anything "natural" about this definition of family—especially since we have cultural anthropologists and other scholars providing us with a history of the changing notion of family as well as various and differing cultural models in our own time? Indeed, family is as much about marriage, commitment, physical resemblance, and shared history as it is about heredity and genetics. Clark's proposed parallel with species thus serves to undermine his own position rather than support it. Like family, species is not just about who your genetic parents were.

It is interbreeding, though, that supposedly created this heredity. Leaving aside, for the moment, the question of whether or not sex with Bigfoot smacks of bestiality, is it possible that we are part of an interbreeding group?

Some argue that the Kantian *Realgattung* should be updated to mean a *Formenkreis* (typically translated as "ring species"). Richard Dawkins explains:

> The best-known case is herring gull versus lesser black-backed gull. In Britain these are clearly distinct species, quite different in colour. Anybody can tell them apart. But if you follow the population of herring gulls westward round the North Pole to North America, then via Alaska across Siberia and back to Europe again, you will notice a curious fact. The "herring gulls" gradually become less and less like herring gulls and more and more like lesser black-backed gulls until it turns out that our European lesser black-backed gulls actually are the other end of a ring that started out as herring gulls. At every stage around the ring, the birds are sufficiently similar to their neighbours to interbreed with them. Until, that is, the ends of the continuum are reached. . . . [47]

Dawkins suggests that chimps and humans might be part of the same ring, but they are deemed to be two different species today because the intermediary steps are extinct. If *Pan, Pongo, Gorilla, Homo,* and whatever a Bigfoot might be are each links in a ringed chain, then the importance of the so-called "missing link" is clear—not in the familiar linear sense of the term, but in the more circular-ringed sense.

Finding bones, though, might not be enough. It is the existence of the living intermediary gulls that makes the herring gulls of Britain joined in a species. This does not fit easily with common sense. Either humans and chimps are the same species or they are not; how could the living existence of a third type of creature fundamentally alter the nature of the first two? Something seems inappropriate. But it is just such a conclusion we are forced to draw. Consequently, a lot is at stake for the notion of humanity in the search for Bigfoot. As Dawkins remarks:

> Remember the song, "I've danced with a man, who's danced with a girl, who's danced with the Prince of Wales"? We can't (quite) inter-breed with modern chimpanzees, but we'd need only a handful of intermediate types to be able to sing: "I've bred with a man, who's bred with a girl, who's bred with a chimpanzee." It is sheer luck that this handful of intermediaries no longer exists. . . . But for this chance, our laws and our morals would be very different. We need only discover a single survivor, say a relict *Australopithecus* in the Budongo Forest, and our precious system of norms and ethics would come crashing about our ears. The boundaries with which we segregate our world would be shot to pieces.[48]

As a respected scientist, Dawkins does not comment on the role of Bigfoot, nor does he hold out hope of finding that missing-ring-link. But it should be clear that the notion of a ring species is something somewhat radical and anti-establishment itself, admitting to a greater interconnection among forms of life than most modern classification systems allow. Of course, as that interconnection is acknowledged, the concept of a species is widened, thus becoming less capable of picking out a *small* group of creatures. "We" gets bigger and more inclusive.

There is an inherent circularity in all of this ring business, however. Suppose we were to find a Bigfoot. To see if it might be part of our ring, we would need to establish its species identity. But of course, its species identity is just what is in question. In other words, to see if it belongs in our ring we would have to test the creature—no doubt resorting to analyzing its hair, screams, genes, etc. Either that, or we would have to try to mate with it to test our interbreeding abilities.

Regardless of the prurient possibilities, there is a more important point to be made here. All of this science is not the typical method for determining humanity. When a new family moves into the neighborhood we do not question their species. We do not attempt to breed with them in the name of science. We do not record and study the sounds emanating from their house, film and scrutinize them as they walk across their lawn, and analyze their various waste products to determine if they are human. We just know.

The same goes for our encounters with squirrels in the park, birds at the feeder, and dogs in the street. Supposedly, we just know that they are not human. Do the folks who have had encounters "just know" whether or not the Bigfoot is human?

One of the problems with relying on selected individual instincts is that those instincts could be quite wrong or at least not fit the instincts of the rest of the community. The other problem is that in the case of Bigfoot, no two instincts are quite the same.

The creature, explains Grover S. Krantz, "is not human, nor even semi-human, and its legal status would be that of an animal if and when a specimen is taken. The fact that it would be classified in the human family of Hominidae does not alter this. . . . Most people who see these creatures have an immediate, gut-level reaction to identify them as animals."[49] On the contrary, argues John A. Keel, several "armed hunters have declared that they could not bring themselves to fire their weapons . . . [because] [t]he creatures seem too human to kill. 'It would be like killing a man in cold blood,' many have said."[50]

We should not be surprised by the conflicting instincts—feral children, after all, presented the same problem. This question of shooting a Bigfoot is interesting, though. The quasi-human form of Amala and Kamala caused Reverend Singh to hold his fire, but does the form of the Bigfoot provide a similar imperative?

Here, too, there is controversy. Some argue that killing a Bigfoot would be akin to murder. They argue that erring on the side of caution is the proper thing to do. Others suggest that killing a Bigfoot is the first best step to understanding him. In this latter vein, Krantz advocates and advises using a weapon of sufficient strength: "[it] should be more powerful than a deer rifle; something good enough to bring down a big grizzly bear or an elk should suffice."[51] For Krantz, Bigfoot's "semihuman appearance" consti-tutes merely an "effective built-in disguise" aiding the creature in his escape from the hunt.[52]

As can be seen, the body of the Bigfoot plays an important role in our definition of its nature. When does looking human make a creature human, and when does it constitute only a "built-in disguise"? How do we know that our neighbor across the street is human and is not merely using a disguise to aid in his search for affordable housing?

The answer to the latter question is simple. Indeed, the question itself is silly. We need not make such judgments about Others because they simply appear to us *as human*. Such a question has echoes of the problem of Other minds and the search for a proof that everyone else is a person and not actually a robot—questions philosophy should have moved beyond long ago. Our experiences of feral children and Bigfoot creatures are intriguing precisely because these individuals are not experienced as human. If not, why not? That is the question.

I can be wrong in my experience of other humans. I can see a form across a room which I take (without judgment) to be a human; but upon closer inspection I realize it is a mannequin. In phenomenological terms, I emptily intended the Other and my expectations were not filled. (A *position-taking* stands out against the *passive synthesis* responsible for my experience of the mannequin as a human, and I judge the form to be a mannequin.) The "gut-level" reaction of which Krantz speaks is a result of the passive synthesis, but the synthesis was not always passive. In the burgeoning consciousness of the infant, "human" is an achievement. Furthermore, we learn something about the being of mannequins. Their being is such that they can appear to be human.

When I experience a house I do not experience merely the side appearing to me now. Rather, I experience the whole house as given to me from this angle. This is how things are known; this is how consciousness works. Things are given in profiles—one profile is perceived while the others are apperceived. What makes science worthwhile is that there are always more profiles to be uncovered. To think that a mannequin is a human is to learn that one of the profiles of a mannequin—part of the Being of the mannequin—is that it can appear to be a human. What, then, does it mean for the being of humans and animals that the Bigfoot can appear as both?

Recall that I have argued that the concept of human arises as a result of the simultaneous coming to sense of the (human) Ego, the (human) Other, and the complex community of which we are a part. Whether the Bigfoot is experienced "gut-level" as animal or human in an adult encounter must depend on the context. Perhaps if the outline of the distant form and the movement of the body are most prominent, he appears as human, but if the mass of fur or the roar first calls one's attention, he appears as animal. The important point is that the passively constructed identity is always called into question and a judgment must occur: true, X is taken *as* Y, but *is* X a Y?

For those of us who have never had personal encounters, the experience is still parallel. Listening to the story of Count Turolla we first take the creatures as animals and then, most probably, question whether they are animals. Thinking back on the precise architecture of the cave, the controlled and even strategic nature of the defensive attack, and of course the jadeite amulet (as the stylized ax-like stone has come to be known), we are not content to let our original experience stand unchecked—we are forced to take a position, make a judgment.

Now, someone might argue that all of this says nothing about our concepts of human and animal and that we have accomplished little with such phenomenological analysis. If we overturn the passively constructed identity of the Bigfoot with a judgment, on what grounds did we base that judgment? Does a beaver become a human when we note her architectural skills? Does a pack of wolves become a human clan when we admire the cunning and group precision of the hunt? Is the songbird's song ever a work of art and if so would this make her human?

It is true that we have not uncovered a set of criteria for being human, but important work has been done. *Bigfoot requires a judgment,* and he represents a crisis in our categorization of the world. This is because our normal conscious engagement with the world relies very little on acts of judgment. Once identities are set and categories are instilled, the scissors (to take a favorite example of Edmund Husserl's) are perceived *as* scissors— we need not make a judgment as to their being a tool or being for cutting; i.e., their being scissors. The same holds true for our neighbors in the campground, our fellow backpackers, the birds in the trees, and the deer up ahead in the clearing. They are taken as humans and as animals. But that shadowy figure behind the grove of redwoods? That set of eyes we realize has been fixed on us for the last several minutes since we stopped on this rock to rest? That sound, that smell, those monstrously large tracks in the mud? Who made them? What do we take *him* as?

Claude Lévi-Strauss has argued that monsters serve as boundaries for human society—defining who we are by saying who we are not.[53] Archaeologist Grant R. Keddie similarly maintains that "[o]ne device for [defining humanity] is to create a clearly nonhuman foil which seems at first glance to be an image of a person but lacks the essential element which make [*sic*] one human."[54] And Jay Miller, a Native American culture scholar, speaks of monsters actually threatening "the *American* definition of humanness"[55] and consequently offering a picture of the ideal modern human as the antimonster. Such arguments seem to be dealing with the proper issues, but drawing the wrong conclusions. It is not the case that the Bigfoot ultimately defines who we are in a negative way. He does not draw a circle around us by constructing a perimeter in which to live. On the contrary, Bigfoot serves only to erode such boundaries and call such definitions into question. By forcing a judgment, he directs us to realize that the senses of human and animal have been constructed *without any clear criteria.* He does not define who we are, but rather calls into question who we assume ourselves to be. His monstrous, furry body pairs with our body and a transfer of sense occurs. The size is threatening (note how we never fear or are forced to question our own nature by a small creature of unknown origin)—this

Other looms above us, capable of crushing our bodies and our uniqueness. He is familiar, yet enigmatic. And standing beside him we see the familiarity of our bodies and yet the enigmatic way in which we define them as human. This monster does not live at the boundary of the human community, but rather destroys the comfortable fiction of such a boundary: if we differ so little from him, then how do we differ from those creatures we have labeled "animals" and have excluded from "us"? "Human" suddenly means much more by meaning much less.

And it is thus that the creature represents a crisis and a discovery. Count Turolla understandably retreats in fear—the world has changed and he is not what he has thought himself to be.

CONCLUSION: THE LUNATIC FRINGE

Men are mad things.
—Two Noble Kinsmen

Perhaps we are the only animals to define ourselves in such a way as to insist on our uniqueness. Perhaps this is a mad pursuit. Yet, crossing the line between human and animal, we are taught in countless ways, can only result in tragedy.

This is the lesson, I take it, of the vampire and the werewolf in our mythology. Here, the human becomes animal—in body and spirit—and nasty things begin to happen. The context of the transformation is one of evil and suffering, and the consequence is always death—death for the human victims and ultimately death for the monster as well. The stories warn us to maintain our human identities, for an animal nature brings forth an animal body which in turn leads to death.[56] There is no fine line to walk. To be animal is to act like an animal, to have the body of an animal, and to die as an animal. In much the same way that Reverend Singh saw the transformation of Amala and Kamala's bodies into animal bodies, so do the vampires and the werewolves of our nightmares transform, abandon their humanity, and become the Other.

But we now know that this alterity is a construct without clear criteria, though it has been a difficult lesson. We have approached the feral child with anxiety and fear. We have completed her transformation into an animal when her ambiguity threatened us, constructing her body and soul. And the Bigfoot has confronted us with all that we are and all that we are not, forcing us to see our bodies and our natures in a new way.

Emmanuel Levinas was concerned that Husserl's argument for intersubjectivity made the Other a modification of the Self, thus stripping the former of his true alterity.[57] The transcendence, the radical otherness of the Other seemed lost—subsumed under the known, the familiar, the Self. One might have similar worries as the boundary between human and animal is eroded. One might fear that we are anthropomorphizing in a philosophically dangerous way, finding enough humanity in a gorilla, a Bigfoot, even a dog, for instance, to bring these creatures into the fold. But the work we have been doing here should show how this need not be the case. If anything, it is the Self that runs the risk of collapsing into the Other, not vice versa. Even some scientists who cling to the notion of species are recognizing that what we call humans are really best understood as the third chimpanzee species under the genus *Homo*—that there are thus common chimpanzees (*Homo troglodytes*), pygmy chimpanzees (*Homo paniscus*), and human chimpanzees (*Homo sapiens*).[58] Such categorization still misses the point, but it is interesting to note the way in which it misses the point. Levinas's worry was never about discovering his own alterity, never about collapsing the Self into the Other. That this may happen is not the ultimate goal of our questioning the boundaries, but it may be a sign that we are on the right path.

We have cast ourselves in an ambiguous role in the story we are telling. In fact, this "we" clearly needs reevaluating, for such a story concerns the whole of the living world regardless of how we dole out the parts. And if there are conclusions to be drawn, then we know that the concept of humanity need not be abandoned, yet it must not be thought of as an isolating characteristic either. To be human is not to be separated from the rest of the living community, but to be immersed in it. It is a world in which all that is living is tied together—our goods intertwined and enmeshed. Categorization is an attempt to unscramble the jumble, but it carries with it unspoken values that lead to real crises of ethical conduct. Some categorization is more conducive to living well (i.e., living morally) than others. Some native peoples, for instance, have categories that point out the ties between us rather than obscure and deny them. Yet the possibility of refusing to classify and categorize life according to its usefulness to humanity, according to its ancestral relation to humanity, according to what makes sense to humanity, has disappeared: the choice to refuse categorization is no longer a live one. So the world is a jumble—let there be chaos! Let there be mysterious ties that refuse breaking! Let feral children roam our intellectual forests! Let there be monsters!

Grover Krantz has mockingly written that if a Bigfoot were ever caught or killed—if we had the body before us—there would "be profound statements from many . . . philosophers . . . and from all of the lunatic fringe."[59] He is probably right. But as we explore who and what we are it makes little sense to silence the voices that question what we have traditionally thought ourselves to be. The power of the narrative pen is great, and the "we" behind "our story" is richer and more complex than some may wish to believe. Within this "we" lives a multitude of subjects—the "human" and the "animal," the familiar Other and the feral Selves of our collective experiences. Unpacking the "we" is telling a story—a new chapter in an old tale of a brave new world that has such creatures in it.

NOTES

1. The account of Singh and the wolf-children which follows is drawn from Douglas Candland's *Feral Children and Clever Animals* (New York: Oxford University Press, 1993), pp. 55–68.

2. Barbara Noske, *Humans and Other Animals* (London: Pluto Press, 1989), p. 184.

3. Gunnar Broberg, "Homo Sapiens," in *Linnaeus: The Man and His Work,* ed. Tove Frängsmyr (Berkeley: University of California Press, 1983), pp. 159–60.

4. Charles Winick, *Dictionary of Anthropology* (New York: Philosophical Library, 1956), p. 339.

5. The examples here are numerous, though one might begin with Dorothy Sayers, "The Human Not-Quite-Human," in *Masculine/Feminine,* ed. Betty Roszak and Theodore Roszak (New York: Harper and Row, 1969); Janice Moulton, "The Myth of the Neutral 'Man,'" in *Sexist Language,* ed. Mary Vetterling-Braggin (New York: Littlefield, Adamas, 1981); Joyce Penfield, ed., *Women and Language in Transition* (Albany: State University of New York Press, 1987); and Jeanette Silveira, "Generic Masculine Words and Thinking," in *Voices and Words of Women and Men,* ed. Cheris Kramarae (New York: Pergamon Press, 1980).

6. This is a strange sort of thought experiment, I know. It forces us to think of alien creatures or Bigfeet—beings without classification and beings which might very well not exist. But the point is relevant for our experience of feral children. And, as we shall see, by forcing us to consider such cases we will get a better understanding of what we mean by "human."

7. Cf. Noske, *Humans and Other Animals,* p. 153.

8. This is a large subject. It touches on the question of the nature of a tool and the nature of technology—questions too grand to concern us at the

moment. It is interesting to note, though, what modern cities and modern technology have done to our "natural" human abilities. It is clear that some knowledge has been lost at a rate at least as great as other knowledge has been gained. Generations of humans—removed from the land, reduced to working for wage labor in a mechanized society—no longer have any real skills of survival such as toolmaking. Without processed food and "mechanized fire," most of us would go hungry. Rare is the individual among us, even, who could grow grain, mill it to flour, and bake a loaf of bread. The acts of eating and providing shelter, etc., are accomplished quite well by nonhumans who are not dependent on external apparatus—tools that have come to rule us.

9. David Premack argues, in "Language in Chimpanzee," *Science* 172 (1971): 808–22, that chimps can think in abstract symbols. Especially intriguing is one chimp named Sarah who learned that a plastic blue triangle represented an apple. When asked to describe the triangle, she indicated "red" and "round." Noske (*Humans and Other Animals,* p. 144) relates the story of how pigeons did the job of picking out pictures with trees as the pictured trees become more and more abstract—better, even, than the most sophisticated computers.

10. Some birds seem capable of learning other species of birds' languages and interpreting the content—a warning, a caution, a signal of found food—even if they can only speak/sing their own.

11. Noske, *Humans and Other Animals,* p. 155.

12. Actually, the French "nose" is an interesting case. All animals are said to have a "museau" except for the dog, who, like a human, has a "nez." The French are well known for treating dogs as if they had a superior status, and this is reflected in the language. Some people say that the French treat dogs better than they treat Americans, though this author would never think to perpetuate such a stereotype.

13. Related examples abound (e.g., German humans "essen" food but German animals "fressen" food), perhaps culminating in the ultimate animal-meat/human-muscle duality which clearly demonstrates the power of language to determine ontology and teleology and not just to label objectively.

14. Mary Ann Warren's (in)famous definition of "person" in her "On the Moral and Legal Status of Abortion," *The Monist* 57, no. 4 (October 1973): 43–61, suffers from this same problem. It is endemic to the genre of list-definitions. Note the ease with which the following argument and line of criticism serve to dismantle a position such as Warren's as well as Winick's.

15. The phrase "well-developed" should be a warning signal here.

16. I say "recent" for a reason which will become clear below in my discussion of a search for the mother of humanity.

17. See Charles Murray and Richard Herrnstein, *The Bell Curve* (New York: Free Press, 1994).

18. See Philip K. Bock, *Modern Cultural Anthropology* (New York: Knopf, 1969), p. 3.

19. See Charles Darwin, *The Descent of Man* (1871; New York: Modern Library), 1949.

20. "The World of National Geographic: Mysteries of Mankind," May 21, 1995.

21. This problem suggests that "human" as an anthropological term is a *vague predicate*. There is a great deal of literature on vague predicates—both as a topic for analytic philosophy (in that vague predicates tend to create paradoxes such as the Sorites paradox) and in the abortion debate concerning the status of the fetus as "person." For an introduction to the latter one might see Jane English's "Abortion and the Concept of a Person," *Canadian Journal of Philosophy* 5, no. 2 (October 1975): 233–43. I will not pursue the argument that "human" is a type of vague predicate here, though most of what I have been saying in another form would count as evidence for such a formalized argument.

22. Darwinism does not face criticism from creationists only. See, for instance, A. R. Manser, "The Concept of Evolution," *Philosophy* 40 (1965): 18–34; Norman Mabeth, *Darwin Retried* (Boston: Gambit, 1971); and I. Bethell, "Darwin's Mistake," *Harper's Magazine,* no. 252 (1976): 70–75, who argue that "survival of the fittest" is a tautology since the only way to identify "the fittest" is to see who survived. Karl Popper is also famous for, among other things, his insistence that Darwin's evolution is untestable and unfalsifiable; see, e.g., *The Philosophy of Karl Popper,* ed. Paul A. Schlipp (La Salle, Ill.: Open Court, 1974, pp. 43–61). And scientists such as Julian Huxley and Willi Hennig have even suggested an alternative scientific twist to Darwin by introducing the notion of a "clade" as a branch of the evolutionary tree; see Hennig's *Phylogenetic Systematics* (Urbana: University of Illinois Press, 1966). As Peter Bowler points out, "transformed cladists claim that the ancestor-descendent link so crucial to evolution cannot be derived from their way of expressing relationships. Outspoken critics of Darwinism, they have extended the charge that the attempt to reconstruct the past history of life is unscientific and have taken up enthusiastically some of the established arguments against natural selection." *Evolution: The History of an Idea* (Berkeley: University of California Press, 1989), p. 345. Such arguments are indeed more numerous than one might at first imagine.

23. And other such figures in the world's religions.

24. See David Carr, *Time, Narrative, and History* (Bloomington: Indiana University Press, 1986); Alasdair MacIntyre, *After Virtue* (Notre Dame, Ind.:

Notre Dame University Press, 1984); Michael Sandel, *Liberalism and the Limits of Justice* (Cambridge: Cambridge University Press, 1982).

25. Cf. my "The Boundaries of the Phenomenological Community: Non-Human Life and the Extent of Our Moral Enmeshment," in *Becoming Persons,* ed. Robert N. Fisher (Oxford: Applied Theology Press, 1995), pp. 777–87; "Deep Community: Phenomenology's Disclosure of the Common Good," in *Between the Species* 10, nos. 3–4 (summer/fall 1994): 98–105; and "They Say Animals Can Smell Fear," in *Animal Others: On Ethics, Ontology, and Animal Life,* ed. H. Peter Steeves (Albany: State University of New York Press, 1999, pp. 133–78).

26. In my "Deep Community" I even suggest that to be human is to be connected to animals, and that a human community that is not in the presence of an animal community—another theme of science fiction—is not a human community at all. This "feral" community could not achieve the status of "human." Note that such an argument need not rely on a strict definition of what constitutes humanity. Our enmeshment, though, is certainly necessary for our being "human."

27. And other living beings!

28. Philip José Farmer, *Mother Was a Lovely Beast* (Radnor, Pa.: Chilton Book Company, 1974), p. 232.

29. Candland, *Feral Children and Clever Animals,* p. 59.

30. Ibid., p. 61.

31. Ibid., p. 66.

32. Candland (*Feral Children and Clever Animals,* p. 61) points out that Singh's contemporary commentator R. M. Zingg is troubled by this apparent impossibility, and goes to great lengths to document cases of reflective human retinas, even reporting the case of an American biologist involved with a shooting at night due to such reflection. Zingg's scrambling for evidence—scientific and biological—attests to the point being made here.

33. I cannot resist two short examples. The first comes from the magazine *Fitness* (June 1995) in a story urging women to aerobicize and marry rich. "How to marry a rich man?" asks the subtitle. "Become incredibly buff." In one story a trainer who met his wife at the gym admits that when he first saw her he said to himself: "she [has] very nice hamstrings" (p. 74). One could argue the case that until recently, hamstrings did not exist in our culture—let alone nice ones. The second example comes from a 1996 CNN report on beauty indicating that in many cultures, including our own, the beautiful human face—especially female—has little or no chin. The smaller the chin, the greater the beauty (and the more properly human?). This is especially intriguing given the importance of the chin in defining humanity for so many scientists/anthropologists—irony with no equal!

34. Dog and cat diet foods serve as a good example here as do doggy sweaters, but again the point is deep. The body of the chicken and steer are certainly social constructs—objects-for-ingestion. Circus and zoo animals are also obvious constructs. Indeed, the power relations mentioned below infect the nature of all animal bodies.

35. Noske, *Humans and Other Animals*, p. 167.

36. The phrase is James Hart's, in *The Person and the Common Life* (Dordrecht: Kluwer, 1992).

37. Ibid., p. 196.

38. Most of what follows is taken from Michael Grumley's *There Are Giants in the Earth* (New York: Doubleday, 1974), pp. 25–36.

39. The stone became known as "the jadeite amulet," and Turolla has since exhibited and published photographs of it. He believes it to have been carved by the creatures he encountered in the cave—yet further evidence that this race of *Monos Grandes* possesses culture, tool skills, symbolic expression, and intelligence, and that they hold the key to prehistory and perhaps our very humanity.

40. The famous Patterson film has been dissected ad nauseam! See, for instance, chaps. 4 and 5 of Vladimir Markotic and Grover Krantz, eds., *The Sasquatch and Other Unknown Hominoids* (Calgary: Western Publishers, 1984). Here the film is analyzed frame by frame, and Dimitri Bayanov suggests that the creature's lack of a chin (!) separates her from humanity (see p. 224).

41. My personal favorite is R. Lynn Kirlin's and Lasse Hertel's vocal tract length estimator,

$$L_3 = \frac{35300 \, (\Sigma k^2/o_{k^2} + 1/O_{\o}^2)}{4\Sigma Kf_k/o_k^2 + f_{\o}/o_{\o}^2}$$

which, I take on faith, says something about vowel pronunciation and the probability that a recording made by Alan Berry is actually of a beast of unknown origin. See Marjorie M. Halpin and Michel M. Ames, eds., *Manlike Monsters on Trial* (Vancouver: University of British Columbia Press, 1980), p. 289. I do not mean any disrespect to the authors (the work, as I understand it, is based on Hertel's master's thesis at the University of Wyoming). I merely refer to the massive equation as a symbol of science's confrontation with Bigfoot and its losing battle to define our distinct humanity.

42. Halpin and Ames, *Manlike Monsters on Trial*, p. 272.

43. Ibid., p. 288.

44. Ibid., p. 243. And all of this without ever seeing a Sasquatch brain.

45. R. I. M. Dunbar, "What's in a Classification? " in *The Great Ape Project,* ed. Paola Cavalieri and Peter Singer (New York: St. Martin's Press, 1993), p. 110.

46. Stephen R. L. Clark, "Apes and the Idea of Kindred," in Cavalieri and Singer, *The Great Ape Project,* p. 118.

47. Richard Dawkins, "Gaps in the Mind," in Cavalieri and Singer, *The Great Ape Project,* p. 82.

48. Ibid., p. 85.

49. Grover S. Krantz, *Big Foot-Prints* (Boulder, Colo.: Johnson Books, 1992), p. 173.

50. John A. Keel, *Strange Creatures from Time and Space* (London: Neville Spearman, 1975), p. 84.

51. Markotic and Krantz, *The Sasquatch and Other Unknown Hominoids,* p. 144.

52. Ibid., p. 145.

53. Cf. e.g., Claude Lévi-Strauss, *The Savage Mind* (Chicago: University of Chicago Press, 1968).

54. Marcotic and Krantz, *The Sasquatch and Other Unknown Hominoids,* p. 23.

55. Ibid., p. 17 (emphasis added).

56. This is a fascinating subject. Note also that werewolves and vampires reproduce by penetrating the bodies of humans—by biting other people. Again there is the theme of body purity and uniqueness.

57. See Emmanuel Levinas, *Totality and Infinity,* trans. Alphonso Lingis (Pittsburgh, Pa.: Duquesne University Press, 1969); idem, *Ethics and Infinity: Conversations with Philippe Nemo,* trans. Richard A. Cohen (Pittsburgh: Duquesne University Press, 1985) idem, *Outside the Subject,* trans. Michael B. Smith (Stanford, Calif.: Stanford University Press, 1994); idem, *Alterity and Transcendence,* trans. Michael B. Smith (New York: Columbia University Press, 1999).

58. See, for instance, Jared Diamond, *The Rise and Fall of the Third Chimpanzee* (New York: Harper Collins, 1991).

59. Krantz, *Big Foot-Prints,* p. 273.

9

THE FOUNDERS OF ETHOLOGY AND THE PROBLEM OF HUMAN AGGRESSION

A STUDY IN ETHOLOGY'S ECOLOGIES

R I C H A R D   W .   B U R K H A R D T   J R .

The twentieth century was not the first period to witness scientists (and others) offering biological insights on the human condition. In the mid-eighteenth century the Swedish naturalist Linnaeus not only classified the human species as a part of nature, he also suggested that "man's" natural inclinations served to maintain the "economy of nature." When human populations grew too large, Linnaeus said, then "envy and malignancy toward neighbors" abounded, and it became "a war of all against all!" Half a century later, Thomas Robert Malthus insisted that the need for food and "the passion between the sexes" were biological requirements of the human species that constituted an insurmountable obstacle to the rosy visions of social equality and biological improvement that various Enlightenment thinkers had recently been promoting. In 1838, mulling privately over his new idea of evolution, the young Charles Darwin wrote in his "M" notebook, "He who understands baboon would do more toward metaphysics than Locke." In his *Origin of Species* of 1859, Darwin finally made his theory of evolution public, yet he continued to keep his thoughts about human evolution to himself. It was not until 1871, in his *Descent of Man,* that he argued that the human race was the product of a long process of biological evolution and furthermore that "a severe struggle" would probably continue to be necessary if the race were to rise further.[1]

Darwin's *Origin of Species* and *Descent of Man* inspired a flood of treatises about the biological dimensions and determinants of human destiny. In 1900, when the German arms manufacturer Friedrich Alfred Krupp founded a thirty-thousand-mark competition for the best treatise on the subject "What can we learn from the principles of evolution for the development and laws of states?" sixty entries were submitted for the prize.[2] The shock of the Great War and then World War II stimulated further thought not only about how evolutionary theory might illuminate social theory but also about the more specific questions of "Why do animals fight?" and "What does animal behavior tell us about why humans fight?"[3] Thus in the 1960s when Konrad Lorenz, Robert Ardrey, and Desmond Morris set forth their views on such subjects—in books respectively entitled *On Aggression, The Territorial Imperative,* and *The Naked Ape*—they were hardly the first to have done so.[4]

Two things, however, were distinctive about the postwar setting in which these last-mentioned discourses were elaborated. One was the flowering of the scientific discipline known as ethology. The Austrian naturalist Konrad Lorenz and the Dutch naturalist Niko Tinbergen had established the conceptual foundations of ethology, "the biological study of behavior," in the 1930s, but it was not until the postwar period that the field gained widespread visibility.[5] Also new in the years after the Second World War was the threat of imminent nuclear war. If biologists worrying about genetic deterioration had earlier in the century written about "mankind at the crossroads," in the 1950s it seemed that the human race was not so much at a crossroads as on the edge of a precipice. The atomic physicists set the hands of the "doomsday clock" only minutes before midnight. Bomb shelters were built in backyards by citizens who then worried not only about how well these structures would protect them from blast and radiation but also about how to deal, when the time came, with neighbors who had not built shelters for themselves. The American television series *The Twilight Zone* offered an episode in which, as missiles were launched, humans fought at shelter doors "like naked animals."[6]

In the 1930s the ethologists focused their research on the study of animal instincts—primarily as exhibited in birds, fish, and insects. Mammals, to say nothing of humans, were not among their original scientific subjects. Yet Lorenz at least, from very early on in his career, cherished the notion that the study of the behavior of animals could illuminate the behavior of humans. The messages he proceeded to offer in this regard changed according to time and place. At the height of the Cold War his warning was that "an unprejudiced observer from another planet, looking upon man as he is today, in his hand the atom bomb, the product of his intelligence, in his heart the aggression drive inherited from his anthropoid ancestors, which this same intelligence cannot control, would not prophesy long life for the species."[7]

The charismatic and controversial Lorenz was the first of the ethologists to pronounce upon the lessons of animal behavior for humanity. He did so in lectures, articles, and popular books. His pronouncements, however, did not go uncontested. Among those who felt a need to put some distance between Lorenz's views and his own was Lorenz's fellow ethologist and longtime friend, Niko Tinbergen. Other ethologists weighed in on the subject in important ways, but to keep the present study from growing too large we will concentrate here on the views of Lorenz and Tinbergen.

Lorenz and Tinbergen each came to the topic of human aggression in a way that was true to his own scientific style and personal temperament. Lorenz came impetuously; Tinbergen came circumspectly. Seen from afar, their respective views on the animal roots of the human condition appear much alike: each represented the human species as biologically ill-equipped to handle the consequences of its rapid cultural evolution. Seen from up close, subtle and not so subtle differences separate them. To make historical sense of their similarities and differences we must work back through a wide range of factors that were constitutive of their respective intellectual formations. Different backgrounds, different personal styles, different experiences, and different settings for their work influenced the respective ways in which each man studied animal behavior and understood his own role as a scientist. Ethology, in other words, bore the impress of multiple ecologies. But where Tinbergen was inclined to acknowledge the social and institutional ecologies that were instrumental in the development of his own work, Lorenz characteristically portrayed his own ideas as a natural outgrowth of immediate encounters with the phenomena of nature.

Let us begin with a quick overview of the scientific accomplishments of Lorenz and Tinbergen, and a brief look at their reception of the Nobel Prize in 1973, as a means of introducing some of the features of the story. It was Lorenz who was primarily responsible for laying the field's early conceptual foundations in the 1930s. Focusing on instinctive behavior in birds, he showed how instinctive behavior patterns could be used like structures to reconstruct phylogenies. He also introduced a range of concepts to account for the physiological causation of instinctive behavior: releasers, innate releasing mechanisms, action-specific energy, threshold lowering, and the like. In addition he was the one who drew attention to the scientific interest of the phenomenon of imprinting. Tinbergen, for his part, contributed experimental and analytical talents that were an invaluable complement to Lorenz's early theory-building. Tinbergen was also the more important of the two in furthering the field's conceptual and practical development after the Second World War. It was he who in 1951 published the first systematic overview of the new field in his book *The Study of Instinct*. And he, furthermore, was the one who worked hardest for ethology's coordinated, balanced growth in the 1950s and 1960s, promoting ethology as the biological study of behavior and identifying new directions for ethology's conceptual and methodological development. In addition, in the years immediately after the war, it was he who offered a particularly compelling example of putting aside deeply felt wartime grievances for the good of the field's postwar recovery.

In 1973 Tinbergen, Lorenz, and Karl von Frisch shared the Nobel Prize for Physiology or Medicine for their respective contributions to the study of animal behavior. Two particular features of the choice of recipients caught the attention of journalists at the time. Tinbergen remarked on these in a letter to his friends Peter and Jean Medawar some three months after the award ceremony in Stockholm. The first was that Tinbergen was the second person in his family to receive a Nobel Prize: his brother Jan had already received the Nobel Prize in economics. Interestingly enough, when the press asked Niko Tinbergen how to account for this, "the ethologist," Tinbergen told the Medawars, "found himself pooh-poohing the idea of exceptional genetic endowment, and pointing to fortunate conditions, as did my brother, independently." The press was also interested in allegations about Lorenz's politics during the Third Reich. Tinbergen explained to the Medawars:

> Konrad Lorenz had, as a (protestant) Austrian been in favour of the Anschluss and had also fallen for Hitler. Unfortunately he published some paragraphs in scientific papers in which he professed to believe in the racially pure society, and although I know that he turned round as soon as he saw what really happened, he has never withdrawn what he wrote (he never does anyway), so it was not astonishing that he was singled out for a (very virulous [*sic*]) attack. And because I was known to have been on the other side of the fence, and also knew in detail how he came to derail, I had to urge him to make a clean breast of it ("I was politically very stupid and gullible") and then, in a series of interviews (the last one in Stockholm) to defend him.[8]

It may be useful to keep a number of the above points in mind as we proceed. That is, we need to remember Tinbergen, the author of *The Study of Instinct,* explaining his accomplishments not in terms of genetic endowment but in terms of fortunate conditions. We also need to ask about the different conditions under which Lorenz and Tinbergen pursued their careers, including whether the different experiences and national allegiances of the two men during the Second World War had any influence on the later development of their science.

We will begin by examining Lorenz's major postwar pronouncements about aggression and the human condition. We will then go back to reconstruct how Lorenz's thinking about the lessons of biology for humankind developed over time. His views in this regard involved two main themes. The first was that the human species is virtually unique among higher animals in its lack of innate inhibitions about killing its own kind. The second was that aggression is an instinct, and that like all other instincts it builds up internally, like a fluid in a reservoir, until eventually it is discharged. Lorenz presented these not as provisional hypotheses but rather as scientific lessons for a species that had gotten out of sync with its own biological heritage. There was a historical argument here, namely, that the cultural evolution of humankind had outpaced the race's biological evolution, and that the race had reached a critical moment in its own history, but there was no reflection on Lorenz's part on the historically situated nature of his own perspectives.

Lorenz made the first of the above claims in several places, most notably in the conclusion of his book *King Solomon's Ring* (first published in German in 1949 as *Er redete mit dem Vieh, den Vögeln und den Fischen* [He talked with beasts, birds, and fishes]), which he wrote to earn money after the war. The book consists primarily of charming stories about Lorenz's experiences as a raiser and observer of jackdaws, graylag geese, and other creatures. Lorenz was also, however, a speaker and writer who liked to raise for his audiences the specter of great dangers facing humankind—dangers that a biologist like himself was uniquely capable of diagnosing. He concluded *King Solomon's Ring* with a question he had posed in an article in a Viennese journal as early as 1935: "The day will come when two warring factions will be faced with the possibility of each wiping the other out completely. The day may come when the whole of mankind is divided into two such opposing camps. Shall we then behave like doves or like wolves? The fate of mankind will be settled by the answer to this question." In 1949 Lorenz followed his question with the observation: "We may well be apprehensive."[9]

Lorenz had prepared the way for his question by indicating that if humans had the option of behaving like doves or behaving like wolves, then behaving like wolves was much to be preferred. Wolves, he explained, had been equipped by evolution not only with powerful weapons—their sharp teeth and strong jaws—but also with powerful, instinctive inhibitions against using these weapons on members of their own species. As he represented it, when two wolves fight, and one gets the better of the other, if the loser submissively exposes its neck to its adversary, then the victor is instinctively inhibited from finishing the loser off. To Lorenz, this was a general law of nature: "When, in the course of its evolution, a species of animals develops a weapon which may destroy a fellow-member at one blow, then, in order to survive, it must develop, along with the weapon, a social inhibition to prevent a usage which could endanger the existence of the species."[10]

Doves exemplified the opposite situation. Because doves lack powerful natural weapons, Lorenz claimed, they have not had to develop inhibitions against injuring their own kind. When two doves fight in the wild, Lorenz maintained, the bird that loses the contest can simply fly away, but if the birds are confined in a cage, the losing bird may be pecked to death because the winner has no innate inhibitions against continuing to the bloody end.

The problem for the human species, Lorenz argued, is that humans are more like doves than wolves when it comes to dealing with their own kind. Not having powerful natural weapons like strong and sharp teeth or claws, humans, in the course of their long biological evolution, had not needed to develop any instinctive inhibitions against killing each other. Unfortunately, in the course of their more recent and rapid cultural evolution, they had developed artificial weapons of tremendous destructive potential, without developing instinctive prohibitions against using them.

Lorenz repeated this view in the 1960s in his book *On Aggression,* a book whose German title revealed better than the English title the main thrust of Lorenz's argument. The German title was *Das sogennante Böse: Zur Naturgeschichte der Aggression* (The so-called evil: On the natural history of aggression). The book's central claim was that "aggression, far from being the diabolical, destructive principle that classical psychoanalysis makes it out to be, is really an essential part of the life-preserving organization of instincts." Not only was aggression essential to species survival, Lorenz maintained, it also constituted phylogenetically "the rough and spiny shoot" which eventually in the higher forms of life and social organization bore "the blossoms of personal friendship and love." Lorenz's message was that the human race had to come to understand its instinctive aggressive drives in order to learn how to deal with them, and that essential to this understanding was a recognition of the positive as well as the negative aspects of aggression.[11] Although man was faced with a predicament of the most urgent sort—"in his hand the atom bomb, the product of his intelligence, in his heart the aggression drive inherited from his anthropoid ancestors"—Lorenz was prepared to offer an "avowal of optimism." He believed the biologist could rescue humankind from its precarious state by teaching humans to change for the better.[12]

On Aggression is a book that ranges widely, from discussions of animal behavior to an evolutionary reinterpretation of Kantian philosophy to an encouragement of the Olympic Games as a means of discharging internationally dangerous aggressions. It is not easily summarized. Here we will sketch Lorenz's model of how instincts work and note the particular attention that he gave to the form of aggression he termed "militant enthusiasm."

Instincts as Lorenz conceived them are not just reactions to external stimuli. Instead, they are drives that build up spontaneously within the body and that need ultimately to be discharged. Lorenz credited the German physiologist Erich von Holst with having demonstrated "the fact that the central nervous system does not need to wait for stimuli, like an electric bell with a push-button, before it can respond, but that it can itself produce stimuli which give a natural, physiological explanation for the 'spontaneous' behavior of animals and humans." The American psychologist Wallace Craig, Lorenz maintained, had discovered essentially the same thing some years earlier when studying the behavior of the blond ring dove. Craig found that, over time, in the absence of the female bird, the threshold value of the stimuli needed to elicit the male bird's courtship behavior grew less and less until finally the male simply directed his bowing and cooing toward the corner of his cage.[13]

As Lorenz saw it, aggression is an instinct that works precisely this way. It is spontaneously generated internally and eventually needs to be released. A problem of "civilized man" was that he suffered "from insufficient discharge of his aggressive drive." The job of "responsible morality" thus became one of reestablishing "a tolerable equilibrium between man's instincts and the requirements of a culturally evolved social order."[14]

Lorenz devoted special attention to a particular form of communal aggression he called "militant enthusiasm." This he identified this as "a powerful, phylogenetically evolved behavior" with distinctive, subjective correlates: "Every man of normally strong emotions knows, from his own experience, the subjective phenomena that go hand in hand with the response of militant enthusiasm. A shiver runs down the back and, as more exact observation shows, along the outside of both arms. One soars elated, above all the ties of everyday life, one is ready to abandon all for the call of what, in the moment of this specific emotion, seems to be a sacred duty."[15]

Lorenz felt certain that "human militant enthusiasm evolved out of a communal defense response of our prehuman ancestors" and that "it must have been of high survival value." Calling it "a true autonomous instinct," he explained: "it has its own appetitive behavior, its own releasing mechanisms, and, like the sexual urge or any other strong instinct, it engenders a specific feeling of intense satisfaction." The problem, however, as history had shown, was that "unbridled militant enthusiasm" was the greatest of dangers.[16]

Lorenz was convinced that humankind could not be shielded from all the stimulus situations eliciting aggressive behavior. Nor would it be wise, he said, to try breeding aggression out of the race by means of "eugenic planning." If aggression were to be bred out of the race, then "everything associated with ambition, ranking order, and countless other equally indispensable behavior patterns would probably also disappear from human life."[17]

The better course, Lorenz allowed, would be to develop an applied science of human behavior that could promote the intelligent channeling of aggression in useful directions. One needed to identify causes everyone could support. Lorenz offered science itself as particularly worthy: "Scientific truth is one of the best causes for which a man can fight and although, being based on irreducible fact, it may seem less inspiring than the beauty of art or some of the older ideals possessing the glamour of myth and romance, it surpasses all others in being incontestable, and absolutely independent of cultural, national, and political allegiances."[18]

The biological assumptions of *On Aggression* were soon enough challenged. Neither Lorenz's account of the evolutionary history of the species nor his explanation of instincts and how they worked met with the general approval of his contemporaries.[19] Our focus here, however, will not be on the objections that others made to Lorenz's claims so much as on how these claims fit into the development of Lorenz's own thinking.

Lorenz was born in Vienna in 1903, the second son of a rich and famous orthopedic surgeon. As a child he was indulged in a passion for raising animals as pets. Later he cheerfully allowed that his practices as a scientist were continuous with those he developed in his youth as an "animal lover." Indeed he claimed that being an animal lover was a prerequisite to being a good observer of animal behavior: "It takes a very long period of watching to become really familiar with an animal and to attain a deeper understanding of its behaviour; and without the love for the animal itself, no observer, however patient, could ever look at it long enough to make valuable observations on its behaviour."[20]

Lorenz credited his childhood love of animals in part to his nanny, a woman named Resi Führinger, who had "a 'green thumb' for raising animals." His passion was also inspired, he said, by having Selma Lagerlöf's classic children's book, *The Wonderful Adventures of Nils,* read to him when he was about six. *Nils* is the story of a boy who is changed into an elf and flies off on the back of a barnyard gander in the company of a flock of wild geese. By Lorenz's account, the story led him to want to become a wild goose himself, or failing that, at least to have one. A closer look at the book reveals what Lorenz's own account does not specify: in Lagerlöf's tale, wild geese are represented as being clearly superior to their domesticated cousins. Already from the bedtime lessons of his childhood, Lorenz was taught that wild animals are stronger and more admirable than their barnyard relatives.[21]

At home and at school (the elite, humanistic Schottengymnasium in Vienna) Lorenz also imbibed the German cultural ideal of *Bildung* that was so central to the self-identification and life goals of highly educated, upper middle-class Germans and Austrians of the period. The ideal encouraged intellectual or cultural development rather than material acquisition or political advancement. Likewise, it valued comprehensive knowledge over narrow expertise. Above all, it stressed the importance of spiritual *culture* as opposed to the external, worldly, and ultimately superficial aspects of modern *civilization*. The intellectual aspirations, scientific style, and general worldview that would be characteristic of Lorenz's thinking in his later career were wholly consistent with the intellectual and cultural ideals he learned in his youth.[22]

Lorenz was already a firm believer in evolution when he enrolled at the University of Vienna in 1923 as a medical student, but it was from his major professor there, Ferdinand Hochstetter, that he learned to study evolution through the methods of comparative anatomy. With Hochstetter's encouragement, Lorenz concluded that these methods could be applied to animal behavior patterns just as effectively as they could be applied to anatomical structures. In other words, behavior patterns could be used just like organs to reconstruct phylogenies. Lorenz soon discovered that he was not the first to have come to this idea. It had already been promoted by Charles Otis Whitman in the United States and Oskar Heinroth in Germany. Be that as it may, the "homologizeability" of behavior patterns became what Lorenz liked to call the "Archimedean point" from which ethology developed.[23]

Lorenz was put in contact with Heinroth about 1927; by 1930 the two were corresponding regularly with each other. Lorenz was thrilled to find in Heinroth an authority whose views and practices appeared very much like his own. Excited by the prospect of being able to establish animal behavior studies on a new and firm foundation, and by the implications these studies seemed to have for human psychology, Lorenz wrote enthusiastically to Heinroth in February of 1931: "Are you aware, Herr Doctor, that you are in fact the founder of a science, namely animal psychology as a branch of biology? . . . Who knows where today's human psychology would be, if one knew for man what was a matter of instinct and what was a matter of intelligence! Who knows what human morality would look like, if one could analyze it like the social drives and inhibitions of a jackdaw."[24]

In a series of important papers published between 1931 and 1935, Lorenz built up a view of how instincts operate and how they fit into the social life of birds. Among the features of instinctive behavior he identified as particularly important were the following.

1. All individuals of a species perform the same instinctive behavior pattern in the same, stereotyped way;

2. Animals are not conscious of the biological purpose of their instinctive behavior patterns;
3. Captivity or ill-health may bring about the pathological breakdown of the components in a behavior chain;
4. Behavior chains are typically not inherited as a whole but instead involve innate and acquired components which are *intercalated* in a functional whole;
5. Instinctive behavior patterns themselves are not modified by experience, though other parts of the behavior chain may be;
6. Ritualized, instinctive behavior patterns are of special value in reconstructing phylogenies.[25]

The most important of Lorenz's early ornithological papers was his 1935 monograph, "Der Kumpan in der Umwelt des Vogels" (The companion in the bird's environment). Here he attempted to organize his observations of bird behavior into a coherent framework and to elaborate a series of concepts on which a continuing program of research could be built. In this paper he developed at length his ideas about how instinctive behavior patterns are elicited by "releasers" (*Auslöser*). Here also he named and described in detail the phenomenon of "imprinting" (*Prägung*).

Lorenz dedicated his "Kumpan" paper to Jakob von Uexküll, the originator of the *Umwelt* concept, who had recently discussed the role of "releasers" and "companions" in animal life.[26] Following Uexküll, Lorenz explained that we humans tend to recognize objects in our environment as *things* as the result of the *compilation* of *multiple* stimuli impinging upon our sense organs. The successful integration of stimuli emanating from objects in the environment allows us to build up a knowledge of the causal relationships of things in our environment —and to survive in the environment. Lower animals such as birds, Lorenz claimed, are adapted to their environments differently than humans are. Birds act not according to insight but rather according to instinctively determined, highly differentiated responses which have been built up through evolution according to their survival value. To be effective, they need only be elicited or *released* by one or at most a very few of the stimuli emanating from the objects in their environment.

Given Lorenz's ideas on how closely adapted the innate behavior patterns of animals are to the sign-stimuli and releasers that elicit them, it is not surprising that he took special note of occasions when animals perform their instinctive behavior patterns *in the absence* of the stimuli that normally release these patterns. The most conspicuous of these cases were what he called "vacuum activities" ("*Leerlaufreaktionen*"), where it appeared that the threshold for eliciting a behavior pattern was reduced to such a point that the behavior pattern "went off" without getting anywhere, like an engine running in neutral. As early as 1932, Lorenz had reported how he had hand-reared a starling which "although it had never trapped a fly in its whole life, performed the entire fly-catching behavioural sequence without a fly—i.e. *in vacuo* [*auf Leerlauf*]."[27] Evidently related to *Leerlaufreaktionen* were cases of "threshold lowering," where instinctive motor patterns became easier to release the longer it had been since they had last run their course.

Up through the publication of his "Kumpan" paper Lorenz endorsed a chain-reflex theory of instincts. He was attracted to the chain-reflex theory because of its nonvitalistic character and because it fit most of the major facts of animal behavior as he knew them.[28] In 1936, however, he became convinced that the chain-reflex theory of instinct was inadequate and need-ed to be replaced. Two figures were particularly instrumental in changing his thinking. One was the American psychologist Wallace Craig. The other was the German physiologist Erich von Holst. Lorenz took particular note of Craig's distinction between the appetitive behavior that begins an in-stinctive behavior cycle and the "consummatory act" that brings the cycle to an end.[29] Where Craig's system needed amending, Lorenz decided, was in Craig's identification of instinctive behavior with the entire behavior cycle. Regarding appetitive and instinctive behavior as fundamentally different from each other, Lorenz insisted that functionally unitary behavior patterns be divided into purposive and modifiable components and nonpurposive, nonmodifiable, instinctive components. Doing so allowed one to recognize that functionally whole behavior patterns involved the intercalation of in-stinctive and learned elements. Failure to separate these distinct compo-nents, Lorenz claimed, was what had led earlier writers such as Herbert Spencer, Conwy Lloyd Morgan, and William McDougall to think that an-imals had insight into their instinctive behavior or that animal instincts were modifiable by experience. Lorenz set forth his views in a major paper delivered in Berlin in 1936 at the Harnackhaus, the new conference site of the Kaiser Wilhelm Gesellschaft.[30]

In the audience at Lorenz's Harnackhaus lecture was Erich von Holst. Holst had been investigating the endogenous production and central co-ordination of nervous impulses.[31] He met Lorenz immediately after the lecture and quickly persuaded him that instinctive behavior patterns were better interpreted as the result of internally generated and coordinated impulses than as chains of reflexes set in motion by external stimuli. This view made sense of appetitive behavior, where an animal, apparently moti-vated by its own internal state, sought out particular external stimuli. It also made sense of the two apparently related phenomena that the chain-reflex theory had not been able to handle satisfactorily—"vacuum activities" and "threshold reduction." Lorenz began to think these phenomena could be explained in terms of a "damming up" of a "reaction-specific energy." As he soon put it: "an animal does actually behave as if some response-specific energy were *accumulated* during periods when a specific pattern is not employed."[32] He would later develop this into his famous psychohydraulic model of the release of innate motor patterns.[33]

In 1936, the same year that Lorenz met Erich von Holst, he also met the Dutch zoologist Niko Tinbergen. Their meeting occurred at a conference on instinct held in Leiden in November 1936. By Tinbergen's own later account, he and Lorenz "clicked" immediately at this their first meeting.[34] Each recognized that the other's strengths complemented his own. Tinbergen was impressed by Lorenz's bold theorizing. Lorenz in turn was ecstatic over what Tinbergen told him of the experimental work that Tinbergen and his students were conducting at Leiden. In 1979, when the present writer asked Tinbergen about the Leiden meeting of 1936, Tinbergen recollected the following:

> We certainly were preoccupied with the "innateness" of so much behaviour and with this selective responsiveness, for which Lorenz at that time had mainly suggestive evidence and I could offer the first set of experimental results, obtained in sticklebacks together with Ter Pelkwijk, with the aid of "dummies." For the rest I remember that we were very much concerned with defending our "objectivistic" approach against the then prevailing notion that the aim of animal psychology was to find out what animals experience subjectively (Bierens de Haan, Portielje).[35]

Tinbergen, like Lorenz, had been an ardent naturalist as a youth. Unlike Lorenz, however, he had found his greatest satisfactions as a naturalist not in raising animals so much as in stalking, watching, and photographing them in the countryside around his home in The Hague. More attuned to field studies than to comparative anatomy, Tinbergen brought to ethology an ecological dimension that was lacking in Lorenz's work. Whereas Lorenz's joys were in raising and breeding animals and having them as companions, Tinbergen took pleasure in being outdoors, watching animals in their natural settings, and matching wits with them. As Lorenz and Tinbergen later agreed, of the two of them, Lorenz was by nature a "farmer," while Tinbergen, in contrast, was a "hunter." These differences were not simply matters of individual temperament. They reflected different personal and cultural experiences. Tinbergen's attitudes toward nature developed from the social as well as the natural environment in Holland in the first third of the century. Nature study was at that time a thriving activity for Dutch youth, and nature study above all meant field study.[36]

Tinbergen went on to study biology at the University of Leiden. By the time he met Lorenz in 1936, he was an instructor at Leiden with an active research program of his own. His department allowed him to take a fellowship leave in the spring of 1937 to travel to Austria and spend three and a half months working with Lorenz at Lorenz's home in Altenberg. It was there that they conducted their classic experiments on the egg-rolling behavior of the graylag goose,[37] and there too that they established a lifelong friendship. It was also there that Tinbergen got an early glimpse of Lorenz's thoughts on the political dimensions of Lorenz's scientific prospects. In a letter home to his parents, dated March 29, 1937, Tinbergen reported Lorenz's views. As Lorenz represented the state of affairs to Tinbergen, biology in Germany, which had recently been pressured to conform to a Nazi line, was once again enjoying freedom and financial support. Leading biologists who had been dismissed from their positions for not sympathizing with the Nazis had been reinstated; concomitantly, the "Party-Swine" who had been inserted in these positions had been thrown out. Funds were even available for work that went against the party line. In Austria under the Catholic dictatorship, in contrast, anyone who was not a Catholic counted for nothing. Lorenz's family had become officially "Catholic" for the sake of Lorenz's career, but Lorenz felt his career possibilities in his home country were limited. He was at that time lecturing on animal psychology at the University of Vienna, but he had to disguise his subject matter by advertising his course under another title.[38]

Tinbergen, however, did not share Lorenz's optimism that science or anything else was getting better under the Nazis. In June 1937, on his way back from Austria, he stopped in Munich to make the personal acquaintance of Karl von Frisch. He recalled years later: "My recollection of this visit is a mixture of delight with the man von Frisch, and an anxiety on his behalf when I saw that he refused to reply to a student's aggressive *Heil Hitler* by anything but a quiet *Grüss Gott.*"[39]

The relation between science and politics during the Third Reich has been the subject of extended analysis.[40] Lorenz's case, not surprisingly, has attracted considerable attention. Here we only have space to identify a few of the more significant elements of a story that remains to be more fully told.[41]

When the Anschluss took place in March 1938, incorporating Austria into greater Germany, Lorenz welcomed the new political order with jubilation. He did so in part because his family regarded itself as culturally German but above all because he believed it would transform the local ecologies most relevant to his own career. He was glad to have the chance to make himself visible to a regime that identified its destiny in biological terms. The kind of professional post that had eluded him under the Catholic dictatorship in Austria now seemed well within reach, and he immediately set about adapting to the new circumstances. Ambitious at one and the same time for his career and for his science of animal and human behavior, and brimming with confidence about his ability to make sense of an ever-widening range of biological, social, and mental phenomena, he began maneuvering within his new ideological and political surroundings. He believed that doing good scientific research, serving the National Socialist state, and advancing his own career could legitimately go hand in hand. He applied for membership in the Nazi party on May 1, 1938 and was accepted June 28, 1938.[42]

Scholars have shown that there was no such thing as a monolithic National Socialist biology with one clear ideological purpose. The scientific landscape of the Third Reich was a complex one, with diverse centers of power. If Lorenz later admitted that he had been attracted to the idea of eugenics as a kind of state religion, this was itself a relatively common enthusiasm among the biologists of his day, and it did not, in and of itself, necessarily identify Lorenz as a follower of a Nazi party line. Indeed Lorenz did not picture himself as a follower but rather as a leader who could help separate good biology from bad. The public posture he cultivated for himself was that of an innovative biologist who was initially interested in pure research but who was also sympathetic with the Reich's race hygiene concerns. He was prepared to suggest, furthermore, that his research on animal behavior might have useful lessons to offer in this regard.

Recent interpretations of Lorenz's activities during this period have ranged widely, from the suggestion that these involved attempts (albeit very cautious ones) "to swim against the current" to the view that they represented Lorenz's endorsement of, and participation in, specific Nazi projects.[43] The terrain of Nazi biology was sufficiently complicated to have elicited behavior on Lorenz's part supportive of interpretations on both ends of the spectrum, and of more in between. Some sense of the complexity of interpreting his case can be derived from the fact that the primary enterprise through which he voiced his sympathies for Nazi concerns about race purity, namely, his campaign to warn against the genetic dangers of "domestication" and civilization, was not something he viewed as a Nazi project per se—nor was it something about which he was later repentant. In the immediate postwar period, when he was disavowing having had any Nazi ties, he continued to write about the genetic and moral dangers of domestication and civilization. However, if, in his own mind, he distinguished his views from those of Nazi party bosses, his use of a rhetoric of "elimination" in his papers of the late 1930s and early 1940s has made it difficult for others looking back on his writings to discern these distinctions so clearly. He pronounced upon the lessons that biology and animal behavior could offer the state at a time and in a way that was broadly consistent with the Nazi goal of creating a biologized German body politic.

In pursuing our theme of ethology's ecologies, we need to look further at how Lorenz's writings reflected the new political circumstances in which he found himself after the Anschluss. As early as his "Kumpan" paper of 1935, Lorenz had claimed that domesticated animals are not good subjects for the study of innate behavior patterns because their innate behavior patterns, like those of animals in poor health, display pathological breakdown. The conditions of domestication, he explained, lead to the disintegration of the complex, well-integrated behavior patterns that allow animals to survive in the wild. Soon after the Anschluss, Lorenz signed up to present a paper at the 1938 Congress of the German Psychological Society. He entitled the paper "On Deficiency Phenomena in the Instinctive Behavior of Domestic Animals and Their Social-Psychological meaning."[44] There he argued that the deficiency phenomena (*Ausfallerscheinungen*) in the instinctive behavior of domestic animals are strictly analogous to the decay phenomena (*Verfallserscheinungen*) in the behavior of human beings in civilization, and that in the two cases the cause was the same: the relaxation of selection. He went on to claim that "the backbone of all racial health and strength" was to be found in the "high valuation of our species-specific and inborn social behavior patterns." The nondegenerate individual, he explained, has an instinctive, intuitive ability to recognize the good or bad ethical (and genetic) character of the social behavior of others, and this instinctive response is truer (and more important for the future of the race) than any reasoned response. The danger to the race, he warned, lay in those undesirable types that proliferated under the conditions of civilization: "Nothing is as important for the health of a people as the eradication (*Ausschaltung*) of *invirent* types, which threaten like cells of a malignant tumor to infiltrate the people's body by reproducing themselves in the most dangerous way."[45] He expressed himself similarly in later writings, as for example when he urged in 1940, with respect to those elements of the populace afflicted with deficiency phenomena, "the earliest possible recognition and elimination (*Ausmerzen*) of the evil."[46] In this form Lorenz argued that the study of innate behavior patterns had a contribution to make to race-political concerns.

Lorenz wrote several different sorts of papers in this period. His most important work from the standpoint of biological systematics was a reevaluation of the affinities of ducks and geese based on a close analysis of their behavior patterns. His most ambitious work overall was a 176–page monograph entitled "On the Inborn Forms of Possible Experience," an attempted synthesis of animal behavior study, Kantian philosophy reworked as evolutionary epistemology, and race hygiene theory. The paper that gave him the greatest trouble from a political standpoint in the immediate postwar period, however, was a piece entitled "Systematics and Evolutionary Theory in Teaching." He published this last-mentioned paper in 1940 in the Nazi biology teachers' journal, *Der Biologe.*

Lorenz began his *Der Biologe* paper by indicating how surprised he had been to learn, upon reading an earlier issue of the same journal, "that in the system of education of greater, National Socialist Germany, there are men who still continue to reject evolutionary thought and the theory of descent as such."[47] He did not proceed to attempt to state the evidence for evolution in a more compelling fashion. Rather, he argued for the essential compatibility of evolutionary theory and National Socialist ideology. His basic point was that the aims of National Socialism were better served by the idea of the continued evolution of the German people than by the "race-political fatalism" of the belief in a perfect and unchanging race. Countering the charge that Darwinists were value-blind materialists, he claimed that providing young German men with a knowledge of phylogenetic processes would imbue them with a commitment to higher values and a recognition of their "own duty regarding the higher racial development of our people."[48]

Lorenz went on to tell how when he had tried to teach evolutionary theory in Austria under the Schuschnigg regime, opponents of evolution had treated evolutionary theory and Nazi ideology as if they were equivalent. The Austrian Ministry of Education, he said, cut biological instruction to a minimum and did not allow evolution even to be mentioned. "Under these circumstances," he explained, "it is understandable that even inherently apolitical scientists became stirred up and were led to draw the correct political conclusions."[49] He happily described how he had taught a student who was initially "a complete Marxist" but who was subsequently convinced of "the untenability of the dream of 'the equality of all mankind'" by hearing Lorenz deliver "a wholly apolitical lecture on comparative phylogeny." Teaching the facts of natural history, Lorenz insisted, was an excellent way to win students over to the ideals of National Socialism. As he put it:

> Certainly socialism and communism spring from a half-digested Darwinism which incorrectly regards the whole of humanity as an equally valuable homogeneous unit. But the self-evident correction, that not

the whole of humanity, but only the race is such a biological unit, now makes National Socialism out of socialism! To discover that this correction can succeed in the course of teaching has been, as I have already mentioned, one of the greatest joys of my existence.[50]

A decade later, in the summer of 1950, Lorenz found his hopes for a chair at the University of Graz scuttled when his 1940 article in *Der Biologe* was called to the attention of the minister of education. Concluding that his chances for any employment in Austria in the near future were slim, Lorenz decided to look elsewhere, specifically in England. He decided further that he had better say something to his friends and supporters there about the 1940 article. He told the British ethologist W. H. Thorpe that he had written his article to counter a series of articles written in *Der Biologe* by "Ernst Krieck, a very important Nazi-bonze, president of the N.S. Lehrerbund and Rektor of Heidelberg University, and a damn fool into the bargain." Krieck, Lorenz explained, had launched a campaign against the teaching of evolution. "Quite naively," Lorenz continued,

> without knowing the importance of this fellow, I wrote a countering article and sent it to the same journal, whose editor, for reasons of his own, published it immediately. This article brought me some very real danger, because, as is my nature, I had ridiculed my antagonist rather pitilessly, a thing which was not usually done to Nazi bonzes. But of course it was written in a generally nazi-like manner and made a point that all eugenic tendencies on which the Nazis laid so much stress, [were] quite senseless, if one assumed the species to be absolutely constant, as originally created by God. So that, if one quotes unconnected passages of this short article, it is actually possible to make me appear as a very dangerous Nazi, although of course, the real trend of the thing, is quite the opposite.

Allowing that quoting isolated passages from his *Der Biologe* paper was precisely what someone had done to undermine his candidacy at Graz, Lorenz assured Thorpe: "If you read that paper, you would actually find that I never had been a Nazi at all, only, fighting for the theory of evolution (which seriously comprises for me much of the creator and creation), I should be ready to talk in Communist, Catholic, or whatever other terminology you want."[51]

Discussing the difficulty of interpreting works on psychology written during the Third Reich, the historian Ulfried Geuter has observed that in certain instances, "What seem to modern readers to be clearly racist expressions turn out on closer inspection to be artful criticism of Nazi views."[52] Perceiving an artfulness in Lorenz's writings is easy enough. Identifying an essence beneath the artifice is not so straightforward. If there was an artfulness in his 1940 *Der Biologe* article, where he sought to signal his biological and political reliability to the German biological community, there was also an artfulness in his later letter to Thorpe, where he represented his criticism of Ernst Krieck as a basically independent and anti-Nazi position. Other German biologists—in particular Ferdinand Rossner and Gerhard Heberer, both of whom were self-consciously Nazi biologists—had already taken Krieck to task in the pages of *Der Biologe*.[53] Lorenz was essentially following in their footsteps when he insisted that not only was evolution true, it was perfectly compatible with the goals of the National Socialist State. In both cases, in his 1940 *Der Biologe* paper and his 1950 letter to Thorpe, he was seeking to cultivate patrons.[54] In each case he constructed an account that was targeted for a specific audience.

Lorenz's claim to Thorpe that he was prepared to modify his terminology as circumstances demanded is substantiated by a number of cosmetic touches that decorate the long manuscript entitled "The Natural Science of the Human Species" that Lorenz wrote while a prisoner of the Russians between 1944 and 1948.[55] In this case, obviously, Lorenz had a much different audience than he had had in the Third Reich. Russian officials would have to approve his manuscript before he would be allowed to take it back with him to Austria. Not surprisingly, Lorenz made no major gestures toward eugenics or racial purity here (though he still expressed a concern with "domestication-induced mutational losses in 'instinctive behavior patterns'").[56] The Russians considered eugenics a fascist enterprise. Instead he cited Karl Marx and went on to allow that the weltanschauung fundamental to "all true natural scientific research . . . was clearly formulated long ago in the philosophy of dialectical materialism."[57] This certainly confirms Lorenz's suggestion to Thorpe that he was willing to adapt his terminology to local circumstances. It also gives one pause, however, when confronted with Lorenz's later pious pronouncement in his book, *On Aggression,* that "should a scientist, in the conscious or even unconscious wish to make his results agree with his political doctrine, falsify or color the results of his work, be it ever so slightly, reality will put in an insuperable veto."[58]

Tinbergen's wartime career contrasted starkly with Lorenz's. The Germans conquered Holland in May 1940 in just five days. It was a bitter experience for Tinbergen to watch with his family as the German bombers and parachutists made their way essentially unchallenged, and yet another bitter experience to have his homeland occupied by a foreign power. In the spring of 1942, when the German authorities tried replacing Jews and anti-

Nazis on the Leiden faculty, Tinbergen was among some sixty faculty members (about 80 percent of the entire faculty) who resigned in protest. He was subsequently arrested and put in a hostage camp as one of the leaders of the faculty resistance. He remained a prisoner for two years. He was released in September 1944, but on the "wrong side" of the front. Through the winter of 1944–45, with Holland in the grip of cold and famine, he lived with his family in the countryside, securing enough food to survive, assisting war victims, spying for the Dutch resistance, and eluding the manhunts of the German Sicherheitsdienst (security service).[59] He told Robert Yerkes later: "The German terror was unbelievably cruel and a terrible burden. I never had suspected before that whole generations could be spoiled so badly and so thoroughly in so relatively short a period as the nazi regime had at its disposal. I refrain from writing you details, and can only [tell] you that the worst you have seen in your newspapers is still short of the truth."[60]

The upshot of Tinbergen's experience was that at the war's end he hated the Germans. It would take some time, he recognized, before he could renew scientific relations with his German associates. He reported to Julian Huxley: "We all have a great longing for international interchange of ideas. I do not intend to cut off all relations with German scientific men. But first I must not see them for a long time, so as to overcome the psychological aversion resulting from the incredible German terror we underwent."[61]

Tinbergen's feelings were particularly mixed with respect to Lorenz. He knew that Lorenz had become an enthusiast for the Third Reich. But he also regarded Lorenz as the founder of his field—and as a friend. When word came in 1945 that Lorenz was missing in action on the Eastern Front and presumed dead, he regretted the news greatly.

Lorenz proved not to be dead after all, but instead a prisoner of the Russians. He remained a prisoner long after the war's end, not returning to Vienna until February 1948. In July 1949 Tinbergen and Lorenz met again for the first time in over a decade at a conference on physiological mechanisms in instinctive behavior held in Cambridge, England. They were reunited at the home of the British ethologist W. H. Thorpe. Thorpe years later recalled the reunion as "a moving event." Lorenz (also years later) recalled: "Though [Niko] had spent years in a German concentration camp and I even longer in a Soviet prisoner of war camp, we found that this had made no difference whatsoever, which Niko put in a nutshell by saying: 'We have won.'"[62]

Lorenz's recollection of Tinbergen's words rings true enough, but his "no difference whatsoever" comment does not. Tinbergen and his country had suffered severely at the hands of the Germans. The fact that Lorenz had been a long-term prisoner-of-war in a Russian camp apparently made a very real psychological difference to Tinbergen. It served, at least in a general sort of way, to balance things out. It made it easier for Tinbergen to forgive Lorenz, put the experience of the war behind them, and get on with the program of research and the discipline-building that the war had interrupted.

One might also note that by the late 1940s the ecologies of world power politics had shifted dramatically from what they had been a decade before. The context of the Russian threat of the present made the behavior of German scientists of the past somewhat less of an issue than it would have been otherwise for scientists in the West. Be that as it may, it is difficult to believe that Tinbergen's example of forgiving Lorenz did not make a considerable difference for ethology's subsequent development. At the same time, it bears remarking that Tinbergen was not averse to putting some distance between himself and Germany. Several months before the Cambridge conference, in order to be an exponent of ethological studies in the English-speaking world but also for deeper, personal reasons, Tinbergen decided to leave Leiden accept a position at Oxford.

Lorenz in the meantime was without a professional post. He had been appointed to a professorship at Königsberg in 1940 but after the war that post no longer existed—Königsberg was now Kaliningrad, in Russian hands. Nor did he have the money to rebuild a research center for himself at his home in Altenberg. He succeeded in securing some support from the Austrian Academy of Science, but only at a very modest level. He was therefore thrilled in 1950 when a professorship of zoology came open in Austria at the University of Graz (Karl von Frisch decided to leave that post to return to Munich), and he himself appeared to be the front-runner. As indicated above, however, his political past (and perhaps also his ideas about human evolution) worked against him, and he failed to get the post. Greatly frustrated, he asked both Thorpe and Tinbergen if they could find him at least a temporary job in England. He complained to Thorpe: "I am 46 years old and time is running away without my doing anything really valuable, except writing my big book, but that means only using up my old capital of knowledge without acquiring any new."[63]

When Lorenz's friend Holst learned that a position was being cobbled together for Lorenz in England, he took the news to the Max Planck Society. Worried about losing top German scientists to other countries, the society moved quickly. In December 1950, the senators of the society were presented with a proposal to create research opportunities for Lorenz, "an animal psychologist of great renown," within the framework of Holst's Max Planck Institute of Marine Biology at Wilhelmshaven. The proposal was endorsed unanimously.[64] Lorenz thereby became firmly established institutionally. In 1957 the Max Planck Society went on to build a whole new institute for him and Holst in Bavaria. It is debatable, however, whether this institutional support led Lorenz to develop any major new ideas. Most of his writings from the 1950s onward appear to have continued to draw primarily on his "old capital of knowledge." Although Lorenz remained a charismatic leader of the field, it was Tinbergen who played the greater role in the postwar period when it came to identifying new directions for ethology and responding constructively to critiques of the field's early assumptions.

Tinbergen's *The Study of Instinct,* published in 1951, was the work that did most to position the new field of ethology with respect to the rest of the life sciences in the postwar period. It showed where ethology had been and where it still needed to go. Here Tinbergen identified, at least implicitly, the four different kinds of questions a biologist should ask about any behavior pattern: What is its physiological causation? How does it develop in the individual? What is its evolutionary history? And what is its function or survival value? Only with the first of these questions, Tinbergen acknowledged, had the ethologists made much progress. As a consequence, *The Study of Instinct* was first and foremost a synthesis of ideas about the physiological causation or "mechanisms" of instinctive behavior.

The ethologists' theory of the causation of instincts was an elegant one, at least in its general outline. It identified "internal" and "external" physiological mechanisms responsible for instinctive behavior. The internal factors (hormones, internal sensory stimuli, and impulses generated by the central nervous system itself) controlled the "motivation" of the animal and served constantly to prime the instinctive mechanisms. "Innate releasing mechanisms" prevented the various instinctive actions from being performed chaotically. Of the external factors, releasing stimuli activated the innate releasing mechanisms with which they were paired, unblocking the performance of the associated instinctive motor pattern (the consummatory act), while directing stimuli "enabled" or "forced" the animal "to orient itself in relation to the environment." In Tinbergen's model the mechanisms underlying instinctive actions were further related to one another by belonging to and being hierarchically arranged within a number of major systems. But Tinbergen was careful to qualify his claims. The ethologist's understanding of instinctive behavior, he allowed, was only provisional: the evidence was still "very fragmentary," the generalizations based on this evidence were of "a very tentative nature," and the diagrams of the operation and hierarchical arrangement of instinctive centers were "no more than a working hypothesis of a type that helps to put our thoughts in order."[65]

It bears remarking that Tinbergen's *The Study of Instinct,* together with another book, *Social Behaviour in Animals,* which he published in 1953, both addressed the question of fighting in animals. Central to his discussion of fighting was the idea of place, or more specifically, *territory*. As he explained in 1953, "restriction to a certain locality is one of the most obvious characteristics of fighting. When a male Stickleback meets another male in spring, it will by no means always fight. Whether it does depends entirely on where it is. When in its own territory, it attacks all trespassing rivals. When outside its territory, it will flee from the very same male which it would attack when 'at home.'"[66] His understanding of the function of fighting was that it served to keep individuals well spaced out. In *The Study of Instinct* he noted that at territorial boundaries, "when the fighting-drive in the two individuals is about equal, . . . lengthy threat performances appear in both of them long before actual fighting occurs." He then went on to observe that "the same instinctive inhibition of the fighting-drive is found in man," but that "our instinctive reluctance to kill" was diminished in modern times by the way one could employ long-range weapons and not witness up close the lethal consequences of their actions.[67]

The most conspicuous challenge to the ethologists' early theorizing came in 1953 from the young American comparative psychologist Daniel Lehrman. In that year Lehrman published in the *Quarterly Review of Biology* a paper entitled "A Critique of Konrad Lorenz's Theory of Instinctive Behavior." Lehrman's central complaint about Lorenz's theorizing was that Lorenz's definitions of instinct and innateness left unexplored the whole question of behavioral development. He leveled other charges as well, among them that the ethologists had moved too quickly and uncritically from the behavior of animals to the behavior of humans.[68] He took Tinbergen to task, for example, for suggesting that a human's pursuit of sports or science depended on internal factors similar to those that led a dog to hunt even when the dog was well fed. He found even more problems in Lorenz's writings, as for example Lorenz's discussion of "falling in love" and more particularly Lorenz's equating of effects of civilization in humans with the effects of domestication in animals. Lehrman noted Lorenz's wartime comments on how civilization stands in the way of the natural elimination of degenerative mutations: "He presents this as a scientific reason for societies to erect social prohibitions to take the place of the degenerated releaser mechanisms which originally kept races from interbreeding. This is presented by Lorenz in the context of a discussion of the scientific justification for the then existing (1940) German legal restrictions against marriage between Germans and non-Germans."[69]

Tinbergen, who knew Lehrman personally from before the war, was inclined to acknowledge that the American's 1953 critique of Continental ethology had some basis, particularly in its assertion that the ethologists had paid too little attention to questions of development when discussing instincts. Lorenz, on the other hand, was not at all receptive to the criticism, nor he did not look kindly on Tinbergen's accommodationist position. In the 1960s he criticized the "English-speaking ethologists" who had let the concept of the "innate" be eroded. In doing so he was thinking in particular of his old friend Tinbergen.[70]

Tinbergen through the 1950s and 1960s continued to credit Lorenz with having introduced biological thinking into the study of animal behavior. At the same time, however, he began to think that Lorenz did not appreciate fully the importance of defining ethology as the biology of behavior, which to Tinbergen meant looking carefully at questions of development and function as well as at questions of causation and evolution. In this period, Tinbergen set himself apart from Lorenz not only in his acknowledgment of the importance of development but also in the attention he gave to the importance of ecological factors in the evolution of instinctive behavior patterns.

Lorenz in the 1930s had advanced the idea that the behavior patterns animals employed in intraspecific signaling evolved independently of ecological factors. This served as the foundation of a special authority claim on his part, namely that when it came to reconstructing phylogenies, instinctive behavior patterns that functioned as releasers were often more reliable than morphological structures, because similarities among releasers were unlikely to be the result of convergence. It also underwrote his practice as a scientist. It legitimated his concentration on the behavior of wild animals living in a state of semicaptivity, as opposed to doing fieldwork. Tinbergen, in contrast, was committed to doing fieldwork.[71]

Shortly after coming to England, and partly in response to prodding from Lorenz and others, Tinbergen decided to undertake comparative studies of closely related species. He decided to do comparative field studies of gulls and comparative laboratory studies of both sticklebacks and *Drosophila*. Where his earlier field research had focused on the herring gull, he, together with a new crop of students, began studying other seabirds as well, in particular black-headed gulls and kittiwakes. Kittiwakes fascinated him from the moment he laid eyes on them in the Farne Islands. They were the most aggressive seabird he had seen, competing severely with one another for nesting sites on cliffs. Over the next several years, on the basis of studies of colonial seabirds—highlighted by the work of his student, Esther Cullen, on the kittiwake—Tinbergen concluded that Lorenz was wrong in claiming that releasers evolved independently of ecological factors. In the case of the kittiwake, a species that gained protection from predators by breeding on narrow ledges on very steep cliffs, a whole host of behavioral peculiarities could be interpreted as "corollaries to this anti-predator aspect of their breeding biology."[72] These included specific releasers, such as special head-turning movements that served to "appease" conspecifics, specialized fighting movements, nest-building behavior, nonremoval of eggshells from the nest site, and more. Tinbergen was greatly impressed by the interrelatedness of these multiple adaptations. He pursued this idea further in a paper with Robert Hinde, stating: "Since the various characters of an animal are developmentally, causally, and also functionally interrelated, selection for change in any one character will have repercussions on many others."[73]

Over the course of the 1950s Tinbergen's work moved from his earlier emphasis on physiological causation, to the study of the evolution and ritualization of signals, to an experimental examination of the ways the behavioral repertoires of different species reflected their adaptation to different selective pressures. Gradually he concluded that what interested him most were the interrelated effects of diverse selection pressures. In the early 1960s his gull studies paid particular attention to the ways in which colonial breeding, synchronized breeding, and the spacing out of territories functioned as antipredator devices. Significantly, he denied any need to endorse Wynne-Edwards's idea of group selection in accounting for such phenomena as spacing out. He felt selection pressures on the individual and family were sufficient to produce the phenomena in question. At the same time, however, he did not take Lorenz to task for having talked uncritically about behavior patterns having been developed for "the good of the species." He knew that his friend and colleague did not respond happily to criticism.[74]

Did Tinbergen's view of human aggression end up being different from Lorenz's? On the occasion of his appointment in 1968 as Professor of Animal Behavior in the Department of Zoology at Oxford, Tinbergen chose as the theme of his inaugural lecture: "On War and Peace in Animals and Man: An Ethologist's Approach to the Biology of Aggression." Contrasting his approach with those taken in the recent bestsellers by Lorenz (*On Aggression*), and by his own student Desmond Morris (*The Naked Ape*), Tinbergen sought to emphasize "how much we do not know." He urged that it was not ethology's results but rather its methods that needed to be applied to the issue of human aggression. Unlike Lorenz with the graylag goose or Julian Huxley with the great-crested grebe, Tinbergen never held up another animal species as a model for humans to emulate. He also warned against extrapolating uncritically to humans from a few selected animal species. The human species, he insisted, needed to be studied in its own right. One thing, in any case, seemed obvious to Tinbergen about early humans: "as a social hunting primate, man must originally have been organized on the principle of group territories."[75]

Tinbergen had the ability to recognize the respective merits of opponents who were disposed to regard one another's views as fundamentally flawed. In his inaugural lecture he maintained that Lorenz and Robert Hinde were not diametrically opposed in their views on the mechanics of aggression; that Lorenz and the American psychologist T. C. Schneirla each had important points to make with respect to the development of behavior; and that Lorenz's *On Aggression,* despite its overassertiveness, its various factual mistakes, and its many possibilities of being misunderstood, "must be taken more seriously as a positive contribution to our problem than many critics have done." He agreed with Lorenz "that elimination, through education, of the internal urge to fight will turn out to be very difficult, if not impossible." Like Lorenz, too, he ended up by suggesting scientific research as one of the best ways of sublimating aggression. In his words: "we scientists will have to sublimate our aggression into an all-out attack on the enemy within. For this the enemy must be recognized for what it is: our unknown selves, or deeper down, our refusal to admit that man is, to himself, unknown."[76]

Seven or eight years later, these subjects were still on Tinbergen's mind. Others had debated whether aggressive behavior was fueled by an internally generated drive or instead was essentially reactive. This to Tinbergen seemed not so important as "the fact that we have inherited the potential . . . for using force in a number of diverse situations." On the basis of information about hunter-gatherer societies still existing in the present, Tinbergen concluded that in the distant past the majority of clashes between human individuals or groups would have been "of the relatively harmless type of 'fight-flight' balance that characterizes similar intra-specific frictions in the vast majority of higher animals in which killing is relatively rare." For modern man over the last ten thousand years or so the situation was different: "[he] has taken the disastrous step to war by using his unique capacity for foresight and experience, and recognising that under certain circumstances killing does pay, because a dead man will not return to fight again."[77]

Tinbergen's explanation was thus reminiscent of Lorenz's, but not identical to it. He did not endorse the idea that aggression is a drive fed by its own action-specific energy. Nor did he think that the main problem with the human species was that it was deficient in its instinctive inhibitions. The problem rather, as Tinbergen perceived it, was that the ancestors of *Homo sapiens,* millions of years ago, had made the "fateful evolutionary 'decision'" of leaving their arboreal habitat, where they had been vegetarians, to enter "a new ecological niche, that of hunter-gatherers who sought their food on more open terrain." The "decision" to take up a new ecological niche inevitably had profound consequences, among the most far-reaching of which was that man, out and about in his hunting range, had used his reason to become a killer.[78]

The way that Lorenz and Tinbergen each gestured toward science for salvation is noteworthy. Yet here too we find different emphases. In *On Aggression* Lorenz wrote:

> Scientific truth is universal, because it is only discovered by the human brain and not made by it, as art is. . . . Scientific truth is wrested from reality existing outside and independent of the human brain. Since this reality is the same for all human beings, all correct scientific results will always agree with each other, in whatever national or political surroundings they may be gained.[79]

Tinbergen, in a different context (not responding to Lorenz, but rather to the editors of a volume who wished him to comment on the future of ethology), looked at the interrelations between science and society from a different angle:

> . . . we have to realise that all scientific endeavour is a function of attitudes in society as a whole. This is certainly true of 'pure' or exploratory science, but to a lesser degree it also holds for the executive, applied branches, the various technologies. In particular exploratory science, the intellectual game of 'science for the sake of science' flourishes only in rich countries and in affluent periods, i.e., when and where, apart from and beyond the resources needed for sheer survival (food, water, housing, clothing, communication, health, education, defense), there is a surplus of manpower and cash that can be allocated to the 'luxury' occupation of being curious. This means that, when trying to forecast the future of our (as of any) science we shall have to make inspired guesses about the future of society as a whole.[80]

In discussing what he called the "two-way traffic between society and science," Tinbergen focused not on the ideological or political dimensions of science, but rather on the importance of making ethology into a more applied science. For this to work, he indicated, "a better knowledge of the interplay of reason and our deep-rooted, typically human motivations will be essential—knowledge, in other words, of our 'true nature', which includes that of both our largely genetic programming and the genetically imposed potential and the limitations of our flexibility. There are signs that economic and social planners are beginning to see that they will need this better understanding of human behaviour; we shall have to try to help them as well as we can."[81]

How should one think historically about the views Lorenz and Tinbergen offered on the subject of aggression? Certainly the two ethologists were not somehow interrogating nature independently of their historical contexts. They were not, as Lorenz once tried to portray his predecessors Whitman and Heinroth, "happily free from even a working hypothesis, . . . just observing the pigeons and ducks they loved."[82] Rather, they were responding to and, to a greater or lesser degree, seeking to reshape their respective environments. At the same time that they were seeking to make sense of animal behavior they were also recruiting allies for their ideas and research programs, positioning their work with respect to that of other investigators in both the life sciences and psychology, reflecting on the broader implications their work might have for understanding the human condition, and last but not least, benefiting from and reacting to each other.

What one thinker takes from another is typically highly selective, corresponding more to the recipient's needs than to all that the donor has to offer. In this regard it is instructive to consider what Lorenz embraced and what he neglected in the writings of the two American writers, C. O. Whitman and Wallace Craig, who figured most prominently in the early development of his thinking. Whitman in a classic article of 1898 had pointed out a special consequence of domestication. Under the conditions of domestication, he said, instinctive behavior patterns break down, and this in turn favors greater freedom of action, which allows for the development of intelligence.[83] Lorenz picked up the theme of the breakdown of instinctive behavior patterns under domestication, but the way he used it tended to reflect the immediate circumstances in which he found himself. As a scientist in the Third Reich, he was inclined to emphasize the dangers that domestication phenomena posed for the race. After the war, without giving up the idea of the degenerative effects of domestication, he emphasized the liberating features of domestication, as Whitman had done.

How Lorenz's ideas compare with Craig's is equally interesting. He found Craig's distinction between appetitive behavior and consummatory acts in instinctive behavior to be immensely useful in elaborating his own theory of instinct. Curiously enough, however, he neglected Craig's analysis of why animals fight.

It is worth recalling how Lorenz in his book, *On Aggression*, cited Craig as having been the first to demonstrate that the threshold value of the stimuli needed to elicit an instinctive behavior pattern decreases as the appetite for the behavior builds from within. It is important to recall further that Lorenz proceeded to treat aggression as an instinct fitting this same model of internal buildup and eventual release. We need to remember in addition the role that the ring dove played in Lorenz's striking claims about the contrasting behavior of doves and wolves. Let us now compare Lorenz's views with Craig's on the subject of animal aggression.

Craig himself was in fact a specialist on ring doves and (like his mentor, Whitman) on the pigeon family in general. With the pigeon family as his model and the confidence that his knowledge of the behavior of other birds and mammals was sufficient to justify his generalizations from his pigeon studies, Craig in his 1921 paper "Why Do Animals Fight?" set out two main theses:

> I. Fundamentally, among animals, fighting is not sought nor valued for its own sake; it is resorted to rather as an unwelcome necessity, a means of defending the agent's interests.
>
> II. Even when an animal does fight, he aims, not to destroy the enemy, but only to get rid of his presence and his interference.[84]

The basic conclusion Craig drew from his pigeon studies was that the pigeon has no special appetite for fighting. It does not seek the fighting situation, nor does it seek to prolong it while engaged in it. To the contrary, Craig explained, "fighting belongs under the class of negative reactions or aversions; it is a means of getting rid of an annoying stimulus." As he explained: "The pigeon, unless his temper is aroused, has no appetence for a battle. He has appetence for a great many other objects; as, water, food, mates, nest: if kept without such appeted objects he shows distress, tries to get out of his cage, and in every way makes clear to us that he is seeking the appeted object. But when he is kept without enemies, he never manifests the least appetence for them."[85]

Now let us contrast Craig's account of fighting behavior in doves with what we have already extracted from Lorenz's later writings. Craig described what happens in a fight between a stronger bird and a weaker bird when the weaker bird does not fly away but instead simply submits. Here we find, amazingly enough, Craig's victorious pigeon performing behaviors Lorenz later ascribed not to the pigeon but to the wolf:

> If the enemy submits, the agent ceases fighting. In pigeons this is witnessed again and again. In the heat of battle the agent may rush upon his enemy, jump on his back, peck him with all his might, and pull out his feathers. But if the reagent lies down unresisting, the agent's blows quickly diminish into gentle taps, he jumps off his

prostrate foe, walks away, and does not again attack the enemy so long as he is quiet. This behavior is typical, and it proves that the pigeon is devoid of any tendency to destroy his rival.

Craig concluded his paper by asserting that although "no bird or mammal follows a policy of non-resistance," it remained the case that "aggressive fighting does not pay," and that "no distinctively 'biological' need for fighting" exists. Conflicts occur among humans and among animals, Craig insisted, because of their interests: "Animals and men fight because they must conserve their interests, and their technique for the adjustment of conflicting interests is too imperfect to adjust all cases of conflict." This, said Craig, is why wars happen, not because there is any biological need to fight.[86]

Did Lorenz know of Craig's article? Yes, Craig sent it to him late in 1934 or early in 1935 along with reprints of some of his other papers, and Lorenz cited the article in his "Kumpan" monograph of 1935. Lorenz's correspondence with Craig in February and March of 1935 led Lorenz to exclaim to Erwin Stresemann that Craig, after Heinroth, understood animals better than anyone else he knew. Much later in his career Lorenz would identify Craig as his "most influential teacher" after Heinroth and Hochstetter.[87] It is possible, of course, that Lorenz did not read Craig's "Why Do Animals Fight?" when Craig sent it to him, or that he read it and then forgot about it. Be that as it may, it was no more than a year later, in November of 1935, that Lorenz, seeking to make a striking claim about human aggression, told a story about doves that was just the opposite of what Craig, the dove expert, had reported.

Donna Haraway has written of twentieth-century primatologists in her book, *Primate Visions*: "The women and men who have contributed to primate studies have carried with them the marks of their own histories and cultures. These marks are written into the texts of the lives of monkeys and apes, but often in subtle and unexpected ways."[88] The same can be said of the ethologists Lorenz and Tinbergen in their diverse treatments of animal and human behavior. Influences of their respective histories and cultures are visible in their writings, but not in entirely straightforward ways.

Neither man, as it turned out, chose to bring his experiences of the Second World War directly to bear on his discussions of human aggression. Indeed Lorenz, when he wrote in *On Aggression* about leaders who inspired militant enthusiasm on the part of their followers, cited Napoleon but did not refer to Hitler.[89] Tinbergen also refrained from revisiting wartime experiences in his scientific or popular writings on ethology. At least indirectly, however, wartime experiences played an important role in his career and his thinking, for they contributed to his decision to leave Holland for Britain, and his transplantation to Oxford became the occasion for his research program to develop in new directions.

More clearly for both Lorenz and Tinbergen, there were strong consistencies in the way each conceptualized his own scientific behavior, related his ideas to particular scientific practices, and made sense of human aggression. We find Tinbergen, the fieldworker and "hunter," ultimately describing the choices he made in setting up his Oxford program in the same behavioral-ecological terms he used to explain the behavior of kittiwakes and black-headed gulls, namely, as compromises worked out in the face of the selective pressures of particular environments. He likewise regarded the enterprise of modern science as being intimately dependent upon the social conditions that allowed it to flourish. And his interpretation of human aggression was one that highlighted the ecological dimensions of the history of the human race.

Lorenz, the animal raiser, appears in contrast to have undervalued the importance of ecological context in the evolution of specific patterns of animal behavior, the importance of external stimuli in the generation of aggressive behavior, and the importance of social, institutional, and political settings in shaping his own thinking. Indeed, though he is widely regarded today as a founder of evolutionary epistemology, he was by and large remarkably uncritical about the human settings that helped structure the patterns of his own thought. He liked to represent his scientific observations and claims as being essentially inductive in character, not filtered by any intellectual presuppositions. But while he thought he was advancing universal truths, his views often bore the distinct marks of his own, historically situated personal development. Perhaps his inattention to the importance of local circumstances had some relation to his having grown up in the *Bildung* tradition, with its valuation of general intellectual, cultural, or spiritual development over the more mundane features of building a career. It may also have been in part because he, like others who pursued careers as scientists under the Third Reich, found it difficult after the war to think about having been in any way co-opted or influenced by such a murderous regime, to say nothing of having in any way, whether inadvertently or intentionally, aided the regime's operation. Be that as it may, Lorenz's presentations of his science seem, from a variety of different angles, to be lacking in their attention to context.

For a historian of science today, Tinbergen's ecologically oriented perspective, rather than an approach that would simply trace the historical filiation of ideas, seems an instructive way of thinking about the history of

animal behavior studies as a whole. It encourages us to look upon ethology
as a complex, contingent, historically situated, and evolving set of practices
and concepts, worked out by communities of researchers, in conjunction
with various allies, in specific institutional, social, and cultural settings. It
provides a means of appreciating the various kinds of work that went into
the construction of ethology and furthermore to see this as a very human
enterprise, involving obstacles and opportunities, politics and passions, and
theories and practices, all intersecting in the project of seeking to develop
an understanding of the biology of behavior. By thinking in terms of "ethology's ecologies," we gain a richer sense of what was involved in the ethologists' evolving project of understanding animal and human behavior.

There were biologists in addition to Tinbergen who had keener insights
than Lorenz did into the ways in which science has been consciously or
unconsciously enlisted on behalf of special interests or how an individual's
entire worldview can be structured by his social and historical situation.
One was Daniel Lehrman. Another was the British geneticist J. B. S. Haldane,
whose own science and politics combined in the 1930s to make him critical
of the racial state that had developed in Germany under Hitler. In 1938,
the year in which Lorenz published his first article on the degenerative
effects of domestication and civilization, Haldane published a book entitled
Heredity and Politics. The conclusion of Haldane's book is an instructive
assessment of the "situatedness" of human knowledge:

> If we hope to be successful in any political or social endeavour there
> are two prerequisites besides good will. We must examine the system
> with which we have to deal, and we must examine ourselves. We must
> find out what we take for granted in the field of social science, and
> then ask ourselves why we take it for granted, a much more difficult
> question. We must remember that the investigator, whether a biolo-
> gist, an economist, or a sociologist, is himself a part of history, and
> that if he ever forgets that he is a part of history he will deceive his
> audience and deceive himself.[90]

If this was something that Lorenz appreciated, it was not something that
featured prominently in the lessons he chose to broadcast to others. He
insisted on the significance of the biological history of the human species
for understanding human behavior, but he was never sufficiently reflective
about how his own, more immediate, cultural, political, and social history
influenced his scientific ideas and practices and the stories he told about
animals and humans.

NOTES

For permission to quote from manuscript materials cited in this paper, the author gratefully acknowledges the Tinbergen and Lorenz families and the following institutions: Bodleian Library, University of Oxford (Niko Tinbergen papers); Cambridge University Library (W. H. Thorpe papers); Woodson Research Center, Fondren Library, Rice University (Julian S. Huxley papers); and Yale University Library (Robert M. Yerkes papers). The research on which the paper is based was supported by grants from the National Science Foundation (NSF 9122970), the John Simon Guggenheim Memorial Foundation, and the Research Board of the University of Illinois at Urbana-Champaign.

1. See Robert C. Stauffer, "Ecology in the Long Manuscript Version of Darwin's *Origin of Species* and Linnaeus' *Oeconomy of Nature*," *Proceedings of the American Philosophical Society* 104 (1960): 235–41; Thomas Robert Malthus, *An Essay on the Principle of Population, as It Affects the Future Improvement of Society* (London: J. Johnson, 1798), chap. 1; Paul H. Barrett, Peter J. Gautrey, Sandra Herbert, David Kohn, and Sydney Smith, eds., *Charles Darwin's Notebooks, 1836–1844* (Ithaca, N.Y.: Cornell University Press, 1987), p. 539; Charles Darwin, *The Descent of Man and Selection in Relation to Sex*, 2 vols. (London: J. Murray, 1871), 2:403.

2. See Paul Weindling, *Health, Race and German Politics between National Unification and Nazism, 1870–1945* (Cambridge: Cambridge University Press, 1989). First prize was awarded to Wilhelm Schallmayer for his work *Vererbung und Auslese als Faktoren zur Tüchtigkeit und Entartung der Völker* (Heredity and selection as factors in the fitness and degeneration of the race). Central to Schallmayer's treatise was the view that civilized peoples were more subject to biological degeneration than primitive peoples because civilized society spared individuals from the selection pressures operating in nature. On Schallmayer, see also Sheila Faith Weiss, *Race Hygiene and National Efficiency: The Eugenics of Wilhelm Schallmayer* (Berkeley: University of California Press, 1987).

3. On the views of many American biologists toward war, see especially Gregg Mitman, "Evolution as Gospel: William Patten, the Language of Democracy, and the Great War," *Isis* 81 (1990): 446–63; "Dominance, Leadership, and Aggression: Animal Behavior Studies during the Second World War," *Journal of the History of the Behavioral Sciences* 26 (1990): 3–16; and *The State of Nature: Ecology, Community, and American Social Thought, 1900–1950* (Chicago: University of Chicago Press, 1992). Here we will pay particular attention to an additional American writer: Wallace Craig, "Why Do Animals Fight?" *International Journal of Ethics* 31 (1921): 264–78.

4. Konrad Lorenz, *On Aggression* (New York: Harcourt Brace, 1966), Robert Ardrey, *The Territorial Imperative* (New York: Atheneum, 1966), and Desmond Morris, *The Naked Ape* (London: Jonathan Cape, 1967).

5. On the history of ethology see W. H. Thorpe, *The Origins and Rise of Ethology* (London: Heinemann, 1979); John R. Durant, "Innate Character in Animals and Man: A Perspective on the Origins of Ethology," in *Perspectives on Biology, Medicine and Society 1840–1940*, ed. C. Webster (Cambridge: Cambridge University Press, 1981), pp. 157–92; and the following articles by the present author: Richard W. Burkhardt Jr., "On the Emergence of Ethology as a Scientific Discipline," *Conspectus of History* 1 (1981): 62–81; "The Development of an Evolutionary Ethology," in *Evolution from Molecules to Men*, ed. D. S. Bendall (Cambridge: Cambridge University Press, 1983), pp. 429–44; "Charles Otis Whitman, Wallace Craig, and the Biological Study of Behavior in America, 1898–1924," in *The American Development of Biology*, ed. R. Rainger, K. Benson, and J. Maienschein (Philadelphia: University of Pennsylvania Press), pp. 185–218; "Struggling for Identity: The Study of Animal Behavior in America, 1930–1945" (with Gregg Mitman), in *The Expansion of American Biology*, ed. Keith Benson, Ronald Rainger, and Jane Maienschein (New Brunswick, N.J.: Rutgers University Press), pp. 164–94; "Le comportement animal et l'idéologie de domestication chez Buffon et les éthologistes modernes." in *Buffon 88: Actes du Colloque international pour le bicentenaire de la mort de Buffon*, ed. J.-C. Beaune et al. (Paris: J. Vrin, 1992), pp. 569–82; "Julian Huxley and the Rise of Ethology," in *Julian Huxley: Biologist and Statesman of Science*, ed. C. Kenneth Waters and Albert Van Helden (Houston, Tex.: Rice University Press, 1992), pp. 127–49; "The Founders of Ethology and the Problem of Animal Subjective Experience," in *Animal Consciousness and Animal Ethics: Perspectives from the Netherlands*, ed. Marcel Dol et al. (Assen: Van Gorcum, 1997), pp. 1–13. See too Philippe Chavot, "Histoire de l'éthologie: Recherches sur le développement des sciences du comportement en Allemagne, Grande-Bretagne et France, de 1930 à nos jours" (doctoral thesis, University of Strasbourg, 1994); and D. R. Röell, *De wereld van instinct: Niko Tinbergen en het ontstaan van de ethologie in Nederland (1920–1950)* (Rotterdam: Erasmus Publishing, 1996).

6. Spencer Weart, *Nuclear Fear: A History of Images* (Cambridge, Mass.: Harvard University Press, 1988), p. 256.

7. Lorenz, *On Aggression*, p. 49.

8. Tinbergen to Peter and Jean Medawar, January 18, 1974, Nikolaas Tinbergen papers, Department of Western Manuscripts, Bodleian Library, University of Oxford.

9. Konrad Lorenz, *King Solomon's Ring* (London: Methuen, 1952), p. 199. I have not identified the original article on "Morals and Weapons of

Animals" which Lorenz indicates he published in a "Viennese journal" in November 1935.

10. Lorenz, *King Solomon's Ring,* p. 197.

11. Lorenz, *On Aggression,* p. 48.

12. Ibid., pp. 49, 248, 265.

13. Ibid., pp. 50–52.

14. Ibid., pp. 243, 246.

15. Ibid., pp. 268–69.

16. Ibid., pp. 270–71.

17. Ibid., p. 278.

18. Ibid., p. 291.

19. *On Aggression* came to be a controversial bestseller. Although not everyone agreed with Lorenz's analysis of human aggression, various reviewers of his book commented on the manifest humanity of the author's writing. Marston Bates wrote in the *New York Times Book Review*: "Mr. Lorenz, with his profound knowledge of animals and deep sympathy for the human condition, has been more successful than any author I know in explaining human actions in biological terms" (June 19, 1966, p. 3). Similarly, Joseph Alsop commented in the *New Yorker*: "Above all, a warm humanity, a kindly humor, and a deep thoughtfulness shine through almost every word he writes" (September 10, 1966, p. 221). In an article entitled "That Old-Time Aggression" in *The Nation,* John Paul Scott accused Lorenz of being fifty years behind in his biology but still described Lorenz himself as "kindly and humanitarian" (January 9, 1967, p. 53). Scott's article is included in the collection of critical reviews of Lorenz (and Ardrey) edited by Ashley Montagu, *Man and Aggression* (New York: Oxford University Press, 1968).

20. Konrad Lorenz, "Foreword," in Niko Tinbergen, *The Herring Gull's World* (London: Collins, 1953), p. xii. Lorenz made the same claim elsewhere, as for example in "The Comparative Method in Studying Innate Behaviour Patterns," in *Physiological Mechanisms in Behaviour,* Symposia of the Society for Experimental Biology, vol. 4 (New York: Academic Press, 1950), p. 235, and "My Family and Other Animals," in *Studying Animal Behavior: Autobiographies of the Founders,* ed. Donald A. Dewsbury (Chicago: University of Chicago Press, 1989; originally published as *Leaders in the Study of Animal Behavior* [Cranbury, N.J.: Associate dUniversity Presses, 1985]), see p. 263. This statement probably reflects the relations between Lorenz's material practices and his research programs more accurately than his claim in 1932 that he was drawn to the study of tame, free-flying birds because it was a good way of adding to one's chances of observing those "experiments 'which nature may be said to make,'" a phrase which Lorenz attributed to Edmund Selous. See Lorenz, "Betrachtungen über das Erkennen der arteigenen Triebhand-

lungen der Vögel," *Journal für Ornithologie* 80 (1932): 69. The practice of keeping tame, free-flying birds preceded and helped shape the scientific programs he pursued, which then in turn fed back upon his research practices.

21. Konrad Lorenz, "Konrad Lorenz," in *Les Prix Nobel en 1973* (Stockholm: Imprimerie Royale P. A. Norstedt & Söner, 1974), pp. 177–84, and "My Family and Other Animals." Selma Lagerlöf's *The Wonderful Adventures of Nils* (Garden City, N.Y., 1935) was first published in Stockholm in 1906. The Swedish author's book was immediately popular in Sweden and was soon translated into German and Danish.

22. On the *Bildung* ideal, see Fritz K. Ringer, *The Decline of the German Mandarins: The German Academic Community, 1890–1933* (Cambridge, Mass.: Harvard University Press, 1969); and Jonathan Harwood, *Styles of Scientific Thought: The German Genetics Community, 1900–1933* (Chicago: University of Chicago Press, 1993).

23. Konrad Lorenz, *Vergleichende Verhaltensforschung: Grundlagen der Ethologie* (Vienna: Springer-Verlag, 1978), p. 3.

24. Oskar Heinroth and Konrad Lorenz, *Wozu aber hat das Vieh diesen Schnabel? Briefe aus der frühen Verhaltensforschung, 1930–1940,* ed. Otto Koenig (Munich: Piper, 1988), p. 42.

25. Konrad Lorenz, "Beiträge zur Ethologie sozialer Corviden," *Journal für Ornithologie* 79 (1931): 67–127; "Betrachtungen über das Erkennen der arteigenen Triebhandlungen der Vögel," ibid., 80 (1932): 50–98; "Der Kumpan in der Umwelt des Vogels," ibid., 83 (1935) 37–215, 289–413.

26. J. von Uexküll, *Umwelt und Innenwelt der Thiere* (Berlin: J. Springer, 1909); J. von Uexküll and G. Kriszat. *Streifzüge durch die Umwelten von Tieren und Menschen* (Berlin: J. Springer, 1934).

27. Lorenz, "Betrachtungen über das Erkennen der arteigenen Triebhandlungen der Vögel," p. 90; and Lorenz, *Studies in Animal and Human Behaviour,* 2 vols. (Cambridge, Mass.: Harvard University Press, 1970–71), 1:93.

28. See Theo J. Kalikow, "History of Konrad Lorenz's Ethological Theory, 1927–1939: The Role of Meta-Theory, Theory, Anomaly and New Discoveries in a Scientific 'Evolution," *Studies in History and Philosophy of Science* 6 (1975): 331–41.

29. Wallace Craig, "Appetites and Aversions as Constituents of Instincts," *Biological Bulletin of the Marine Biological Laboratory* 34 (1918): 91–107. On Craig, see Burkhardt, "Charles Otis Whitman, Wallace Craig, and the Biological Study of Behavior in America."

30. K. Lorenz, "Über die Bildung des Instinktbegriffes," *Die Naturwissenschaften* 25 (1937): 289–300, 307–18, 324–31.

31. E. von Holst, "Versuche zur Theorie der relativen Koordination," *Pflügers Archiv für die gesamte Physiologie des Menschen und der Tiere* 237 (1936): 93–

121; and "Vom Dualismus der motorischen und der automatisch-rythmischen Funktion im Ruckenmark und vom Wesen des automatischen Rhythmus," ibid., pp. 356–78.

32. Lorenz, "Über die Bildung des Instinktbegriffes," p. 327; *Studies in Animal and Human Behavior,* 1:307–8. Many people have noted the similarity between Lorenz's and Freud's hydraulic action models. Lorenz does not mention Freud in any of his early papers, but he does mention Freud (and criticizes Freud's "death wish") in *On Aggression,* p. x.

33. Konrad Lorenz, "The Comparative Method in Studying Innate Behaviour Patterns," pp. 255–57.

34. N. Tinbergen, "Nikolaas Tinbergen," in *Les Prix Nobel en 1973,* pp. 197–200.

35. N. Tinbergen to R. W. Burkhardt, June 6, 1979.

36. For biographical information on Tinbergen, see his own autobiographical comments in "Nikolaas Tinbergen," and especially his "Watching and Wondering," in Dewsbury, *Studying Animal Behavior,* pp. 431–63. See also R. A. Hinde, "Nikolaas Tinbergen," *Biographical Memoirs of the Royal Society* 36 (1990): 547–65; Gerard Baerends, Colin Beer, and Aubrey Manning, "Introduction," in *Function and Evolution in Behaviour: Essays in Honour of Professor Niko Tinbergen, F.R.S.,* ed. Gerard Baerends, Colin Beer, and Aubrey Manning (Oxford: Clarendon Press, 1975), pp. xi–xxii; and Röell, *De wereld van instinct.* See too Gerard P. Baerends, "Early Ethology: Growing from Dutch Roots," in *The Tinbergen Legacy,* ed. M. S. Dawkins, T. R. Halliday, and R. Dawkins (London: Chapman & Hall, 1991), pp. 1–17.

37. K. Lorenz and N. Tinbergen, "Taxis und Instinkthandlung in der Eirollbewegung der Graugans," *Zeitschrift für Tierpsychologie* 2 (1938): 1–29.

38. Tinbergen letter from Altenberg to his father and mother, March 29, 1937, Nikolaas Tinbergen papers.

39. Tinbergen, "Nikolaas Tinbergen," p. 199, and "Watching and Wondering," p. 447.

40. An excellent overview of recent literature is provided by Jonathan Harwood, "German Science and Technology under National Socialism," *Perspectives on Science* 5 (1997): 128–51.

41. For diverse views of Lorenz's actions as a biologist under the Third Reich, see especially A. Nisbett, *Konrad Lorenz* (New York: Harcourt Brace Jovanovich, 1976); Theodora Kalikow, "Konrad Lorenz's Ethological Theory: Explanation and Ideology, 1938–1943," *Journal of the History of Biology* 16 (1983): 39–73; Robert Richards, *Darwin and the Emergence of Evolutionary Theories of Mind and Behavior* (Chicago: University of Chicago Press, 1987); F. M. Wuketits, *Konrad Lorenz: Leben und Werk eines großen Naturforschers* (Munich and Zürich: Piper, 1990); P. Leyhausen, review of Wuketits, *Kon-*

rad Lorenz, in *Ethology* 89 (1991): 344–46; J. R. Krebs and S. Sjölander. "Konrad Zacharias Lorenz," *Biographical Memoirs of the Royal Society* 38 (1992): 221–28; Ute Deichmann, *Biologists under Hitler* (Cambridge, Mass.: Harvard University Press, 1996). Lorenz's wartime career is discussed at greater length in the author's forthcoming volume on the history of ethology.

42. The dates of Lorenz's application and acceptance to the Nazi party are given by Kalikow, "Konrad Lorenz's Ethological Theory," p. 56.

43. The quote is from Leyhausen, review of Wuketits, *Konrad Lorenz,* p. 344. The contrasting view is Deichmann's *Biologists under Hitler,* pp. 185–98.

44. K. Lorenz, "Über Ausfallerscheinungen im Instinktverhalten von Haustieren und ihre sozialpsychologische Bedeutung," in *16. Kongress der Deutschen Gesellschaft für Psychologie in Bayreuth* (Leipzig: Johan Ambrosius Barth, 1939), pp. 139–47.

45. Ibid., p. 146.

46. K. Lorenz, "Durch Domestikation verursachte Störungen arteigenen Verhaltens," *Zeitschrift für angewandte Psychologie und Charackterkunde* 59 (1940): 1–81.

47. K. Lorenz, "Nochmals: Systematik und Entwicklungsgedanke im Unterricht," *Der Biologe* 9 (1940): 24.

48. Ibid., p. 32.

49. Ibid., pp. 30–31.

50. Ibid., p. 32.

51. Lorenz to Thorpe, August 17, 1950, W. H. Thorpe Papers, Cambridge University Library.

52. Ulfried Geuter, *The Professionalization of Psychology in Nazi Germany* (Cambridge: Cambridge University Press 1992), p. xvii.

53. The article that stimulated Lorenz's own article was Ferdinand Rossner, "Systematik und Entwicklungsgedanke im Unterricht," *Der Biologe* 8 (1939): 366–72. See too Gerhard Heberer, "Die gegenwärtigen Vorstellungen über den Stammbaum der Tiere und die 'Systematische Phylogenie' E. Haeckels," ibid., pp. 264–73.

54. Two days after writing to Thorpe, Lorenz wrote a very similar letter to Julian Huxley. There he said of his article in *Der Biologe*: "But of course the whole confounded thing is written in Nazi terminology (I should write in the terms of any old terminology in order to make the value of the theory of evolution understood!) and if one quotes disconnected passages out of this article one can make me a damn Nazi indeed. Also I do not deny that I was, at the time, rather taken with the idea of making Eugenics a sort of state religion—I really did not suspect then that it was only an excuse to kill off Jews and other 'racially inferior' peoples." Konrad Lorenz to Julian

Huxley, August 19, 1950, Julian Huxley Papers, Woodson Research Center, Fondren Library, Rice University.

55. Konrad Lorenz, *The Natural Science of the Human Species. An Introduction to Comparative Behavioral Research. The "Russian Manuscript" (1944–1948),* ed. Agnes von Cranach (Cambridge, Mass.: MIT Press, 1996).

56. Ibid., p 76.

57. Ibid., p. xxxi. Another reference to dialectical materialism appears on p. 196. See too a remark on p. 138: "Karl Marx's saying that quantity gives rise to quality is nowhere more appropriate than when applied to the phylogenetic developmental processes of organic creation."

58. Lorenz, *On Aggression,* pp. 288–89.

59. See Tinbergen to Margaret Nice, June 23, 1945, Margaret Morse Nice Papers, Cornell University Library.

60. Tinbergen to Robert M. Yerkes, October 18, 1948, R. M. Yerkes Papers, Yale University.

61. Tinbergen's letter to Huxley was one of two letters published under the heading "Scientific Affairs in Europe," in the November 10, 1945, issue of *Nature* 156 (1945): 576–78. *Nature* did not report the date of Tinbergen's letter, and the original letter is not among the Huxley papers at Rice University.

62. Lorenz, "My Family and Other Animals," p. 277.

63. Lorenz to Thorpe, June 31, 1950, W. H. Thorpe Papers.

64. See Senatsprotokoll, 19.12.1950, in "Verhaltensphysiologie, allgemein (1)," Max Planck Gesellschaft Archives, Berlin. That there were no dissenting votes is stated by Lorenz in a letter to Huxley, December 21, 1950, Huxley papers.

65. Tinbergen, *The Study of Instinct,* pp. 101, 127.

66. Tinbergen, *Social Behaviour in Animals* (London: Methuen, 1953), pp. 62–63.

67. Tinbergen, *The Study of Instinct,* pp. 177–78.

68. Daniel S. Lehrman, "A Critique of Konrad Lorenz's Theory of Instinctive Behavior," *Quarterly Review of Biology* 298 (1953): 337–63.

69. Ibid., p. 354.

70. Konrad Lorenz, *Evolution and Modification of Behavior* (Chicago: University of Chicago Press, 1965), pp. 2, 102, 105–6.

71. See R. W. Burkhardt Jr., "The Development of an Evolutionary Ethology," in *Evolution from Molecules to Men,* ed. D. S. Bendall (Cambridge: Cambridge University Press, 1983), pp. 429–44.

72. N. Tinbergen, "On the Functions of Territory in Gulls," *Ibis* 98 (1956): 408.

73. R. A. Hinde and N. Tinbergen, "The Comparative Study of Species-Specific Behavior," in *Behavior and Evolution,* ed. A. Roe and G. G. Simpson

(New Haven, Conn.: Yale University Press, 1958), p. 260.

74. Tinbergen criticized Wynne-Edwards's views in Tinbergen, "Behavior and Natural Selection," in *Ideas in Modern Biology,* ed. John A. Moore (Garden City, N.Y.: Natural History Press, 1965), pp. 519–42, esp. pp. 536–37; and Tinbergen, "Adaptive Features of the Black-Headed Gull, *Larus ridibundus* L.," *Proceedings of the 14th International Ornithological Congress* (Oxford: Blackwell, 1967), pp. 43–59, esp. pp. 55–56. See too a letter from Tinbergen to Ernst Mayr, dated April 17, 1963, in the Ernst Mayr papers, Harvard University.

75. Tinbergen, "On War and Peace in Animals and Man: An Ethologist's Approach to the Biology of Aggression," *Science* 160 (1968): 1411–18. Similar views were expressed by Tinbergen in a 1964 lecture entitled "The Search for Animal Roots of Human Behaviour," not published until 1973 in Niko Tinbergen, *The Animal in Its World: Explorations of an Ethologist, 1932–1972,* 2 vols. (London: Allen & Unwin, 1972–73), 2:161–74. See too Tinbergen's 1972 Croonian lecture, "Functional Ethology and the Human Sciences," ibid., pp. 200–231.

76. Tinbergen, "On War and Peace in Animals and Man," p. 1418.

77. N. Tinbergen, "Ethology in a Changing World," in *Growing Points in Ethology,* ed. P. P. G. Bateson and R. A. Hinde (Cambridge: Cambridge University Press, 1976), p. 516.

78. Niko Tinbergen, "On the History of War," in *Aggression and Violence: A Psychobiological and Clinical Approach,* ed. I. Valzelli and I. Morgese (Milan: Edizioni Saint Vincent, 1981), pp. 31–32.

79. Lorenz, *On Aggression,* pp. 288–89.

80. Tinbergen, "Ethology in a Changing World," p. 508.

81. Ibid., p. 524. The editors of the volume in which Tinbergen's paper appeared put their own gloss on Tinbergen's suggestion: "Certainly we are wholly in sympathy with his view. But he is of course not implying that ethologists should give up fundamental work." They warned that "an exclusive focus on problems of immediate practical importance could deprive ethology of the possibility of theoretical growth. Furthermore, the conceptual structure necessary for the practical problems of the 1990s will not necessarily arise from examination of the problems of today." P. P. G. Bateson and R. Hinde, "Editorial: 8," p. 531.

82. Lorenz, "The Comparative Method in Studying Innate Behaviour Patterns," p. 222.

83. C. O. Whitman, "Animal Behavior," in *Biological Lectures Delivered at the Marine Biological Laboratory of Wood's Hole ... 1898* (1899), pp. 285–338.

84. Craig, "Why Do Animals Fight?" p. 267.

85. Ibid., p. 268.

86. Ibid., pp. 276–77.

87. Nice, *Research Is a Passion with Me* (Toronto: Consolidated Amethyst Communications Inc., 1979) pp. 140–41, mentions the seven-page letter from Craig to Lorenz. Lorenz's reaction to Craig's letter is described by Lorenz in a letter to Erwin Stresemann, March 13, 1935, Erwin Stresemann papers, Staatsbibliothek, Berlin. The continuing correspondence between Craig and Lorenz provided the core of Lorenz's Harnackhaus lecture and the basis of Lorenz's later identification of Craig as his "most influential teacher" after Ferdinand Hochstetter and Oscar Heinroth. See Lorenz, "Konrad Lorenz," p. 179.

88. Donna Haraway, *Primate Visions: Gender, Race, and Nature in the World of Modern Science* (New York: Routledge, 1989), p. 2.

89. Lorenz, *On Aggression,* chap. 13.

90. J. B. S. Haldane, *Heredity and Politics* (London: G. Allen & Unwin, 1938), p. 182.

10

ANIMAL PARTS/HUMAN BODIES
ORGANIC TRANSPLANTATION IN EARLY TWENTIETH-CENTURY AMERICA

SUSAN E. LEDERER

"The dream of surgery," observed Mayo Clinic surgeon Carleton Dederer in 1920, "will have been realized when it has become possible to transplant a vital organ from one individual to another."[1] Although Dederer's research involved the transfer of kidneys and ovaries from one dog to another, he shared, with other American surgeons, the desire to perform transplantation to aid human patients. In the first three decades of the twentieth century surgeons sought operative solutions to problems of trauma and disease. Grafting tissues, skin, bone, and organs taken from human bodies, both living and dead, surgeons attempted to restore the appearance, structure, and function of human patients.[2] In addition to tissues donated by friends and family members, surgeons used human body parts purchased as commodities or retrieved from the birthing room, dissecting room, and executioner. The difficulties and scarcities associated with such supplies prompted the use of a variety of animals, both exotic and domestic, as sources for tissues and organs.

The incorporation of animal parts into human bodies in early twentieth-century America called into question traditional assumptions about the boundaries between animal and human bodies. The use of skin, bone, corneas, and testicles from animals graphically illustrated the shifting line Thorstein Veblen had identified in the late nineteenth century between the natural and the unnatural in American culture.[3] Although these early efforts at heterotransplantation were mostly abandoned by the late 1920s as knowledge of immunological specificity developed, the initial embrace of "organic transplantation" challenged notions of human distinctiveness and biological individuality, especially when transplanters harvested parts from animals increasingly recognized as "almost human," the nonhuman primates.

British novelist H. G. Wells explored some of the cultural implications of surgically altering the animal-human boundary. In *The Island of Doctor*

Moreau (1896), Wells created a memorable and influential portrait of an exiled vivisector, whose grafting experiments in the House of Pain produce "humanised animals," unnatural hybrids (wolf-hyena-man, ox-hog-man, puma-woman) who eventually turn on their creator and kill him. Invoking the classic experiments of surgeon John Hunter and the manufacture of such "monsters" as rhinoceros rats, Moreau explains to the hapless visitor to the island where he conducts his secret researches: "You begin to see that it is possible to transplant tissue from one part of an animal to another, or from one animal to another; to alter its chemical reactions and methods of growth; to modify the articulations of its limbs; and, indeed, to change its most intimate structure."[4] Although some reviewers criticized the scientific practicality of the kinds of transplants performed by Doctor Moreau, French surgeon Alexis Carrel found Wells's portrait of the surgeon and his experiments sufficiently compelling to lend copies of the novel to his friends and professional colleagues and to meet to discuss the "quaint and queer" aspects of the book.[5] In the first part of the twentieth century, Carrel became inseparably linked in the American public sphere with the "revolution in surgery" that included the transplantation of organs, animal and human.

THE WIZARD OF OZ

Even before he joined the staff of the Rockefeller Institute for Medical Research as head of the Department of Experimental Surgery, Carrel's surgical exploits had attracted public attention. In the summer of 1906, reports in Chicago and New York newspapers of his work on the transplantation of veins and arteries raised the possibility of organ transplantation in human beings.[6] Although Carrel conducted this early work with University of Chicago colleague Charles Guthrie, co-author of many of his papers on transplantation of the kidney, ovary, thyroid gland, and limbs in animals, Guthrie soon faded from popular accounts of the organ transplants.[7] In magazines and newspapers Carrel received sole credit for making an ancient dream of curing bodily ills a reality. "The idea of removing a diseased member and replacing it with a sound one is by no means new," observed the editors of *Scientific American* in 1911. "An old painting in Florence represents a miraculous operation of this kind in which the sacristan of the Church of St. Como [*sic*] and St. Damian is the patient, the saints are the surgeons, and the leg substituted for the sacristan's cancerous limb is taken, without regard to color, from a dead Moor."[8] This story, readers learned, was quoted by Carrel, who had earned the honor of converting the legend of the medieval saints into fact.[9] Carrel performed the "miracle of the black leg" not on human beings but on dogs, successfully grafting in 1907 the black leg of a dog onto a white animal of the same height.[10]

Carrel's celebrity intensified when his work on blood vessel surgery and organ transplantation earned him in 1912 the Nobel Prize in medicine and physiology. He was only the third U.S. resident to receive the prize, and his fame reached dizzying heights and sparked speculation about the human implications of the surgeon's ability "to play with the animal machine as if it were made of tubes and rods of brass and iron." Identifying Carrel as New York's version of the Wizard of Oz, writer Carl Snyder offered readers of *Collier's* a graphic calculation about available body parts which, placed in cold storage, could be used by surgeons for transplantation into human beings. Citing the more than fifty thousand people injured annually in American factory, train, and automobile accidents, Snyder elaborated: "Depending upon the degree of mutilation—whether the bodies are blown to pieces, or chewed up, or merely punctured by a bullet, or killed electrically, here at a modest calculation are at least 50,000 good arms, as many legs, and perhaps a slightly less number of lungs, livers, hearts and other organs."[11]

Letters written to Carrel from people across the country suggest that many Americans had already considered the possibility of human transplantation and what it might entail. Popular articles on Carrel produced a predictable crop of letters from people either seeking transplants or offering to serve as donors in return for financial compensation. In 1908, for example, a fourteen-year-old boy who had lost a leg in a streetcar accident four years earlier read an account in the *Chicago Examiner* of Carrel's "wonderful success in grafting the leg of a dead dog to the leg of his companion" and wrote to the surgeon to offer him the opportunity to "graft a new foot on my stump anytime you please if you are inclined to do so."[12] Among the letters Carrel received in 1913 came requests for grafting of arms, hands, legs, breasts, feet, eyes, clitorises, fingers, and ovaries. Whereas some expressed willingness to undergo surgical operations in exchange for remuneration, others expressed the hope that criminals about to be executed could be persuaded to donate their body parts for transplantation.[13]

Cash for human organs and tissues was not without precedent in this period. The well-publicized sale of a human ear for the purpose of transplantation suggests that many Americans found the idea of trafficking in body parts entertaining rather than unethical. In 1903 New York newspapers had carried the following advertisement: "$5,000 will be paid for right ear, 2½ inches long, 1¼ inches wide, with perfect curves and full lobe; the ear may be from either male or female, and must be from a person in perfect health; offers by mail considered."[14] Contacted by reporters, Dr. Andrew

Linn Nelden explained that the ear was intended for a miner who had lost his own in an accident.

Nelden had apparently first made the rounds of hospitals seeking a prospective donor. Concern about the transmission of syphilis made the health of the potential donor a prime consideration. "It is necessary to get some one whose blood is absolutely pure," he informed reporters. "Such persons are not so numerous among those who would be likely to part with an ear."[15] After locating two possible donors, Nelden asked each to sign a written contract indemnifying the surgeon and the recipient from legal liability in case of a bad outcome. Such disclosures apparently frightened these prospective donors, compelling Nelden to advertise. In a front-page story in the *New York Times,* readers learned that 150 persons called upon Dr. Nelden in response to his advertisement. After the physician selected a young German man as the donor, he was forced to perform the operation in Philadelphia when the Manhattan district attorney threatened to interfere with the case. According to a report in the *Philadelphia Inquirer,* the Philadelphia district attorney promised there was nothing in Pennsylvania law that would make it a criminal offense to cut off a man's ear unless it was done without consulting him about the price.[16]

The operation, performed in a private hospital on November 19, 1903, required that the donor and recipient be physically linked for twelve days to ensure that blood circulation could be achieved in the grafted ear.[17] Notable about the incident was the matter-of-fact tone in reports of the transaction. Aside from jocularity in the newspaper headlines ("lend me your ears!"), no comment was made about the immorality of selling a body part, the mutilating effect on the donor, or the surgeon's cutting into a healthy person for the benefit of a third party. While it is possible that the comparative rarity of ear transplants and sales of body parts contributed to a lack of concern about the morality of the practice, it is also true that the much more common practice of providing financial compensation for people willing to undergo direct blood transfusion similarly elicited little comment.[18]

If some Americans demanded and received compensation for their donations of blood and tissues, others were apparently prepared to give of themselves and expect nothing in return. Newspapers and magazines celebrated these tissue donors and their willingness to go under the knife to aid injured family members and strangers, as the response to "Crippled Newsie" Rugh's extraordinary donation suggests.

In September 1912 Rugh read about twenty-two-year-old Ethel Smith, seriously burned when the gasoline tank on her motorcycle exploded. Learning that "skin-grafting alone could save her life," Newsie appeared at the office of Dr. J. A. Craig and offered to donate his "withered" leg for the grafting operation. When informed that so much skin was required that an amputation would be needed, Rugh reportedly hesitated only a moment before giving his consent to the operation.[19] Donor and recipient met on adjoining tables in the operating room before undergoing chloroform anesthesia. After 150 square inches of skin were removed from the man's leg and grafted onto the girl's body, Rugh received an additional dose of chloroform before his leg was amputated at the hip. A few days after Smith was discharged from the hospital, Rugh developed pneumonia (news reports noted the anesthetic given for the amputation was too much for his weak lungs) and died.

The press coverage of Rugh's death emphasized his unselfish sacrifice. The special report to the *New York Times* noted: "when his foster mother knelt beside the bed and hid her face in the edge of the boy's pillow, he reached out a weak hand and stroked her hair. 'Don't cry, Mammy,' he begged. 'I never 'mounted to nothin' before, and now you know I done sompin' fer somebody.'"[20]

Reports of Rugh's heroism moved many Americans to donate funds to erect a memorial in his name. A number of people recommended that Rugh be awarded a medal from the Carnegie Hero Fund, established in 1904 with a five-million-dollar grant from Andrew Carnegie in order that "the heroes and those dependent upon them should be free from pecuniary cares resulting from their heroism."[21] As one of Rugh's supporters noted, "it wasn't, indeed, a very good leg that Willie sacrificed, and possibly he is better off without than with it, but there seems to be no reason for supposing that he would have parted with the limb, poor specimen as it was, had he not heard that unless a very considerable amount of living cuticle could be secured the victim of the accident would not recover."[22] Although the fund did eventually recognize some "medical heroes," Rugh received no posthumous recognition from the commission.[23]

The transplantation of tissues and organs excited tremendous interest in the American popular media in the first two decades of the twentieth century. Reporters described the prospect of a future in which the body's worn-out or damaged organs could be replaced by donated or discarded healthy organs and tissues in glowing terms with little apparent reservations. Some physicians conceded that wholesale transplantation would not be easily accomplished. Gynecologic surgeon Robert Morris, who performed ovarian transplants in the early twentieth century, recalled how "prospective donors and recipients of grafts exhibit extremely interesting differences in attitudes toward the subject." Whereas some of the women he approached to donate ovarian tissue (scheduled to be removed for therapeutic reasons) rejected his suggestion "with a great deal of feeling and exclamations," others proved eager to render aid by providing a "piece" of themselves. Morris further recalled gender differences in attitudes toward donation: "When a request for donation of blood for transfusion comes up in an emergency, men seem to be much more responsive than women—they may even vie with each other for the opportunity to make the sacrifice. Women, on the other hand, are much more ready than are men to sacrifice a solid organ."[24] Women had so little fear of the operation for removal of the ovaries, Morris explained, that they sometimes suggested the "self-sacrifice" of their ovaries to benefit some other woman who could benefit by their implantation.

The fact that one of Morris's patients about to receive an ovarian graft wanted to know whether the donor was a Methodist or an Episcopalian suggests that the source of donated tissue interested (perhaps worried) some recipients, even if it did not prevent their acceptance of the organ. Morris himself raised questions about some of the social consequences stemming from using donated ovaries when he reported in 1906 the birth of a living child following a case of ovarian grafting. "It will be interesting to note," Morris observed, "which parent the child of Mrs. W. most resembles. According to Haeckel hereditary characteristics are due to cell memory, and the cell memory of an engrafted ovary may not be changed by the influence of its new host."[25] Morris did conclude that the woman who gave birth to the child should be regarded as the real mother, as she had furnished the nutrition for development of the infant. This notion of cell memory may explain why another ovarian transplanter, performing grafts at the same time as Morris, insisted that the woman who donated ovarian tissue be of the same race as the woman who received the tissue.[26]

Not all Americans welcomed the advent of organ transplantation. American antivivisectionists questioned the utility of such procedures, labeling John D. Rockefeller, the man whose "need for a new stomach and kidney" had prompted Carrel's research, as "the most credulous of men in matters that affect his health."[27] Critics of animal experimentation also found "gruesome" the prospect that murderers sentenced to death should have their eyes removed prior to their execution in order to use the corneas to restore the sight of blind patients.[28] Although their reservations about the source of tissue in this case stemmed from opposition to the death penalty, suggestions that the bodies of executed criminals be used as sources of tissue for transplantation confirmed their suspicions that "human vivisection was the inevitable outcome of animal experimentation and the brutishness begotten thereof."[29]

ANIMAL BODIES

In 1907, speculating about the potential clinical application of his experimental work in animals involving transplantation of kidneys, ovaries, limbs, and thyroid glands, Alexis Carrel raised several issues that would have to be addressed before large-scale human use could be undertaken. One of the difficulties was locating a reliable and suitable supply of healthy organs. Conceding that bodies of executed criminals and men killed in accidents could be harvested for their organs, he expressed reservations as to whether this would produce sufficient material in good condition. Organs from anthropoid apes, he suggested, would perhaps make acceptable substitutes from the biological standpoint. But here too practical questions arose. The expense and the difficulties in managing the animals made their large-scale use unappealing. "The ideal method," Carrel explained, "would be to transplant on man organs of animals easy to secure and to operate on, such as hogs, for instance. The future of transplantation of organs for therapeutic purposes depends on the feasibility of hetero-transplantation. Research must be directed along this line but as yet we have not been able to do more than perform a few preliminary experiments."[30]

Heteroplastic transplants (tissue and organs from different species), in Carrel's experience, unlike autoplastic grafts (tissues from the same animal) and homoplastic transplants (the use of tissue from animals of the same species), raised their own problems. Even when the surgical technique of transplanting the organ and establishing a blood supply within the host went perfectly, he explained, the transplanted tissue could be destroyed by the serum of the recipient, "as it happens in heteroplastic transplantations of the thyroid glands, when the zoological distance of the animals is very marked."[31] Although he expressed the hope that a means to immunize the organs of a nonhuman animal against the human serum could be developed, he was not sanguine that this would happen in the near future.

Carrel's pessimism followed nearly three decades of American surgical experience with animals as sources for skin for treating badly burned and injured human beings. Faced with growing numbers of such injuries as scalp avulsion (the extensive laceration and separation of the scalp which occurred, for example, when a woman's long hair became entangled in machinery), physicians and surgeons in manufacturing centers turned to skin grafting as a means to treat those injured in the mills.[32]

One of the issues immediately confronting surgeons was locating sufficient skin for grafting. Physicians looked first to the patient as a potential donor. Collecting skin from an injured patient was not always possible. In the case of young children, already traumatized by severe burns or extensive injuries, shaving portions of skin from uninjured parts of the child's body was not satisfactory to children and parents.[33] Physicians then attempted to find friends, family members, and others willing to undergo the procedure.[34] But many potential donors found the process of being flayed physically painful and aesthetically unacceptable. Covering the eyes of "hysterical adults" and "very nervous children" with a bandage so they could not "see the pain" was one solution.[35] Other physicians considered the use of anesthetics to make donors more comfortable, but this not only increased the danger for the donor but also required more attention from the doctors. Although New York surgeon George Fowler dismissed the discomfort of skin donation as "really slight" and "accompanied only by a peculiar burning sensation," he believed that using such anesthetic agents as ether, chloroform, or cocaine was neither prudent nor practical: "Where a number of people volunteer to furnish the skin for transplantation, and but a single strip of skin is taken from each, it will be obviously impracticable to administer an anesthetic to each donor. On the other hand, but few will be found to volunteer to give a large amount of skin, and endure the inconveniences and risks of an anesthetic; nor yet to allow themselves to be flayed alive, with all that the term implies."[36] The experience of skin donation made some donors reluctant to undergo the procedure a second time. When Zera Lusk, a New York physician, required skin to treat a patient severely burned in an accident at the salt works, he was initially able to obtain eight grafts shaved from the palm of one of his surgical attendants. The following day Lusk reported "when I asked to repeat the operation he declined. His 'hand was tender,' that I had 'cut too close,' and though it didn't bleed, was 'sore.'"[37]

The difficulties raised by human donors encouraged some grafters to turn to animals as sources of skin. Pigeon skin grafting, as one Massachusetts physician explained in 1893, offered several advantages. Removing skin from the bird did "not necessitate an anesthetic; its failure does not discourage because squabs come as cheap as a can of ether, and you can graft without even the consent of the patient, or in fact, the patient hardly realizing what you are doing."[38] Problems of feathers, N. B. Aldrich noted, could be avoided by selecting young squabs whose feathers had not developed under the wings, and half-grown birds, which he plucked after killing.

Dogs, cats, chickens, frogs, and rabbits offered similar advantages to pigeons as a source of tissue. Readily available and inexpensive, these animals could be supplied by either the physician or the family and friends of the patient.[39] The obvious problems of fur (in the case of dogs, cats, and rabbits) could be avoided, as in the case of pigeons, by using young animals.

In 1890, for example, when M. E. Van Meter, a physician in Red Bluff, Colorado, required skin to treat the severe burns of a fourteen-year-old boy, he first took grafts from the boy's father and brother. Needing even more skin, the physician removed skin from two young puppies of the "Mexican hairless breed," and applied them to the boy's arm, achieving a "superior result."[40]

Perhaps the most commonly selected animal for grafting was the frog. Like dogs, frogs were easily acquired (although less available in winter months). Surgeon George Fowler advised using large, healthy frogs, maintained for several days in a container containing clean water. "The animal is held by an assistant by grasping its extremities and head, " he explained, "while the operator, pinching up a fold of skin, snips it through transversely to the long axis of the frog's body, and just behind its eyes, for from a quarter to half an inch, according to the size of the frog."[41] Fowler predicted that the size of the strips obtained from the process would reflect the steadiness on the part of the assistant holding the animal.

How did patients and their families respond to the surgical union of animal skin and human bodies? As the advocate for pigeon skin suggested, American patients may not always have been aware of the source of skin they had received. Physicians may have withheld such information in the best interests of their patients, or a patient's medical condition (some surgeries were undertaken when the patient was comatose or near death) may have prevented their learning about the type of graft used. Given the catastrophic nature of the injuries to these patients and their desperate situations, these individuals and their families may not have cared that pigeon or frog skin was being used in an effort to treat their damaged bodies.[42]

Some British and French physicians reported that some patients refused to permit skin grafts using frog skin. "These amphibia," observed British physician G. F. Cadogan-Masterman, "are so repulsive to most people, and especially so to women and children, that after two [unsatisfactory] trials I gave it up."[43] American surgeons reported no such reactions from their patients. Surgeons like George Fowler, a leading American proponent for frog skin grafts, noted that the pigment in frog skin disappeared after seven to ten days, which may have served to reassure anxious patients about the resulting appearance of their grafts. C. S. Venable, a Texas physician, offered similar assurances about using pig skin for grafting; "lest one be deterred through fear of the patient becoming part swine," he happily related that the pigment soon disappeared and no bristles grew when the grafts were cut above the hair follicles. "However," he continued, "should such an unforeseen catastrophe as the advent of bristles obtain, the prognosis even then was good, as the follicles would atrophy in a very short time."[44] Venable's account suggests that some physicians were prepared for the prospect that dog hair, rabbit fur, or pig bristles would actually develop on the patient's skin as a result of a successful graft. Fortunately for all involved, this did not occur. But it raises questions about what patients might have believed about the outcome of their grafts.

The possibility that American patients may have found the animal origins of their grafted skin interesting rather than problematic is suggested by physician Samuel Lambert's discussion of one patient's response to a pig skin graft. In 1934 the New York surgeon regaled physicians at the Charaka Club with a tale of a "rising young surgeon at a well known New York medical school" who, in the first decade of the twentieth century, treated the badly burned thigh of a socially prominent woman with skin taken from a live pig. The unnamed surgeon dissected a six-inch square of skin from the back of a young male white pig, leaving one six-inch side still intact on the animal. He then attached the living pigskin to the woman's leg. Although both the patient and the pig recovered from the anesthesia, complications soon developed. Nursing care provided "to care for the calls of nature for the Lady" did not meet the needs of the pig. Special arrangements, including tissue products from the Star Pulp Mills, the predecessors of Scott Tissue, were implemented with little success. In addition to the pig's eliminatory problems, the animal's constant movement of the skin flap caused the patient considerable pain. The surgeon was able to recruit several undergraduate students to maintain the pig in a constant state of etherization. After several days, however, the enthusiasm of the students waned; the surgeon decided to sever the pig's spinal cord to paralyze the animal. The incision, instead of immobilizing the animal, killed it. The pig was detached from the woman, who subsequently underwent grafts with both her own skin and that taken from other human donors.[45]

With considerable humor, Lambert related how the woman, following her recovery, insisted on exhibiting her resulting scar tissue to interested women physicians. Although he had not personally seen the scar, Lambert learned from a colleague that the area "really looked not unlike a bristleless pig skin." Apparently, the patient believed that in fact, she retained some of the pig skin graft, for her surgeon had neglected to disclose to her that "the pig experiment was an entire failure."[46] Although there are a number of intriguing aspects to Lambert's tale, I emphasize here the nature of the woman's response to the idea that the pig skin graft had united with her own skin; rather than rejecting the union, she celebrated her experience and sought to benefit others (while simultaneously preserving her modesty by restricting viewing of her leg to women physicians).

In a recent history of transplantation immunology (1997), immunologist Leslie Brent has criticized the use of "misleading" references from the older literature and to Lambert's account in particular: "a highly disreputable transaction between a woman patient and a pig, resurrected by Saunders, strikes one as wholly frivolous as well as worthless, if indeed it ever occurred."[47] Lambert's light tone and his inclusion of details typically absent from case reports published in medical journals (references to medical mistakes and eliminatory and personnel problems) reflected his intended audience, his fellow members of the Charaka Club, a New York–based society for physicians interested in history, literature, and music, rather than the fictional nature of his narrative.

Some of Lambert's references can be verified, including his discussion of an early and failed effort to transplant an animal kidney into a human patient: "One large hospital in New York saw a young lamb put to bed with a would-be suicide to have the lamb's kidney sewn into the circulation of the human sufferer in order that this organ of a healthy animal might substitute its function for that of the damaged kidneys of the poisoned human until the crisis of the toxic dose had passed."[48] Although Lambert did not identify the patient, hospital, surgeon, or date, such an "organic transplant" was in fact performed in 1923 by Harold Neuhof at Bellevue Hospital in a desperate effort to save the life of Mrs. Adele Robertson. According to the detailed report in the *New York Times*, Robertson's failure to respond to the usual treatment for mercury poisoning prompted the "animal sacrifice to medical science" in which a sheep kidney was "spliced" into the artery in the woman's thigh.[49]

SYMPATHY FOR THE BRUTES

The animal side of the heteroplastic transplant received little systematic attention from physicians or the public. In some cases, details about the animal source furnished a humorous dimension to newspaper accounts of organ transplantation. In 1923 press reports of the efforts to restore the sight of a boy blinded in a fireworks explosion included not only description of the substitution of the lens from a pig's eye for the boy's destroyed cornea but the fact that the "porker" would spend its days "in peace and plenty on a Connecticut farm" if the operation succeeded. In the subsequent reports of the progress of the pig's eye graft appeared the offer by a museum to purchase for five hundred dollars the pig which had furnished portions of its right eye for the graft, an offer refused by the surgeon on the case.[50]

In light of their opposition to animal experimentation and vaccination, American antivivisectionists sometimes expressed objections to the use of animals as sources of tissue. The use of a live dog as a source of bone prompted the most sustained and critical response from American antivivisectionists. In November 1890 a surgical procedure involving a dog and a fourteen-year-old boy at the Charity Hospital on Blackwell's Island excited comment in New York City newspapers. In an effort to avoid the amputation of his malformed leg, John Gethins and his parents agreed to an operation in which two inches of a dog's foreleg were grafted onto his shin bone; the boy and dog had to remain joined for twelve to fourteen days in an effort to promote growth of the engrafted bone. Firmly encased in a plaster jacket to prevent his movement, the animal, a black spaniel named Yig, described by reporters as "a very good-natured dog," shared a bed with the boy in a private room in the hospital for nearly two weeks before surgeons concluded that the graft had failed.[51] In "a prospective act of humanity," surgeon A. M. Phelps, professor of orthopedic surgery at the University of New York and chief surgeon at the Post-Graduate Hospital, severed the union between the boy and the dog, stitched the stump of the dog's leg, and allowed both of his "patients" to recuperate.[52]

It was "natural," observed the editors of the *Boston Medical and Surgical Journal*, "that an attempt to temporarily unite a human being and a dog in a union as close as that of the Siamese twins should have excited the interest of a newspaper reporter and also of the lay mind."[53] Daily press reports about the bone graft experiment prompted a series of letters critical of the "wanton brutality" of encasing the animal in plaster and emphasizing the spaniels "pitiful moanings," the result of the devocalizing procedure undertaken to prevent him from disturbing the boy and other hospital patients.[54] The boy's plight generated no similar outcry; during his convalescence, he apparently received a number of "postal cards from persons praying that the effort to save his leg might be a failure."[55]

In an effort to refute the "absurd rumors" created by the wide interest in the bone grafting experiment, Phelps offered a detailed explanation of his experiment and a sharp riposte to his antivivisectionist critics. Recognizing that selecting the dog as a source of tissue contributed to the interest and criticism of his experiment, Phelps emphasized that the careful attention and nursing care received by the animal during the surgery, in the period of eleven days in which the dog and boy "became friends, administering to each other's comfort," and following the decision to end the grafting experiment, all of which ensured that little suffering accompanied the bone graft. "It is useless," he insisted, to reply to those who have denounced the operation as cruel and unnecessary. Those who understand the motive which actuates the surgeon can comprehend how, with all sympathy for the brute, his sacrifice of limb may be demanded for the good of his master, man. They too, can appreciate the reluctance of the surgeon to inflict wanton suffering, whether upon man or brute, and can understand how such an operation only seemed commendable when a more than commensurate benefit was promised. To those whose eyes are blind to human suffering, and whose sympathies are all for the brute, I have nothing to say.[56]

Given the considerable opposition within the antivivisection movement to vaccination, there was surprisingly little comment about the unnatural union of human and animal skin, bone, and tissue. In the 1920s, pamphlets against vaccination continued to warn about the dire consequences of injecting animal poison into the human bloodstream. Propaganda from the American Medical Liberty League, an organization with ties to several antivivisection societies in the 1910s and 1920s, alerted parents to the apocalyptic effects of smallpox vaccination, which produced lymphatic blockages "due to the engrafting upon the human of the cells and pus from the bovine." Like other invaders, the bovine cell reproduced at a much more rapid rate than the human cell. "Such a graft therefore must enormously overtax the human circulation, in having to harbor and harmonize, in a degree, this foreign cell life. The very thought of grafting beast into human is so revolting, instinct as well as reason cries out against it."[57]

In the 1910s and 1920s, American antivivisectionists continued to focus on the cruelty of the "freak experiments" on animals conducted by Alexis Carrel and his colleagues at the Rockefeller Institute, remaining suspicious about their implications for human beings.[58] As Jon Turney has observed, Carrel appeared to have behaved just like "the anti-vivisectionists' stereotype of the unfeeling experimental physiologist."[59] This image was considerably enhanced by newspaper stories describing him (in favorable terms) as a man who takes an animal apart "with the eagerness of a small boy who describes to papa just what the clock did when it was taken apart."[60] In the 1930s Carrel, with the collaboration of aviator Charles Lindbergh, would go on to perfect the disassembly of the body—animal and human—into parts with the creation of the perfusion pump.[61] Labeled the "glass heart" in the popular press, the machine was designed to keep whole body organs alive outside the body. Like all of Carrel's researches, the pump, which had been used to preserve only nonhuman animal organs, quickly inspired human applications. It would be possible, speculated one popular writer, "to hook a human uterus bearing an embryo into the system and have it produce a baby. Normal development over short periods of time has already been recorded for the uterus of a cat. But no kittens have developed. A similar experiment with the reproductive apparatus of the human being would be almost prohibitively expensive."[62]

MONKEY GLANDS

In the 1920s the reproductive apparatus itself became the focus of intense activity and interest. Although the transplantation of both ovaries and testes (using mostly cadaveric organs) had been performed for nearly two decades, the work of Viennese physiologist Eugen Steinach and Russian physician Serge Voronoff generated enormous enthusiasm for gland surgery. Unlike the Steinach operation which involved ligating the spermatic ducts (vasectomy), Voronoff's procedure entailed grafting testicular tissue from chimpanzees or baboons into men. In 1920 Voronoff first published the results of ape gland grafts in human patients. By 1925 he had performed his surgical procedure on more than three hundred men, attracting patients from around the globe.[63]

By 1920 the indiscriminate use of animal tissue in human bodies was no longer respectable, even in rejuvenation circles. The heteroplastic implant for rejuvenation, biologist Paul Kammerer explained in 1924, created difficulties: "the farther apart tissues are in relationship, the less likely they are to blend. The best results of blending are achieved by tissues of the same individual. The next best results come from the blending of tissues of different individuals of the same kind. In only a few cases has there been a satisfactory blending of tissue of different kinds."[64]

Voronoff conceded that the best donors for human males were other males, even as he acknowledged that it would hardly be charitable to deprive a young man of a source of energy in order to profit an elderly man. (At the same time, he indulged the fantasy that the restoration of vital energy to a man like Pasteur might well be worth the "slight mutilation on a robust porter.")[65] Not only would it be uncharitable, it would not be possible. Men, he explained, would rather give up an eye than one of their glands. Although he had received two offers to sell him the organs, the amount required by the sellers would restrict the grafting operation to millionaires. This "despicable traffic in organs" had already produced cases in which legal papers were drawn up to formalize sale of organs, and reports in the press describing men "knocked unconscious and then robbed of the long-sought-for organ."[66]

In the face of such constraints, Voronoff turned to the close evolutionary relations of humans, chimpanzees, orangutans, and gibbons. Similarities between human and simian tissues and blood, argued Voronoff, made the transfer of ape testicular material closer to a homograft than a heterograft. Using anthropoid apes as a source of tissue did not solve all Voronoff's problems. The animals were expensive to acquire (chimpanzees reportedly cost him five hundred dollars each) and available in only limited quantities, and their large size and intelligence made them hard to handle both inside and outside the operating room. Voronoff's efforts to breed animals for his surgical use met with little success; he welcomed the efforts by the French government to conserve the primate supply in their colonial outposts.[67]

In the United States the press closely monitored Voronoff's progress, dutifully reporting details of his movements, his efforts to obtain monkeys, and the response to his medical claims from physicians and surgeons.[68] Unlike French surgeons who were forbidden by law to use organs obtained from executed criminals and other cadavers, American surgeons had limited access to such material for transplantation.[69] In 1914, six years before Voronoff announced his testicular transplant procedure, American urologist Victor Lespinasse expressed surprise at how easy it was to obtain fresh human testicular material.[70] California prison physician Leo Stanley's access to organs from executed criminals made possible an extensive research program into the effects of testicular grafting.[71] In Chicago surgeon Max Thorek took up the Voronoff procedure, performing a number of monkey gland procedures at the American Hospital. Like Voronoff, Thorek insisted on using either human tissue for transplant or material taken from apes. Thorek was one of the few transplanters to offer detailed discussion about species differences and their implications for the success of testicular transplants. He distinguished, for example, between higher anthropoids (baboons, chimpanzees) which were acceptable as "donors" and the lower anthropoids (small rhesus, lemurs, ringtails) which he deemed unsuitable for implantation purposes because "their blood agglutination tests are too distant, their life cycle and *vita sexualis* too remote to give the desired results to be of proper therapeutic value in this work."[72] Thorek's insistence on a close biological relation between donor and recipient made him particularly critical of one of Voronoff's more disreputable (and successful) American imitators, John R. Brinkley, "the goat gland doctor," who continued to attract a large following of satisfied customers even after the Kansas State Medical Board revoked his medical license in 1930.[73]

The popularity of gland grafting in the United States and the large-scale incorporation of animal sex glands into human bodies raises questions about cultural responses to this use of animal tissue. Unlike the earlier skin grafters who used frogs and dogs largely because of their availability and ease of use, monkey gland grafters argued that the close biological relationship between humans and apes was essential to the success of the transplant. Did this closer biological relationship in turn influence cultural acceptance of the procedure? The remarkable thing about the monkey gland grafts is the extent to which Americans seized the opportunity to rejuvenate themselves. American physicians indicated no concerns about the incorporation of monkey or ape material into their patients. Reports in the press reflected only optimism about such medical innovations rather than distaste or reluctance on any moral or religious grounds.

The association of the monkey gland operation with human sexuality and human sterilization did prompt some Catholic theologians to address the moral status of the procedure.[74] This religious response to the Voronoff operation has received little or no attention from historians of rejuvenation and monkey gland grafting. In a textbook on medical ethics, Charles McFadden explored religious dimensions of medical mutilation and organic transplantation and the Voronoff procedure in particular. McFadden pronounced both aspects of the Voronoff operation—the transplantation of human testicular material from a living human donor and the grafting of the reproductive organs of monkeys into men—immoral. Using human testicular material from a live donor, the Villanova University professor explained, required the cutting of the healthy donor body without any corresponding benefit to the individual. McFadden did not address the morality of using testicular material from cadavers or executed criminals. But in a related discussion of cornea transplantations and reports in the popular press of criminals willing to donate an eye or poverty-stricken women seeking to sell a cornea, he concluded that it would be immoral to take the cornea from the healthy eye of a living person. A living donor could supply a cornea, only if some other defect in the eye rendered the person blind. There would no problem, however, in taking the corneas from the eyes of a dead person, including an executed criminal, to restore the sight of another.[75]

The moral evaluation of the incorporation of monkey glands into the human body required a different line of reasoning. "There is ordinarily no deordination in using the lower animals for the benefit of man," McFadden noted. Humans were free to assimilate the flesh of lower animals in the digestive system and to take in animal serums in the battle against disease. But the monkey gland procedure did not seem to fit these acceptable uses.

Instead he found it repelled human nature and offended human dignity. "The unnatural character of the operation," he elaborated, "rests in the fact that the transplanted organ is said to continue to function in a non-human manner, effecting notable physical and psychical changes in the subject. If this be so, the operation is manifestly immoral."[76] Whether other religious traditions shared McFadden's views about the repellent nature of monkey grafts clearly deserves greater attention.

In addition to the religious responses, the popular culture of the 1920s, 1930s, and 1940s may provide some insight into the negotiation of the animal-human boundary prompted by widespread adoption of gland grafting. Preliminary exploration of some of the novels and films from these decades suggests that the ape-human boundary in particular interested both artists and audiences. In the 1920s, films as diverse as *Darwin Was Right,* a 1924 farce involving experiments with the elixir of life and the substitution of three escaped chimpanzees for three babies, and the 1922 melodrama *The Blind Bargain,* featuring Lon Chaney as an evil doctor obsessed with performing ape gland experiments, toyed with the permeability of the ape-human border.[77] Following the success of the 1932 Paramount release *Island of Lost Souls* (based on Wells's Doctor Moreau), a series of films in the 1940s also featured the horrible consequences of ape gland grafting experiments and injections of gorilla spinal fluid.[78]

Novelists similarly probed the ape-human boundary. Harry Stephen Keeler's 1928 novel *Sing Sing Nights,* for example, featured the surgical problem of transferring a human brain to the body of a gorilla and "the psychological and social results of such a combination of man-brain and animal-body."[79] In addition to crediting surgeon Alexis Carrel with yet another miracle of limb transplantation (the transposition of the arm of a French private to the stump of a French general), Keeler's novel capitalized on "a farcical trial" in a tiny Tennessee town, "a trial attended by journalists from all over the world, a trial in which a young teacher of Evolution was being held to punishment for teaching that man and monkey were in some way related."[80] Whether the Scopes trial and its implications for human-monkey relationships in turn influenced popular understanding and acceptance of the monkey gland transplants has not been explored by historians of gland grafting.

In the first three decades of the twentieth century the transplantation of tissues from both human and animal bodies generated enormous interest and optimism. The biological rejection of foreign tissue, which by the 1920s was becoming increasingly apparent to surgeons and immunologists, was not accompanied by any significant cultural rejection of the process or the sources of donated tissue and organs. Issues that have come to be seen as troubling in the current context of organ transplantation, including buying and selling organs, entertained rather than repelled Americans.[81] The use of animals as sources of skin, bone, corneas, nerves, and kidneys prompted wonder rather than revulsion. Only the widespread interest in monkey gland transplantation seemed to spark more serious reassessment of the boundary separating apes and humans, a renegotiation that may have stemmed from other developments in the 1920s, including the challenges to Darwinian doctrine.

NOTES

1. Carleton Dederer, "Successful Experimental Homotransplantation of the Kidney and the Ovary," *Surgery, Gynecology, and Obstetrics* 31 (1920): 45–50.

2. Surgeons also used nonliving materials, including paraffin, for correcting such conditions as saddle-nose deformity (commonly associated with syphilis). See Beth Haiken, "Plastic Surgery and American Beauty at 1921," *Bulletin of the History of Medicine* 68 (1994): 429–53.

3. Mark Seltzer, *Bodies and Machines* (New York: Routledge, 1992).

4. H. G. Wells, *The Island of Doctor Moreau,* ed. Robert M. Philmus (Athens: University of Georgia Press, 1993), p. 46. Hunter's experiments included transplanting human teeth into the comb of a rooster, and grafting the spur of a young cock onto a hen and vice versa to determine the influence of sex on transplants; see John B. deC. M. Saunders, "A Conceptual History of Transplantation," in *Transplantation,* ed. John S. Najarian and Richard L. Simmons (Philadelphia: Lea & Febiger, 1972), pp. 3–25. In *The Island of Doctor Moreau,* "rhinoceros rats" are the work of Algerian soldiers; in the 1860s physiologist Paul Bert conducted experiments on rats in which he implanted the tip of the tail of a rat under the skin of its back. The transplanted tail grew, forming new bone and establishing circulation. See Nikolaus Mani, "Bert, Paul," in *Dictionary of Scientific Biography,* vol. 2 (New York: Scribner's, 1970), p. 61.

5. Dr. Howard Lilienthal to A. Carrel, April 30, 1908, Alexis Carrel Papers, Box 45, Folder 1909, Georgetown University Archives. Zoologist P. Chalmers Mitchell disputed the scientific possibility of interspecies grafting in a review of *Moreau* for the *Saturday Review,* April 11, 1896. In a letter to the *Saturday Review* (published November 7, 1896), Wells not only criticized Mitchell's mistaken characterization but provided a citation to a successful graft involving the spinal cord from a rabbit in a human being, published in the *British Medical Journal,* October 31, 1896. This exchange is discussed in Philmus, *The Island of Doctor Moreau,* pp. 197–210.

6. Jon Turney, "Life in the Laboratory: Public Responses to Experimental Biology," *Public Understanding of Science* 4 (1995): 153–76.

7. Samuel P. Harbison, "Origins of Vascular Surgery: The Carrel-Guthrie Letters," *Surgery* 52 (1962): 406–18, discusses the difficulties between the two collaborators.

8. "The Transplantation of Members and Organs," *Scientific American,* suppl. no. 72 (1911): 236–37.

9. See Thomas Schlich, "How Gods and Saints Became Transplant Surgeons: The Scientific Article as a Model for Writing History," *History of Science* 33 (1995): 311–31, for an explanation of the ubiquity of Cosmas and Damian in scientific discussions of organ transplantation, including the 1982 attempt by "humorous laboratory workers" to emulate the success of the saints by sewing the leg of a black rat onto a white rat.

10. Theodore I. Malinin, *Surgery and Life: The Extraordinary Career of Alexis Carrel* (New York: Harcourt Brace Jovanovich, 1979), pp. 46–47. As most of Carrel's scientific publications describe the dog limb transplants on animals of the same color, it raises the question whether he chose to repeat the miracle of the black limb for popular audiences. A drawing of the canine version of the black limb miracle appeared in "Assez coupé, il faut recoudre," *Lectures pour tous,* 1913, reprinted in *Alexis Carrel 1873–1944, Cahiers Médicaux Lyonnais,* special issue (1966): 74. The Cosmas and Damian miracle was reprised in "Are the Parts of the Human Body Interchangeable?" *Current Opinion* 68 (1920): 358–59.

11. Carl Snyder, "Carrel—Mender of Men," *Collier's,* no. 50 (1912): 12–13. Snyder did not mention that Carrel's work on the preservation of human tissue included skin and bone taken from an infant, who died during labor; see Alexis Carrel, "The Preservation of Tissues and Its Applications in Surgery," *Journal of the American Medical Association* 59 (1912): 523–27.

12. Roy Kemink to A. Carrel, 1 Dec. 1908, Carrel papers, Box 45, Sec. 15-1, Folder 8.

13. See letters in Carrel papers, Box 45, Section 15-1, Folder 18. Carrel instructed his secretary to inform many of his correspondents that laws in the United States did not permit the donation of healthy organs.

14. "The Replacement of a Lost Ear," *New York Medical Journal* 78 (1903): 948–49. This was not the first American advertisement for a human ear, although the offer was considerably more generous. In January 1902 a Chicago surgeon advertised for two subjects willing to undergo an ear "amputation" for the sum of three hundred dollars. Although two willing subjects presented themselves, the surgeon received conflicting reports about the legality of such a transaction. See "A Strange Problem of Ear Surgery," *British Medical Journal* 1 (1902): 161.

15. "Offers $5,000 for an Ear," *New York Times,* November 8, 1903

16. "Lend Me Your Ears, Price of One $5,000," *Philadelphia Inquirer,* November 19, 1903.

17. I have not been able to locate any reports about the outcome of the surgery.

18. Direct blood transfusion, pioneered by Carrel and others, required an incision into the donor's skin, exposure of the donor artery, and sewing it to the vein of the recipient. For agreeing to the physical demands and dangers (both infection and loss of too much blood), donors generally received fifty to one hundred dollars.

19. "Gives His Leg, Girl Saved," *New York Times,* September 30, 1912.

20. "Newsie Died for Stranger," ibid., October 19, 1912.

21. Thomas S. Arbuthnot, *Heroes of Peace* (New York: Carnegie Hero Fund Commission, 1935).

22. "Certainly Earned a Medal," *New York Times,* October 1, 1912.

23. The "kinds of peril" explicitly rewarded by the Carnegie Hero Commission included "drowning, suffocation in wells, railway trains, electric cars, burning, suffocation at fires, runaway teams, cave-in at mines, electric shock, attacks by enraged animals, attempted murder, falls, death by exposure, explosions, mad dogs, death by machinery, snake bites, contagious diseases, etc." One example of "medical heroism" was Leonard Williams, a thirty-four-year-old tool-dresser, who in 1917 received a silver medal and one thousand dollars for attempting to rescue a fellow laborer from epidemic cerebrospinal meningitis. Williams stayed to nurse the stricken man after he was abandoned by everyone else in the community. Carnegie Hero Fund Commission, *Annual Report* (Pittsburgh, 1917), p. 35.

24. Morris, *Fifty Years a Surgeon* (London: Geoffrey Bles, 1935), p. 166.

25. Robert T. Morris, "A Case of Heteroplastic Ovarian Grafting, Followed by Pregnancy, and the Delivery of A Living Child," *Medical Record* 69 (1906): 698. Unlike Carrel, Morris used the term "heteroplastic" to refer to material donated from another human rather than an animal. This use of "heteroplastic" seemed to be confined to discussions of ovarian grafting.

26. See Franklin H. Martin, "Transplantation of Ovaries," *Surgery, Gynecology, and Obstetrics* 7 (1908): 6–21.

27. "The Only Explanation," *Life,* no. 54 (1909): 68.

28. "Gruesome," *Journal of Zoophily* 21 (1912): 377.

29. Ibid. For discussion of the vivisection of criminals, see Susan E. Lederer, *Subjected to Science: Human Experimentation in America before the Second World War* (Baltimore: Johns Hopkins University Press, 1995).

30. Alexis Carrel, "The Surgery of Blood Vessels, Etc.," *Johns Hopkins Hospital Bulletin* 18 (1907): 18–28.

31. Alexis Carrel, "Thyroid Gland and Vascular Surgery," *Surgery, Gynecology, and Obstetrics* 8 (1909): 609.

32. By 1924, there were 173 cases of total avulsion of the scalp reported in the literature; see Clarence A. McWilliams, "Principles of Four Types of Skin Grafting," *Journal of the American Medical Association* 83 (1924): 183–89. See Claire Straith and Morrison D. Beers, "Scalp Avulsions: Report of Early Homo and Zoo-Grafting and Recent Split Scalp Grafting," *Plastic and Reconstructive Surgery* 6 (1950): 319–26; and N. B. Aldrich, "Grafting with Pigeon Skin," *Boston Medical and Surgical Journal* 128 (1893): 336.

33. Some physicians did not seem worried about the children's disinclination to undergo skin donation. In reporting a case involving a seven-year-old boy whose thumb and metacarpal bone were blown off by the explosion of a cannon firecracker, the doctor noted "Grafts were taken from his thigh without anesthesia. He made quite a fuss, but then, he always did whenever the wound was dressed." See Julius T. Rose, "Skin Grafting without Anesthesia," *Medical Record* 72 (1907): 809. For greater concern about a child patient, see G. Seeley Smith, "A Case of Frog-Skin Grafting," *Boston Medical and Surgical Journal* 132 (1895): 79.

34. In some cases surgeons used large numbers of volunteers for a single patient. In 1872 when Miss M. N., a sixteen-year-old girl working at a bench in a shoe shop, caught her long hair in one of the revolving belts, her scalp, forehead skin, and part of her right cheek were entirely torn off. Although a physician immediately attempted to reattach her scalp, the procedure failed; she underwent a series of skin grafts once a week for a period of three years. During this period she received skin from 128 people, many of them "mere children," from whom the physician cut some 1300 bits of skin. See W. Symington Brown, "Skin Grafting," *Boston Medical and Surgical Journal* 101 (1879): 829–33.

35. Julius T. Rose, "Skin Grafting without Anesthesia," *Medical Record* 72 (1907): 809.

36. George R. Fowler, "On the Transplantation of Large Strips of Skin for Covering Extensive Granulating Surfaces, with Report of a Case in which Human and Frog Skin Were Simultaneously Used for This Purpose," *Annals of Surgery* 9 (1889): 184.

37. Zera Lusk, "A New and Original Method of Obtaining Material for Skin-Grafting," *Medical Record* 48 (1895): 800–803.

38. N. B. Aldrich, "Grafting with Pigeon Skin," *Boston Medical and Surgical Journal* 128 (1893): 336.

39. Alexander Miles, "Extensive Burn of Leg Treated by Grafting with Skin of Dog," *Lancet* 1 (1890): 594–95, noted that he was able to obtain a

young greyhound as a skin donor for a badly burned schoolboy with "the co-operation of the friends of the child."

40. M. E. Van Meter, "Note on the Use of Skin from Puppies in Skin-Grafting," *Annals of Surgery* 12 (1890): 136–37.

41. Fowler, "Transplantation of Large Strips," p. 190.

42. In some respects, the use of frog skin may not have seemed that different from the application of leeches to the body. Both are external rather than internal treatments. As a therapeutic practice, leeching retained its popularity among some Americans after the turn of the century, and pharmacies continued to import leeches for sale.

43. Quoted in "Dermepenthesis," *Medical Record* 33 (1888): 638–39. Masterman found the skin of young wild rabbits more satisfactory. Recognizing that wild rabbits were not as plentiful in America, he recommended rooster skin to his American colleagues. Why rabbit or rooster skin was more acceptable to women and children is not addressed. See also Thomas Gibson, "Zoografting: A Curious Chapter in the History of Plastic Surgery," *British Journal of Plastic Surgery* 8 (1955): 234–42.

44. C. S. Venable, "The Use of Pig Skin in Extensive Grafts," *Medical Record* 84 (1913): 822–23.

45. Samuel Lambert, "The Vagaries of a Vivisectionist Turned Clinical Surgeon and the Story of the Lady Who Lay with a Pig for Five Nights and Five Days on Professional Advice," *Proceedings of the Charaka Club* 9 (1938): 38–43.

46. Ibid., p. 42.

47. Leslie Brent, *A History of Transplantation Immunology* (San Diego, Calif.: Academic Press, 1997), p. 378.

48. Lambert, "Vagaries of a Vivisectionist," p. 39.

49. "Sheep's Kidney Grafted into Woman," *New York Times,* January 6, 1923. For a professional account of this "heterograft" in which the patient remains unnamed, see Harold Neuhof, *The Transplantation of Tissues* (New York: D. Appleton and Co., 1923), pp. 260–63.

50. See "Blind Boy May See through Eye of Pig," *New York Times,* January 23, 1923; "Says He Sees by Pig's Eye," ibid., January 25, 1923; "Believes Pig's Eye Works," ibid., January 26, 1923; and "Pig's Eye Tests Fail," ibid., February 3, 1923.

51. "A Novel Surgical Operation," ibid., November 19, 1890. See also "The Boy and the Dog," ibid., November 23, 1890, for the excitement on the ward caused by a delirious patient, requiring the administration of morphine to calm the animal.

52. A. M. Phelps, "Transplantation of Tissue from Lower Animals to Man," *Medical Record* 39 (1891): 221–25, explicitly identifies the dog as one of his two patients.

53. "Bone Transplantation at the Charity Hospital," *Boston Medical and Surgical Journal* 124 (1891): 220.

54. "Dr. Phelps's Experiment: Is It Anything More than Useless Vivisection?" *New York Times,* November 26, 1890. For other criticisms, see letters from "Justice," "Humanity," and John P. Haines, president of the ASPCA, in "Public Opinion: Dr. Phelps's Experiment," ibid., November 30, 1890.

55. Phelps, "Transplantation of Tissue," p. 224.

56. Ibid., p. 225.

57. F. P. Millard, *What You Do When You Vaccinate?* (undated pamphlet, American Medical Liberty League), American Medical Association Historical Health Fraud and Alternative Medicine Collection, Chicago.

58. See "Freak Experiments," *Journal of Zoophily* 23 (1914): 93; and "Transplantation Should Be Tried on Man," ibid., 22 (1913): 60.

59. Turney, "Life in the Laboratory," p. 166.

60. *The Light* (San Antonio, Tex.), November 17, 1912, press clipping, antivivisection files, Rockefeller Archives Center, Sleepy Hollow, N.Y.

61. Alexis Carrel and Charles A. Lindbergh, *The Culture of Organs* (New York: Paul B. Hoeber, 1938). See Martin S. Pernick, "Back from the Grave: Recurring Controversies over Defining and Diagnosing Death in History," in *Death: Beyond Whole-Brain Criteria,* ed. Richard M. Zaner (Dordrecht: Kluwer, 1988), pp. 17–74, for Carrel as the man who revolutionized our conception of the relationship between an organism and its parts.

62. J. D. Ratcliff, *Modern Miracle Men* (New York: Dodd, Mead, 1939), p. 210.

63. Chandak Sengoopta, "Rejuvenation and the Prolongation of Life: Science or Quackery?" *Perspectives in Biology and Medicine* 37 (1993): 55–66. John R. Herman, "Rejuvenation: Brown-Sequard to Brinkley," *New York State Journal of Medicine* 82 (1982): 1731–39; D. Schultheiss, J. Denil, and U. Jonas, "Rejuvenation in the Early 20th Century," *Andrologia* 29 (1997): 351–55.

64. Paul Kammerer, *Rejuvenation and the Prolongation of Human Efficiency* (London: Methuen, 1924), p. 63.

65. Serge Voronoff, *Life: A Study of the Means of Restoring Vital Energy and Prolonging Life* (New York: E. P. Dutton, 1920), p. 82.

66. Kammerer, *Rejuvenation,* p. 62. In the United States, stories of gland robbery also appeared in the popular press; see "Youth Robbed of Glands: Attack in Chicago Believed Perpetrated by Rich Aged Man's Hirelings and Surgeon," *Los Angeles Times,* November 22, 1923. It is interesting to consider these stories in light of present-day accounts of both sale and theft of organs. See Nancy Scheper-Hughes, "Theft of Life: The Globalization of Organ Stealing Rumors," *Anthropology Today* 12 (1996): 3–11.

67. David Hamilton, *The Monkey Gland Affair* (London: Chatto and Windus, 1986), pp. 90–91, discusses Voronoff's failed monkey colony and his response to conservation efforts. For nonhuman primates as part of the apparatus of colonial medicine, see Donna Haraway, *Primate Visions: Gender, Race, and Nature in the World of Modern Science* (New York: Routledge, 1989), pp. 19–25.

68. The *New York Times* published more than forty articles about Voronoff in the years 1920–24. For more on Voronoff's press, see Hamilton, *Monkey Gland Affair.*

69. Louis Dartigues, "Le rajeunissement humain par les greffes animales," *Aesculape* 14 (1924): 129–34.

70. V. D. Lespinasse, "Transplantation of the Testicle," *Chicago Medical Recorder* 36 (1914): 402.

71. L. L. Stanley, "An Analysis of One Thousand Testicular Substance Implantations," *Endocrinology* 6 (1922): 787–94.

72. See Max Thorek, *The Human Testis* (Philadelphia: Lippincott, 1924), p. 384. Also useful is Thorek's autobiography, *A Surgeon's World* (Philadelphia: Lippincott, 1943), pp. 174–91.

73. Brinkley's difficulties with organized medicine are analyzed in Jessica Jahiel, "Rejuvenation Research and the American Medical Association in the Early Twentieth Century: Paradigms in Conflict" (Ph.D. diss., Boston University, 1992).

74. P. O'Neill, "The Voronoff Operation," *Irish Ecclesiastical Record,* 5th ser., 53 (1939): 415–17.

75. Charles J. McFadden, *Medical Ethics for Nurses* (Philadelphia: F. A. Davis Company, 1946), p. 218. For an extensive explication of Catholic teaching on mutilation, see Bert J. Cunningham, *The Morality of Organic Transplantation* (Washington, D.C.: Catholic University of America Press, 1944). Cunningham does not discuss the morality of heterografts, except in passing, noting that neither ovarian nor testicular transplants from simian donors were effective means to the restoration of sexual vigor.

76. McFadden, *Medical Ethics,* p. 218. McFadden retained his assessment of the Voronoff operation in subsequent editions of his text; see Charles J. McFadden, *Medical Ethics,* 4th ed. (Philadelphia: F. A. Davis, 1956), pp. 307–8.

77. The latter film, which no longer exists, has been painstakingly reconstructed by Philip J. Riley; see *A Blind Bargain* (Brigantine Island, N.J.: MagicImage Filmbooks, 1988).

78. Some of these films are discussed in the "Apes and Monkeys" category in Bryan Senn and John Johnson, *Fantastic Cinema Subject Guide* (Jefferson, N.C.: McFarland, 1992), pp. 75–83.

79. Basil Stokes-Hetherington to Morris Fishbein, August 23, 1928, Morris Fishbein papers, Box 8, Folder 4, Regenstein Library, University of Chicago.

80. Harry Stephen Keeler, *Sing Sing Nights* (New York: E. P. Dutton, 1928). Carrel is discussed on p. 352; the Scopes trial on pp. 377–78.

81. See, for example, Donald Joralemon, "Organ Wars: The Battle for Body Parts," *Medical Anthropology Quarterly* 9 (1995): 335–56.

Notes on Contributors

Piers Beirne is Professor and Chair of Criminology at the University of Southern Maine. Prior to working in Maine he taught sociology and criminology in England, at the University of Wisconsin–Madison, and at the University of Connecticut–Storrs. He is co-editor of the journal *Theoretical Criminology*, and his recent books include *Inventing Criminology* (1993) and *Issues in Comparative Criminology* (1997), edited with David Nelken.

Richard W. Burkhardt Jr. is Professor of History at the University of Illinois at Urbana-Champaign. His research interests include the history of evolutionary theory, of the study of animal behavior, of naturalists' voyages, and of zoos. He is the author of *The Spirit of System: Lamarck and Evolutionary Biology* (1977).

Angela N. H. Creager is Associate Professor of History at Princeton University. She writes on twentieth-century biological research, and is author of *The Life of a Virus: Tobacco Mosaic Virus as an Experimental Model, 1930–1965* (2002).

Mary E. Fissell is Associate Professor in the Department of the History of Science, Technology, and Medicine at the Johns Hopkins University. Her current research focuses on women's bodies and popular medical books in early modern England. She is the author of *Patients, Power, and the Poor in Eighteenth-Century Bristol* (1991), as well as essays on popular medicine, patients' narratives of illness, and medical ethics.

Paul H. Freedman is Professor of History at Yale University where he has taught since 1997. Previously he was on the faculty of Vanderbilt University. He is the author of two books on the medieval church and the peasantry in Catalonia. His most recent monograph is entitled *Images of the Medieval Peasant* (1999) and he also edited with Caroline Bynum a volume on death, apocalypse, and bodily transformation entitled *Last Things* (2000). He is currently working on spices and the idea of the exotic in the Middle Ages.

William Chester Jordan is Professor of History at Princeton University. His research focuses on the social, political, and economic aspects of medieval European life. He is the author of *The Great Famine: Northern Europe in the Early Fourteenth Century* (1996). From 1994 until 1999 he served as Executive Director of the Shelby Cullom Davis Center.

RUTH MAZO KARRAS is Professor of History at the University of Minnesota. She is the author of *Common Women: Prostitution and Sexuality in Medieval England* (1996), *Slavery and Society in Medieval Scandinavia* (1988), and *From Boys to Men: Formations of Masculinity in Late medieval Europe* (2003), as well as numerous articles in the areas of gender and sexuality in the Middle Ages.

SUSAN E. LEDERER is Associate Professor in the Section of History of Medicine at Yale University School of Medicine and in the History Department at Yale. A historian of American medicine, she is the author of *Subjected to Science: Human Experimentation in America before the Second World War* (1995). She is currently completing a manuscript entitled "Flesh and Blood: Transfusion and Transplantation in Twentieth-Century America."

ROB MEENS teaches in the History Department of the University of Utrecht and writes on early medieval cultural history. Author of *Het Tripartite Boeteboek* (The tripartite penitential) (1994), which analyzes penitential texts of the period, he is currently studying early medieval attitudes towards purity.

JOHN M. MURRIN is Professor of History at Princeton University. He is a co-author of *Liberty, Equality, Power: A History of the American People* (2d ed., 1999), and in 1999 served as president of the Society for Historians of the Early American Republic.

JAMES A. SERPELL is Associate Professor of Humane Ethics and Animal Welfare at the School of Veterinary Medicine, University of Pennsylvania. His publications include: *In the Company of Animals* (1986), *Animals and Human Society: Changing Perspectives* (1994), and *Companion Animals and Us* (2000).

H. PETER STEEVES is Associate Professor of Philosophy at DePaul University. He is the author of *Founding Community: A Phenomenological-Ethical Inquiry* (1998), and the editor of and a contributor to *Animal Others: On Ethics, Ontology, and Animal Life* (1999).

INDEX

Adam of Eynsham, 36
Adams, Carol, 202
Ady, Thomas, 164
Aelian, 199
Aesop's Fables, 79, 80, 99, 102, 107 n. 12
aggression, ix; animal, xvi; bestiality and, 206; ethology and, 265–95; human, xvi; as instinct, xvi, 270–71; sublimation of, xvi
Agrippa, Cornelius, 95
Albertus Magnus, 60, 62, 95
Alderman, Thomas, 155 n. 75
Aldrich, N. B., 312
Alexander the Great, 240
Alsop, Joseph, 298 n. 19
altruism, xvi
Amala. *See* feral children
America, colonial: bestiality in, xii, 115–44; lesbian activity in, 116; sodomy in, xii, 115–44
American Medical Liberty League, 317
Anaxagoras, 231
animal abuse: bestiality as, xiv, 193–217
animal-human relations: biological similarities, xv; boundaries, 230, 231, 318–22; diversity of opinions on, xii; familiars, 157–84; goats and, 50–66; horses and, 3–18; nonphysical differences, 231–35; organ transplantation and, 318–22; physical differences, 235–40; problematization of, ix–x; sexual assault and, 193–217; vermin and, 77–104
Animal Liberation (Singer), xv
animal(s): affect in, xviii n. 7; bodies as social constructs, 263 n. 34; boundaries with humans, ix, 88, 230, 231, 318–22; carnivorous, 88; classifications of, 3–18, 17; cognition in, xviii n. 7; communication by, x; as companions, xi; consumption of, x, 3; culture and,

235; edibility of, 88; extermination of, 81; familiars, 157–84; human eating versus animal eating, 83, 88; language used by, xv, 235; as metaphors for persons, 38; motivations for dietary rules, 14–16, 17; notions of culture and, xv; organic transplantation of parts, 305–22; otherness of, x; as pests, xi; respect for, 222 n. 34; prohibitions on eating, 14–16; rights of, xv; sexual assault on, 193–217; supernatural powers of, xiv; symbolic meanings of, ix; tool-making by, xv, 237; as victims in bestiality, 142
animism, 199
anthropocentrism, 196
anthropomorphism, 81
antivivisectionism, svii, 316, 317
Arbecoc, 5
Ardrey, Robert, 266
Aristotle, 64, 65, 199, 240, 241
Arnoll, John, 138, 142
Art of Courtship, 84, 102
Astomi, 39
Augustine, 36, 46 n. 39, 61

Ball, John, 37
Barnes, Julian, 3
Barnyard Love (video), 194, 195, 214
Barrett, John, 138
Bartoldus, 64, 65
Bates, Marston, 298 n. 19
Bayley, Samuel, 138
Bayts, Margaret, 169
beanus: xii, 56, 58, 59, 60, 63, 68 n. 20
Bebel, Heinrich, 34
Beirne, Piers, xiv, xv, 193–217
Bellingham, Richard, 132
Bennett, John, 131
Bentham, Jeremy, 201, 222 n. 32
Beowulf, 38